D1299762

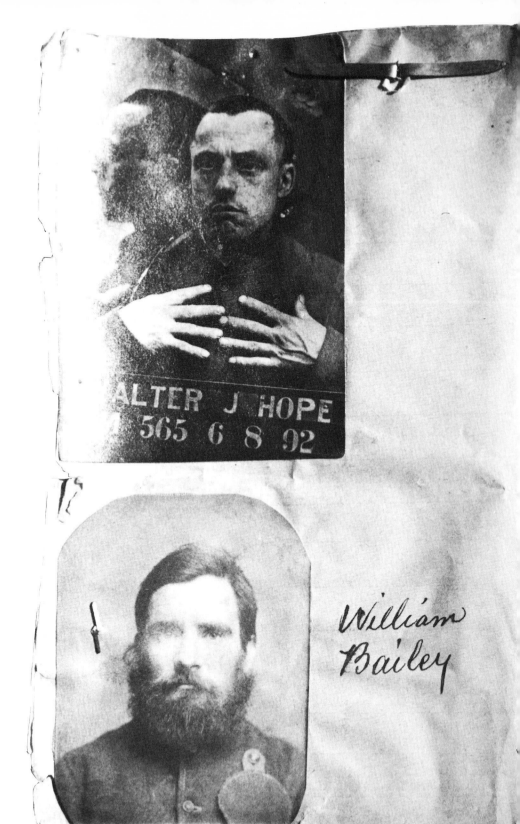

ALTER J HOPE
565 6 8 92

William
Bailey

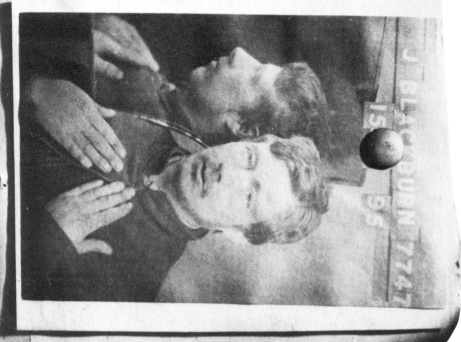

CRIMINAL ANCESTORS

A Guide to Historical Criminal Records
in England and Wales

This book is dedicated to the memory
of the late Arthur James Hawkings of
Bristol whose last words to me were,
'Carry on Sherlock Holmes.'

CRIMINAL ANCESTORS

A Guide to Historical Criminal Records
in England and Wales

D A V I D T . H A W K I N G S

SUTTON PUBLISHING

First published in the United Kingdom in 1992
Sutton Publishing Ltd
Phoenix Mill · Thrupp · Stroud · Gloucestershire

Paperback edition, with corrections, first published in 1996

British Library Cataloguing in Publication Data

Hawkings, David T.
  Criminal Ancestors
  A guide to historical criminal records in England and Wales.
  I. Title
  364.942

ISBN 0-7509-1084-4

Cover illustration: *Thomas Hartnell, robbery with violence (Public Record Office)*

Typeset in 10/12 Times.
Typesetting and origination by
Sutton Publishing Limited.
Printed in Great Britain by
WBC Limited, Bridgend.

CONTENTS

PREFACE

Family and local historians cannot afford to ignore the criminal law in their researches if they hope to build a comprehensive picture of an earlier age. A significant proportion of the population fell (and continue to fall) unwillingly into its clutches. Still more were and are involved as victims, witnesses, jurors, Justices of the Peace and constables.

A study of records relating to the criminal law can shed light on the activities and movements of some of our ancestors to say nothing of resolving the reason for a person's disappearance. One such chance find in my own family related to a nineteenth-century shepherd who disappeared from view. I came upon the reason for this when I found him circulated in the *Police Gazette* to police forces nationally as wanted on suspicion of sheepstealing. The entry contained a complete description of the offender, including his age, last residence, his dress, and circumstances of the alleged offence. On a higher plane, criminal records can also give a good indication of contemporary problems and the ways in which society regulated itself.

The English criminal law is one of the constituents of the mortar which binds our society together. Because the lives and liberties of individuals could literally hang in the balance of the interpretation of a word or argument, the law has developed over the years as an overlay of texts, glosses on those texts, reported precedents and statutes. The legal profession has often been accused of restrictive practices and lawyers seldom saw the need to make the law readily understood by the layman. Complex areas of law and procedure evolved to mitigate the ferocity of a severe legal code which at one stage contained in excess of two hundred capital statutory offences. With continuing evolvement of the law it is not surprising to find that the subject is complex, difficult to unravel and not attractive to the amateur historian.

The prison system can be equally mystifying. This has been part local, part national and, if transportation is also considered, even part international. The criminal law has always been administered locally, at least in part. This has led to a fragmentation of those records which have survived and are now to be found in museums, record offices and other collections as well as the Public Record Office.

The many layers of complexity and difficulties in finding and interpreting records have put off all but the most knowledgeable or determined researcher. Criminal records have remained a largely untapped source of information for historians.

This book has been a long labour of love for David Hawkings and the research has required detective skills in excess of those displayed by some of our police ancestors. The author has produced a map of these largely uncharted territories for other researchers to follow. I am pleased to note that this book is one of a small number of important recent works in this difficult area. Others are Ian Bridgeman and Clive Emsley's work on police archives, quoted in Appendix 5, and the forthcoming microfilm reprint of nineteenth-century *Police Gazettes*. I am sure that these will all lead to more research on the history of crime, the criminal law, policing and punishment.

David Hawkings is to be congratulated on another front. This is no stale work of reference, important though that would be. By extensive use of case studies and examples he brings the subject to life with a number of criminal cameos which give a flavour of the harsh existence and often rough justice of the day. The many practical examples of the information which can be found show our ancestors as real people, warts and all, and make this a book to be read and enjoyed as well as an invaluable research and reference tool.

L.A. Waters MA,
Police Superintendent,
Founder Secretary of the Police History Society

ACKNOWLEDGEMENTS

I am indebted to the following without whose help and guidance this book would have been impossible to research: the archivists and staff of the seventy-four City and County Record Offices throughout England and Wales who kindly answered my enquiries; in particular my thanks go to the following record offices for giving me of their time during my visits: Anglesey, Bedfordshire, Berkshire, Cornwall, Dorset, West Devon, Guildford, Hampshire, Lancashire, Portsmouth, Northamptonshire, Surrey, West Sussex, Somerset, Wiltshire, the Corporation of London Record Office and the Greater London Record Office.

My thanks go to the staff of the Public Record Office both at Chancery Lane and Kew for their unceasing help during my numerous visits. Those who gave me specialist advice and guidance there were Mr C.D. Chalmers, Dr N. Cox, Mr N.E. Evans, Dr Meryl Foster, the late Dr Daphne Gifford, Dr Elizabeth Hallam-Smith, Dr J.B. Post and Mrs E. Shenton.

Thanks also goes to the staff of the National Library of Wales and in particular to Mr Glyn Parry who assisted me with research into the records of the Courts of Great Sessions of Wales.

Mr C. Pickford, County Archivist of Bedfordshire Record Office kindly selected photographs from Bedford Gaol registers and Dr G.A. Knight, County Archivist of Lincolnshire Archives Office was helpful in selecting some Quarter Sessions records for reproduction.

Mr D. Bromwich, Librarian of the Somerset Local History Library, Taunton, provided detailed information on Somerset gaols.

Grateful thanks must go to Mr D.J. Blackwood of the Records Department of the Home Office for giving me his support during this project, and to the governors of the forty-five surviving historic prisons for answering my enquiries.

Miss Pamela Clark of the Royal Archives, Windsor Castle, helped with the references to Queen Victoria and Dr C.M. Woolgar, Archivist of Southampton University Library, furnished me with details from the Wellington Papers.

A special thank you must go to Superintendent Les Waters, one time Secretary of the Police History Society, who gave me considerable encouragement and advice and wrote the preface to this book.

The staff of the British Library and Newspaper Library at Colindale, the Print Department of the British Museum and the Guildhall Library, City of London who assisted during my visits.

The Commandant and Librarian of the Police Staff College, Bramshill kindly allowed me access to the college library and Dr P. Davies, curator of the Prison Service Museum, gave me support and guidance.

Mr W. Tricker and Mr P. Pearman gave me photographic advice and assistance and Mrs Mollie Gillen, Mrs Linda Elkins, Miss Stella Colwell, Mr L. Mitchell and Miss Jill Chambers gave me important detailed information.

The documents reproduced from Quarter Sessions, Courts of Great Session of Wales, Assizes, the Palatinate Courts and other records held by the Public Record Office together with Wellington Papers held at Southampton University being Crown Copyright material are reproduced by permission of Her Majesty's Stationery Office.

Details of records in Police Archives given in Appendix 5 are reproduced by kind permission of Professor Clive Emsley of the Open University.

Material from Northampton Police Museum is reproduced by kind permission of Mr M. Buck, late Chief Constable, and photographs from the Huntingdon Prison Registers by kind permission of Superintendent L. Waters.

The plates of Pentonville Prison and Clerkenwell Sessions House are reproduced by permission of the Trustees of the British Museum. The plate of Fleet Prison is reproduced by permission of the Guildhall Library, City of London.

The picture of hulks with convicts at work at Woolwich is reproduced by courtesy of Mr Wesley Harry. The plates of Tothill Fields Prison and Surrey House of Correction are reproduced by courtesy of Mr Clifford Elmer. Pages from Bedford Gaol registers are reproduced by kind permission of Mr C. Pickford, Bedford County Archivist.

Transcripts of documents from Somerset Lunatic Asylum are reproduced by permission of the Somerset County Archivist.

ABBREVIATIONS

Ang. RO	Anglesey Area Record Office, Llangefni
Beds. RO	Bedfordshire Record Office, Bedford
Berks. RO	Berkshire Record Office, Reading
Corn. RO	Cornwall Record Office, Truro
Dor. RO	Dorset Record Office, Dorchester
Lancs. RO	Lancashire Record Office, Preston
Lincs. AO	Lincolnshire Archives Office, Lincoln
NLW	National Library of Wales, Aberystwyth
Ports. RO	Portsmouth City Record Office, Portsmouth
Powys AO	Powys Archives Office, Llandrindod Wells
PRO	Public Record Office, London and Kew
Q.S.	Quarter Sessions
Som. RO	Somerset Record Office, Taunton
SUL	Southampton University Library
Sur. RO	Surrey Record Office, Kingston-upon-Thames
W. Sus. RO	West Sussex Record Office, Chichester
Wilts. RO	Wiltshire Record Office, Trowbridge

INTRODUCTION

Early in my genealogical researches I established that my own family originated in West Somerset. I therefore carried out a general search of the whole of the 1851 population census returns[1] for West Somerset in an attempt to locate those family members who had 'gone missing'. The census returns revealed a Richard Hartnell recorded in Wilton Gaol, Taunton; his place of birth was given as Hillfarrance, Somerset, the parish where a family of Hartnells was then living and known to be related to me. It was not difficult to ascertain that Richard Hartnell[2] was also related to me. Reference to the gaol and court records showed that Richard Hartnell had been convicted at Taunton Assizes on 2 April 1851 for stealing fifteen pieces of firewood and sentenced to fourteen days imprisonment. He had been arrested on 21 March, the date of the offence, and immediately imprisoned but his time in gaol up to his trial (eleven full days) did not count as part of his sentence. He was released on 15 April 1851. The gaol records also listed the items of clothing he was wearing at the time of entering the gaol and that he had no money with him. Furthermore his physical description was given: he was 5 feet 10 inches tall, had fresh complexion, blue eyes and brown hair with a scar over his left eye. It was also recorded that he was aged twenty-nine years, married and lived in Milverton.

Such a discovery was indeed a surprise though an old member of the family recalled later that 'a certain branch of the family had been disowned for being of doubtful character'. Later research uncovered three more family criminals. Technically they were criminals though a large number of the crimes of the nineteenth century, and earlier, were trivial by today's standards. Criminals or not, such detailed information contained in criminal records certainly adds colour to the otherwise mundane family tree.

In attempting to find my way through the maze of legal records I discovered that there was no written work which would provide a guide. No publication

---

[1] Taken on Sunday 30 March 1851.

[2] This Richard Hartnell was an uncle of Thomas Hartnell referred to in Chapter 21 and a brother of Elizabeth Hartnell who had married the author's great, great, grandfather Thomas Cornelius Hawkings in 1841.

could be found which would outline the use of these records. After many years of research a detailed account has been provided of the criminal records in England and Wales. Such a project would not be complete without a survey of records held in the various repositories throughout England and Wales and, after questioning every record office, a listing of prison registers and calendars of prisoners was compiled and is given in Appendix 2. A survey of the criminal records held by the Public Record Office is also given in Appendix 4.

The material described covers all that has been found to contain biographical references to criminals from the sixteenth to the nineteenth century including the records of the criminal courts but it does not include the various courts which dealt only with civil disputes. It does, however, include records of debtors and bankrupts (non criminals); those persons who often found themselves in debtors' prisons or in county gaols alongside convicted criminals. Each chapter describes a major subject and examples are given from various sources throughout the country.

Earlier criminal records are considered outside the scope of this study. Such records as those of the medieval itinerent justices[3] which date from the beginning of the thirteenth century are not included. Nor does it include the notorious Star Chamber[4] which was abolished in 1640. Military courts, and the High Court of Admiralty which tried piracy and other crimes committed on the high seas, cover a large field yet to be explored and will be the subject of a separate study.

Those family historians who are prepared to delve into criminal records will not go unrewarded. It is probable that somewhere in one or other of the branches of every family at least one criminal will be found. Family members may also be recorded on the right side of the law. Every able-bodied tradesman was likely to be called upon to act as a parish constable. Lists of jurors are also on record and those caught up unwillingly in criminal matters, the victims and witnesses, have also left their statements for us to read.

This book therefore provides a guide for all those wishing to use the criminal records of England and Wales[5] for research purposes. Not just for family historians but anyone who is interested in the crimes of our ancestors; for social historians, criminologists, legal historians and for the merely curious. The statements of defendants, victims and witnesses contain all manner of detail which reveals a way of life long forgotten. In describing their own version of a crime incidental information is included. Methods of transportation, of cultivating the land, the food they ate, the clothes they wore, the houses they lived in, the animals they bred, the type of work they were employed at, may all be found among the myriad of legal depositions. And the language itself records many

---

[3] PRO, document Classes JUST 1, JUST 3, and JUST 4.

[4] PRO, document Classes STAC 1 to 10.

[5] Occasionally Scottish and Irish criminals are also mentioned.

words and phrases, and local dialects no longer in use. Numerous examples from the various types of records are given in this book to show the way in which they are written and presented, making it more than just a documentary report. It contains many colourful and heart-rending illustrations of the harshness and cruelty of the legal system of our past.

Care has been taken in transcribing the examples of documents given in this book and any peculiarity of spelling or grammar is as in the original. In some cases, however, in order to clarify the meaning of a document punctuation has been added or changed. The information given in original documents in tabular form has often been rearranged to simplify its presentation.

David T. Hawkings
West Drayton
February 1992

PRISONS AND PRISON LIFE

Until the end of the eighteenth century the punishment for over one hundred crimes was death though this was often commuted to transportation to America. The penalty for lesser offences was either the stocks or pillory, corporal punishment, or a fine varying in degree dependent on the crime and also on the ability of the offender to pay. Gaols were usually only used to secure prisoners while awaiting trial, though many debtors were gaoled for years until their debts were paid.

GAOLS AND HOUSES OF CORRECTION

Up to the seventeenth century, as well as county gaols there were many small gaols and lock-ups kept by municipal corporations, and by nobles and bishops. There was no clear responsibility on county justices or sheriffs for the upkeep of these gaols or for the maintenance of the prisoners. An act of 1609 required the justices of each county to set up Houses of Correction (later to be known as Bridewells) which were to be under their direct control. A House of Correction was originally quite a different building to a gaol. This was the establishment in which vagrants and vagabonds were confined and where those who were able-bodied were put to useful and productive work. It was believed that their labours would help correct their unacceptable behaviour. The labours in the House of Correction were considered a form of deterrent while those souls held in gaols were often left idle and unemployed. Their only hope of comfort was (for those who could afford it) to pay the keeper for 'extras'. In time many County Gaols and Houses of Correction came to be situated under the same roof and supervised by the same keeper; this was given statutary recognition by the Gaol Act of 1823. This Act required Justices of the Peace, regulated through the County Courts of Quarter Sessions, to be responsible for the building and upkeep of these combined establishments under the name of 'prisons'. The

DIETARIES.

The following are the amended Dietaries ordered at the Somerset Epiphany Session, 1850.

Class 1.

Convicted Prisoners confined for any Term not exceeding Seven Days.

	Males.		Females.	
Breakfast	Oatmeal Gruel	1 pint.	Oatmeal Gruel	1 pint.
Dinner	Bread	1 lb.	Bread	1 lb.
Supper	Oatmeal Gruel	1 pint.	Oatmeal Gruel	1 pint.

Class 2.

Convicted Prisoners for any Term exceeding Seven Days and not exceeding Twenty-one Days.

	Males.		Females.	
Breakfast	Oatmeal Gruel	1 pint.	Oatmeal Gruel	1 pint.
„	Bread	6 oz.	Bread	6 oz.
Dinner	Bread	12 oz.	Bread	6 oz.
Supper	Oatmeal Gruel	1 pint.	Oatmeal Gruel	1 pint
„	Bread	6 oz.	Bread	6 oz.

Prisoners of this class employed at hard labour, to have, in addition, 1 pint of soup per week.

Class 3.

Convicted Prisoners employed at hard labour for Terms exceeding Twenty-one Days, but not more than Six Weeks; and convicted Prisoners not employed at hard labour for Terms exceeding Twenty-one days but not more than Four Months.

	Males.		Females.	
Breakfast	Oatmeal Gruel	1 pint.	Oatmeal Gruel	1 pint.
„	Bread	6 oz.	Bread	6 oz.
	SUNDAY AND THURSDAY.			
Dinner	Soup	1 pint.	Soup	1 pint.
„	Bread	8 oz.	Bread	6 oz.
	TUESDAY AND SATURDAY.			
„	Cooked Meat without Bone	3 oz.	Cooked Meat without Bone	3 oz.
„	Bread	8 oz.	Bread	6 oz.
„	Potatoes	½ lb.	Potatoes	½ lb.
	MONDAY, WEDNESDAY, AND FRIDAY.			
„	Bread	8 oz.	Bread	6 oz.
„	Potatoes	1 lb.	Potatoes	1 lb.
Supper	Same as Breakfast		Same as Breakfast	

Class 4.

Convicted Prisoners employed at hard labour for Terms exceeding Six Weeks but not more than Four Months; and convicted Prisoners not employed at hard labour for Terms exceeding Four Months.

	Males.		Females.	
Breakfast	Oatmeal Gruel	1 pint.	Oatmeal Gruel	1 pint.
„	Bread	8 oz.	Bread	6 oz.
	SUNDAY, TUESDAY, THURSDAY, AND SATURDAY.			
Dinner	Cooked Meat without Bone	3 oz.	Cooked Meat without Bone	3 oz.
„	Potatoes	½ lb.	Potatoes	½ lb.
„	Bread	8 oz.	Bread	6 oz.
	MONDAY, WEDNESDAY, AND FRIDAY.			
„	Soup	1 pint.	Soup	1 pint.
„	Bread	8 oz.	Bread	6 oz.
Supper	Same as Breakfast		Same as Breakfast	

Class 5.

Convicted Prisoners employed at hard labour for Terms exceeding Four Months.

	Males.		Females.	
	SUNDAY, TUESDAY, THURSDAY, AND SATURDAY.			
Breakfast	Oatmeal Gruel	1 pint.	Oatmeal Gruel	1 pint.
„	Bread	8 oz.	Bread	6 oz.
Dinner	Cooked Meat without Bone	4 oz.	Cooked Meat without Bone	3 oz.
„	Potatoes	1 lb.	Potatoes	½ lb.
„	Bread	6 oz.	Bread	6 oz.
	MONDAY, WEDNESDAY, AND FRIDAY.			
Breakfast	Cocoa made of ¾ oz. of Flaked Cocoa or Cocoa Nibs, sweetened with ¾ oz. of Molasses or Sugar	1 pint.	Cocoa made of ¾ oz. of Flaked Cocoa or Cocoa Nibs, sweetened with ¾ oz. of Molasses or Sugar	1 pint.
„	Bread	8 oz.	Bread	6 oz.
Dinner	Soup	1 pint.	Soup	1 pint.
„	Potatoes	1 lb.	Potatoes	½ lb.
„	Bread	6 oz.	Bread	6 oz.
Supper	Oatmeal Gruel	1 pint.	Oatmeal Gruel	1 pint.
„	Bread	8 oz.	Bread	6 oz.

Class 6.

Prisoners sentenced by Court to Solitary Confinement.

Males.	Females.
The ordinary Diet of their respective Classes.	The ordinary Diet of their respective Classes.

Class 7.

Prisoners for examination, before Trial, and Misdemeanants of the first Division, who do not maintain themselves.

Males.	Females.
The same as Class 4.	The same as Class 4.

Class 8.

Destitute Debtors.

Males.	Females.
The same as Class 4.	The same as Class 4.

Class 9.

Prisoners under Punishment for Prison offences, for Terms not exceeding Three Days.

1 lb. of Bread per diem.

Prisoners in close confinement for Prison offences under the provision of the 42nd section of the Gaol Act.

	Males.		Females.	
Breakfast	Gruel	1 pint.	Gruel	1 pint.
„	Bread	8 oz.	Bread	6 oz.
Dinner	Bread	8 oz.	Bread	6 oz.
Supper	Gruel	1 pint.	Gruel	1 pint.
„	Bread	8 oz.	Bread	6 oz.

Note.—The Soup to contain, per pint, 3 ounces of cooked Meat without Bone, 3 ounces of Potatoes, 1 ounce of Barley, Rice, or Oatmeal, and 1 ounce of Onions or Leeks with pepper and salt. The Gruel to contain 2 ounces of Oatmeal per pint. The Gruel on alternate days to be sweetened with ¾ oz. of molasses or sugar, and seasoned with salt. In seasons when the potato crop has failed, 4 ounces of split peas made into a pudding, may be occasionally substituted: but the change must not be made more than *twice* in each week.—Boys under 14 years of age to be placed on the same diet as females.

The foregoing Dietary having been submitted to me, I hereby certify the same as proper to be adopted in the Gaols for the County of Somerset.

(Signed)

Whitehall, 31st January, 1850. G. GREY.

From Wason's Albion Printing Office, Shepton-Mallet.

Prison Diet, 1850, ordered at Somerset Quarter Sessions

justices appointed the 'keeper' and his supporting staff, and visiting justices oversaw the daily management of the prisons. The records of the Quarter Sessions Courts, therefore, contain much detail about prisons and their building and maintenance, and the appointment of prison governors and their staff. Diet was always a concern and often diet sheets are to be found as well as medical reports from prison surgeons. The following report from the visiting justices to Wandsworth House of Correction, Surrey, is an example of the detail to be found.

To Her Majesty's Justices of the Peace for the County of Surrey in General Quarter Session assembled at Reigate on the 5th April 1870.[1]
We the undersigned visiting Justices of the House of Correction at Wandsworth report as follows.
Since the last Quarter Session four meetings have been held at the prison at each of which the several parts of the prison have been inspected and the prisoners visited.
The general condition of the building is good but we beg to direct the attention of the Court to the roofs which in consequence of the great number of slates which are blown off by every severe gale are a constant source of expense. This appears to be chiefly owing to the slates within a certain distance of the extraction shafts being laid on iron instead of wood battens which renders the wire fastenings hitherto in use very insecure. In the hope of remedying this evil we have caused the part of the slates round the *D* wing shaft to be relaid and fastened with copper pegs. This work has been done by Mr Bundley of Bermondsey at a cost of about £43 and should it prove to be effectual we shall at some future time recommend the Court to order that the other roofs be similarly treated.

We also beg to call the attention of the Court to the road in front of, and running parallel to the prison premises which is, and been for a long time in a very bad state. We have applied to the Board of Works for this District to repair the road which the Board declines to do but offers if the whole road be put into proper repair to take it into their own hands for the future. As there are other parties who are equally interested in the maintenance of the road the County cannot be expected to contribute more than a fair proportion towards the repairs which has been estimated at £85, and we recommend the Court to authorize the expenditure of that sum provided the other parties will agree to bear their proportion of the expenses and provided also that the repairs are to be done to the satisfaction of the County Surveyor.

The Governor reports that the Officers have generally done their duty and conducted themselves to his satisfaction, but we regret to report that one instance to the contrary has occurred and that an Officer has been detected in communicating in a very improper manner with a discharged prisoner. This Officer has been severely reprimanded and fined a months pay and we should have thought it our duty to recommend his discharge but for his previous good character during his six years service.

The Governor also reports that the general conduct of the prisoners has been good, that the discipline has been effectually maintained and that the prisoners have been employed in the usual labour.

We have had under our consideration the subject of mat making and we find that the

---

[1] Sur. RO, QS2/1/83.

Officer who superintends that work also superintends the receipt and issue of junk and coir fibre the rubbing up of the oakum &c., in addition to the ordinary duties of a sub-warder. We are of opinion that it is not possible for one man to perform such a multiplicity of duties and as we think that if this Officer were relieved of his divisional duties the trade of mat making might be considerably increased. We recommend the Court to give the Visiting Justices authority to employ another sub-warder at the usual wages viz to commence at 21/6d and rise 1/– a week each year to 27/6d and employ the present Officer in superintending the mat making and other works.

Sub-warder Austen has left the service having sent in his resignation and Simeon King Eldridge has been taken on in his stead. Eldridge joined on the 12th February and having satisfactorily completed his months probation we recommend the Court to confirm his appointment. We have not found it necessary to appoint another female Officer to supply the place of Stoddart whose resignation was reported at the last Quarter Session.

Three prisoners have died during the Quarter viz: – on the 30th December *902* Henry Davis aged 70 of apoplexy. On the 1st January *4930* James Williams aged 18 of pneumonia, and on the 21st February *1541* John Key aged 28 of heart disease. In each case the Coroner's Jury returned a verdict of natural death.

One female and three male prisoners have been moved to Fisherton House Lunatic Asylum by order of the Secretary of State for the Home Department they having been duly certified to be insane viz: – on the 2nd February *643* Henry Windrich aged 20. He was convicted at the Assizes on the 2nd August last of unlawfully wounding and sentenced to eight calendar months imprisonment. Nothing peculiar was observed about him till the middle of January when he became very strange in manner and very much excited. There is reason to believe that he has before been out of his mind. On the 12th February *923* William Garlick aged 28. He was received here on the 24th Dec. last under sentence of a Court Martial and first showed symptoms of insanity towards the end of January. On the 19th March *31* Thomas Taylor aged 19. He was received here on the 4th October last on conviction of an assault for six calendar months. Shortly after which he showed symptoms of mental derangement and was for a long time treated in the Infirmary. And *433* Mary Ann Yetton aged 40. She was received here on the 1st of February on conviction of wilful damage for four calendar months and first began to show symptoms of insanity in February. She has before been in a Lunatic Asylum. The County Solicitor has been instructed to endeavour to ascertain the settlement of all these Lunatics.[2]

At the request of the Secretary of State for the Home Department arrangements have been made with the Commissioner of the Police of the Metropolis for a party of the Police to visit the prison twice a week for the purpose of inspecting the prisoners and these visits commenced on the 12th February.

We have accepted tenders for the supply of provisions for the ensuing six months and we recommend the Court to confirm the same as follows:

---

[2] It was necessary to determine the 'rightful place of settlement', i.e. the legal place of residence of each lunatic. A criminal lunatic after serving his sentence was transferred to the County Lunatic Asylum. The cost of his maintenance (unless he had the means to pay himself) fell on the Poor Law Union within which his rightful place of settlement was situated.

Hubbard	Beef and Mutton at	6s 1d	per 14 lb
Neill and Waugh	Scotch Barley	13s	cwt
	Oatmeal	14s 6d	
Percival	Rice	10s 9d	
	Split Peas	6s 9d	bush [bushel]
	Treacle	17s 9d	cwt
	Raw sugar	34s 6d	
	Raw cocoa nuts	68s	
	Tea	2s	lb

with the understanding that if the duty is taken off any of the above named articles the price is to be reduced in proportion.

George Hearn & Co.	Soap	26s 6d	per cwt

Lastly we report that we have examined the several bills for the Quarter and directed them to be forwarded to the Clerk of the Peace for order of payment.

Dated the 28th March 1870

Thomas Tilson, Wm. Hardman, Robert Hudson, S.R. Curzon, L. Loyd, J. Mews, Jas. Phillips, R.R. Roberts, Henry T. Lambert, Jno. R.F. Burnett, Wm. Fred. Harrison, Henry Sterry.

A report of the State and Condition of the County Bridewell at Abingdon with the Number and Description of Prisoners confined therein at the Easter Sessions April 4th 1826.

No.	Names	Age	By Whom Committed	For what Offence	Orders
			Felony unconvicted		
1	Richard Sandford	23	B. Wroughton	Stealing Wood	Sessions
2	John Smith	28	Wm. Bowles	Stealing Wood	Sessions
3	Mary Jones	23	Jas. Cole Esq.	Felony	Assizes
			Misdemeanors unconvicted		
4	Gabriel Debank	31	Wm. Bowles Esq.	Poaching in the Night	Sessions
5	Richard Matthews	45	Wm. Morland Esq.	Sending a threatening letter	Sessions
6	Thomas Bungay	20	Rev. J.F. Cleaver	Bastardy	Sessions
7	William Ilott	18	Thos. Goodlake Esq.	Bastardy	Sessions
			Felony convicted		
8	Ann Tuck	23	Windsor Boro Sessions	Felony	1 year hard labour
			Misdemeanors convicted		
9	John Langstone	46	J. Bowles & T. Duffield Esqs.	Bastardy	3 months hard labour
10	Thomas Preston	23	Rev. Wm. Mills	Poaching	3 months
11	John Packer	20	T. Duffield Esq.	Poaching	3 months
12	John Whiting	19	Rev. Wm. Mills	Poaching	3 months
13	George Willis	15	Rev. J.F. Cleaver	Leaving his service	6 weeks hard labour
14	Martha Withers	22	Rev. J.F. Cleaver & E. Berins	Bastardy	4 months hard labour
15	William Prater	25	Rev. J.F. Cleaver	Bastardy	3 months hard labour
16	John Witts alias Brown	24	Thos. Goodlake Esq.	Poaching	3 months
17	Thomas Evans	46	T. Goodlake & B. Wroughton Esqs.	Leaving his wife & family	3 months hard labour
18	James Wilkins	46	T. Bowles Esq.	Bastardy	3 months hard labour
19	Christopher Becketts	42	T. Duffield Esq.	Stealing Wood	14 days hard labour
20	George Ford	22	T. Duffield Esq.	Leaving his service	1 month hard labour

John Walker
Keeper

Some reports even included a complete list of all prison inmates with details of their crimes, a useful source when the prison register is missing. The table on page 5 is taken from an entry for 1826 from a Berkshire Order Book:[3]

Medical reports usually gave only numbers of sick prisoners but occasionally a list is given naming sick inmates together with their illnesses. The following is an example:

Report of the sick in the Gaol at Ilchester, October 12th, 1820[4]

Name	Class	Disease
James Backhouse	Debtor	gout
Samuel Stacey	Time	syphlis
George Coles	Debtor	syphlis
John Read	Felon	syphlis
James Innes	Felon	syphlis
Samuel West	Debtor	scalded leg
Ann Cooper	Vagrant	cough
John Johnson	Time	gravil
Christopher Ingram	Time	cough
Joseph Hayward	Debtor	sore leg
Francis Erdale	Debtor	strain on ye kidneys
Elizabeth Wilkins	Convict	venting
Jeremiah Hodge	Time	cough
Edward Silk	Debtor	cold

Lists of the 'Officers and Servants' of the various prisons within a county are also to be found among these reports and give their salaries.

In the eighteenth century throughout the country living conditions in most gaols were very bad. When John Howard became High Sheriff of Bedfordshire in 1773 he was so alarmed at what he found in his own county that he toured the country inspecting many other gaols and in 1777 published his findings, *The State of*

[3] Berks. RO, Q.S.O. 13.

[4] Som. RO, Q/SR Mich. 1820.

Prisons in England and Wales. He detailed many recommendations in order to improve conditions but the only radical changes made (by an Act of 1784) were the segregation of men from women and for the provision of separate cells.

From the beginning of the seventeenth century many condemned criminals were given the alternative, transportation to America, and up until the American War of Independence it is estimated that about forty thousand prisoners had been so dispensed with.

PRISON HULKS

From 1775 those criminals sentenced to transportation could no longer be sent to America and the prisons in England and Wales became seriously overcrowded. In 1776, as a *temporary expedient*, many convicts were housed on two prison hulks, the *Censor* and *Justitia*, (disused warships) moored in the Thames at Woolwich. Each day the convicts were taken ashore and employed in the building of the Royal Arsenal at Woolwich and the nearby embankments. Some were also used in cleaning up the River Thames. These miserable wretches slaved away for ten hours a day though in the severity of winter this was reduced to seven hours. The labouring convicts became something of a tourist attraction and many hundreds of visitors appeared every day to watch them at work.
The diet on board these hulks at the outset of their use was far from adequate:

5 days per week:
Ox-cheek boiled or made into soup with pease and bread or biscuits.

2 days per week:
Oatmeal and cheese, pease and bread or biscuits.

4 days per week: 2 pints of beer.

3 days per week: river water (imperfectly filtered).

In the first few months the meat was often putrid and the biscuits were green with mould. But the prison reformer John Howard, after a visit to the hulks in October 1776 influenced Duncan Campbell, overseer of convicts, to make some changes which marginally improved the quality (but not the quantity) of the food.

At one time friends of convicts were allowed to visit the hulks and give the convicts additional food but this had to be stopped because often hidden within the food parcels were saws and other instruments of escape. Some crippled convicts were used as gardeners to tend a plot of land near the Royal Arsenal to grow vegetables, but most of their produce went to the officers on board the hulks and not to the convicts as officially intended.

Further prison hulks were later established at Chatham, Sheerness, Portsmouth and Plymouth. Much concern was shown about the living conditions

Prison hulks at Woolwich showing convicts at work on the embankment

on the prison hulks and public outcry pressed the Government to search for an alternative to America for the transportation victims. Eventually, in 1784, another Act was passed authorizing the transportation of convicts though it was not until 13 May 1787 that the first fleet carrying 778 convicts as well as free settlers, sailed to New South Wales, arriving in January 1788. The *temporary expedient*, the prison hulks, continued to be used to house convicts prior to their transportation and many transportees waited for two years or more before they were conveyed to New South Wales, a voyage which at the outset of transportation took eight months. To survive the atrocious conditions on the hulks followed by this long voyage, being most of the time sealed below deck, was indeed a miracle and some convicts died before reaching their destination.

Life on a prison hulk was described as 'hell on earth' and the Government authorized an enquiry into the conditions and management of the hulks at Woolwich. This resulted in the 'Report and Minutes of Evidence taken upon Inquiry into the General Treatment and Condition of the Convicts in the Hulks at Woolwich' published in 1847. This report covers twenty-nine pages of detailed enquiries and statements, a part of which is reproduced here. 'Moral and Religious Instruction' was lacking and cleanliness was an 'unknown'. The report continues '. . . the utter disregard and neglect of the ordinary means of cleanliness on board these ships . . . was most disgraceful and discreditable. In the hospital ship, the *Unité*, the great majority of the patients were infested with vermin and their persons in many instances, particularly their feet, were begrimed with dirt. . . . and the unwholesome odour from the imperfect and neglected state of the water closets was almost insupportable.' Many convicts suffered from scurvy and the food 'is not the best suited for his condition'.

The rules for punishment of convicts were completely ignored. 'It is laid down by Regulation 20 that in no case is moderate whipping to take place upon adult prisoners until the Superintendent is acquainted with the nature of the offence and his approval to the punishment is obtained, and which in no case is to exceed 24 stripes.'

In the year 1839, a series of instructions were issued by the Secretary of State for the guidance of the Superintendent of all the convict establishments, together with a code of rules and regulations for their general government, which still remain in force. They are both comprehensive and suitable to the purpose for which they were framed.

It will be perhaps useful, and give a clearer insight to the subject, to describe briefly the present extent of the convict establishment at Woolwich. It comprises the *Warrior*, an old 74: the *Justitia*, formerly used as a storeship, and built in India; the *Unité*, an old French frigate; and the *Wye*, a ship sloop. These are thus appropriated: – the *Warrior* is laid alongside the Dockyard wharf, and lodges the daily labourers required for that service; the *Justitia* hulk, which lies about a mile distant, but in a similar position at the Arsenal, supplies the daily labourers required by the Ordnance department. Both these ships are connected with the shore by stages. A plot of ground belonging to the Arsenal was obtained for the use of the establishment by grant from the Ordnance. It stands in front of the *Justitia* hulk, and has been enclosed on three sides, the river completing the square. The enclosure is formed by a series of low wooden sheds appropriated to the purposes of a dead-house, wash-house, surgery, and workshops, looking inwards, and the square is closed by gates, preventing all access to the Arsenal. The convict hospital ship, the *Unité*, is moored out in the stream at about 100 yards from the *Justitia*, and can only be reached by boat. The *Wye*, a smaller hulk used for the reception of invalids, was, prior to the inquiry, moored alongside the *Unité*, but, having sprung a leak, had been removed, and her place shortly after temporarily supplied by another ship called the *Morning Star*.

The plan adopted for accommodating the convicts on board the ships is convenient, and well adapted for the purposes of inspection. The decks are divided longitudinally, leaving a passage in the centre for the guard to patrol in during the night. The space on each side is parted into small rooms, where the convicts, in classes of from 10 to 20 men in each, eat their meals and sleep. The central corridor is formed by a barrier of open iron railings on each side. The men sleep in hammocks, and were the passage well lighted at night with gas, it would be even a more effective check against disorder than it is at present. The hospital-ship is not divided into classes, the decks being left flush, and the patients sleeping on iron bedsteads.

I am of opinion that this plan of accommodating convicts might be found very convenient in convict barracks upon shore, where separate sleeping cells are not provided. The central corridor should be divided from the space on each side allotted for sleeping by strong barriers of open iron railing to the roof, and be of sufficient dimensions for them to take their meals and assemble in when not at labour. The men should sleep in hammocks ranged laterally in single rows, at about $3\frac{1}{2}$ feet from the floor, so that, by the aid of a strong light, the patrolling officer would have every prisoner under his eye.

In reporting upon the proceedings, I propose, as the most convenient course, first to dispose of such of the allegations made by Mr. Duncombe in the House of Commons as refer to the cases of individuals, and which are chiefly confined to charges against the Medical Officer of cruelty and ill-treatment of the sick, giving my opinion upon each case separately, and leaving the other accusations of a more general nature to be treated under the several heads to which they characteristically belong.

I copy the charges made by Mr. Duncombe in the following cases from the report of his speech in the *Times* newspaper, which is admitted by him to be substantially correct:–

Case 1: The Case of George Monk

1. George Monk, or Taylor, belonging to the *Warrior*, a lunatic; he was admitted on board with a broken leg; he was allowed to lie in bed in his own water and filth until such time as a large piece fell out, putrid with his urine, from the bottom of his back bone; he was sometimes handcuffed to each side of the iron bed which he lay on, at other times with a strait jacket on; he, if he were living, bore the mark on his back. This man was afterwards removed to Bethlehem [Lunatic Asylum].

1. *Case of George Monk*. – The evidence on this case does not in any way support the charge of neglect or cruelty. George Monk was a lunatic, and was in the hospital in consequence of having broken his leg by accident. His violence and restlessness under treatment, were so great that he on one occasion displaced the fractured bone, and the surgeon was obliged to place him under restraint; handcuffs and other means being resorted to to secure him from impeding his own cure. He was for a time unable to attend to his personal wants, and appears to have had a bed sore on the back; but there is no evidence to prove this arose from neglect. The witness, George Rushworth, who was over him as nurse for three months, and gives a somewhat exaggerated description of the case, says, 'I took to him, and every time he dirtied himself I used to clean him and get him a clean bed.' The convict recovered from the effects of the accident, and was sent to Bethlehem, where he undoubtedly ought to have been removed before the accident occurred.

Case 2: The Case of Peter Bailey

2. An old man of the name of Peter Bailey. When Mr. Perry called, he told Mr. Bossy that the poor man ought to be sent home, and they passed on to other prisoners. This poor man got daily worse; he asked Mr. Bossy if he could see a religious person belonging to his own persuasion. He asked him what that was. He told him he belonged to the Wesleyan Methodists, and Mr. Bossy said, laying great stress on his words, 'What brought you here?' He then began to relate a life of the most simple nature, at which Bossy began to laugh. 'Sir,' said he, 'you have more occasion to pity me than to laugh at me.' Bossy turned round to him and said to him. 'It is of no use your imagining that you will ever go home, for home you will never see; you will die on that bed you are lying on; for, were your friends at the gates of the Arsenal, they might come to see you; that would be all the consolation you should derive.' He died a few days afterwards. I called to see him the Friday before he died; he told me that he had a pain at his heart ever since Mr. Bossy's conversation with him, and said, 'He has broke my heart.'

2. *Case of Peter Bailey.* – Much evidence has been adduced on this allegation, but I come to the conclusion, that Peter Bailey was treated with kindness, and received every attention from Mr. Bossy. The circumstances which gave rise to this case are to be regretted, but they were accidental, and peculiarly liable to misconstruction. Mr. Perry, the Inspector of Prisons, on an occasion of his visiting the hospital ship, the *Unité*, observed the declining appearance of Peter Bailey, and in his hearing said to Mr. Bossy, '*This poor man ought to be sent home.*' These words appear to have made a very strong impression upon this man's mind, no doubt more than ordinarily susceptible and irritable from disease, and on his finding that no result followed this observation of Mr. Perry, he seems to have taken it greatly to heart, and to have made it the frequent subject of conversation with his fellow prisoners, attributing his not receiving a pardon to Mr. Bossy, saying that he had broken his heart. The surgeon in not recommending Peter Bailey for discharge appears to have acted in this case upon the same general principle which governed him in others, that it was not the custom of the establishment to apply for the liberation of aged, infirm, or sick prisoners, until they had served one half of their terms of transportation. Restricting my observations for the sake of convenience to the case of Peter Bailey for the present, I shall feel it my duty to remark further upon his application of this as a general principle in another part of the Report. With respect to the charge of Mr. Bossy having intended to mock, or of his having used derisive language to this prisoner, I consider it quite groundless. The surgeon, well aware that the convict's hopes of liberty were not likely to be realized, appears to have endeavoured to convince him of their futility, and to reconcile him to his situation, and being of the same religious persuasion, a Wesleyan methodist, he interested himself more than ordinarily, by procuring for him the attendance of a minister of that sect.

Case 3: The Case of William Theobald

3. The next man that came under my notice was William Theobald, belonging to the *Justitia*. This man was subject to epileptic fits, besides great weakness of body. Mr. Bossy called one day when he was in a fit and said, 'He should soon cure him.' He ordered a bucket of water to be brought to him; he got upon his bed, he ordered a tin to be given to him, and he commenced pouring the water on his head, which had no effect. The next day he saw him, and told him he should have him well flogged if he found him in any such fits as those again. He died on the 31st of July, 1844. The diet that he was receiving at the time of his death was three pints of skim milk, and three quarters of a pound of bread.

3. *Case of William Theobald*. – The evidence given in this case appears to me to establish, that the medical treatment of William Theobald by the surgeon was judicious and proper, and the allegation of his threatening to have the prisoner flogged if he saw him in such fits again is unsupported, and appears, under the circumstances, improbable.

Case 4: The Case of James Brandish

4. The next was James Brandish, a maniac. This man was admitted while in a fit, roaring out very lustily. This was his second time of admission into the hospital. When I saw him he was shouting out on each occasion. The first time when Mr. Bossy saw him he began to laugh at him, and told him 'Those fits would not do there.' Brandish had a fit after this, which appeared to deprive him of the power of opening his jaws. Bossy placed his thumb on his cheek and pressed against his teeth; he then opened his mouth. Bossy began to laugh, and said, 'It's all gammon, Mr. Brandish. I will have you well flogged if you don't alter your course of conduct. I will have you sent to the *Justitia* and well flogged.' After the doctor went away I examined his mouth, and I found that his cheek was cut opposite where he pressed it with his thumb. They frequently handcuffed his hands to each side of the bed, and kept him lying in this position in his dirt and water until a large piece mortified out of the bottom part of his back, about the same place as that of George Monk. He became completely childish. The doctor frequently threatened to have him flogged. He allowed him wine before he died, a part of which he took off a few days before his death, with his usual threat of having him flogged. He died October 6, 1844.

4. *Case of James Brandish*. – This case has occupied a considerable portion of time and attention, and from the period which has elapsed, it being nearly three years since the man died, and the contradictory character of the testimony, it is somewhat difficult to arrive at a just conclusion.

James Brandish was admitted into hospital with epileptic fits, first in April, 1844, and several times subsequently until his death, which happened in the October of the same year. He appears, on his first reception at the hulks from Milbank, to have been of weak intellect, bordering upon insanity, which gradually increased with the frequency of his fits. Mr. Bossy seems to have doubted whether the indications of insanity were not assumed. Whether in forming such an opinion he acted with discrimination and judgment is a question which could only be answered by a professional view of the case at the time. The patient, however, continued, with the exception of short intervals, to sink under the influence of his attacks, becoming gradually more imbecile and helpless, and was at last reduced to a state of insensibility, being wholly dependent upon the attention of the nurses and officers for the commonest offices. During his paroxysms it seems that his mouth was frequently closed, and that it became necessary to employ means to open it, and I cannot find that the surgeon in so doing used the slightest unnecessary violence, but on the contrary, rather evinced professional dexterity. With respect to the allegation of James Brandish having been neglected, it is established that Mr. Bossy when visiting the patient on one occasion, found him in a very neglected condition as to personal cleanliness; and Mr. Blyth, the assistant surgeon, in his examination relative to Brandish's case, is asked the following questions:–

Have you any recollection of there being any disputes between Mr. Phillips and Mr. Bossy upon the subject of this man? – I have a recollection of Mr. Bossy being very angry with everybody about him, but his anger was specially directed to the master of the hospital.

As to his neglecting Brandish? – Yes, but that he had been neglected for a week I can safely say is impossible. I believe so.

You do not know? – No, I do not know.

You perfectly recollect the circumstance of Mr. Bossy being very angry with Mr. Phillips and the master of the vessel for neglecting this prisoner? – Yes, I do.

The fact of James Brandish having been neglected when in the hospital admits of no doubt; and that the neglect was not of a trifling nature may also be assumed from the evidence of the convicts, making allowance for some exaggeration, and the degree of anger it seems to have elicited at the time from Mr. Bossy. The responsibility for the proper treatment of all the patients in the hospital devolving upon the principal medical officer, he is no doubt answerable for this neglect.

Case 5: The Case of William Cooper

5. The next was William Cooper; he was nurse in the hospital. I will here state how the office of nurse is fulfilled: on a man being admitted to the hospital he is put on what is termed low diet, which consists of eight ounces of bread, two pints of tea, and one pint of mutton soup; this is diet for the day. The medicine which is prescribed for all diseases when they enter is a purging draught and a calomel pill; the patient is then confined to his bed for three or four days perhaps, when Bossy pronounces him to be recovering; he then orders him to get up and make himself useful as a nurse in waiting on the other patients, and keeping watch at night; those watches sit up all night, three of them taking it in turns, and dividing the watch into two hours and a half each. At this time the poor man perhaps is not able to walk, which I have frequently seen the case, the nurse often worse than the patient whom he is attending. This Cooper was one of these nurses. When he arrived at the hulks he was bad with a liver complaint, which was swollen to an enormous size. It projected two inches. I heard Bossy tell some young men, who, I believe, were his and his brother's apprentices, that there was a bag of matter lying in the pit of his stomach, and he then ordered him to lie down on a bed, and to strip his breast; when he commenced knocking and squeezing it, his sides and breast, but in particular that part where he said the bag of matter was. The next day this poor man was unable to get up. He complained bitterly to me of the treatment that Bossy gave him in bruising and pinching him in the way that he did, and he ever after complained of the pain that he endured from that pinching. He said he believed that Bossy wanted to break that bag of matter which he had described to his apprentices. – He died shortly after.

5. *Case of William Cooper.* – No evidence has been adduced in support of this allegation, Mr. Duncombe having stated that his informant had been discharged from the hulks and his attendance not procurable. The statement of the surgeon, which appears reasonable, must be admitted as a full and exculpatory explanation of the circumstances of the case.

Case 6: The Case of Henry Heighton

6. *Henry Heighton.* – Treated for six months for consumption, and kept from the hospital to the last moment. When, on his deathbed, was ordered out to work, which he declared he was unable to do. Mr. Bossy threatened him with punishment. He got up, and in a few hours death eased him of his troubles. In his last moments he declared he was a 'murdered man.' He entered the hospital on the 25th of May, and died the 9th of June, 1846 – 15 days.

6. *Case of Henry Heighton.* – The case of Henry Heighton has been satisfactorily traced from its commencement on the 12th of March, 1846, when he was admitted into hospital as a case of fever, discharged on the 22nd of April, re-admitted May 25th, to its final termination in his decease on the 9th June in the same year.

The statement that Henry Heighton was treated for six months for consumption is incorrect, nor has the allegation that he was kept from the hospital to the last moment been supported by evidence. The assertion, that when on his death-bed he was ordered out to work, which he was unable to do, is unfounded, as also of the surgeon threatening him with punishment, or his getting up, and declaring in his last moments he was a murdered man. The charge of his being ordered out to work appears to have arisen from the improper practice of employing patients in the hospital as watches and nurses over the sick. Robert Ellis, a convict, states, that the clerk or the doctor's mate, both convicts, ordered Heighton out of bed as a watch, when he was unable to perform the duty. It does not however appear, even if this was the case, that he attempted the duty, and it is quite clear, he was neither punished nor threatened with punishment for his non-compliance. This man's case appears to have received every attention from the hands of the medical officers. The evidence given by Mawman Brown, fully illustrates the impropriety of employing convicts as clerks in compiling the books; and allowing them access to the journals and writings. On the inquiry, he produced an extract which he had copied from the Prescription Books, giving the medical treatment of Henry Heighton as an out-door patient from April 30 to May 25. Having admitted that he was Mr. Duncombe's informant upon this case, I refer to his answers to the following questions to show the grounds on which he made the charge.

> You have given information to Mr. Duncombe, relative to the case of Henry Heighton, a prisoner, who died in the hospital, on the 9th of June, 1846, have you not? – Yes.
> Are you yourself cognizant of the truth of those statements or not, or do you derive them from other prisoners? – I have taken them from that book (*pointing to a book on the table*).
> Are the facts which you have stated to Mr. Duncombe, relative to Henry Heighton, facts, which you have ascertained yourself, or from any other prisoner? – The statement I have given relative to Henry Heighton, with reference to what occurred while he was at this ship, comes from my personal knowledge; what transpired at the hospital is from what was reported to me.

Case 7: The Case of Henry Driver

7. *Henry Driver* (Milbank prisoner). – Died through similar treatment; said to be a schemer by Bossy. Entered the hospital the 21st of May, died the 26th of May, 1846 – four days. This unhappy wretch had no sooner departed this life than the body, still warm, was carried over to the dead house, and the knife at work, operating and dissecting. Entrails taken from the body, and thrown into the river, where dozens had gone before. When the dissection was over the vacuum was filled up with flannel, and then sewn up for the jury to sit on.

7. *Case of Henry Driver*. – The allegation that the post-mortem examination of Henry Driver took place the day he died, is disproved by direct evidence of its having been performed in the morning of the day succeding his decease. The statement that his entrails were taken from the body and thrown into the river, where dozens had gone before, is greatly exaggerated, and the surgeon's explanation may be received as nearer the truth, who says,–

> I have no doubt the description given by one of the prisoners, who says, he took the bucket and that a great deal of blood went out of that bucket, and something hung upon the ears of the bucket, I have no doubt it was fibrine, which had probably been washed out from some of the cavities in consequence of the effusion; and in Driver's

case, there were extensive layers and portions of lymph of this kind. That would be taken out with the fluid that was taken from his body, and being in the bucket would be at the bottom of the bucket, and when the fluid was poured off might possibly adhere to the ears to which the rail is fastened, and this gave rise to the idea that it was a portion of the entrails of the body.

I shall feel it my duty in another portion of this Report, to describe and observe upon the gross impropriety of confiding the care of the dead-house wholly to convicts, and of the apathy, carelessness, and want of decent propriety which prevailed, among the officers of the establishment, in not feeling the necessity of cloaking its painful details as much as possible from the public view.

The explanation of the surgeon relative to the placing a substance in the interior of the man's body, appears satisfactory.

The allegations in Henry Driver's case, were extended in the inquiry to a charge of unnecessary harshness in the surgeon for his ordering the patient to be scrubbed in cold water, when labouring under disease, and on the day he was ordered into hospital.

The incident on which this charge is grounded, arose entirely from one of the numerous irregularities which pervaded the convict establishment – inattention to the prisoners' personal cleanliness. On Henry Driver's appearing before the surgeon, among the daily complaining sick, his feet were in so filthy a condition, that he was ordered over by Mr. Bossy to the washhouse to be cleaned. This appears to have been no unusual practice. The officer who was directed to take him over to be washed, Mr. Sutherland, would not speak positively as to the terms in which he gave the order to the washerman, whether he was to be scrubbed or whether he had designated the water to be cold or hot.

The circumstance happened in May, 1846, when the temperature was high, and his having been washed in warm water as is stated, through the commiseration of his fellow prisoners, it cannot be supposed that he experienced any ill effects therefrom.

Case 8: The Case of Timothy Hetherington

8. *Timothy Hetherington*. – He should mention the case of a lunatic, named Hetherington, who was flogged on board the *Justitia*. This man was reported for something, and ordered a dozen lashes by the Overseer. Upon being taken down the man immediately ran to the Overseer and kicked his shins; upon which he was ordered another dozen. Hetherington was immediately ironed and taken to his cell, where he attempted to cut his throat, but did not do so effectually; and he was now in Bethlehem.

8. *Case of Timothy Hetherington*. – This case, referred to by Mr. Duncombe, is one not directly involved, like the preceding, in the medical treatment of the prisoners; but refers to the propriety of the infliction of corporal punishment upon a prisoner named Timothy Hetherington, which took place as far back as the 16th of June, 1843. This convict had been removed from Kirkdale, was subject to epileptic fits, and frequently treated for them in hospital, and discharged; he was also admitted into the hospital ship on one occasion as insane, as is shown by the following entry in the Journal:–

May 25, 1842. – Timothy Hetherington, age 30, received from Liverpool; sentence, life; disease, mania; belonging to the *Justitia*, discharged June 11.

It is stated in Mr. Capper's Report, that when this man was brought up for punishment, it was not known that he had been previously insane; this, however, is manifestly incorrect, as is shown by the preceding extract from the hospital books, which prove he had been under treatment for that malady. There can be no doubt that this punishment was most improperly inflicted. The prisoner was unquestionably insane at the time; and even if not so, being subject to epilepsy he would not have been a proper subject for corporal punishment. He twice attempted his life afterwards, and was finally removed to Bethlehem Hospital, on the 21st of August, 1843. It is most difficult, at this length of time, to decide upon which medical officer the responsibility of this punishment rests. Mr. Hope, the principal surgeon, was infirm and incapable of executing his duties at the time. Mr. Bossy was surgeon of the *Warrior* only, but still performing Mr. Hope's duties; Mr. Phillips, the assistant-surgeon, is said to have been present; Mr. Bossy to have been on the spot a few minutes afterwards. Mr. Bossy does not consider himself as responsible for the punishment, and I can only dismiss the case with this observation, that it is one of the links of a long chain of irregularities in the management of the convict establishment.

The labour to which the convicts are subjected in the Dockyard varies greatly in its intensity, and requires great nicety and discretion in adjusting it to the varying strength and capability of the convicts. The hardest descriptions of work are the landing and discharging of coal, excavating, the raising and drawing of timber and other heavy materials, and the cleaning of shot. The convicts labour in gangs from 10 to 20 in each, superintended by a paid officer and convict wardsmen, under the title of gangsmen; the latter wear a badge, with the word *gangsman* on the arm, which allows the wearer to pass to and fro in the yard without being accompanied by a guard. They work the same number of hours as the paid labourers in the employment of Government.

The value of convict labour in convict establishments has, I think, been generally underrated. The utility of having a body of men who may be ready upon any sudden public emergency to supply steamers with coals, or to assist in extinguishing fires, has been fully shown in the evidence – the convicts having been called upon and employed for many hours in assisting to extinguish a fire in a large quantity of coal, which had ignited from spontaneous combustion, and also in coaling one of Her Majesty's war steamers, loading with provisions for Ireland. On both these occasions the conduct of the convicts was most praiseworthy, and the services rendered by them were very valuable, so much so, Sir, that you were pleased to recommend and obtain Her Majesty's pardon for those who assisted in putting out the fire.

In consequence of the number of guards on board the *Warrior* and *Justitia* not being sufficient to furnish one to every gang of prisoners, their places have been supplied by paid labourers in the Dockyard and Arsenal; and from those persons so employed not being under the control of the officers of the convict establishment, they exercise but a very imperfect superintendence, and are, moreover, strongly suspected of being the private channels by which the convicts carry on correspondence with their friends, and also through whom the introduction of prohibited articles is facilitated.

In the employment of convicts in public works, it becomes the first care to associate them as little as possible with the paid labourer or mechanic. It appears from the evidence of several of the officers and the inspectors of police, that the privies in the Dockyard and Arsenal are common to all, and that they are resorted to by the convicts and paid labourers together for the purpose of communicating with their friends without, and receiving prohibited articles. It has also been stated that the friends of convicts have come down as strangers to visit the Arsenal and Dockyard, and being previously informed of the fact that the privies were common to all, they have there met and communicated with each other.

Upon these points I cannot too strongly recommend that the number of guards attached to the convict establishment should be increased, so as to provide one for the superintendence of each working gang, and thereby supersede the necessity of employing prisoners as gangsmen; also that privies should be forthwith constructed in the Arsenal and Dockyard for the sole use of the convicts, which might be placed under the charge of a sentry, to enforce such regulations as would prevent the improprieties to which I have referred.

I consider that portion of the evidence which refers to the health and diseases of the convicts will be found not the least valuable. The low and humid ground in the neighbourhood of Plumstead, and on the opposite shore of Essex, by generating malaria, is undoubtedly the cause of the prevalence of ague on board the *Justitia* and hospital ship. It will be found that the officers, as well as the convicts, are subject to its attacks, and that no less a number than 157 prisoners were treated for it between the 1st of January, 1847, and the 7th of April in the same year. The circumstance of the *Warrior* being higher up the river and lying on a chalk soil, appears to be the only reason which can account for the few cases of ague occurring among the convicts lodged in that ship. The prevalence of ague in this district appears to be aggravated by a preceding summer of unusual heat, when the decomposition of vegetable matter is consequently more active. The evidence of the Surgeon would lead to the conclusion that it would be desirable to move at least the hospital ship to a position nearer the Dockyard, could a suitable spot be found not interfering with the navigation of the river. Where the *Justitia* is placed, there is a considerable deposit of mud, which is described by the Surgeon as emitting very unpleasant, if not deleterious, effluvia in hot weather. It seems that the soil beneath the mud is gravel, and were the ordinary methods resorted to of cleaning the beach at ebb tide, I have no doubt much of the nuisance might be abated.

The principal medical officer of the convict establishment at Woolwich, is Mr. Peter Bossy, a member of the College of Surgeons, and a licentiate of the Apothecaries' Company, with a salary of £250. This gentleman, since his appointment of surgeon to the convict establishment, has purchased a business, and in conjunction with his brother, enjoys a large private practice in Woolwich, and its neighbourhood. His emoluments are further increased by taking apprentices, an advantage which he admits is ascribable to the office he holds, from its affording great facilities to the study of the medical profession.

Looking to the importance and size of the convict establishment, and the situation of the hulks at a distance from each other, and the constant personal attendance and supervision which must therefore be required from the principal medical officer, I feel it incumbent on me to express an opinion, that I consider his engaging in private practice to be incompatible with the satisfactory performance of his public duties. It is true that Mr. Bossy says, and there is no doubt of the fact, that his partner and brother, Dr. Bossy, is always ready to supply his place in case of his absence, and that his professional ability is unquestionable; but I think a government establishment should not be exposed to the condition of dependency upon irresponsible persons for the performance of public duties. It was elicited in evidence from Mr. Bossy, that his brother had been allowed by him to perform capital operations on board the hospital ship, and that they were successful, but I consider his having been permitted to do so without the sanction of superior authority, as improper. Mr. Bossy further states that he acquainted the Superintendent, Mr. Capper, of his intention to engage in private practice, and that it was not objected to, this privilege having been allowed to his predecessor in office.

The gentleman who holds the office of Assistant-Surgeon in the establishment is a Mr. Alexander Blyth, who was transferred from the same service at Chatham. He is 27 years of age, is not a qualified surgeon, having no diploma, and indeed may be said to be still in a state of pupillage, having up to the present time, been attending lectures at Guy's Hospital. His salary is £100 per annum, and he resides on board the hospital ship. I must here notice the irregularity of permitting this gentleman, for a period of four months in each of the last two years, to be daily absent from the hospital from early in the morning to the afternoon, for the purpose of attending lectures in London, in order to qualify himself for a diploma. On these occasions the hospital has been frequently left without a medical attendant, and the Assistant-Surgeon has visited his patients in the hospital at an unusually early hour in the morning, for the purpose of being in time for the lectures.

The surgery-man, H.A.S., (a convict,) has been most improperly permitted to select the prisoners for watches or nurses over the sick during the night, without any reference to, or sanction of, the medical officer. He has also been in the practice of compounding medicines in the absence of the Assistant Surgeon, and is entrusted with the charge of a variety of medical preparations and compounds of a dangerous character, such as croton oil mixture, laudanum, &c., which he administers to the prisoners according to the directions in the Prescription Book. It is true that this convict had been formerly connected with the medical profession, but the impropriety of entrusting a prisoner cannot be stronger marked than from a recent occurrence, in which it was imputed to him that he had administered croton oil instead of cod liver oil to a patient.

The evil consequences resulting from the vicious principle of employing convicts in offices of trust, are nowhere so apparent as in the management of the hospital, where this practice has been carried to an extent almost amounting to absurdity, by appointing the sick to attend upon the sick. The duties of nurses and of watches during the night are imposed upon the patients, and many instances are shown in evidence of their having been physically incapable of performing them from illness. That the sick and dying, under such circumstances, must have been most imperfectly attended to, is sufficiently obvious, even without the numerous confirmatory facts in the evidence.

Among the evils inseparable from the employment of convicts in responsible offices, is the bringing them in such close contact with the officers as must diminish the moral distinctions between the parties, and weaken that respect which the governed should always entertain for the governing power.

Several of the officers employed in the Convict Establishment at Woolwich are manifestly incapable of performing their duties satisfactorily, in consequence of age and infirmity, others are so tainted by long habit with the vicious system of employing the convicts in work for themselves, and other irregularities, and the evidence developes against others cases of such a suspicious character, that after giving the subject every consideration, I feel I can do no less than advise a thorough re-organization of their whole body.

This report was a damning indictment to the management of the prison hulks and the Home Office was petitioned to abandon their use. But it was not until the accidental burning of the last hulk, the *Defence*, at Woolwich on 14 July 1857 that this system of incarceration finally came to an end in England.

Prison hulks were also in use in Bermuda and Gibraltar. Those criminals sentenced in Britain to transportation were often (from 1824) sent to Bermuda and others (from 1842) were transported to Gibraltar. From Bermuda and Gibraltar convicts were sometimes conveyed to Australia. Six hulks were used in Bermuda: *Antelope*, *Coromandel*, *Dromedary*, *Weymouth*, *Medway* and *Tenedos*. All but the *Antelope* appear to have been in use up until 1862, five years after the abolition of prison hulks in England.

A record of only three prison hulks has been found in use in Gibraltar: *Europa*, *Euryalus* (which was sold in 1860), and *Owen Glendower* (which continued in use as a prison hulk until 1875 and was sold in 1884).

It is important for the historian who is tracing the movement of a convict to note that the sentence of transportation did not automatically result in banishment to one of our colonies. Indeed, young able-bodied men were often given the chance to join the army or navy as an alternative to transportation. References to all changes of sentences, whether remissions, redirection to the army or navy, or the granting of pardons, are to be found in Home Office Warrants. See Chapter 17.

Some concern was shown as to the convicts' health because the colonies did not wish to import feeble convicts or those infected with 'any putrid distemper'. Many convicts, therefore, who were old and infirm or suffered from serious infections spent out their transportation sentence confined to the prison hulks, and from 1837 those convicts whose transportation sentence was seven years or less were not usually transported but served out their sentences on the hulks in England or in government prisons.

GOVERNMENT PRISONS

Some government prisons were built from the beginning to the middle of the nineteenth century to house convicts, and these prisons were supervised directly by the Prison Department of the Home Office. (All prisoners given sentences of transportation or a period of 'penal servitude', i.e. prison with hard labour, were called convicts or government prisoners. All other gaoled offenders were prisoners, *not* convicts.)

The 'Model Prison' at Pentonville, London, opened in 1842 (British Museum)

In 1835 the Home Secretary was empowered to appoint officers of Convict Prisons and Inspectors of County Gaols. In 1846 a Surveyor General of Prisons was appointed and in 1849 five Inspectors of Prisons. From 1850 the Home Secretary was also responsible for the appointment of a body of Directors of Convict Prisons who superseded earlier separate Boards of Commissioners. The Home Office also controlled the prison hulks.

An Act of 1853 introduced the system of penal servitude as a substitution for transportation. In practice transportation continued until 1868 when the last convict ship, the *Hougoumont*, carrying 280 convicts, arrived in Western Australia in January 1868. The 1853 Act resulted in all convicts in England and Wales (excepting those who were transported) being confined in government prisons. At that time there were twelve government prisons in England:

Pentonville
Wakefield
Leicester   } male convicts held in separate confinement[5]
Millbank

Chatham
Portsmouth   } male convicts employed at public works
Portland

Woking
Dartmoor   } male invalid convicts

Brixton
Fulham   } female convicts

Parkhurst   male juvenile offenders

Life in Government Prisons

A strict rota system was drawn up to regulate the movement and discipline of convicts in government prisons. There were three periods of custody for male convicts:

1. Separate confinement.
2. Associated labour.
3. Ticket-of-Leave in the colonies or at home.

The convict first went to either Wakefield, Leicester or Millbank and was kept in separate confinement. Each convict was provided with work, the most

[5] Millbank also took females.

capable being put to weaving at a hand loom. Others were given tailoring, shoemaking or mat making. A convict who at any time committed an offence was put in a refractory cell, a strongly constructed room, sometimes padded for the insane.

From Millbank (or Wakefield or Leicester) the convict was then transferred to Pentonville and again kept in separate confinement. At one time convicts had to wear masks over their faces in an attempt to prevent them from recognizing each other. This, however, proved quite futile as the men recognized each other's voices. The scheme was soon abandoned.

At Pentonville the convicts were occupied with tailoring, shoemaking, mat making, and the production of woollen cloth and coarse shirting. Millbank and Pentonville were in fact the manufacturers of the clothes and shoes for all the government prisons including the clothing given to convicts when they were discharged from prison.

Convicts were kept in separate confinement for a minimum of nine months. If a convict spent his first six months well behaved and industrious he was allowed to wear a badge which entitled him to receive a single visit from a relative or friend. At the end of another three months he could earn a second badge and was then allowed a second visitor. The second badge also allowed him to obtain a gratuity of 4d, 6d, or 8d a week depending on the quality of his work. This money was kept for him and he was not allowed to receive it until his discharge. His day started at 6 a.m. when he was given half an hour to wash and dress. From 6.30 a.m. to 7.30 a.m. he worked in his cell. The next half hour was allowed for breakfast followed by an hour in the chapel. The next two hours were taken up with school instruction and exercise. From 11 a.m. to 1 p.m. he worked again in his cell followed by an hour for dinner. The next hour was allowed for exercise and from 3 p.m. to 5.30 p.m. he worked again. Supper took place from 5.30 p.m. to 6 p.m. followed by work until 8 p.m., then an hour for reading and writing and to bed at 9 p.m. This routine was modified on Sundays to allow for full morning and evening divine service. Each convict was allowed to borrow books from the library which he could retain in his cell and was given writing materials.

From Pentonville at the end of a minimum of nine months the convict was taken to one of the public works at either Portland, Chatham or Portsmouth. At Portland the convicts were employed in excavation in the quarries, at work in the machine shop or labouring for the Admiralty. The best behaved were used as bakers, cooks and storekeepers.

At Chatham the convicts were employed at St Mary Island in building the naval dockyard and at Portsmouth they worked in the dockyard or on Southsea Common under an armed guard.

The diet at Pentonville (as in nearly all prisons) was most basic:

Breakfast $\frac{3}{4}$ pint of cocoa made from flaked cocoa and milk and sweetened with mollasses.

Dinner	4 ounces meat, $\frac{1}{2}$ pint soup, 1 lb potatoes.
Supper	1 pint gruel sweetened with mollasses, $1\frac{1}{4}$ lb bread and salt.

The convicts at Portland, Chatham and Portsmouth were given a more varied diet to compensate for their excessive labours:

Breakfast	12 ounces bread, 1 pint of tea with sugar and milk for four days a week. On the other three days the tea was substituted with 1 pint cocoa.
Dinner	6 ounces meat, 1 lb potatoes or rice, 6 ounces bread four days a week. 5 ounces meat, 1 pint soup, 10 ounces suet pudding three days a week.
Supper	1 pint gruel.

Convicts who had risen to the first stage of the highest grade were also allowed on Sundays 2 ounces of cheese, 3 ounces of bread, $\frac{1}{2}$ pint of beer and tea for supper instead of gruel if preferred. The highest grade of convicts also received baked mutton in lieu of beef on Thursdays and Fridays and baked beef on Sundays and Mondays.

Male offenders who were under seventeen years of age and who were serving a sentence of penal servitude in Millbank were sent direct to Parkhurst as also were boys under seventeen years who were sentenced to up to two years imprisonment in county gaols. On arrival each boy was placed in a probationary ward in a cell to himself. The boys attended school together and were allowed to play in the exercise yard for three periods each day. School was attended for three hours in the morning and three hours in the afternoon, for four days each week. The afternoon of Wednesdays and Saturdays was occupied in cleaning and sweeping the corridors, staircases, cells and passages of the wards. Each boy had issued to him a hammock and bedding, table, stool, and set of cleaning brushes and a hand broom, bible, prayer book, hymn book, writing slate and lesson books and one book at a time from the prison library. The boys were employed at field labour on the prison farm from 8 a.m. to noon and from 1 p.m. to 6 p.m. except when attending school.

After four months a boy, if he had conformed to the rules and received no punishments was granted a second class, red, good conduct badge (shield of red with 2 embroidered on it) which he wore on his right sleeve. He was then allowed to correspond with his parents or friends once every three months, to have 3d per week accredited to his account, to have a 'goodly hunk' of baked plum pudding added to his dinner every Sunday and to attend reading and writing instruction from 7 to 8 p.m. on every weekday. After a further three months if he had received no punishment his badge was exchanged for a first class, red, good conduct badge (shield of red with 1 on it). When this badge had been worn for three months without disgrace it was exchanged for a second class, blue, good conduct badge (blue shield with 2 on it) and 6d per week was accredited to his account. At the end of six more months he was then able to obtain a first class, blue badge. After wearing this badge for eight months and if he had arrived within eighteen months of the expiration of his sentence he was placed in the second division of the liberty class when he was allowed to write a letter once a week and was given an additional 3d a week towards his gratuity. In nine more months he could advance to the first division of the liberty class. The boys were then allowed to set aside the prison uniform and dress in plain mechanics' working suits and to have some variation from the ordinary prison diet. To those of highest calibre a small garden was allotted in which they were allowed to work in the summer evenings and at recreation during the day. The boys in the liberty class could then earn, by good conduct, minor positions of trust.

Most of the boys who were sentenced to a term of transportation were (often after two years or more), in due course, transported to Tasmania or Western Australia.

In 1851 Mary Carpenter said of Parkhurst in her 'Reformatory Schools':

> With such a state of feeling, with nothing to exercise and give free vent to their restless and adventurous spirit, with no direct and sufficiently powerful stimulus in the way of remuneration for work efficiently done, their pent-up energies should break out into frequent acts of disrespect to the officers, violence, wanton damage to property, and even theft, as well as disorder and prohibited talking, for which an average of 445 boys incurred in 1844, 4105 separate punishments (among them 165 whippings), making an average of above ten per diem!

Up until then Parkhurst was obviously largely unsuccessful in the reformation of these boys. But by 1861 with the introduction of the incentive schemes described above there had been a vast improvement. An anonymous writer[6] in the *Cornhill Magazine* (June 1861) wrote:

> The whole object of the training at Parkhurst is to fit boys for useful and credible life when restored to liberty, and I am told that very many of them are brought to co-operate willingly in the system to which they are subjected.

Female Convicts

Most female convicts were initially sent to Millbank where they were employed in the first two months at coir-picking[7] and the next five months at bag making and coarse needlework. They were then selected as cooks, cleaners and laundry women. After ten to twelve months they passed to Brixton where they 'cleansed

---

[6] The article is attributed to Thornton Smith.

[7] *Coir*, fibre of the coconut used for making mats and ropes.

washing' for the staff and officers, for themselves and for the male convicts in Millbank and Pentonville. They were also employed at needlework for all the convict prisons.

In Fulham Refuge women were trained for domestic service, given instruction in baking, cooking, laundry and housework and some became farm servants. Washing was also undertaken there for other convict establishments.

Tickets of Leave

By the Act of 1853, following a period of good behaviour, a convict could be granted a period of remission which allowed him to leave the confines of the prison and 'live at large'. He was granted a conditional pardon and through the Secretary of State he was then issued with a ticket of leave. He took with him part of the gratuity he had earned while in prison; he was not allowed the whole amount at once but the balance was sent to him by post in several instalments over a period of six months. This procedure acted as something of an incentive for his good behaviour. If he failed to return to an honest living he forefeited the remainder of his gratuity and was returned to prison. Copies of these licences together with captions are preserved in the Prison Commission records (see Chapter 16).

The number of licences issued from 1853 to 1861, with the numbers of licences revoked and convicts reconvicted, is summarized in two tabulations (one for men, one for women) on pages 26 and 27.

Penal Servitude

Together with the treadmill the crank was used for prisoners sentenced to hard labour. It had the additional advantage from the prison authorities viewpoint that the prisoner was shut up in his cell. The crank was made up of a narrow iron drum mounted horizontally in a frame with a handle on one side which, when turned caused a series of cups or scoops in the interior to revolve. At the lower part of the inside was a thick layer of sand or gravel which the cups scooped up and carried to the top of the wheel where they emptied themselves rather like a dredging machine. A dial plate fixed in front of the crank showed how many revolutions the machine had made. A man could make about 20 revolutions in a minute moving a weight of up to 12 lbs per revolution, that is 1200 revolutions per hour. It was usual to stipulate that a prisoner completed 10,000 turns per day which would take him about 8 hours and 20 minutes. Some prisoners were able to turn the crank much faster than others and to retard their efforts the gaoler could turn a screw which tightened the mechanism and rendered the crank more difficult, and therefore slower, to rotate. Hence gaolers became known as 'screws'.

Corporal punishment could be given to any prisoner by order of a visiting justice. The flogging was witnessed by the prison surgeon who had the authority to stop it at any time if he believed that the prisoner could not take the full punishment without severe effect on his health. Corporal punishment was not formally abolished until the Criminal Justice Act of 1967.

The treadwheel at Portsmouth Prison (from *Sidelights on Convict Life*, G. Griffith, 1903)

Cell with a prisoner at the 'crank' in Surrey House of Correction (from *The Criminal Prisons of London and Scenes of Prison Life*, H. Mayhew and J. Binny, 1862)

RETURN of the NUMBER of MALE CONVICTS released under ORDERS of LICENCE in each Year, from October 1853, to April 1861; showing the NUMBER returned to the CONVICT PRISONS, either by having had their LICENCES REVOKED for trifling Offences, or by being sentenced to PENAL SERVITUDE or TRANSPORTATION.

Years	No. Licensed	1853 Rev	1853 Rec	1854 Rev	1854 Rec	1855 Rev	1855 Rec	1856 Rev	1856 Re	1857 Rev	1857 Rec	1858 Rev	1858 Rec	1859 Rev	1859 Rec	1860 Rev	1860 Rec	1861 Rev	1861 Rec	Total Rev	Total Rec	Grand Total	% Rev	% Rec	Period Y	Period M
1853*	335	1	..	7	10	3	5	2	4	2	5	..	..	..	..	..	..	..	..	15	24	39	4·5	7·1	7	6
1854	1,895	..	..	14	19	63	53	38	64	19	33	5	10	2	3	2	..	..	..	143	182	325	7·5	9·6	7	7
1855	2,528	..	..	..	..	40	47	126	190	99	64	36	24	12	15	1	7	..	2	314	348	602	12·5	13·7	6	3
1856	2,007	..	..	..	..	..	..	49	131	122	106	52	52	26	33	8	13	..	1	257	337	594	12·8	16·7	5	3
1857	674	..	..	..	..	..	..	..	..	15	34	31	20	14	22	8	5	1	1	69	82	151	10·2	12·1	4	3
1858	318	..	..	..	..	..	..	..	..	..	..	7	10	12	12	6	4	..	..	25	26	51	7·8	8·1	3	8
1859	260	..	..	..	..	..	..	..	..	..	..	..	..	5	4	3	10	1	1	8	15	17	3·0	6·1	3	8
1860	818	..	..	..	..	..	..	..	..	..	..	..	..	..	..	2	15	..	..	2	15	10	0·2	1·8	2	8
1861†	345	..	..	..	..	..	..	..	..	..	..	..	..	..	..	..	..	1	9	1	9	10	0·2	2·6	1	0
Totals	**9,180**	1	..	21	29	106	105	215	389	257	242	131	116	71	89	30	54	2	14	**834**	**1,038**	**1,872**	**9·0**	**11·3**		

* From October to December 31st, 1853. † To 31st March, 1861.

The following shows the percentage per annum of Male Convicts return to Convict Prisons, either by revocation of licence, or under fresh sentences, to Penal Servitude or Transportation, during the 7¾ years the system has been in operation:—

			Per ct.	Yrs.	Per ct.
Of the Number	335	licensed from Oct. to 31st Dec. 1853	11·6	or in 7¾	1·5 per ann.
"	1,895	in the year 1854	16·11	" 7¾	2·2 "
"	2,528	" 1855	26·2	" 6¾	4·1 "
"	2,007	" 1856	29·5	" 5¾	5·5 "
"	674	" 1857	22·3	" 4¾	5·1 "
"	318	" 1858	15·9	" 3¾	4·5 "
"	260	" 1859	9·1	" 2¾	4·0 "
"	818	" 1860	2·0	" 1¾	1·5 "
"	345	to 31st March, 1861	2·8	" 3 mos.	0·12 "

As regards the nature of the Crimes for which the 834 Male Convicts had their licences only revoked, and the 1,038 who have been re-convicted for fresh offences, the following is an analysis:—

OFFENCES OF A GRAVER CHARACTER.

Murder	2
Forgery, uttering forged notes or base coin	44
Burglary	106
Robbery	41
Robbery with violence	16
Highway robbery	6
Cutting and wounding with intent	6
Felony, housebreaking, sheep-stealing, &c.	284
Arson	4
Total	**509**

MINOR OFFENCES.

Larceny	650
Offences against vagrant act	126
Assaults on police	34
Desertion	18
Picking pockets	27
Wilful damage	14
Assault	118
Offences against game laws	21
Theft, misdemeanour, and other offences	355
Total	**1,363**

Total	509
Minor offences	1,363
Total	**1,872**

Numbers of Male Convicts' Licences, 1853 to 1861 (from the *Cornhill Magazine*, August 1861)

RETURN of the NUMBER of FEMALE CONVICTS released under ORDERS of LICENCE in each Year, from October 1853, to June 1861; showing the NUMBER returned to CONVICT PRISONS, either by having had their LICENCES REVOKED for trifling Offences, or by being sentenced to PENAL SERVITUDE or TRANSPORTATION.

Years.	No. Licensed	1853. Rev.	1853. Rec.	1854. Rev.	1854. Rec.	1855. Rev.	1855. Rec.	1856. Rev.	1856. Rec.	1857. Rev.	1857. Rec.	1858. Rev.	1858. Rec.	1859. Rev.	1859. Rec.	1860. Rev.	1860. Rec.	1861. Rev.	1861. Rec.	Total Re.	Total Rec.	Grand Total.	Per Centage Rev.	Per Centage Rec.	Period Y.	Period M.
1853*	40	—	—	—	—	—	—	—	—	—	—	—	—	—	—	—	—	—	—	2	1	3	5·	1·5	7	8
1854	115	—	—	—	—	1	—	1	1	—	—	—	—	—	—	—	—	—	—	18	14	32	14·7	12·1	6	5
1855	221	—	—	1	—	2	1	10	7	5	2	1	3	—	—	—	—	—	—	33	30	63	14·9	13·5	5	5
1856	55	—	—	—	—	—	—	10	11	14	8	7	9	—	—	—	—	—	—	7	7	14	12·7	12·7	4	5
1857	18	—	—	—	—	—	—	—	—	5	3	1	1	2	1	—	2	—	—	—	2	2	—	11·1	3	5
1858	29	—	—	—	—	—	—	—	—	—	—	—	1	1	1	—	1	—	—	1	1	2	3·4	3·4	2	5
1859	183	—	—	—	—	—	—	—	—	—	—	—	—	1	1	4	1	—	—	4	8	12	2·1	4·2	1	5
1860	103	—	—	—	—	—	—	—	—	—	—	—	—	—	—	—	3	5	5	—	2	2	—	1·9	0	5
1861†	103	—	—	—	—	—	—	—	—	—	—	—	—	—	—	—	—	—	—	—	—	—	—	—	—	—
Totals	764	..	..	..	..	3	1	21	19	24	13	9	14	4	3	4	8	7	—	65	65	130	8·5	8·5		

* From October, 1853. † To June, 1861.

The following shows the percentage per annum of Female Convicts returned to Convict Prisons, either by revocation of licence, or under fresh sentences, to Penal Servitude or Transportation, during the seven years and eight months the system has been in operation:—

		Per ct.		Yrs. M.		Per ct.
Of the No. 40 licensed from Oct. 1853 to 31st Dec. 1854	..	6·5	or in	7 8	..	0·8 per ann.
" 115 "	In the year 1855 ..	26·8	"	6 5	"	4·0 "
" 221 "	1856 ..	28·4	"	5 5	"	5·2 "
" 55 "	1857 ..	25·4	"	4 5	"	5·9 "
" 18 "	1858 ..	11·1	"	3 5	"	3·2 "
" 29 "	1859 ..	6·8	"	2 5	"	3·3 "
" 183 "	1860 ..	6·3	"	1 5	"	4·4 "
" 103 "	to 1st June 1861 ..	1·9	"	0 5	"	.. "

As regards the nature of the Crimes for which the 65 Female Convicts had their licences only revoked, and the 65 who have been re-convicted for fresh offences, the following is an analysis:—

OFFENCES OF A GRAVER CHARACTER.			
Uttering base coin	..	..	2
Unlawful possession	..	..	3
Horse-stealing	..	..	
Robbery	..	..	2
Receiving stolen goods	..		1
Wounding	..	..	1
Housebreaking	..	..	4
		Total ..	14

MINOR OFFENCES.			
Larceny	..	..	72
Wilful damage	..	..	2
Breach of peace	..	..	3
Vagrancy	..	..	5
Theft	..	..	26
Disorderly conduct	..		4
Picking pockets	..	..	4
		Total ..	.. 116

Uttering base coin	..	..	2
Unlawful possession	..	..	3
Horse-stealing	..	..	
Robbery	..	..	2
Receiving stolen goods	..		1
Wounding	..	..	
Housebreaking	..	..	4
	Total ..		14
	Minor offences	..	116
	Total ..	..	130

Numbers of Female Convicts' Licences, 1853 to 1861 (from the *Cornhill Magazine*, August 1861)

All male convicts had their hair cropped short. About three months before a convict was to be released he would ask the Governor of the prison, 'Please sir may I grow?' That is he wished to grow his hair longer so that he would not be identified in public as an ex-convict. During his time in prison he was able to earn money by various labours and on his release he would be given £2 as part of this 'gratuity'. The remaining amount would be sent to him at regular intervals but he would need to obtain a signature from a clergyman or magistrate, confirming that he was leading an honest and respectable life. Many ex-convicts found it impossible to obtain honest work and soon returned to a life of crime. Others, although determined to tread the 'straight and narrow', were met by a 'Fagan's Man' whose aim was to lure them back into crime.

In 1857 Samuel Whitbread, MP for Bedford, established the Discharged Prisoners' Aid Society at 39 Charing Cross Road, London. The aim of the society was to give advice to convicts on leaving prison and to assist in finding them employment, and for the few who set up business on their own, help was given in finding tools and materials for their work. Female convicts were encouraged to return to their families or to enter domestic service.

Although, of course, all classes of persons committing crimes were in theory subject to the same penalties, a man of substantial financial means could appoint a barrister to defend him who by verbal jostling with legal jargon gave the defendant a far better chance of ensuring his acquittal. And those such wealthy defendants who *were* found guilty of criminal activities were more likely to be fined than imprisoned. It was usually the penniless, unable to raise the funds to pay fines, who found themselves being imprisoned for what are often, by today's standards, considered very petty offences.

Those by their status and class selected as justices to apply the law very often showed little or no compassion towards the underprivileged. They meted out ruthless sentences knowing full well that they were committing their 'victims' to a period of hardship and deprivation, and young offenders received just as severe a punishment as adults. Prison life for most was indeed severe. In 1872 young George Davey (aged ten years), no doubt driven by his love of animals, stole two tame rabbits for which he was committed to one month's hard labour. The photograph of him (see page 142) reflects utter bewilderment. What mental scars did this experience leave on him at such an early age? Did this 'punishment' act as a deterrent for others; his young friends? Was this a lesson to be learned to turn him to a life of penitence and sobriety? It is doubtful! More likely that this dreadful ordeal created in him deep anger and lifelong bitterness. It is probable too that he spent the rest of his life rebelling against the authorities. Did this set him on a life of crime?

Certainly imprisonment did not prove to be a deterrent; many prisoners when released were reconvicted. Perhaps because, when set free, their spirit was broken making it difficult if not impossible for them to earn an honest living. In 1895 Sir Herbert Gladstone set up an enquiry to report into the prisons and condemned the system as it was then. Prisoners were no longer to be treated as unworthy hopeless wretches but were to be encouraged in industrious activities and good moral living. Useful work was to replace futile and unproductive laborious activities such as the treadmill and the crank. Instruction in various skills was to be taken in groups and time in separate confinement reduced. Habitual criminals were to be separated from others to reduce the risk of 'contamination'. Gladstone's recommendations were implemented by the Prison Act of 1898.

An analysis given with the Habitual Criminal Register for the period 1869 to 1876 (PRO, PCOM 2/404) shows, as would be expected, that London with the greatest population had the highest crime rate, i.e. number of crimes committed. When, however, crime figures for the principal towns and cities are arranged in proportion to the size of population the highest rate was Stafford at 1.881 per thousand persons, second was Worcester at 1.757, and third Taunton at 1.745. London was surprisingly the lowest at 0.461 per thousand.

THE 1877 PRISON ACT AND THE PRISON COMMISSION

In 1877 the county gaols were brought under Government management on the appointment of the Prison Commission. The Prison Commission was established under the Prisons Act 1877 as a statutory board to administer and inspect prisons in England and Wales in accordance with the general or special direction of the Secretary of State. It took over the executive powers and the property rights of the Home Secretary but some powers remained with the Home Office including the appointment of a chairman from among the commissioners of the Prison Inspectorate and of the senior officers of each prison, the approval of appointments of staff made by the commissioners and the regulation of visiting committees of justices. The commissioners were appointed by Royal Warrant on the recommendation of the Secretary of State. The Commission was a body corporate of not more than five members. Its duties included the maintenance of all prisons, the appointment of subordinate prison staff, the inspection of prison buildings and the condition of prisoners and the exercise of powers formerly vested in visiting justices and inspectors of prisons. It also submitted annual reports on every prison to the Home Office for presentation to Parliament. The reports included details of manufacturing processes carried out by prisoners within the prisons. The commissioners were assisted in their work by a central staff, by the Prison Inspectorate and by visiting committees of justices, which acted under regulations drawn up by the Home Office. In 1881 the staffs of the Directors of Convict Prisons and the Prison Commission were merged and under the Prisons Act 1898 the office of commissioner was made to carry that of director as well. The Commission thus became responsible for all prisons in England and Wales. It was closely associated with the Criminal Department of the Home Office and was frequently referred to as the Prison Department of the Home Office. In 1908 the Commission took charge of borstal institutions and in

1948 remand centres and detention centres. From 1877 to 1895 the Commission was responsible for maintaining a register of habitual criminals. In the latter years this was returned to the Metropolitan Police Office. The Commission developed secretariat, set up establishment and finance branches, as well as an Industries and Stores Division concerned with industries in the prisons and borstals and a Works Division dealing with buildings.

The directors of convict prisons were abolished in 1948 and in 1963 the Prison Commission was transferred to the Home Office.

JUVENILE OFFENDERS

For centuries no distinction was made between adults and children when being sentenced in court. Many youngsters were cast into gaol with adults, only to be further corrupted by hardened criminals. It was general practice to hold all those who were waiting to be charged for criminal offences in gaol, and many spent months behind bars awaiting trial.

Thus a juvenile was exposed, in gaol, to debauchery and violence. By the time he had reached his trial, even if he was then found not guilty, it was probably too late, he had experienced the corruption which his term in gaol had yielded and was thus influenced to follow a life of crime.

Until the early nineteenth century no one of influence appears to have shown any concern for the plight of young children who were imprisoned. The law did not differentiate between children and older offenders and juveniles shared the gaols with all manner of evil criminals to be 'contaminated' by their wicked ways in crime and debauchery.

It was in 1815 that Peter Bedford, a Quaker from Spitalfields, was inspired to form a society 'for investigating the causes and alarming increase in juvenile delinquency in the metropolis'. He devoted all his spare time to work among young criminals. A supporting committee was formed from fifty benevolent men who visited the London gaols and listed over seven hundred names of the associates of imprisoned juveniles. Investigation revealed that thousands of boys and girls were living by crime being encouraged and organized by hardened criminals. One committee member, T. Fowell Buxton, visited other gaols in England and found that conditions varied. In a few gaols children were taught to read and write and were given employment to assist them in earning an honest living when they were released. But most gaol conditions were just as dreadful as John Howard had found forty years earlier.

After a visit to Bristol Gaol, Buxton wrote:

Amongst a multitude of persons, whom the jailer described as having no other avocation or mode of livelihood but thieving, I counted eleven children; children hardly old enough to be released from a nursery; hardly competent to understand the first principles of moral obligation, here receiving an education which, as it must unfit them for everything useful, so it must eminently qualify them for that career which they are doomed to run. All charged or convicted of felony, without distinction of age were

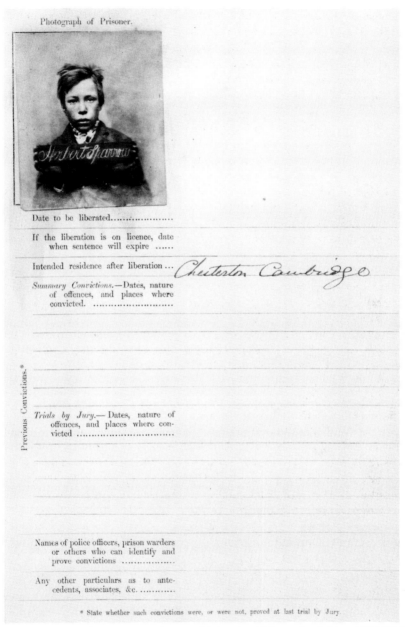

Herbert Sparrow, aged fourteen years, larceny, 21 days hard labour, Cambridge, 1877 (PRO, PCOM 2/300)

Girls' school at Tothill Fields Prison, Westminster (from *The Criminal Prisons of London and Scenes of Prison Life*, H. Mayhew and J. Binny, 1862)

in heavy irons; almost all were in rags; almost all were filthy in the extreme; almost all exhibited the appearance of ill health. . . . When I first went to Newgate, my attention was directed by my companion, Mr Bedford, to a boy whose apparent innocence and artlessness had attracted his notice. The schoolmaster said he was an example to all the rest, so quiet, so reserved, and so unwilling to have intercourse with his dissolute companions. At his trial he was acquitted, upon evidence which did not leave a shadow of suspicion upon him; but lately I recognized him again in Newgate, but with a very different character. He confessed to me that on his release he had associated with the acquaintances he had formed in prison; of his ruin, I can feel but little doubt, and as little of the cause of it. He came to Newgate innocent, he left it corrupted.

In 1813 Elizabeth Fry paid her first visit to Newgate and began her great work of prison reform. In 1817 she started a school there. She was greatly encouraged by the Sheriff of London and the Governor of Newgate though they believed she took on a hopeless task. She also formed an association for the improvement of female prisoners and in 1818 she spoke to a committee of the House of Commons and explained the changes she thought necessary to improve the dreadful conditions in Newgate. Her aim was to make prison life a means of reformation and not degradation. Mrs Benjamin Shaw, influenced by Elizabeth Fry, opened 'A School of Discipline' in Chelsea to receive and assist children when they were discharged from Newgate.

In 1818, in Warwickshire, a 'Farm Colony' was established at Stratton-on-

Dunsmore. This was run by a voluntary organization who received boys from the Warwick and Birmingham Gaols and trained them in farm work. They were also guided in religious and moral living.

In 1830 Mary Carpenter became interested in the poor children of Bristol and in the 'Ragged Schools' which had been founded by John Pounds in 1818. In 1846 she opened her own Ragged School in Lewins Mead, Bristol. It was a day school for twenty boys taken from wandering the streets to civilize them. Some had already been in gaol but she found that imprisonment had done nothing to reform them. She managed to turn a few from a life of crime but realized that the Ragged Schools were inadequate. In 1851 with the help of Matthew Davenport Hill and a Mr Hubback she organized a conference with Lord Lyttleton as president. Mary Carpenter did not speak at the conference as she said it was 'Tantamount to unsexing herself'. Resolutions were adopted which approved her scheme for three kinds of schools. These were: free day schools, feeding industrial schools and reformatory schools.

Mary Carpenter established a reformatory school at Kingswood just outside Bristol. Her aim was reformation not retribution. In 1853 a committee of enquiry into the treatment of juvenile offenders was set up in the House of Commons. Mary Carpenter in her evidence stated:

A child will never behave well in prison for any moral sense; I have in point of fact found that those who behave best in prison are really more likely to do badly when they come out. I would enlist the will of the child in the work, and without this I do not think that any true reformation can be effected. There should be that degree of confidence shown to the children which will make them feel that they are workers together with the teacher.

Following this enquiry the first Youthful Offenders Act was passed in 1854. It recommended the use of reformatories. Inspectors of prisons could inspect an existing reformatory school and, if it met with approval, children could be committed for not less than two years and not more than five years.

After two years at Kingswood Mary Carpenter realized that placing boys and girls in the same school was undesirable. In 1854 she therefore opened Red Lodge, a school for girls. It was discovered that some parents would deliberately ensure that their children were prosecuted in order to get rid of them. To overcome this the 1855 Youthful Offenders Act ruled that magistrates could fix an amount, not exceeding 5 shillings per week to be paid by the parents of the children held in detention. Boys at these schools were taught the cultivation of land, and girls 'the operation of domestic economy'.

By the end of 1857 forty-five schools had been certified as reformatories. Thirty-four were for boys, ten for girls and one for boys and girls. For those children who misbehaved corporal punishment was generally found to be ineffective and the more usual punishment was a few days in solitary confinement with bread and water. The schools had been mostly established by private individuals and supported by local authorities. In 1860 full control was transferred to the Home Office. Fourteen days imprisonment before entering a reformatory school was applied until 1877 when this became ten days or longer.

Sir William Harcourt (Home Secretary 1880 to 1885) was deeply concerned with the harsh treatment of young offenders and sought to reduce their sentences. Queen Victoria was disturbed by what she felt was undue tenderness towards them and had not approved of some remissions of sentences. Sir William was requested to return detailed reports. In a letter to the Queen on 16 September 1880 he wrote:

> Many of these cases were for very trifling offences, as, for instance, a boy of nine years for throwing stones, several boys of eleven and twelve for damaging grass by running about in the fields; a girl of thirteen for being drunk; several boys of twelve and thirteen for bathing in a canal, and similarly for playing at pitch and toss; a boy of nine for stealing scent; a boy of thirteen for threatening a woman, three boys of eleven for breaking windows; a boy of ten for wilfully damaging timber. This morning a case is reported of a boy of ten years old sentenced to fourteen days hard labour or a fine of £1 15s 3d for 'unlawfully throwing down a boarded fence', and the Governor of Prisons reports this child as a small, delicate boy who can neither read nor write. Sir William humbly begs leave to represent to your Majesty that protracted imprisonment in such cases has an injurious effect both upon the physical and moral nature of children of tender years. The child who has been guilty only of some mischievous or thoughtless prank which does not partake of the real character of crime finds himself committed with adult criminals guilty of heinous offences to the common gaol. After a week or fortnight's imprisonment he comes out of prison tainted in character amongst his former companions, with a mark of opprobrium set upon him, and he soon lapses into the criminal class with whom he has been identified. That this sort of punishment has not a reformatory, but degrading effect, is painfully evident from many of the cases reported. Most of them were first convictions, but in those where there have been previous imprisonments, the child was over and over again brought up on fresh charges generally exhibiting a progressive advance in criminal character.

The Queen thereupon sent her approval, and in a letter to Harcourt from Balmoral, Sir Henry Ponsomby wrote:

> Her Majesty was really interested in all you said about the youthful criminals. She would like to whip them, but it seems that that cannot be done. What she objected to was not being forewarned of these numerous remissions.

In 1882 Sir William Harcourt presented a bill for the abolition of imprisonment for convicted children prior to sending them to reformatory schools. It was not until 1899 that imprisonment for children was finally abolished.

Borstal Prison had pioneered a system for the rehabilitation of young offenders and in 1908 this system for those between sixteen and twenty-one years of age was sanctioned by Parliament. Borstals were later replaced by Youth Custody Centres which are now called Young Offenders' Institutions.

CRIMINAL

REGISTERS

In 1791 annual registers (PRO, Class HO 26) of all persons indicted for criminal offences (whether found guilty or not) in the county of Middlesex, which included the City of London, began to be compiled. The early registers list the name of each of the accused together with the date when brought to prison, a physical description of the prisoner, his place of birth, the place to which he was committed and by whom, a summary of the crime, when and where tried and before whom, the sentence of the court and the date of discharge. For those dying in prison the date of death is given and the name of the prison hulk or ship is given for those sentenced to a term of transportation. This style of record was maintained until 1802 after which entries become less informative giving only name, date of trial, summary of the offence and the sentence of the court. The Middlesex Criminal Registers continued as a separate series until 1848. From 1849 Middlesex is entered with the other counties.

It was not until 1805 that criminal registers were kept for the other counties of England and Wales. These (PRO, Class HO 27) are arranged annually and the counties within the annual volumes are arranged alphabetically. It should be noted that there are some anomalies in the alphabetical arrangement. Hampshire is listed as Hants 1805 to 1837 and as Southampton from 1838. Shropshire is listed as Shropshire 1805 to 1808 and from 1809 as Salop. From 1805 to 1814 all Welsh counties are to be found listed after all English counties and from 1815 to 1854 they are alphabetical with English counties. From 1855 they are again listed after all English counties. Bristol is listed after Gloucestershire and London with Middlesex. Monmouthshire is always treated as part of England and is therefore to be found alphabetically arranged with English counties.

Ages are given together with the degree of literacy (whether the prisoner could read or write) from 1834 to 1848. From 1850 onwards the volumes were made up from separately completed forms and then bound together annually. In some instances part of one county has been missed from the main content of the volume and has been added at the end. When searching a particular county it is important therefore to check at the end of each volume to ensure that the required county has been fully covered. With the ending of the separate registers for Middlesex in 1849 Middlesex was then entered alphabetically with English counties. Criminal registers continue in an unbroken series up to 1892.

Registers of habitual criminals were also kept and these appear in PRO, Classes PCOM 2 and MEPO 6. Old Bailey prisoners are listed in PRO, Class HO 16. A detailed listing of all criminal registers in the Public Record Office is given in Appendix 4.5.

Examples from Middlesex registers are given in this chapter and a selection of entries from county registers is tabulated on pages 39 and 40. Abstracts are also given here from Old Bailey calendars and habitual criminal registers.

PRO, HO 26/56

Date when brought to Newgate		18 July 1791
Number of Commitment		24
Prisoner's Name		Sarah Douglas, widow
Description	Age	63
	Height	5 feet 4 inches
	Hair	Brown
	Eyes	Light
	Complexion	Fresh
Born		Nottingham
To what place committed		New Prison
By whom		Bond
Crime		Stealing table linen, Mr Ibbetson's
When and where tried		22 July 1791, Old Bailey
Before whom		Recorder
Sentence		Transportation 7 years
Date when discharged		Died [no date given]

PRO, HO 26/2

Name	Alexander Elder
Height	5′ 5″
Complexion	Dark
Born	London
Trade	Seaman
To What Place Committed	Newgate
By Whom	Neve
The Crime	Stealing stays &c., Mr. Fletcher's
When Tried	25 February 1793
Before Whom	Grose
The Sentence	Death, Executed at Newgate 1 May 1793

ENGLAND & WALES

REGISTER OF THE NAMES OF ALL PERSONS COMMITTED FOR TRIAL

or

BAILED FOR APPEARANCE

at the

ASSIZES and SESSIONS IN THE YEAR 1850

and the

RESULT OF THE PROCEEDINGS

VOL. I

Criminal register for 1850, (PRO, HO 27/91)

Examples from Criminal Registers (PRO, HO 27)
[From 1834 to 1848 degree of literacy and age are given]

NAME	DEGREE OF LITERACY [Read or write]	AGE	SENTENCED		OFFENCE	SENTENCE
			PLACE	DATE		
Charles Way	R & W	36	Somerset Q.S.	5 Jan 1835	Larceny	1 month prison
James Paul	R	27	Norfolk Assizes	28 March 1835	Night poaching	14 years trans.†
Henry Bottomly	R & W	21	Suffolk Q.S.	6 March 1835	Horse stealing	Life trans.
William Brown	Imp*	54	Lincoln Assizes	16 July 1836	Maliciously stabbing with intent	Death – Reprieved Life trans.
Thomas Godley	R & W	19	Yorkshire, Leeds Borough Sessions	20 April 1836	Larceny	7 years trans.
Edward Blakemore	Well	32	Stafford Q.S.	4 Jan. 1837	Receiving stolen goods	Not guilty
Ralph Rawling	Imp	50	Durham Assizes	28 Feb. 1838	Burglary (simple)	15 years trans.
Charles Longhurst	Imp	24	Kent Q.S.	5 July 1838	Fraud	6 months prison
John Locke	No	20	Devon Q.S.	18 March 1839	Burglary (simple)	6 months prison
Elizabeth Slocombe	N	27	Pembroke Adjd. Q.S.	5 March 1840	Larceny	12 months prison & thrice whipped
John Couper	Well	36	Liverpool Boro' Sessions	20 July 1840	Forgery of a receipt for money	2 years prison
James Gray	N	57	Hertford Q.S.	28 June 1841	Stealing a Fixture	6 weeks prison
Edward Hawkins	N	22	Somerset Assizes	13 March 1844	Entering enclosed land armed by night to take game	2 months prison
William Parsons	N	16	Somerset Q.S.	26 Oct. 1846	Larceny from the person	9 months prison
James Venn	Imp	20	Gloucester Assizes	29 March 1848	Robbery, before convicted of felony	14 years trans.
George Bryant	Well	29	Gloucester Assizes	9 August 1848	Sacrilege	Not guilty

* Imperfect
† transportation

Examples from Criminal Registers (PRO, HO 27)

| NAME | SENTENCED | | OFFENCE | SENTENCE |
	PLACE	DATE		
John Richardson	Lancashire Assizes [Palatinate Ct. of Lanc.]	Lent 1809	Uttering forged bank notes	Death – Executed
Hannah Fisher	Derby Assizes	Lent 1816	Concealing the birth of her child	6 months prison
Robert Wood	Huntingdon Assizes	Lent 1816	Receiving stolen goods	Not guilty
John Potter	Westmorland Assizes	Summer 1816	Setting fire to an outhouse	Not guilty
John Saunders.	Devon Q.S.	July 1816	Embezzlement	6 months prison
Griffiths Roberts	Carnarvon Great Sess.	Spring 1817	Murder	Insane
James Bell	Durham Lent Assizes [Palatinate Ct. of Durham]	Lent 1822	Stabbing a person	Death – Reprieved
Richard Blackmore	Somerset Assizes	Summer 1828	Assault (on an infant) with intent to ravish	2 years prison
Charles Streake	Oxford Q.S.	Easter 1832	Receiving stolen goods	3 months prison and whipped
William Henderson	Denbigh Q.S.	27 June 1848	Fraud	No bill
Charles Whitehouse	Hereford Q.S.	2 July 1849	Larceny by servant	8 months prison
Henry Bandy	Bedford Assizes	16 July 1850	Burglary and stealing, before convicted of felony	10 years trans.
Daniel Blackstaff Donovan	Middx. C.C.Ct.*	8 July 1850	Maliciously causing an injury dangerous to life to murder.	Death recorded Committed suicide in prison
Jane Beattie	Derby Assizes	25 July 1850	Bigamy	Not guilty
Samuel Blagden	Monmouth Assizes	6 April 1880	Bestiality	10 years prison
Elizabeth Morgan	Monmouth Q.S.	19 October 1880	Keeping a bawdy house	8 calendar months prison
Thomas Acton	Warwick Q.S.	4 Jan. 1883	Obtaining goods by false pretences	3 months prison
Robert Rimmer	Lancashire Q.S.	7 April 1884	Shop breaking and larceny	1 month prison
Henry Pearce	Bristol Assizes	16 March 1891	Robbery	7 years penal servitude

* Central Criminal Court

48

County of *Buckingham*

RETURN of all persons Committed, or Bailed to appear for Trial, or Indicted at the *General Quarter Session of Peace* held at *Aylesbury* on the *31st* day of *December* 1849, shewing the nature of their Offences, and the result of the Proceedings.

No.	NAMES	Offences of which those tried were Convicted or Acquitted, and of which those Discharged without Trial were charged on Indictment or Commitment.	Convicted and Sentenced				Acquitted and Discharged
			Death	Transportation	Imprisonment (state if also Whipped or Fined)	Whipped, Fined, or Discharged on Sureties	
1	Hannah Hill	Larceny – before Convicted of Felony			1 week		
2	Richard Bovingdon	Larceny			2 Months		
3	Humphrey Short	Larceny			2 Months		
4	John Williams	Larceny			1 Month		
5	Joseph Harman	Larceny - before Convicted of Felony			3 Months		
6	William Harman	Larceny			1 Month		
7	Frederick Saunders	Larceny					Not Guilty
8	Abraham Ridgely	Larceny					No Bill
9	Thomas Plumridge	Larceny from the person			1 Month		
10	William Rakestraw	Larceny			2 Months		
11	William Abbey	Housebreaking			3 Months		
12	Charles Wright	Receiving stolen Goods			3 Months		
13	Jesse Walker	Larceny			1 Month		
14	John Hall	Housebreaking - before Convicted of Felony		7 years			
15	Alexander Read	Assaulting a constable in execution of his Duty			1 Month		
16	George Cheshall	Using threatening language					No Prosecution
17	Thomas Flowers	Larceny			2 Months		
18	James Addaway	Larceny					Not Guilty
19	Joseph Lewin	Larceny - before Convicted of Felony					Not Guilty
20	Robert Smith	Larceny					Not Guilty
21	John Keep	Larceny					Not Guilty
22	Henry Nerry	Larceny			2 Months		
23	John Towersey	Larceny			2 Months		
24	Henry Finch	Larceny			6 weeks		
25	William Turner	Larceny			12 months		
26	William Rodwell	Larceny			1 week		
27	William Aldridge	Larceny			1 Month		
28	David Bignell	Larceny by Servant			2 Months		
29	John Bignell	Larceny by Servant					No Prosecution
30	Elizabeth Hall	Larceny			2 weeks		

Home Office Return. 2th 2

T

Criminal register showing entries for Buckinghamshire Quarter Sessions, 31 December 1849 (PRO, HO 27/91)

PRO, HO 19/11B
Criminal Register of Cases 1850 to 1851 (arranged alphabetically)

Name		Hawkins, Richard
Conviction	Where	Wiltshire Lent Assizes
	When	March 1851
	Of What	Highway Robbery
Sentence		20 years
Character		Before convicted
Remarks		Millbank [prison]
Result		—

Name		Webb, Jesse
Conviction	Where	Gloucester Summer Assizes
	When	August 1849
	Of What	Stealing a blanket
Sentence		7 years
Character		Character good
Remarks		*Justitia* [prison hulk]
Result		F.P. [free pardon] 9 August 1850

PRO, MEPO 6/1
Metropolitan Police Habitual Criminal Register, 1881

Name	Thomas Kidner
Date of Birth	1862
Place of Birth	North Petherton, Somerset
Married or Single	Single
Trade or Occupation	Labourer
Complexion	Pa [Pale]
Hair	Dk. Br. [Dark Brown]
Eyes	Hz [Hazel]
Height without Shoes	5′ 10″
Build	Prop [Proportionate]
Shape of Face	Long
Distinctive Marks and Peculiarities	Scar on right hand, birth mark on belly, mole on back of neck
Prison from which Liberated, and Date of Liberation	Shepton Mallett 14/4/81
Destination on Discharge	West Newton, North Petherton, Somerset
Period of Police Supervision	3 years
Remarks	2 pre [previous] con [convictions] in the name of Kidner, Thomas

CALENDARS OF PRISONERS

PRE-TRIAL CALENDARS

Before a court sat it was necessary for a list to be drawn up of those persons accused of crimes and who were to be tried at the court hearing. Such documents are called Calendars of Prisoners and can often be found among the court papers or written into Order Books and Process Books. Towards the end of the eighteenth century the calendars began to appear in printed form and many survive in separately compiled files in the Public Record Office and many County Record Offices. The name of the prisoner is given, his crime and by whom committed into custody with the date of the warrant for his arrest. The prisoner's age and trade is often given together with his degree of literacy, i.e. whether he could read or write. It is not unusual to find the sentence of the court appended against each name though the outcome of each trial should be found in Order Books or Fine Rolls.

POST-TRIAL CALENDARS

By the middle of the nineteenth century[1] calendars also began to be printed *after* the trial and so recorded the sentence of the court as well as the details given in the pre-trial calendars. These calendars do sometimes include references to any previous convictions of the prisoners and indicate any alias used.

Calendars of prisoners for Quarter Sessions cases may be found among Quarter Sessions records often filed with the actual records of the court proceedings in County Record Offices. Many counties have separated their calendars from other Quarter Sessions material and are therefore quickly

---

[1] A few counties, e.g. Dorset and Middlesex, did in fact produce post-trial calendars from the beginning of the nineteenth century.

consulted. For all such cases a county listing has been compiled and is given in Appendix 2.1. It should be noted that some County Record Offices hold a limited number of calendars for several counties besides their own. These are also given in Appendix 2.1.

Although Assize records are officially deposited at the Public Record Office, London, many County Record Offices hold Calendars of Prisoners for Assizes. These are also listed in Appendix 2.1.

Several collections of Calendars of Prisoners for both Quarter Sessions and Assizes are held at the Public Record Office. These appear in Classes PCOM 2, HO 16, HO 77, HO 140, and CRIM 5 and are listed in Appendix 4.2.

The HO 140 series is of particular interest. Commencing in 1868 it purports to be a complete series for Quarter Sessions and Assizes for every county in England and Wales and also includes the Channel Islands.

Most printed calendars have a name index at the beginning which greatly assists the researcher to locate a particular name within the calendar.

Abstracts of pre- and post-trial calendars of prisoners for both Quarter Sessions and Assizes are given in this chapter.

PRO, PCOM 2/347

North Riding of Yorkshire
Quarter Sessions 4 January 1859
House of Correction at North Allerton

No. 21

Name	David Robinson
Age	23
Trade	groom
Degree of Instruction	Imp [Imperfect]
Committed by	The Venerable Archdeacon Edward Churton, Craike, Easingwold
Date of Warrant	29 December 1858
When received into Custody	29 December 1858
Offence	Stealing a leaden cistern, the property of John Haxby, at the Township of Easingwold on the 6th November 1858

NORTH-RIDING OF YORKSHIRE.

A CALENDAR OF PRISONERS

WHO HAVE TAKEN THEIR TRIALS AT THE

GENERAL QUARTER SESSIONS OF THE PEACE,

Held at NORTHALLERTON, on TUESDAY, the 29th day of JUNE, 1880.

J. R. W. Hildyard, Esq., Chairman.

SIR CHARLES WILLIAM STRICKLAND, BART., *Sheriff.*
GEORGE GROVES, *Gentleman, Deputy Sheriff.*
THOMAS LAWRENCE YEOMAN, Esq., *Clerk of the Peace.*
WILLIAM CHARLES TREVOR, *Gentleman, Deputy Clerk of the Peace.*

N.B.—N, signifies neither read nor write—R, read—Imp., read and write imperfectly—Well, read and write well—Sup., superior education.

Index.

Cover page with index of the Calendar of Prisoners for Yorkshire North Riding Quarter Sessions, 29 June 1880 (PRO, PCOM 2/347)

HER MAJESTY'S PRISON, NORTHALLERTON.

No.	NAME.	Age.	TRADE.	Degree of Instruction	Name and Address of Committing Magistrate.	Date of Warrant.	When received into Custody.	Offence as charged in the Commitment.	When Tried.	Before whom Tried.	Verdict of the Jury.	Particulars of previous Convictions charged in the Indictment and proved in Court.	Sentence or Order of the Court.
1	SUSANNAH BURNSIDES.	22	Single woman.	N.			8th April, 1880.	The said Susannah Burnsides on the 4th day of April last, at the borough of Middlesbrough, stealing five pounds in money, and one purse, the property of William Bishop; and the said James Rice on the same day at the said borough, feloniously receiving the same well knowing them to have been stolen.					Trial adjourned, prisoners admitted to Bail in their own recognizances of £10 each, to appear and surrender at the next Sessions.
2	JAMES RICE.	25	Hawker.	N.	C. J. Coleman, Esq., *Stipendiary Magistrate for Borough of Middlesbrough.*	7th April, 1880.	8th April, 1880.						
3	JAMES ENGLAND. *Leeds, Oct. 1801—obtaining money falsely...*	36	Printer.	W.	A. W. English, Esq., Aislaby, Whitby.	10th April, 1880.	10th April, 1880.	Stealing one silver watch, the property of Turton Smithson, at the township of Whitby, on the 18th day of November, 1878.	30th June, 1880.	J. R. W. Hildyard, Esq., *Chairman,* Hutton Bonville Hall, Northallerton.	Guilty	7th April, 1879—obtaining money falsely — 12 cal. months.	Imprisonment with hard labour for six calendar months in Her Majesty's Prison at Northallerton.
4	JANE VENTRESS. *Whitby, 17th Feb., 1880—larceny—14 days.*	35	Married woman.	N.	A. W. English, Esq., Aislaby, Whitby.	10th April, 1880.	10th April, 1880.	Stealing one sheet, the property of Mary Stubbs, at the township of Whitby, on the 9th day of April last.	Ditto	A. W. Simpson, Esq., *Chairman,* Scarborough.	Pleaded guilty.	17th Feb., 1880—larceny—14 days.	Imprisonment with hard labour for two calendar months in Her Majesty's Prison at Northallerton
5	ANNIE NUGENT. *Middlesbrough and Durham, Feb. 1878, to March, 1880—drunkenness and indecency 36 times—11 months and 27 days*	29	Married woman	Imp.	C. J. Coleman, Esq., *Stipendiary Magistrate for Borough of Middlesbrough.*	23rd April, 1880.	24th April, 1880.	Stealing one pound fifteen shillings, the monies of William Brown, at the borough of Middlesbrough, on the 16th day of April last.	Ditto	J. R. W. Hildyard, Esq.	Guilty	6. 19th May, 1879— larceny from the person—9 cal. months. 7. 8th Feb., 1869— stealing beef— 21 days.	Imprisonment with hard labour for six months each in Her Majesty's Prison at Northallerton.
6	JOSEPH TYERMAN	45	Blacksmith	R.									
7	JAMES MEGGISON *Middlesbrough, 8th Feb., 1869—stealing beef from a stall—21 days.*	44	Shoemaker	Imp.									
8	(ON BAIL.) ALFRED WRIGHT.	22	General Dealer	N.	Hon. W. F. Dawnay, Bossall, York.	3rd May, 1880.	30th June, 1880.	Stealing a hen, the property of John Ward, at the township of Huntington, on the 24th day of April last.	Ditto	A. W. Simpson, Esq.	Guilty		8. Imprisonment with hard labour for four calendar months in Her Majesty's Prison at Northallerton.
9	JOHN POLLARD. *Admitted to Bail, 4th May, 1880.*	16	Labourer	R.									9. Imprisonment with hard labour for fourteen days in Her Majesty's Prison at Northallerton
10	THOMAS GAY. *Whitby, 18th Oct., 1867—stealing a bottle of whiskey—1 cal. month	Jan., 1874—obtaining money by false pretences—2 cal. months	23rd May, 1878—rogue and vagabond—14 days.*	33	Jet worker.	N.	A. W. English, Esq., Aislaby, Whitby.	8th May, 1880.	8th May, 1880.	Embezzling the sum of ten shillings, received on account of his master, William Lewis, at the township of Whitby, on the 1st day of May last.	Ditto	J. R. W. Hildyard, Esq.	Pleaded guilty.	18th Oct., 1867— stealing a bottle of whiskey — 1 cal. month.	Imprisonment with hard labour for six calendar months in Her Majesty's Prison at Northallerton.
11	ELIZABETH MILLINGTON *Middlesbrough, 20th Jan., 1873—stealing a chair—4 cal. months...*	39	Married woman	N.	C. J. Coleman, Esq., *Stipendiary Magistrate for the Borough of Middlesbrough.*	17th May, 1880.	18th May, 1880.	Stealing a piece of beef, the property of Peter Daniels, at the borough of Middlesbrough, on the 16th day of May last.	Ditto	Ditto	Pleaded guilty.	10th April, 1878— stealing a chair —4 cal. months.	Imprisonment with hard labour for twelve calendar months in Her Majesty's Prison at Northallerton.
	Ditto				Ditto			Stealing two pieces of bacon, the property of William Hodgson and another, at the borough of Middlesbrough, on the 16th day of May last.			A true bill found but no evidence offered on the part of the prosecution.		

Page of Post-Trial Calendar of Prisoners for Yorkshire North Riding Quarter Sessions, 29 June 1880 (PRO, PCOM 2/347)

PRO, HO 140/45

County of Flint, General Quarter Sessions, 9 April 1879, at Mold,
HM Prison Chester Castle

Number	1
Name	Evan Andrew
[Previous Convictions]	Chester Castle 18 June 1878, stealing a hen. 14 days Hard Labour in Her Majesty's Prison at Chester
Age	40
Trade and Residence	Labourer, Caerwys
Degree of Instruction	Imp [Imperfect]
Name and Address of Committing Magistrate	R. Sankey, Esq., Holywell
Date of Warrant	4 February 1879
When Received into Custody	5 February 1879
Offence as Charged in the Commitment	Stealing one hen of the value of two shillings the property of one Joseph Simon Williams at Caerwys on 1 February 1879
When Tried	9 April 1879
Before Whom Tried	P.P. Pennant, Esq., Deputy Chairman, Nantlys, St Asaph
Verdict of Jury	Pleaded guilty of larceny after a previous conviction for felony
Particulars of Previous Convictions charged in the Indictment and Proved in Court	At Holywell Petty Sessions 18 June 1878, stealing a hen, 14 days
Sentence or Order of the Court	Two calendar months Hard Labour in HM Prison Chester Castle

PRO, HO 140/45
Bristol Quarter Sessions 20 October 1879

HM Prison Bristol

Number	12
Name	George Pearce
Age	20
Trade	Salesman
Degree of Instruction	Well
Name and Address of Committing Magistrate	Henry Overton Wills, Esq., Redland Knoll, Bristol
Date of Warrant	29 September 1879
When Received into Custody	29 September 1879
Offence as Charged in the Commitment	Stealing in the dwelling house of Matthew Whiting the sum of £6-13-6, his monies, at Bristol, 28 September 1879
When Tried	20 October 1879
Before Whom Tried	Deputy Recorder, Alexander Mortimer, Esq.
Verdict of the Jury	Pleaded Guilty of Larceny in the dwelling house above the value of £5
Particulars of Previous Convictions Charged in the Indictment, and Proved in Court	– – –
Sentence or Order of the Court	3 calendar months with hard labour

PRO, HO 140/140
Somerset Assizes, 13 July 1892 at Wells
Shepton Mallet Prison

Number	17
Name	John Hawkins, bailed 11 July 1892
Age	– – –
Trade	– – –
Degree of Instruction	– – –
Name and Address of Committing Magistrate	C.J.W. Allen, Esq., Lyngford House, Taunton
Date of Warrant	11 July 1892
When Received into Custody	– – – 1892
Offence as Charged in the Commitment	Wilfully make sign and subscribe a false declaration at the foot of a notice of his intended marriage with intent to procure a marriage between himself and Jane Casnell, at Taunton 2 April 1892
When Tried	13 July 1892
Before Whom Tried	Mr Justice Charles
Verdict of the Jury	Not Guilty of making a false declaration to procure marriage
Particulars of Previous Convictions Charged in the Indictment and Proved in Court	– – –
Sentence or Order of the Court	Discharged

PRO, HO 140/73
Lancashire Quarter Sessions, 27 November 1884

Preston Prison

Number	41
Name	William Richardson
Age	29
Trade	Sailor
Degree of Instruction	Imp [Imperfect]
Name and Address of Committing Magistrate	J. Hull, Esq., H.E. Sowerbutts, Esq., Preston
Date of Warrant When Received into Custody	19th Nov. 1884 19th Nov. 1884
Offence as charged in the Commitment	Stealing one rope, and 80 yards of rope, the property of one James Kay, at Preston, 14th Nov. 1884.
When Tried	27th Nov. 1884
Before whom Tried	C.R. Jackson, Esq.
Verdict of the Jury	Guilty of feloniously receiving stolen property well knowing the same to have been stolen
Particulars of Previous Convictions charged in the Indictment and proved in Court	− − −
Sentence or Order of the Court	4 calendar months hard labour

PRO, HO 77/2
Newgate Calendar 1794 to 1795

January 1795
Middlesex Verdicts

Case No.	Tried Before	Name	Verdict	Crime	Age
6	Recorder	William Patch	G	fel	33
33	Heath	Philip Gibson	G	fel	35
13	Ch. of Bar	William Collins	G	fel	18
26	Heath	Randall Smith	G	fel	55

London Verdicts

Case No.	Tried Before	Name	Verdict	Crime	Age
11	Ch. of Bar	Thomas Yeoman	N.G.		
10	Heath	Mary Clark	G	fel	46
37	Heath	Elizabeth Eaves alias Bishop	N.G.		
34	Heath	Ann Hawkins	G	fel	27
19	Heath	Michael Love	G	Death	17
8	Ch. of Bar	Martha Palethorpe	G	fel	33
7	Heath	James Watkins	N.G.		
7	Heath	William Russel	G	fel	55
9	Recorder	John Sluice	G	fel	58
22	Heath	Elizabeth Salvill	G	fel	33
32	Ch. of Bar	Ann Atkins	G	fel	41
11	Heath	Susannah Lee	G	fel	30
5	Ch. of Bar	William Lister	G	fel	34
24	Recorder	Edward Saville	N.G.		
18	Recorder	Sarah Cowley	G	fel	60
31	Recorder	James Movies	G	fel	40
16	Recorder	William Myatt	G	fel	19
20	Recorder	Andrew Sedgwick	N.G.		
17	Recorder	Hannah Bardwick	N.G.		
35	Ch. of Bar	Mary Marchant	G	fel	24
35	Ch. of Bar	Mary McClugh	N.G.		

[G guilty; N.G. not guilty; fel felony]

PRO, HO 16/1
City of London and County of Middlesex

A return of the several prisoners committed for trial at the Sessions of Oyer and Terminer, and Gaol Delivery held at the Old Bailey in the month of January 1815, shewing the nature of their Crimes and the results of their commitments.

NAME	CRIME AS CHARGED IN INDICTMENT	AS BY VERDICT OF JURY	SENTENCE
Richard Jones ⎱ William Jones ⎰	Larceny above 5s privately in a shop	Guilty	Death
David Kelly	Highway Robbery	Guilty of stealing from the person but not violently nor putting the person in fear	Transported 7 yrs.
Elizabeth Ringrose	Burglary	Guilty of stealing in the dwelling house but not of breaking out of the dwelling house	Judgement respited
James Vinn	Larceny above 5s privately in a shop	Guilty of stealing but not privately in the shop	Privately Whipped and imprisoned 9 cal. months in the House of Correction at Clerkenwell.
Jane Beaumont	Larceny	Bill not found	Delivered by proclamation
Richard Mools	Larceny	No prosecution	Delivered by proclamation
Robert Panton	Murder	Guilty of manslaughter only	Fined 1s and imprisoned 6 cal. months in Newgate
Thomas Gillham	Obtaining money by false pretences	Guilty	Publicly Whipped and discharged.

COURTS OF
QUARTER SESSIONS

In 1363 Keepers of the Peace were formally called Justices and were empowered to meet four times a year to hold their Courts of Quarter Sessions. These four sessions were termed Epiphany, Easter, Midsummer and Michaelmas. Quarter Sessions Courts dealt with all manner of civil matters as well as administering the criminal law.

County Quarter Sessions were held in all counties in England and Wales except in the county of Middlesex. Although the City of Westminster held its own Quarter Sessions there were no Quarter Sessions held for the county of

Sessions House, Clerkenwell, 1826 (British Museum)

Middlesex. The Old Bailey Sessions were held every month where London and Middlesex trials took place (see Chapter 6).

It was usual for each County Session within a year to be held in a different town in the county. Each session aimed to complete all its proceedings in a day. By the nineteenth century there had been such an increase in the amount of business of the courts that it was often necessary to continue the court proceedings on another day, usually within a week of the main hearing. This second session was referred to as an Adjourned Session and was treated administratively as a separate session. Second sessions were formally authorized by the Act 59 Geo. III c. 28 (1819). All documents, including calendars of prisoners, are therefore filed separately and referred to as, for example, 'Somerset Epiphany *Adjourned* Sessions'.

In addition to County Quarter Sessions, towns and cities also held quarterly sessions. These are known as Borough or City Sessions.

Many types of crimes were tried at Quarter Sessions, from petty larceny to assault, arson and rape. It is not unusual to find cases of very serious crimes referred on to Assizes. The Courts of Quarter Sessions also dealt with a wide range of civil matters.

Records of Quarter Sessions are held in County and Borough Record Offices. A summary of surviving sessions records in England and Wales is given in J.W.S. Gibson's booklet *Quarter Sessions Records*, published by The Federation of Family History Societies, 1st edition, 1982.

Depositions

Of the range of documents found among court records the most detailed and informative are the depositions. A deposition is a statement made under oath by a witness before a magistrate or constable. It often gives the informant's place of abode and usually his trade or occupation. It bears his signature (if he could write) at the end of his statement. A person with a common name may only be definitely identified by his signature, comparing it with his signature at marriage or from some other document.

Indictments

Records of some court proceedings omit the place of abode of an accused person or those bringing the charge. The indictment is therefore of particular use in giving this information. An indictment is often a small printed parchment document filled in to record the name of the accused, his place of abode and the offence with which he was accused with the date and place of the event. Other persons directly involved in the crime whether accomplices, victims or witnesses may also be mentioned.

Examinations

These are statements made under oath by accused persons before a justice and are similar to depositions made by witnesses.

Order Books

These together with Process Books and Minute Books record the proceedings of the court. Order Books particularly record verdicts and sentences though sometimes such details are also found in Process Books. Lists of sentenced criminals are to be found for each session and, like calendars of prisoners may be used as a finding aid for individual persons.

Note: The type and amount of records which survive vary considerably from county to county. In some counties no depositions exist and the researcher must rely on calendars of prisoners and/or indictments as the only source of criminal proceedings.

Lancs. RO, QJI/1/188
Indictment,[1] Lancashire Easter Sessions, April 1814

Thomas Buffrey late of the Township of Manchester, labourer, in the County of Lancashire on the 22nd day of February in the fifty fourth year of the Reign of our Lord George the Third by the Grace of God of the United Kingdom of Great Britain and Ireland, King, Defender of the Faith, at the Township aforesaid in the County aforesaid, one silver watch of the value of one penny, one piece of silver the value of one penny, one piece of brass the value of one penny, one piece of steel the value of one penny and one piece of gold the value of one penny the goods and chattels of Henry Smith then and there found and being by force and arms feloniously did steal, take, and carry away against the Peace of our said Lord the King, his Crown and Dignity.

Witnesses   Henry Smith
             Henry Hulse

Guilty   Transportation for 7 years

Corn. RO, DD.RO. 3685
Indictment, Michaelmas Sessions, 1801

Borough of Helston in Cornwall

The Jurors for our Lord the King upon their oaths present that Peter Landeria of the said Borough, butcher, on the first day of June in the forty first year of the reign of our Sovereign Lord George the Third, King of the United Kingdom of Great Britain and Ireland and on divers other days and times between that day and the day of taking this Inquisition with force and arms at the Borough aforesaid in the County aforesaid in a certain place there close to and adjoining upon a certain public street and the King's Common Highway there called Meneage Street and near to the dwelling houses of divers liege subjects of our said Lord the King there unlawfully and injuriously did uphold, maintain and keep a certain house or place for the slaughter of Bullocks, Calves and other Cattle and the blood and offals of the animals so slaughtered unlawfully and injuriously did permit and suffer to become putrid and offensive by means whereof divers of the subjects of our said Lord the King were during the term aforesaid and still are in great danger of an infectious distemper and disorder and of having their health materially

---

[1] Some counties, including Lancashire, do not have surviving records such as depositions and examinations. In these cases the indictment may be the only record of the case.

injured and impaired to the great detriment, danger, and common nuisance as well, of many of the liege subjects of our said Lord the King passing and repassing by the said house or place so upheld and kept for the purpose aforesaid and by, through and along the said public street and King's Common Highway and also of those inhabiting and residing thereabouts to the evil example of all others in the like case offending and against the peace of our said Lord the King, his Crown and Dignity.

Helston, 15 July 1801
Borlaise, Town Clerk

Peter Landeria pleaded Not Guilty and was Acquitted.

Berks. RO, Q/SR/P1
A conspiracy to break out of gaol

To the Worshipful His Majesty's Justices of the Peace for the said County of Berkshire at their General Quarter Sessions held at Newbury in and for the said County of Berkshire on Tuesday the 19th day of April 1737.

The Humble Petition of John Wiseman keeper of His Majesty's Gaol at Reading for the said County of Berkshire. Sheweth that whereas about the month of October last a conspiracy was formed between Mary Groves, Richard Madson and others in concert with several prisoners, some convicted others committed for felony, among whom the son of the said Mary Groves was planning to break the said Gaole and discharge the said prisoner, and saws, picklock keys and other tools and instruments were provided and lodged for that purpose, and your petitioner having likely discovered the said conspiracy a night or two before the same was intended to be put in execution your petitioner also found where the said tools and instruments were lodged and took the same and also caused several persons to be apprehended on account thereof two of whom, viz the said Mary Groves and Richard Madson liveing in London your petitioner caused to be there apprehended and committed for the said offence, and your petitioner was bound in a recognizance to prosecute them and was obliged at his own expence to move them from London to Reading to take their tryal for the said offence at the last Assizes where by reason of a favourable Jury they were acquitted, and in the carrying on of which prosecution your petitioner was at great expence.
Your petitioner therefore humbly hopes that as the said offence was of a heinous nature and publick concern, that he shall be reimbersed the charges of the said prosecution and that Your Worshipp will be pleased to grant him an order upon the Treasurer to pay him the same amounting to the sum of seven pounds as appears by the annext bill, wherein your petitioner hath charged nothing for his own trouble but only such money as he expended out of his own pocket.

And your petitioner shall ever pray,

[signed] John Wiseman

An account of the expenses of John Wiseman in taking and removing from London to Reading and in prosecuting of Mary Groves and Richard Madson for providing saws and other instruments in order to break the County Gaol:

Paid for horse and man to London and expenses in taking Mary Groves	1 – 1 – 0
Paid at ye Crown Office for two Habeus Corpus	1 – 8 – 0
Paid ye Keeper for bringing ye prisoner from London to Reading	4 – 4 – 0
Paid for two Bills of Indictments	0 – 7 – 0
	£7 – 0 – 0

To be paid by Treasurer
In the year 1736

Powys AO, Brecon SR 1801 E
Brecon Quarter Session Rolls, Easter Sessions, 1801

Conveyance of convicts to Portsmouth

Whitehall, 19th January 1801

Sir,

His Majesty having been pleased to give directions that three male convicts now under sentence of Transportation, in the Gaol at Brecon should be removed from thence on board the Hulks at Portsmouth, or Langston Harbour near Portsmouth, and committed to the charge of Andrew Hawes Bradley, Esquire, Overseer of the Convicts on board the said Hulks. I am commanded to signify to you the King's pleasure that you do cause the said Convicts if upon being examined by an experienced Surgeon they shall be found free from any Putrid or Infectious Distemper to be removed on board the said Hulks where they are to remain until their sentences can be carried into execution or otherwise disposed of according to Law.

I am Sir
Your Obedient
Honourable Servant
Portland

P.S. You will send with the
Prisoners an account of
their ages and respective
Sentences.

The High Sheriff of Brecon

A Bill of the Expences in Conveying the hereunder named Male Convicts from Brecon County Gaol, on board the hulks lying in Langston Harbour near Portsmouth.

1	Phillip Phillips	Transported for Life
2	John Owen	For the Term of 7 years
3	Thomas Davies	For the Term of 7 years Carriage Charges &c

	£	s	d
From Brecon to Gloc^r per Mail Coach } 4 outside 1 inside	5	2	0
Coachman & Guards fees		5	0
Towards lodging Convicts in Gloc^r Gaol 1 night		7	6
Carriage from Gloc^r to Bristol	2	7	6
Lodging the Convicts 1 night in Newgate, Bristol and support there		12	0
Carriage from Bristol to Portsea	6	15	0
pd to sundry Coachmen &c		7	0
Carriage from Porsea to Langston Harbour		7	6
Pd Boatmen to Convey the Convicts on Board the hulk		2	0
Carriage Expences in Returning to Brecon. 2 passengers	6	0	0
Maintenance &c in the Journey	5	4	6
Guards for conveying the Convicts, £2 2s each	4	4	0
	£31	14	0

Powys AO, Radnor QS OB/3
Radnorshire Quarter Sessions, Order Book

The King on the Prosecution of James Griffiths

V

James Jenkins for an Assault

At this Court came the Defendant James Jenkins of the Town of Presteigne mercer and acknowledged himself indebted to our Sovereign Lord the King in the sum of £20 – 0 – 0
Mary Jenkins of the same place, widow in the sum of £10 – 0 – 0
John Evans of the same, yeoman in the sum of £10 – 0 – 0

Upon the following condition that if the Defendant James Jenkins do and shall personally appear at the next General Quarter Sessions of the Peace and plead to a Bill of Indictment found against him at this present Sessions on the prosecution of James Griffiths for an Assault and shall also at the following Sessions Traverse, Quash or Submit to the said Bill of Indictment and not depart without leave of the Court.

Discharged at Michaelmas Sessions, 1805

Ang. RO, W/QA/G/1087a
Petition of Griffith Roberts a prisoner confined in the County Gaol

To your Worshipful the Magistrates now assembled at the Adjourned Trinity General Quarter Sessions to be held at Beaumaris in the County of Anglesey on the 26th day of July 1843.

This is the humble petition of Griffith Roberts now a prisoner in the County Gaol at Beaumaris hoping that your Worships will take my humble petition under your due consideration. This being my first offence and I trust in God that it shall be my last. Having been confined in the County Gaol to hard labour since the 4th day of January your humble Petitioner hopes through your tender mercy towards my wife and young family who are entirely destitute of maintenance and support on account of my confinement I hope and trust that your Worships will mitigate and shorten my sentence according to your wise discretion and your humble Petitioner will ever Pray.

his
Griffith X Roberts
mark

This is to certify that the within named Griffith Roberts is a quiet and industrious behaviour since here and seems often pondering on his past habit of life. And I further say that I have had less trouble with him in performing his labour than any one that here has been.

H. Jones
Keeper

Ang. RO, W/Q/AG/1090
Free Pardon

Whereas Fanny Hughes was at a Quarter Sessions of the Peace holden for the County of Anglesey in January 1849 convicted of larceny and sentenced to be imprisoned six months for the same we in consideration of some circumstances humbly represented unto us are graciously pleased to extend Our Grace and Mercy unto her, and to grant her Our Free Pardon for the crime of which she stands convicted. Our Will and Pleasure therefore is that you cause her the said Fanny Hughes to be forthwith discharged out of custody, that for so doing this shall be your Warrant.

Given at Out Court at St. James's the second day of June 1849 in the Twelfth Year of Our Reign.

By Her Majesty's Command

To Our Trusty and Wellbeloved
the Keeper of the Gaol at
Beaumaris in the County of
Anglesey, and all others
whom it may concern.

Ang. RO, W/QA/G/1025
Court Orders 1849

Thomas Hughes, aged 19, 5 ft 7 ins. Read imperfect

Lloyd John Price, Esquire one of Her Majesty's Justices of the peace for the said County [Anglesey], to the Constable of the parish of Pentraeth in the said County, and to the keeper of the Common Gaol at Beaumaris, in the said County. These are to command you the said Constable in Her Majesty's name, forthwith to convey and deliver into the custody of the said Common Gaol the body of Thomas Hughes, labourer charged this day before me the said Justice on the oath of Thomas Jones and others, for that he the said Thomas Hughes on the 21st day of March in the year of our Lord one thousand, eight hundred and forty nine at the parish of Pentraeth in the said County, did feloniously steal take and carry away one coat of the value of fifteen shillings, one trousers of the value of two shillings, one waistcoat of the value of three shillings and one pair of shoes of the value of four shillings of the goods and chattels of me Thomas Jones against the peace of our Sovereign Lady the Queen, her Crown and Dignity. And you the said keeper are hereby required to receive the said Thomas Hughes into your custody in the same

Common Gaol and him there safely to keep until he shall be thence delivered by due course of Law. Herein fail you not. Given under hand and Seal the 2nd day of May in the year of our Lord 1849.

Lloyd J. Price

W. Sus. RO, QR/W 537
William Bartlott charged with attempted rape

West Sussex Epiphany Sessions, 13 January 1777, at Midhurst.

Willm Bartlott committed January ye 11.1777 by Willm Mill Leeves, esq., charged upon the oath of Mary Fogden of the parish of Boxgrove with an intent to ravish and carnally know her against her will.

Be it remembered that on the eleventh day of January in the year of our Lord, one thousand seven hundred and seventy seven Richard Fogden of the parish of Boxgrove in the County of Sussex aforesaid, yeoman personally came before me one of his Majesty's Justices of the Peace for the said County and acknowledged himself to be indebted to our Sovereign Lord the King in the sum of twenty pounds. The condition of this Recogniz-ance is such, that if Ann the wife of the aforesaid Richard Fogden shall personally appear at the General Quarter Sessions of the Peace to be holden in and for the said County and then and there give such Evidence as she knoweth upon a Bill of Indictment to be exhibited by the said Richard Fogden and Mary Fogden his daughter or one of them to the Grand Jury, against William Bartelott late of the City of Chichester in the said County of Sussex, labourer for an assault committed by him the said William Barttelot with an Intent to committ a Rape on the body of her said daughter Mary Fogden. Then this Recognizance to be void.

The Examination of Mary Fogden daughter of Richard Fogden of the parish of Boxgrove in the County aforesaid, yeoman, taken upon her oath this eleventh day of January 1777. Who saith that she is of the age of twelve years and upwards and that about the hour of eleven o'clock in the forenoon of yesterday the tenth day of this instant January as she was passing over Halnaker Down in the parish aforesaid to her father's house she was accosted by a young man whose name she hath since learnt is William Barttelott and who is now present and who inquired of her the way to Chichester, which this Examinant informed him. That the said William Barttelott immediately laid his hands on her and by force and violence threw her on the ground, pulled up her petticoats and unbuttoned his own breeches and laid down upon her and endeavoured to put his cock into her against her will and consent and threatened her this Examinant that if she cryed out he would cutt her throat. And this Examinant further saith that as soon as the said William Barttelot left her she went home and immediately acquainted her mother how she had been used by the said William Barttelot.

[signed] Mary Fogden

The Examination of Ann the wife of Richard Fogden of the parish of Boxgrove in the County aforesaid, yeoman taken on her oath this eleventh day of January 1777. Who saith that she is the mother of Mary Fogden now aged twelve years and upwards and that yesterday the 10th instant about two o'clock in the afternoon she was told by her said daughter that about eleven o'clock in the forenoon of the same day she her said daughter was passing over Halnaker Down in the parish of Boxgrove aforesaid she met a man who threw her down and had almost killed her that he unbuttoned his breeches and wanted to put his cock into her. That her said daughter then described the said man as being of age and size between a man and a boy with a blue coat on and having a bundle. And this Examinant further saith that such description corresponds with William Barttelot now present standing charged with the said offence and who by such description was afterwards pursued and taken.

Sworn before me   The mark of the above named
Wm Mill Leeves   X
                                                   Ann wife of Richard Fogden

Sentence
Recommited till Saturday next then to be conveyed to Chichester and publicly wipt at the wipping post with 20 lashes on his bare back till being bloody to be then recommited again for one month and then receive 20 lashes more till his back is bloody each wipping about the middle of the day and then discharged.

Ports. RO, S3/183
Richard West, an army deserter

Portsmouth Borough Sessions, 26 October 1781

Richard West voluntarily confesseth that in the month of January 1780 he enlisted as a private man into the Cinque Ports Regiment or Battalion of Foot and received two shillings from the Officer who commanded the recruiting party at Frome, Somersetshire. That the next day after his so enlisting he absconded without going before a Justice of the Peace in order to declare his assent or dissent to such enlisting, and that on or about the thirteenth day of June last past he enlisted into the Portsmouth Division of Marines, and this day at Portsmouth was apprehended as a deserter from the said Cinque Ports Regiment by John Smith now present, Corporal in Captain Walcot's Company in the same Regiment and secured by him.

[signed] Richard West

Taken at Portsmouth aforesaid
the 27th Sept. 1781 before me
Edward Linzee, Mayor

John Smith, corporal in Captain Walcot's Company in the Cinque Ports Regiment or Battalion of Foot maketh oath that this day at Portsmouth he apprehended the above named Richard West as a deserter from the said Regiment and caused him to be secured.

[signed] Jno Smith

Sworn at Portsmouth aforesaid
the 27th Sept. 1781 before me
Edward Linzee, Mayor

[No further material regarding the outcome of this case has been found.]

Berks. RO, Q/SR 213
Robert Silver charged with stealing pigeons, a copper and a cock

Berkshire Easter Sessions, 17 April 1787, at Newbury

Robert Silver, aged 40 years, committed 6 March 1787 by G.T. Goodenough, Esq., on the oath of James Marlow of Binfield, charged with feloniously taking and carrying away several fowls, the property of said James Marlow.

The King against Robert Silver

For stealing pigeons of the value of 10d the property of Anna Maria Reeve and Jane Reeve, spinsters.
Benjamin King, Miss Reeve's coachman proves the pigeon house having been broke open and the pigeons stole thereout.

Barth°. Stiff of Bracknole, victualler, of buying live pigeons of Robert Silver to be shot at.

The King against Robert Silver

For stealing a copper of the value of 10d the property of [blank] Tighe, widow.

Anthony Hadland. That the copper was pulled from out of the brick work and taken away, saw the copper at Mr Goodenough's and measured the lead which went round it and fitted.
Edward Pither proves the same as Hadland and the copper stolen had a cock like the one produced.
Mr William Randall proves having mended coppers at the house and that the copper found is a copper which he had once mended.
John Henham proves that in searching the house of Robert Silver for nets found a copper which appeared to have been pulled down from new brick work.
Mr Goodenough proves finding the copper at Silver's house.

The King against Robert Silver

For stealing a cock of the value of 6d the property of James Marlow. James Marlow proves that at different times he lost a cock (which he knows to be his property) and suspects that Silver stole same.
Mr Dee, constable of Binfield, proves that in searching the house of Silver he found a cock and having heard Marlow lost a cock he took it to him which he said was his property.
John Henham proves that in searching Silver's house for nets he saw the cock and which Dee took to Marlow and Marlow said it was his property.

The several Examinations of Benjamin King, servant to Miss Reeves of Holyport in the parish of Bray in the said county and Bartholomew Stiff of Bracknole in the parish of Warfield in the said county, victualler, taken on oath this 26th day of March 1787.
Who saith in the evening of Christmas 1785 the pigeon house belonging to his mistress at Holyport aforesaid was broken open by the door being wrenched open and about two dozen of pigeons stolen thereout, and this examinant suspects that some person or persons did steal the same. And that some of the pidgeons so stolen were blue and white.

[signed] Benjamin King

And the said Bartholomew Stiff says that at or about Christmas 1785 one Robert Silver of Binfield in the county aforesaid, labourer, brought 29 or 30 pidgeons alive to the house of this examinant and he suspecting that they had been stolen, kept Silver drinking and in conversation while he sent to Binfield to Mr Morton's whom this examinant had heard had lost pidgeons, but receiving an answer upon a servant of Mr Morton's seeing the pidgeons that they were not his pidgeons, this examinant then questioned said Silver whence he got them and on his saying that he bought them in a market this examinant paid him 14s 6d for the same. And says that some of them were blue and white and some of them all blue.

the mark of
X
Bartholomew Stiff

The examination of Anthony Hadland of Warfield in the said county, broker, taken the 26 day of March 1787.
Who on his oath says that a few days before Christmas in the year 1785 he was informed that Mr T. Tigh's farm house had been broken open and a copper stolen thereout. That he inspected the place, tracked 2 men and saw where they had put the copper down on the grass. That in October last he was sent for by Mr Goodenough to Binfield, where he saw a copper which he was informed had been then found in the house of Robert Silver at Binfield aforesaid. That he returned home and sent the lead which had been put round the top of the copper when it was fix'd up at Mrs Tigh's house. That he saw the lead tied round the top of the copper and it appeared to him to be the lead belonging to the copper.

[signed] Anthony Hadland

The Examination of John Henham of the parish of Bray in the said county, gamekeeper, taken on oath the 26th day of March 1787.
Who on his oath says that on or about the 24th day of October last he assisted the constable by virtue of a Justice's Warrant in searching the house of Robert Silver at Binfield for nets, and therein found a washing copper which appeared to have been pulled down from some brick work where it had been fixed. That having heard a copper had been then lately stolen from the farm house of Mrs Tighe of Warfield he carried it to the house of Mr Goodenough a Justice of the Peace by his orders. That having also heard that one Farmer Marlow of Binfield had lost some fowls, one of which had been described particularly he this examinant saw one on the premises of the said Silver which answered such description. That he immediately put it into the hands of the constable Wm. Dee who in his presence was directed by the said Justice to carry it to the said Farmer Marlow who said he knew the same to be his property.

[signed] John Henham

The Examination of Edward Pither, gardener of the parish of Warfield in the said county, taken on oath the 26 March 1787.
Who on his oath says that about Christmas 1785 when he lived servant with Mrs Tighe of the same parish the front door of her farm house situate near her dwelling house was broke open and a washing copper pulled down from the brick work, stolen and carried away. That the copper now produced appears to him to be the same as that which was stolen as aforesaid, and which copper had a cock like the one now produced.

Sworn Before us   [signed] Edward Pither
Pen. Powney
G.S. Goodenough

Proofs respecting the burglary at Mrs Tighe's out house at Warfield, Berks, no one being therein, a little before Xmas 1785.

Anthony Hadland and Ed^d Pither	Proves that the fore door of the house was wrenched open and that a boiling copper was lost thereout.
Henham and Mr Goodenough	Prove the finding a copper at Robt Silver's house at Binfield.
Eleanor Cooper and David Priest and Wm Smith	Prove the property of the copper to be Mrs Tighe's.

The information of James Marlow of the parish of Binfield in the said county, yeoman, taken the 24th day of October 1786.

Who saith that he hath at different times lost chicken from his hen roost and particularly about a twelve month ago he lost a cock which he verily believes and hath no doubt he shall be able to prove was stolen by Robert Silver of Binfield, labourer and this informant further saith that the cock now produced to him by Wm. Dee the constable, is the property of this informant and which he hath heard and verily believes was found by the said constable in the possession of the said Robert Silver.

> The mark of
> X
> James Marlow

The information also of the aforesaid William Dee the constable of Binfield aforesaid taken on oath as above.

Who saith that yesterday the 23rd Inst. he was ordered by a Warrant under the hand and seal of Penyston Powney one of His Majesty's Justices of the Peace for the said county to search the house of the aforesaid Robert Silver and that he found a cock as before mentioned running about the yard of the said Robert Silver's house at Binfield and that having heard that James Marlow had lost fowls at different times he carried the said cock to him who immediately and without hesitation declared the cock to be his property upon which this informant left it in the possession of the said James Marlow.

> [signed] William Dee

Verdict   Guilty
Sentence   To be transported beyond the seas for seven years

Sur. RO, QS 2/6/1798, Easter Sessions Papers
John Baker Dove charged with stealing 215 wooden spokes

Surrey Easter Sessions, 17 April 1798, at Reigate

John Baker Dove committed the 29th March 1798 by Arthur Jones Esq., charged on the oaths of Joshua Russell and William Moore, with feloniously stealing taking and carrying away, at Reigate in the said county, two hundred and fifteen rough oak wheel spokes, the goods and chattels of the said William Moore, and his partner Robert Boxall.

The information of Joshua Russell of Reigate, taylor, William Upfold of Reigate, labourer, William Moore of Reigate, carpenter and Jasper Bryant of Reigate, labourer and William Charman of Reigate, builder, taken on oath this 29th day of March 1798 before me Arthur Jones, esq., one of His Majesty's Justices of the Peace for the said county.

First this informant Joshua Russell for himself saith that he is the collector of the tolls of the Reigate Turnpike at a gate called Woodhatch Gate and that he has for some time past seen a parcel of small pieces of rough oak timber called spokes piled up near the Toll House in which he lives and that being called up between one and two o'clock in the morning of Wednesday the 28th day of March instant in the way of his business as gatekeeper he heard a horse cough a little below the garden adjoining his house and suspecting something was going on wrong he kept on the watch. And that soon afterwards this informant heard a noise like the loading of a cart and about a quarter of an hour afterwards a person came partly towards the Turnpike House made a stop and went back again immediately and as soon as the man turned back that this informant heard a cart or waggon drive away and that informant suspecting that some persons had been stealing the spokes so piled up near his house went to the Angel public house and called up Abraham Hobsman and William Upfold who ran after the cart with this informant. That informant who outran the other two overtook the cart which went down the Turnpike Road. That he looked into the cart and saw pieces of timber in it very like the rough spokes now produced with which the cart was fully loaded. That the cart was drawn by three horses. That this informant went by the left side of the cart and asked the man who drove it whose team it was. And that the man answered he did not know. And this informant saith that he is positive that the man who drove the cart was John Baker Dove of Reigate aforesaid, labourer now in custody on a charge of feloniously stealing and carrying away a quantity of spokes the property of William Moore and Robert Boxall and that witness then returned back to his house.

And this informant William Upfold for himself saith that being called upon at the Angel public house where he lodged by informant Joshua Russell he went with him in pursuit of the said cart and came up with it and saw it.

And this informant Joshua Russell further saith that understanding that the said spokes lying near his house were the property of the said William Moore he went up to Reigate immediately after he had left the said John Baker Dove driving the cart and informed him of what had happened. And these informants Joshua Russell and William Moore for themselves say that about seven o'clock the same morning they went to Woodhatch to the pile of spokes and that from that spot they tracked a broad wheel cart along the Turnpike Road as far as the gate by Bartlott's Cottage, thro' the gate along the lane to Whitehall from thence all the way along the lane to Cockshott Hill and from thence down the Turnpike Road to the yard of Thomas Turner and John Turner of Reigate aforesaid, wheelwrights (now in custody on a charge of receiving the said spokes so stolen and taken away as aforesaid knowing them to have been stolen) into which yard the track turned.

And this informant Jasper Bryant for himself saith that about half past 5 o'clock in the morning of Wednesday the 28th day of March instant he saw the said John Baker Dove driving a broad wheel cart with three horses down the Turnpike Road into the Town of Reigate about 40 or 50 rods from the Yard of the said Thomas Turner and John Turner the said yard being situate between Woodhatch and the place where informant saw the said John Baker Dove driving the said cart and that the cart was not loaded and that informant spoke to the said John Baker Dove.

And this informant William Moore saith that upon going to the place where the spokes had been piled, and upon examining the pile he missed a quantity and numbered them and discovered that two hundred and fifteen of them were gone. And that informant having procured a search warrant to search the yard and buildings of the said Thomas Turner and John Turner he went on the same day with the constables to make the search and in an open shed there found a pile of spokes with two sacks spread over them and some fresh sawn timber set up against them with the appearance of being put there for the purpose of concealing the said spokes and that this informant is clear that the spokes so found were part of those which were piled up at Woodhatch aforesaid. And that the same are the property of this informant and of Robert Boxall and that the spokes now produced are part of the spokes which were so found in the shed of the said Thomas Turner and John Turner.

And this informant Joshua Russell further saith that in the evening of the 27th day of March instant between 6 and 7 o'clock in the evening he saw the said John Baker Dove and John Turner sitting in a public room in the Bell public house in Reigate with several other persons in the room.

And this informant William Charman for himself saith that he is constable of the Borough of Reigate that having a warrant against the said John Baker Dove, Thomas Turner and John Turner he went to the said Bell public house in search of the said John Turner where he found the said John Baker Dove and John Turner with several other persons and that he then apprehended them. And this informant saith that he searched the buildings of the said Thomas Turner and John Turner and found a parcel of spokes there which the said William Moore claimed to be his property, and that the same were concealed in the manner stated by the said William Moore.

And this deponent William Moore for himself saith that he verily believes that the said John Turner received the said spokes knowing them to have been stolen but that he verily believes that the said Thomas Turner was not in any manner privy thereto.

[signed] Joshua Russell

The mark of
X
Wm. Upfold

[signed] Wm Moore

The mark of
X
Jasper Bryant

[signed] William Charman

The examination of John Baker Dove of Reigate, labourer taken before me Arthur Jones, esq., this 29th day of March in the year of our Lord 1798. The said John Baker Dove labourer being charged with feloniously stealing and carrying away on the 28th day of March instant at the parish of Reigate aforesaid two hundred and fifteen rough oak wheel spokes the goods and chattels of William Moore and Robert Boxall. He the said John Baker Dove upon his examination now taken before me saith that he is guilty of the offence so charged upon him.

[signed] John Baker Dove

The examination of John Turner of Reigate, wheelwright taken before me Arthur Jones, esq., the 29th day of March in the year of our Lord 1798. The said John Turner being charged on suspicion of having feloniously received two hundred and fifteen rough oak wheel spokes the goods and chattels of William Moore and Robert Boxall on the 28th day of March instant at the parish of Reigate aforesaid, he the said John Turner well knowing the same to have been stolen, he the said John Turner upon examination now taken denieth he is guilty of the offence so laid to his charge.

[signed] John Turner

Taken before me
Arthur Jones

Continued to next Session

Sur. RO, QS 2/1/30, Order Book

Midsummer Sessions at Guildford, 10 July 1798
County Gaol
John Baker Dove convicted of Felony is committed to your custody for the Term of one
year there to be kept to hard labour.

Som. RO, Q/SR Michaelmas 1819
Francis Jennings charged with stealing an elm post

Somerset Michaelmas Sessions, 18 October 1819, at Taunton

The Jurors for our Lord the King upon their oath present, that Francis Jennings late of
the parish of Wellington in the County of Somerset aforesaid, labourer on the sixth day of
September in the fifty ninth year of the Reign of our Sovereign Lord, George the Third by
the Grace of God of the United Kingdom of Great Britain and Ireland, King, Defender
of the Faith, with force and arms at the parish of Wellington in the County of Somerset
aforesaid, one elm post of the value of four shillings of the goods and chattels of John
Bird then and there being found, then and there did feloniously steal, take and carry away
against the Peace of our said Lord the King his Crown and Dignity.

The information and complaint of Henry Thorne of Wellington in the said County of
Somerset, weaver taken on oath this 6th day of September 1819. Who saith that this
morning at about half past four o'clock he was at work in his garden at a place called
Rockwell Green. He saw Francis Jennings of the same place, labourer with a large elm
post upon his shoulders and suspecting he had stolen it this informant concealed himself
under that part of his garden hedge which separates it from a field called Pitholes in which
the said Francis Jennings then was, and in which there is no path way. That he saw the said
Francis Jennings then throw the post into the hedge and that the post now produced is the
same which the said Francis Jennings threw into the hedge. And this Informant further
saith that soon afterwards he called on James Pyne to go with Informant into the field to
ascertain if any thing else were placed in the hedge by the said Francis Jennings but they
found nothing else. That he then gave notice to the Constable Robert Hawkins [sic] of
what he had seen and that he and the said Constable went into the said field called Pitholes
in pursuit of the said Francis Jennings where they found him asleep and took him into
custody.

[signed] H. Thorne

The Information and Complaint of Robert Hawkins of Wellington in the said County of
Somerset, carpenter, Constable of Wellington, taken on oath this sixth day of September
1819. Who saith that the elm post now produced is of the value of four shillings.

[signed] Robert Hawkings[2]

The information and complaint of James Bryant of Wellington in the said County,
labourer taken on oath this sixth day of September 1819. Who saith that the post now
produced is the property of his master Mr John Bird of Greenham Barton. That the same
with two others were seen by him on Tuesday last in a hay loft belonging to Mr Bird which
was locked. That on going to the said hay loft this morning he found that the same had

---

[2] The author's great-great-great-grandfather.

SOMERSET, (TO WIT.) **These are to Certify** that at the General Quarter Session of the Peace of our late Sovereign Lord King George the *Fourth* held at *the City of Wells* in and for the County of Somerset, on Monday, the *fourteenth* Day of *January* — in the *eighth* — Year of the Reign of our late Sovereign Lord George the *Fourth* — and in the Year of our Lord, 18*28* before *William Dickinson John Phelips Esquires* —

and others their Companions, Justices of our said late Lord the King, assigned to keep the Peace of our said late Lord the King, in and for the County of Somerset aforesaid, and also to hear and determine divers Felonies, Trespasses and other Misdemeanors committed in the same County, *John Treasure* late of the Parish of Stone Easton in the County of Somerset labourer was in due form of law indicted tried and convicted for that he on the sixteenth day of December in the eighth year of the Reign aforesaid with force and arms at the Parish aforesaid in the County aforesaid one duck of the value of eighteen pence of the goods and chattels of Dame Elizabeth Anne Hippisley then and there being found then and there feloniously did steal take and carry away against the said late Kings Peace And the said John Treasure was thereupon ordered and adjudged by the Court to be imprisoned and kept to hard labour in the House of Correction at Wilton for one Calendar month, and to be once privately whipped.

Given under my hand this eighth day of October in the year of our Lord one thousand eight hundred and thirty two.

Edw. Coles,
Clerk of the Peace.

Somerset Quarter Sessions, 14 January 1828. John Treasure convicted of stealing a duck; one calendar month hard labour and to be once whipped (Som. RO, Q/SR Epi 1828)

been entered by ripping open one of the boards on the side of the said hay loft and that the post now produced with two others were missing.

		his
Before me		James X Bryant
W.P. Thomas		mark
Verdict	Guilty	
Sentence	Fined 1 shilling and to be imprisoned in Wilton Gaol for 2 months and further until the fine is paid. To be publically whipped at Row Green for the space of 100 yards backwards and forwards on a Thursday during his imprisonment between the hours of one and two o'clock.	

Lincs. AO, HQS/A/1
James Bavin charged with stealing a pair of breeches

Lincolnshire Michaelmas Sessions for the Parts of Holland, October 1819, at Spalding

James Bavin of the parish of Holbeach in the Parts of Holland in the county of Lincoln, labourer on the seventeenth of July 1819 . . . with force of arms at the parish of Holbeach one pair of breeches of the value of ten pence of the goods and chattels of one Charles Ashby . . . did feloniously steal take and carry away against the peace.

The information and complaint of Charles Ashby of Holbeach in the said Parts and County, shepherd taken on Oath before me one of His Majesty's Justices of the Peace in and for the said Parts, this 16th Day of August 1819.
Who saith, That five weeks since last Sunday he took a pair of Woolen Cord Breeches his property to the house of Francis Addy at Holbeach aforesaid for the purpose of getting them washed. That on the Sunday next following the said Francis Addy came to Complainant and told him that his Breeches had been stolen. That the Breeches this day shewn to him by Wm Hipworth constable of Holland are this complainant's property and the same which were taken to Francis Addy's as aforesaid.

[signed] Charles Ashby

The Information and Examination of Francis Addy of Holbeach in the said Parts and County, labourer taken on Oath . . . this 16th August 1819.
Who saith that he is ground keeper for Mr Ashby of Fleet and that as he was dressing some of his Master's sheep in a pen near to his (examinant's) dwelling house on Saturday the 17th day of July last he saw the prisoner James Bavin in company with Thomas Hall cross examinant's yard when he asked them what they wanted. Bavin and Hall replied they were looking out for a job and asked examinant if he could inform them of one. On examinant telling them he could not they walked off.

[signed] Francis Addy

The Information and Examination of Mary Addy of Holbeach in the said Parts and County . . . this 16th August 1819.
Who saith that five weeks since last Sunday Charles Ashby of Holbeach aforesaid brought a pair of woolen cord breeches to examinant's house for the purpose of having them washed and that examinant accordingly washed them and hung them to dry on a hedge near to examinant's house on the Friday afternoon following. That on examinant going for the breeches on the evening of the following day she found that they were stolen. That

the breeches this day shewn to her by Wm Hipworth constable of Holbeach are the same which were stolen from off the garden hedge as aforesaid.

her
Mary X Addy
mark

The Information and Complaint of Thomas Hipworth of Holbeach . . . this 16th August 1819.
Who saith that on Sunday the 15th instant he was informed by Charles Ashby that he (Ashby) had a pair of breeches stolen from off Francis Addy's garden hedge at the same time giving examinant a description of them, and that he (Ashby) rather suspected that James Bavin had stolen them. Examinant in consequence took Bavin into custody a few hours after when he found upon the person of Bavin the Breeches now produced and which Ashby identifies as his property, the same that was stolen as aforesaid.

[signed] Thos Hipworth

The Information and Examination of Thomas Hall of Holbeach . . . this 16th August 1819.
Who saith that better than three weeks since on a Wednesday or Thursday, he this examinant went with James Bavin into the East Fen near to Boston to endeavour to get work. That on the washway road near to Meltons they were asked by a man who was sitting by the road side, and a perfect stranger to this examinant if they wanted to buy a pair of breeches for that he was broken down. He is positive the man was sitting down at the time they came up to him. Bavin stopped and looked at the breeches and bargained for them at five shillings. That he, this examinant, saw Bavin pay for the breeches now shewn to this examinant by Thomas Hipworth the constable of Holbeach, and are the same so purchased. That he positively speaks to them being the same. That Bavin put on the breeches before he got to Boston.

his
Thomas X Hall
mark

The voluntary Examination of James Bavin of Holbeach . . . this 16th August 1819 charged on suspicion of having stolen a pair of woolen cord breeches the property of Charles Ashby of Holbeach aforesaid labourer. Who saith that he this examinant together with Thomas Hall, about a fortnight since but certainly not three weeks ago, went into the East Fen near to Boston to get work, and that as they were going they were asked by a man who overtook them on the washway road, betwixt Fosdike and Meltons, whether they wanted to buy a pair of breeches for that he was broken down. Examinant said he would buy them if he could and examinant did buy them for five shillings. That Hall did not stop with this examinant but walked on for about 20 or 30 yards and then stopped. That the breeches produced by Hipworth the constable are the same that examinant bought. That the man of whom he bought them was a stranger to this examinant.

his
James X Bavin
mark

[James Bavin was found guilty and sentenced to seven years transportation but he was not actually transported. He appeared in court again 6 May 1824 at the Holland Sessions and was convicted of stealing a goose and given again a sentence of seven years transportation. This time he was embarked on the Asia *for New South Wales in 1825.]*

Dor. RO, Quarter Session Rolls
John Richards charged with embezzlement

Dorset Epiphany Sessions, 6th January 1835 at Dorchester.

John Richards, aged 29, of Blandford, Dorset, charged with having on 1st September 1834 at Fordington, embezzled a certain sum of money the property of Richard Fippard. He was also charged with embezzling money, the property of Robert Taber of Bere Regis, and also for stealing carpenter's tools from John Hutchins of Fifehead Neville.

The information of Amelia Fippard now residing at Grove Buildings in the parish of Fordington, Dorset taken 6th November 1834. Who saith as follows: 'I am the wife of Richard Fippard now a prisoner in Dorchester Gaol and on the first of September last John Richards came to my house and offered to take & convey to my husband any thing that I had to send to my husband. He said that he was just let out of prison & had been in the same yard with him. I asked him what my husband wanted & he told me that he wanted a little tobacco which he could sell in the prison & buy bread with it, of which my husband, he said was in want, & as much money as I could spare & a piece of bacon would be useful. I gave John Richards a quarter pound of tea & some moist sugar and between three & four pounds of bacon, two half crown pieces & a pound of tobacco. He, Richards tied it all up in one of my husband's handkerchiefs (except the pound of tobacco which I gave him separately) as he said that he would throw that over the wall. He said that he shall send in the articles in the handkerchief to a smuggler of his acquaintance who would deliver them to my husband & he engaged with a boy, the son of Thomas Ellis, keeper of the Little Jockey to carry it to the prison & told me to send my little girl to see that he did it, & my little girl saw him go inside the prison yard gates some way towards the prison & then Richards who had accompanied the little girl to the prison yard gates came with her to me at my house & said. "So we have sent it in have we not my little dear?" & she said, "Yes we watched him out of sight." And he then left me & I gave him twopence for the boy. I went some time after wards to see my husband & he asked me before the turnkey Cox whether any one had ever called on me & told me that he had never received any thing & desired me never to send any thing to him as it was contrary to the rules, if he wanted linen he would always send by the turnkey. I gave John Richards a shilling for his trouble.'

[signed] Amelia Fippard

The information of Isabella Hardy now residing at Wells, Somerset, taken 6th January 1835. Who saith as follows: 'I am the niece of Mrs Fippard, I was on a visit to my Aunt on the first of September last, on Sunday John Richards called on my Aunt & she sent me out with the children. I did not hear him say anything, but the next day about eight or nine o'clock being the first of September my Aunt Mrs Fippard gave me a small bundle tied up in a blue Handkerchief & desired me to carry it to the door of the beer house called the Little Jockey & wait for John Richards, whom I had seen on Sunday. I did so & he met me near the house & took the parcel in the same state in which I received it & carried the parcel into the house & remained there two or three minutes & then came out with a boy whom he called Ellis & told me to go with him to the prison gates to see that the parcel was delivered there for my Uncle. This parcel I saw Richards give to the boy in the passage of the Jockey in the blue handkerchief in which I received it & he put it under his coat & we went all together to the outside gates of the Gaol & saw the boy with the parcel under his coat because it was a wet day, go as far as the corner of the nursery of the gaol. Richards then said now you can tell your Aunt that you saw the parcel delivered & we went together as far as the beginning of the north walk & he then said that he was going down street to his wife & left me to go home alone, but should be there as soon as me. I found him at my Aunt's & he said that I had seen the parcel safe in the gaol & I said that I had, I do not know what the parcel contained as I did not see it tied up in the blue handkerchief, but I knew it contained bacon because my Aunt Brice went for the bacon whilst I was sent to take care of her children. I have seen the boy since & should know him again.'

This was not taken in the prisoner's presence as the deponent came too late from Wells.

[signed] Isabella Hardy

The information of Anne the wife of Frederic Brice now residing at Grove Buildings in the parish of Fordington, Dorset taken 1st January 1835. Who saith as follows: 'On Monday the first of September last the prisoner John Richards was in my sister's Amelia Fippard's house, he said that he had just come out of prison, that he was there for smuggling & that he would send any thing into the prison to Amelia Fippard's husband who desired him to say that he wished for bacon or any thing that she could send him. My sister told me to go & buy some bacon. I went for some & paid two shillings & three pence for it & gave it to my sister who gave it to Richards, who said that one piece would be sufficient. He then took it & cut it half through in the fat part so as not to separate the pieces into two parts. My sister then gave him two half crowns, which he put into the cut observing that she thought he must have been a smuggler, as he knew how to smuggle that. He then closed the bacon. I went for Isabella Hardy, whilst my sister was preparing tea and sugar to send her husband. I then gave a blue cotton handkerchief of Amelia Fippard to John Richards to tie up the bacon & other articles in, but what became of them afterwards I do not know.'

[signed] Ann Brice

The information of George Ellis now residing at Dorchester in the county of Dorset, taken 15th December 1834. Who saith as follows: 'About four months ago I was standing by my father's parlour door, along with Henry Watts, where this man (the prisoner John Richards) who is now present came to me and said, "If you will go down to the prison with this parcel I will give you three halpence". I said I would. I took the parcel and asked him if it was tobacco, because I knew that it was not allowed at the prison. He said No! it was bacon. I went with him as far as the outer gate of the prison. He told me then to run. I ran down to the prison door and delivered the parcel but I do not know to whom I gave it. I never opened the parcel which I think was tied up with string.'

[signed] George Ellis

The information of Russell Ayres [sic] now residing at Dorchester taken 15th December 1834. Who saith as follows: 'I know the boy Ellis who is now present. Some time ago, but I do not know how long, this boy came to the prison door and brought a piece of pork or bacon, which he said was for Mr Byatt a smuggler. I do not remember whether the meat was wrapped up in a parcel or not, but I know that I examined the meat particularly lest there should be anything concealed in it. I found nothing and am convinced that there was nothing but the bacon which was afterwards given to Byatt.'

[signed] Russell Eyres

The voluntary declaration of John Richards, under examination on a charge of embezzling money committed to his charge by Amelia the wife of Richard Phippard [sic]. He being first cautioned, saith: 'Mrs Phippard gave me two half crowns and some bacon. I cut a hole in the bacon and put the half crowns into it. I tied it up and gave it to Mrs

Phippard who gave it to the servant girl, and afterwards took it from her and gave it to the boy Ellis.'

[signed] John Richards

The information of Decimy the wife of Robert Taber now residing at Bere Regis, Dorset, taken 6th January 1835. Who saith as follows: 'On the 27th of September last John Richards now present came to me at a Booth on Woodbury Hill & said that he was Superintendent Turnkey in Dorchester Gaol that my husband who was then in prison under sentence desired him to call on me that he had been at my house & was directed here to find me on Woodbury Hill, that my husband told him that if I could send him any thing he should be glad of it. I then replied that I hope that I should not commit an error, he said leave that to me, that will be all right. I have a note from Mrs Beasant of Bere with half a crown, which she gave me for her brother Sexey, now a prisoner in gaol with two pieces of ginger bread & one piece of cheese which he shewed me. I wrote a note & enclosed one shilling & gave it to Richards for my husband. I asked his name & he said Askill & if I asked for that name at the Phoenix at Dorchester he could convey any thing to him at any time. I told him that I would reward him for his kindness & gave him a cup of beer & would see him again. I never saw him afterwards, but found that he had not told me the truth. My husband never received it.
I afterwards recollected that Richards said to me did you not recollect me standing with my husband or behind my husband when he (my husband) took his trial.'

[signed] Decimy Taber

The information of Robert Taper [sic] now residing at Bere Regis, Dorset, taken 6th January 1835. Who saith as follows: 'I was dismissed from the Gaol on the last day of October and during the whole time I was in prison I never received any thing from my wife or any one else after my trial & I cautioned my wife not to send any thing as some men had been punished for having it.'

To the question put to the prisoner 'Did you see any thing coming over the wall on the 29th Sept? 'I say I never did.'

his
Robert X Taper
mark

The information of John Hutchins now residing at Fifehead Neville, Dorset, carpenter, taken 7th January 1835. Who saith as follows: 'On the fifth day of May last John Richards came to my shop and asked me to let him have materials to make a chest of drawers and to allow him to make them in my shop to which I consented. John Richards had no tools of his own and on the following morning the sixth of May I left home but previous to going out I told Richards who was then in bed in my house that he would find tools in the shop necessary for his use. I returned in the evening but did not go into the shop but understood that Richards was gone to Sturminster to fetch his working cloathes, he did not return on the morning of the seventh of May. I went into the shop and missed some tools. I then went to Sturminster to enquire for Richards and at the blacksmith's shop I saw James Rose the Turnpike Man and asked him if Richards had offered any tools for sale and he informed me he had seen Richards and asked me if I could swear to the tools if I saw them, I told him I could. Rose then produced a doved tailed saw, a round, a brad awl, plane and a gimblet, which I identified as my property. I took the tools from Rose and paid him the money he advanced to Richards. The tools now produced are those I had from James Rose.'

[signed] John Hutchings

The information of James Rose now residing at Toll Gate House in the parish of Sturminster Newton, Dorset, taken 7th January 1835. Who saith as follows: 'On the sixth day of May last I was standing by the blacksmith's shop at Sturminster Newton, John Richards came up to me and asked if I knew one Rose a butcher, I told him yes but that he was not at home. Richards then went into the public house and had some beer and a pipe of tobacco and soon afterwards came out again and asked me if I would lend him three or four shillings. I said I did not know any thing about him and could not lend him the money, he then took out of his pocket the tools now produced a dovetail saw, plane, awl, & gimblet and said he would leave them with me as a security and said he would return the money by butcher Rose and he promised me a shilling if I would lend the money. He said he wanted the money to go to Stalbridge to see William Harris. I lent him three shillings and sixpence and paid for a pint of beer and a pipe of tobacco and Richards left the tools with me. Richards said he should return in a day or two but if he did not he would send the money by butcher Rose who could take the tools for him when he went to Stalbridge & I returned the tools to John Hutchings on his paying me the three shillings & ninepence.'

[not signed]

The statement of John Richards prisoner charged with stealing carpenter's tools made before us this seventh day Jany 1835. 'This happened two months before I was in prison & took my trial for stealing tools from Mr. Beasant of Puddletown. Mr Hutchins' son in law Thomas Mullett wrote a letter to my wife concerning the tools which I am now accused of stealing stating that the money that I took up on the tools & likewise money which I owed him before were paid in a few months, he and his father in law would arrange matters to make it up.'

[signed] J^o Richards

Verdict   Guilty
Sentence   14 years transportation

CIVIL PROCEEDINGS

In addition to criminal proceedings, examples of which have been given above, Quarter Sessions also dealt with civil actions, the two most important of which for family historians are settlement disputes and bastardy charges. If a person was found 'wandering and begging' in a parish and therefore unable to support himself and his family he was questioned as to his 'rightful place of settlement'. Such 'Rogues and Vagabonds' could be supported by the parish Poor Rate but unless they had a legal right to be maintained by that parish they would be sent back to their home parish. Their home parish was not necessarily their place of birth. A large number of factors could apply. A man could, for example, claim a settlement in a parish having served an apprenticeship there regardless of where he was born. Because of the complexity of the settlement laws it was not always clear as to which parish a person rightfully belonged and as a result thousands of these wanderers were taken to the Courts of Quarter Sessions to be questioned and their rightful place of settlement determined. A *Removal Order* was issued by the court and they would then be escorted to that parish. The officers of the receiving parish often challenged the decision of the court and such enquiries and disputes into settlement will be found among the Quarter Sessions rolls and papers.

Many a girl, though unmarried, found herself 'big with child' and was likely to be a burden on the parish poor funds. It was therefore in the interest of the overseers of the poor of her parish to ascertain who the father was. Such enquiries were made at Quarter Sessions when the girl would state who had 'carnally known her'. (Inevitably there were some cases where a girl was unable to be certain of the father.) Having determined who the father was the two were pressed to marry, though often, particularly in the case where the father was a married man, the father was compelled to pay maintenance for the child. Bastardy was not a criminal offence but if a man found guilty of a criminal offence had already been found guilty of bastardy he was likely to suffer a more severe penalty than a first offender. At the Essex Epiphany Quarter Sessions at Chelmsford in 1844 James Hawkins, aged forty-two and single, was given seven years' transportation for stealing six fowls. This appears to be a very harsh sentence for such a crime but the Millbank Prison Register[2] records that he had been convicted fourteen times previously for bastardy.

The whole cost of setting up the Court of Quarter Sessions and for arresting and detaining accused persons in gaol fell on the county funds. Similar expenses at Assizes were paid for by the Treasury. It was, therefore, in the interest of the local justices to commit as many prisoners as was reasonably possible to Assizes and thus reduce the expense to the county (see Chapter 10).

[3] PRO, PCOM 2/21.

ASSIZE COURTS

Since the twelfth century itinerant justices have travelled the counties of England holding their courts to administer both civil and criminal law. By the middle of the sixteenth century these courts had developed into six specific *circuits* under the control and organization of *Clerks of Assize*. The records of these circuits are listed in Appendix 4.1. It was usual for the courts within each circuit to be held twice a year in each county (Lent and Summer) but by the middle of the nineteenth century a third (Winter) circuit was sometimes introduced to cope with the increased number of criminal cases.

Assize Circuits always covered all English counties with the exception of Cheshire, Durham, Lancashire and Middlesex. It should be noted that there was a circuit re-arrangement in 1864 when some counties were transferred from one circuit to another. See Appendix 7. There was another major change in 1876:

a   The Home Circuit and Norfolk Circuit were combined to form the South Eastern Circuit.

b   Part of the Northern Circuit was split off to form the North Eastern Circuit taking in the counties of Northumberland and Yorkshire together with Durham which had previously had its own Palatinate Court. At the same time Lancashire was included in the Northern Circuit. Lancashire too had previously had its own Palatinate Court.

c   The North and South Wales Circuit (which had been formed in 1830[1]) was split into two divisions:

   i   North Wales Division which included Cheshire.
   ii South Wales Division.

In 1945 these two divisions were combined to form the Wales and Chester Circuit.

Assize Courts were abolished in 1971 when Crown Courts were established

---

[1] Prior to 1830 Wales had its own Courts of Great Sessions (see Chapter 8).

throughout the country. (Liverpool and Manchester Crown Courts had already been set up in 1956.)

Like Quarter Sessions Courts, Assize Courts also dealt with all manner of civil actions as well as criminal cases. The maintenance of roads and bridges was the responsibility of the parish in which they were situated. Failure to keep them in good repair was brought to the attention of either Quarter Sessions or Assizes. The following example is taken from PRO, ASSI 21/20:

Western Circuit of Assizes, Wiltshire
Held at New Sarum 29 July 1796

The inhabitants of the parish of Hillmarton for not repairing the Highway called Marsh or Goat Acre Lane (as in the Indictment) containing in length 5 furlongs and 33 poles.

Let the execution of the judgement of £100 at the last session be again respited 'till the further Order of the Court. It appearing by the usual certificate and affidavits that the road hath been put into good and sufficient repair.

'Nuisances' were also brought before both Quarter Sessions and Assizes, as in this instance, from PRO, ASSI 23/9:

Western Circuit of Assizes, Somerset
Summer Assizes, 1811

William Blackmore   Nuisance at Sampford Arundel by erecting and continuing to erect a dwelling house and shop upon the King's Highway at Sampford Moor whereby same was narrowed and obstructed.

[No other record of this case has been recorded but it is likely that Blackmore would have been given a minimal time in which to demolish the building and clear the obstruction caused. Note that this was a civil offence and Blackmore would not therefore appear in the Criminal Registers at the Public Record Office.]

PRO, ASSI 45/25/2
Richard Nesbit charged with robbery

Northern Circuit   Yorkshire 21st March 1754

Town and County of Kingston upon Hull
The examination of Richard Nesbit taken the fifteenth day of March 1754 before George Thompson Esq. Mayor of the said Town and one of his Majesty's Justices of the Peace for the said Town and County.

The Examinant being charged with suspition of feloniously robbing a person on the King's Highway near Hayton in the county of York of ten shillings in money a shirt a silk handkerchief and a pair of stockings, saith that on the twelfth day of this Instant March he overtook a young man between three and four miles on this side of the City of York that he this examinant and the said young man walked together and called at several places upon the road and the said young man told this examinant that he was tired and thereupon this examinant offered to carry a bundle for the said young man which the said young man thereupon gave this examinant to carry for him and this examinant accordingly carried the said bundle for the said young man till they came between Hayton and Shipton and the said young man being very much tired and both he and this examinant having drank freely on the road he this examinant laid down the said bundle and said he would carry it no further and desired the young man to give him something for his trouble who thereupon gave this examinant one shilling and said that he had not any more money from the said young man and in laying down the said bundle saith several things fell out and that he found a shirt and a pair of stockings in his pocket when he got to his lodgings at Shipton but being in liquor knows not whether the said young man put them into his pocket or he this examinant put them in himself. And that the said young man tied a silk handkerchief about the head of this examinant soon after they met and this examinant further saith that he left the said shirt stockings and handkerchief at the house of William Bone in the parish of Sculcotts in the said County of York with another handkerchief and a pair of stockings belonging to this examinant on the thirteenth day of this Instant March and that he hath no acquaintance with the said William Bone.

Taken before me   The mark of
George Thompson, Mayor   X
                                                                    Richard Nesbit

The information of William Bone of the parish of Sculcotts in the East Riding of the County of York, gardner, taken upon oath this fifteenth day of March 1754.
This Informant on his oath saith that on the thirteenth day of this instant March a man from Market Weighton in the said County of York came to the house of this Informant and this Informant being then in the garden his this Informant's wife called him this Informant into the house and told him this Informant that a man whom she did not know had left a bundle with her and that there was a man in the house wanted to challenge it and asked him this Informant whether it should be delivered or not and the said man that came to challenge the said bundle told this Informant that he came in pursuit of a man who had robbed his son upon the highway near Hayton in the said County of York of ten shillings in money and a shirt a silk handkerchief and a pair of stockings. And thereupon this Informant delivered the bundle the said man had left to the person who came to claim it. And that bundle consisted of one shirt two handkerchiefs and two pair of stockings and this Informant further saith on his oath that Richard Nesbit a soldier in Captain Shadwell's Company of Invalids in Kingston upon Hull aforesaid came to him this Informant and demanded the bundle which he said he had left. And this Informant told the said Richard Nesbit he could not deliver it and then the said Richard Nesbit said he knew how to come by it and that he would call some other time and this Informant further saith he suspects the said Richard Nesbit did feloniously rob the son of the said person who challenged the said bundle.

Taken before me   [signed] William Bone
George Thompson, Mayor

The information of George Hall of Market Weighton in the County of York, labourer taken upon oath the sixteenth day of March 1754.
This Informant on his oath saith that on the twelfth day of this instant March between seven and eight of the clock in the morning a man overtook this Informant about four miles from York in the road between York and Market Weighton aforesaid and this Informant having a bundle of cloths the said man offered to carry the bundle for him upon which this Informant thanked the said man and let him have the said bundle to carry and this Informant and the said man called at several places upon the said road and eat and drank together and each paid their proportion of the reckoning and the said man carried the said bundle until they came to Barnby Moor where this Informant took the said bundle and carried it himself and travelled along with the said man on the said road as far as the parish of Hayton in the said County of York and in a close there through which a

Assizes Northern Circuit, Yorkshire, 21 March 1754. The examination of Richard Nesbit, charged with robbery (PRO, ASSI 45/25/2)

common footway lieth the said man asked him this Informant for something for carrying his this Informant's bundle which this Informant refused to give him upon which the said man bid this Informant stand and deliver his money he this Informant told him he would not whereupon the said man threatened to kill him this Informant, if he did not and lifted up an oak stick which he had in his hand as if he intended to strike him this Informant and then the said man threw this Informant down and took a purse out of this Informant's pocket in which were ten shillings which the said man took and then threw the purse down and put this Informant into great fear after which the said man opened this Informant's said bundle and took thereout a shirt a pair of worsted stockings and a coloured silk handkerchief and then the said man took this Informant's walking stick and left his own and ran away as fast as he could towards Burnby upon which this Informant went forward as fast as he could to Market Weighton and acquainted his father in Law William Seller of Market Weighton aforesaid, thong maker, with what had happened who made enquiry and pursued the said man upon whose pursuit and enquiry Richard Nesbit was apprehended and committed to gaol at the town of Kingston upon Hull aforesaid on suspicion of the said robbery. And this Informant further saith on his oath that the said Richard Nesbit is the very person who did assault and put him this Informant in fear and steal take and carry away from him this Informant the said ten shillings, shirt, stockings, and handkerchief in the said close or common highway as aforesaid he this Informant having now seen the said Richard Nesbit in the said gaol at Kingston upon Hull aforesaid.

Taken upon oath before me
George Thompson, Mayor

                            The mark of
                                  X
                            George Hall

The Information of John Richardson one of the constables of the town of Kingston upon Hull taken upon oath this sixteenth day of March 1754.
This Informant on his oath saith that on Wednesday last William Sellers of Market Weighton in the County of York, thong maker came to him this Informant and desired him to apprehend a man who was coming by and had robbed his son in Law and this Informant desired the said William Sellers to go to Mr Mayor for a warrant and that he this Informant in the mean time would look after the said man. That this Informant thereupon did follow the said man from place to place and saw him leave a bundle at the house of William Bone a gardner in the parish of Sculcotts in the county of York and immediately go away and this Informant still continued to follow him till at last he lost sight of the said man and this Informant further saith on his oath that on the fifteenth day of this month being informed the said man he had followed was one Richard Nesbit a soldier belonging to the garrison at Kingston upon Hull aforesaid he this Informant acquainted Mr Mayor with it who immediately sent to the commanding officer of the said garrison to deliver up the aforesaid Richard Nesbit which the said commanding officer accordingly did and Mr Mayor having taken the Examination of the said Richard Nesbit committed the said Richard Nesbit to gaol on suspition of having committed the aforesaid robbery and for a further examination.

Taken upon oath before me
George Thompson, Mayor

                            [signed] John Richardson

The information of William Seller of Market Weighton in the County of York, thong maker taken upon oath the sixteenth day of March 1754.
This Informant on his oath saith that on Tuesday last the twelfth day of this instant March George Hall son in Law to this Informant came to this Informant's house at Market Weighton aforesaid and told him this Informant a man had robbed him the said George Hall in the parish of Hayton in the said County of York of ten shillings in money a shirt a

pair of stockings and a handkerchief and that the said man had taken away the said George Hall's stick and left his own stick. Thereupon the next day he this Informant enquired after the said man and pursued him and overtook him with a bundle under his arm between Beverley and the town of Kingston upon Hull and suspected him to be the man that had robbed his said son in law because he knew the stick which the said man had to belong to his said son in Law and then went before him and applied to John Richardson one of the constables of Kingston upon Hull aforesaid to apprehend the said man as he passed by but the said John Richardson desired this informant to go to Mr Mayor for a warrant and in the mean time he the said John Richardson told this Informant he would look after the said man and while this Informant went to get a warrant the said man had got away but had left the said shirt, stockings and handkerchief at the house of William Bone a gardiner in the parish of Sculcotts in the said County of York who delivered them to this Informant and some others in company with him and this Informant further saith on his oath that Richard Nesbit committed to the gaol in the town of Kingston upon Hull aforesaid on suspition of committing the aforesaid robbery is the same man whom he overtook between Beverley and the town of Kingston upon Hull aforesaid with the bundle and his son in Law's stick.

Taken upon oath before me   [signed] William Seller
George Thompson, Mayor

The further examination of Richard Nesbit.
This Examinant saith that his examination within written is true and further saith not.

The mark of
X
Richard Nesbit

PRO, ASSI 42/7

Northern Circuit   Gaol Book   Yorkshire 21st March 1754
Richard Nesbit pleaded not guilty. For feloniously robbing George Hall in the King's Highway

[No record of the sentence of the court for this case has been found.]

PRO, ASSI 42/7

Northern Circuit, Gaol Book
Yorkshire

The General Gaol Delivery of our Lord the King of his County of York held at the Castle of York in and for the said County on Saturday the sixteenth day of July in the third year of the reign of our Sovereign Lord George the Third [1763] now King of Great Britain &c before Sir Henry Gould knight one of the Justices of his majesty's Court of Common Pleas George Perrott esquire one of the Barons of his Majesty's Court of Exchequer and others their fellow Justices of our said Lord the King assigned to deliver his Gaol there of the prisoners therein being and also Justices of our said Lord the King assigned to inquire hear and determine all Treasons, Misprisions of Treason, Murder, Felonies, Contempts, Nusances, Offences and other Misdemeanors committed in the said County and after Justices of our said Lord the King assigned to keep the peace in the County aforesaid and also to hear and determine diverse Felonies, Trespasses and other Offences committed in the said County.

Saturday evening, present Mr Justice Gould and Mr Baron Perrott.
Adjourned to Monday 18th inst. at 11 o'clock in the forenoon.

Grand Jury

Sir Digby Legard of Ganton	Baronets
Sir George Caley of Brompton	
Edwin Lascelles of Gawthrop	
Roger Talbot of Wood End	
Giles Earle of Benningbrough	
Thomas Hassell of Thorp	
Peregrine Wentworth of Wakefield	
Wm. Gossip of Thorp Arch	
Thos. Robinson of Welburne	
Leonard Thompson of Sheriffe Hutton	
Thos. Arthington of Arthington	Esquires
Matthew Boyton of Rawcliffe	
John Dealtry of Catton	
Ralph Bell the younger of Thirsk	
Gregory Elsley of Mount St. John	
John Dalton of Slenningford	
Simon Butterwick of Thirsk	
Timothy Ford of West Hesleston	
Thomas Barstow of Fulford	

John Lobley of Baildon, gent, exempted and fine remitted.
Gilbert Dixon of Sheffield, gent, exempted and fine remitted.
Gervase Broughton of Bentley, gent, coroner of the West Riding fined £5 for not appearing at this present Assize as by duty of office as Coroner he ought to have done.

Wednesday morn before Mr Baron Perrott
Jury

Christopher Powell	Robert Inchboard	Thos. Hodgson
John Parsons	Thos. Walker	John Robinson
Nathaniel Bagnall	Thos. Powell	John Applegarth
John Harrison	Wm. Bilton	Richard Ellis

John Hall otherwise Bloom pleads guilty. For stealing a bay mare price £10 property of John Harrison 4th July last at Beverley.

Jane Hacksup the wife of John Hacksup pleads guilty.
For fel [feloniously] stealing 8 yds of linen cloth val [value] 8s the property of John Hutton in his Bleaching Yard at the parish of Kirk Fenton.

Joshua Hartley late of Leeds in the County of York, merchant for wilful and corrupt Perjury in an answer in Chancery.
Joshua Hartley of Leeds in the County of York, merch. Ackn [Acknowledged] £400.
That Joshua Hartley appear at the next Assizes and tried, traverse with effect on an indictment for wilful and corrupt Perjury and do not depart the Court without leave.

Samuel Jackson pleads guilty.
Mark Farrer als Farrar pleads not guilty.

For stealing diverse goods val [value] 2s 4d property of Jonas Shackleton at Wadsworth, and another count for stealing some goods property of persons unknown.

Thos. Hill the younger pleads guilty. For fel [feloniously] stealing an Ewe sheep price 5s property of Henry Atkinson at Kirksmeaton.

William Thompson late of North Frodingham labr. [labourer] pleads not guilty. For wilfull and corrupt Perjury.

Eleanor Darnbrook pleads not guilty. For stealing in the dwelling house of John Heath senior twenty one Gs [guineas] val [value] £22 1s his property.

Isabel Lambert pleads not guilty. For fel [feloniously] breaking and entering the dw [dwelling] house of John Harland in the day time at Yearby (no person therein being) and stealing thereout 1 guinea and 12s in money numbered the property of said Harland.

Elizabeth the wife of Wm. Morrell otherwise called Elizabeth Seavers singlewoman pleads guilty. For stealing in a booth in Easingwood Market goods val [value] 12s 8d property of Robert Omblay (who was therein sd booth).

Peter Wright of Baldsersby in the County of York yeoman. For a nusance.

Thursday morn present Mr Baron Perrott
Same Jury

Wm. Thompson pleads not guilty. For wilfull and corrupt Perjury on a Trial of an Indictment before the Justices of the East Riding at Beverley Sessions in April last.

Joseph Whalley pleads not guilty. For the wilfull and corrupt Perjury on a Trial at Yorkshire Lent Assizes 1763.

Thomas Wilkinson pleads not guilty. For feloniously stealing a brown gelding price 6s 6d property of John Bywater at pish [parish] of Leeds.

Martha Cookson pleads not guilty. For the murder of Tawer Kay the wife of Squire Kay of malice aforethought by strangling.
Squire Kay pleads not guilty. For being feloniously present and aiding abetting and assisting sd. Cookson to commit sd. murder.

PRO, ASSI 33/8

Norfolk Circuit, Gaol Book
Suffolk

The delivery of the Gaol of our Lord the King of the County of Suffolk Wednesday 9th August in the 37th year of the reign of George 3. 1797.

Kerenhappuck Jones, singlewoman
Puts herself upon the Court. Jury says Not Guilty nor fled. Acquitted

1st May 37 George 3 [1797] being big with a certain male child on the same day and year was delivered of the aforesaid child which was born alive and a Bastard and that she not having the fear of God before her, but being moved on the same day and year at Beccles willfully assaulted said child and with both hands cast and threw said child into a privy of Jno. Scarlet whereby said child was choaked and suffocated.

2nd Count. Same time and place being with child was delivered of said child which was born alive and a Bastard and that she not having fear but being moved feloniously assaulted said child carried said child into a grove or plantation there feloniously exposed and deserted said child whereby said child died.

Suffolk 24th March 38th year of the reign of George 3 [1798].

The King against John Lincoln
After 1st August 1797 viz 25th January 37 Geo. 3 at Beccles unlawfully receiving 20 lbs wt. of Gunpowder val. [value] 40 [sic] and 1 piece of flannel val. [value] 1d goods of our Lord the King by a cart ill disposed from before then feloniously against the Stat. and against the peace.

[Verdict not given]

Bedfordshire	6th March in the 40th year of the Reign of George 3 [1800] at Bedford.
James Albone, labourer	21st Sept. last at Biggleswade stealing 2 deal boards val. [value] 3s and 6 pecks of coals val. [value] 2s
	Puts himself upon the Country. Jury says not guilty nor fled. Acquitted
Norfolk	15th March in the 40th year of the reign of George 3 [1800] at Thetford.
William Yaxley, labourer	8th July 36 George 3 [1796] at Gresham, stealing 2 geldings price £2, goods of Mr Cook.
	Puts himself at the mercy of the Court. Jury says Guilty, no goods. To be hanged by the neck till he be dead. Reprieved on being Imprisoned in the House of Correction for 1 year.

PRO, ASSI 25/22/17
William Stacey and eleven others charged with murder

Western Circuit, Hampshire, Lent Assizes 1832

Indictment
County of Southampton to wit. The Jurors for our Lord the King upon their Oath present that William Stacey late of the parish of Stratfield Turgis in the county of Southampton, labourer, Daniel Pearman late of the same place labourer, Charles Steele late of the same place labourer, Charles Woolford late of the same place labourer, Peter Norman late of the same place labourer, Joseph Groves late of the same place labourer, John Everard late of the same place labourer, Charles Englefield late of the same place labourer, Daniel Neville late of the same place labourer, Edward Belcher late of the same place labourer, Richard Bye late of the same place labourer, and James Caesar late of the same place labourer not having the fear of God before their eyes but being moved and reduced

by the instigation of the Devil on the ninth day of December in the year of our Lord one thousand eight hundred and thirty one with force and arms at the parish of Stratfield Turgis in the County of Southampton aforesaid in and upon one John Woolford in the peace of God and our Lord the King then and there being feloniously wilfully and of their malice aforethought did make an assault and that the said Daniel Neville a certain Gun of the value of five shillings then and there loaded and charged with gunpowder and divers leaden shot which Gun he the said Daniel Neville in both his hands then and there had and held at to and against the said John Woolford then and there feloniously wilfully and of malice aforethought did discharge and shoot off at to and against the said John Woolford and that the said Daniel Neville with the leaden shot aforesaid then and there by force of the Gunpowder aforesaid shot and sent forth as aforesaid out of the said Gun so by the said Daniel Neville feloniously wilfully and of his malice aforethought discharged and shot off then and there did strike penetrate and wound the said John Woolford in and upon the left thigh of him the said John Woolford giving to him the said John Woolford then and there with the leaden shot aforesaid . . . one mortal wound of the depth of five inches and of the breadth of one inch of which mortal wound he the said John Woolford then and there instantly died and that the said William Stacey, Daniel Pearman, Charles Steele, Charles Woolford, Peter Norman, Joseph Groves, John Everard, Charles Englefield, Edward Belcher, Richard Bye, and James Caesar then and there feloniously wilfully and of their malice aforethought were present aiding and assisting abetting comforting and maintaining the said Daniel Neville to do and commit the said felony and murder aforesaid in form aforesaid and so the Jurors aforesaid on their Oath say that the said William Stacey, Daniel Pearman, Charles Steele, Charles Woolford, Peter Norman, Joseph Groves, John Everard, Charles Englefield, Daniel Neville, Edward Belcher, Richard Bye, and James Caesar the aforesaid John Woolford at the parish of Stratfield Turgis in the County of Southampton aforesaid on the day and year aforesaid in the manner and form aforesaid feloniously wilfully and of their malice aforethought did kill and murder against the peace of our Lord the King his Crown and Dignity.

Witnesses:

    Jonathan Miller
    Octavius Workman
    William Cane
    Joseph Stacey
    Henry Broom
    Samuel Clift
    John Bosier
    George Kersley
    Thomas Bosier
    John Elliott
    George Benett
    George Bosier
    Joel Ham
    Thomas Young
    James Brooks

The following was found among the Duke of Wellington Papers:

SUL Wellington Papers 4/1/4/3/1

                                            Odiham March 3rd 1832

My Lord Duke,
    We beg to report for your Grace's information that the 12 men charged with shooting John Woolford were tried yesterday. On the indictment for the murder they were all

acquitted, there being no evidence of a preconcerted intention to commit it and no means of ascertaining the person who fired the gun. To the indictment for the misdemeanor of being out at night armed for the destruction of game they all pleaded guilty and were this morning sentenced, 10 of them to transportation for 14 years, and the other 2 for 7 years. Your Grace will find their names on the other side.

And we have the Honor

to remain

Your Grace's most Obedient Servants

Cole, Lamb and Brooks

William Stacey
Charles Woolford
Richard Bye
John Everard
Joseph Groves
Charles Englefield
James Caesar
Daniel Pearman
Edward Belcher
Daniel Neville

The above were transported for 14 years.

Charles Steele
Peter Norman
For 7 years.

Peter Norman is the man who desired Caesar not to shoot.

PRO, ASSI 26/11
Joseph Tancock and Mary Prouse charged with murder

Western Circuit
Somerset Summer Assizes, 3 August 1875, at Wells

The examination of Mark Cottrell, Charles Wyatt, John Redwood, William Dalley and George Kidgell all of Wellington in the County of Somerset, taken on oath this third day of August in the Year of our Lord, one thousand eight hundred and seventy five at the Police Station, Wellington, in the County aforesaid, before the undersigned, one of Her Majesty's Justices of the Peace for the said County, in the Presence and Hearing of Joseph Tancock and Mary Prouse who are charged this day before me for that they the said Joseph Tancock and Mary Prouse on the 2nd day of August 1875 at Wellington, feloniously, wilfully and of their malice aforethought, did kill and murder one Richard Baker against the Peace of our Sovereign Lady the Queen.

Mark Cottrell on oath saith: I am a mason residing at Rockwell Green in the parish of Wellington in this county. I was yesterday engaged at work at a place called Foxdown in this parish. About five minutes before two o'clock in the afternoon I and the deceased Richard Baker were going to our work. When we were going up the hill I saw the two prisoners. Tancock was sitting down and the female was standing up. Upon seeing me the prisoner Tancock jumped up from where he was sitting and ran towards us and said 'Dick Baker you Buggar I'll kill you before I leave you'. The prisoner Tancock ran at Baker and struck him with both fists in the face and knocked him down and with the same he struggled over Baker and his fist met with him in the head and with the same some blood spurted out from Baker's head. Tancock laid on Baker and the female prisoner came and caught Baker by the hair of his head. I pulled her away from Baker. Another person then pulled Tancock off Baker. I then helped Baker up and ran down the hill. We called back and said we should go and have a warrant for him. We first went to Mr Mancey's house and not finding him in we went back to the Foreman and told him we were going for a warrant. We then went to the Magistrate Clerk's Office for a warrant where Baker became so faint that Mr Kidgell a medical gentleman was called in. Baker was then put into a dog trap and drawn home. Baker never spoke a word all day to the prisoner Tancock I was with Baker the whole day. The prisoner Tancock did not work at all that day.

Cross examined by the prisoner Tancock. You did make use of the word to Baker.

Cross examined by the prisoner Prouse. You did pull him by the hair of his head.

Re-examined. It was not a wilfull kick. Tancock was the worse for drink. Dalley was the person who pulled Tancock off Baker. When I pulled the woman away from Baker she struck at me and used bad language.

[signed] Mark Cottrell

Charles Wyatt on Oath saith: I am a carpenter and work at Foxdown and was at work there yesterday. During the dinner time about half past one I heard an unusual noise under where I was having my dinner. I went down and saw a man called Winter and the prisoner Tancock listening against the door. I said to the prisoner 'Joe you ought to know better'. I saw the prisoner Tancock was the worse for liquor. Tancock went and sat on the bench when the female prisoner came in and said to the male prisoner, 'Joe they say I are drunk as well as thee'. He said 'Who said that?' She said 'that little chap who went down over the hill'. Then he said 'thats that bloody Dick'. The prisoner Tancock said to the man 'Thee stick to me'. The other said 'I will'. Then Tancock says 'we will give him a good leathering'. The other man said 'I'll shew him a bit of Devon'. The prisoner Tancock tucked up his cuffs and said 'come on we will go down and kill the buggar.'

Cross examined by the prisoner Tancock you did say 'I will kill the Buggar.'

[signed] Charles Wyatt

John Redwood on oath saith: I am a carpenter residing in Wellington. Yesterday I was going towards Foxdown about ten minutes before two o'clock I saw the prisoner Tancock sitting down in the hedge and the female prisoner standing the other side of the road. There were one or two other men near the male prisoner. I saw two other men walking towards Foxdown. They were just behind me. When they got near to where the male prisoner was sitting he got up and made towards Baker and struck him. He was one of the two men. He struck him on the side of the head. Baker fell and the prisoner Tancock fell upon him. I saw the female prisoner hold Baker by the coat or the hair. I cant tell which. Tancock got up and got hold of Baker and they pulled him up. After Baker was up the prisoner Tancock struck him again with both hands. Baker fell down. I saw people interpose. I saw Baker's mate help him up and that they went down the hill. I saw Baker afterwards near Improvement Place and spoke to him. I saw some blood at the side of his head.

Cross examined by the prisoner Tancock 'I saw you knock him down the second time.'

[signed] John Redwd [sic]

William Dalley on oath saith: I am a mason and working at Foxdown. A little before two o'clock yesterday afternoon I was sitting by the road side, the prisoner Tancock and a person called Jeffrey were sitting there also. I saw the deceased man Baker and a man called Cottrell come up the hill. When they were within five or six land yards of the prisoner Tancock he got up and walked towards Baker and struck him. The blow knocked him against the hedge. They caught hold of one another by the coat and fell on the ground. Baker was under just then the female prisoner was quarrelling on the other side of the road with one other man and I was looking at that. I first pushed the female prisoner away and then I and Cottrell went and pulled the prisoner Tancock off Baker and then we got Baker up. Baker and Cottrell then went away.

[signed] William Dalley

George Kidgell on oath saith: I am a medical practitioner residing at Wellington. As I was passing the Registry Office I was called in to attend the deceased man Baker. I found him sitting in a chair and appeared to be faint. I spoke to him but he did not answer and was drivelling at the mouth. He was semi conscious. I examined him and found a slight cut over the right temple I could not then discover other marks of violence. The right eye was dilated and the other rather contracted. The appearance of the right eye denoted some mischief on the brain. I saw him twice afterwards during the same afternoon. When I saw him the second time I found he was cold and could not swallow. The next time I saw him he had got warm and was in a perfuse perspiration. I was told he had been in convulsions. I have today assisted in making a post mortem examination of the body. There was a slight wound on the scalp, blood was escaping from the nose. There was great extravasation of blood over the right temple under the scalp corresponding with the external wound. On opening the skull I found a clot of blood about three ounces in weight between the bone and the dura matter. In my opinion that was produced by violence, a knock down blow on the head coming in contact with the hard road would cause this. In my opinion the cause of death was extravasation of blood as described and the result of violence. There was no mark of a blow on the back part of the head. When I examined the deceased just after his death I found the marks of a blow on the chest just under the collar bone.

[signed] George Kidgell

Joseph Tancock and Mary Prouse stand charged before the undersigned one of Her Majesty's Justices of the Peace in and for the County of Somerset this third day of August in the Year of our Lord one thousand eight hundred and seventy five for that they on the 2nd day of August 1875 at Wellington feloniously, wilfully and of their malice aforethought did kill and murder one Richard Baker against the Peace of our Sovereign Lady the Queen her Crown and dignity and contrary to the Statute in such case made and provided and the said Charge being read to the said Joseph Tancock and Mary Prouse and the witnesses for the prosecution Mark Cottrell, Charles Wyatt, John Redwood, William Dalley, George Kidgell being severally examined in their presence the said Joseph Tancock and Mary Prouse are now addressed by me as follows: 'Having heard the evidence, do you wish to say any thing in answer to the charge? You are not obliged to say anything unless you desire to do so; but whatever you say will be taken down in writing, and may be given in evidence against you upon your trial,' and before the said accused persons made the following statements, I stated to them and gave them clearly to understand that they had nothing to hope from any promise of favour, and nothing to fear from any threat which may have been holden out to them to induce them to make any admission or confession of their guilt, but that whatever they should then say might be given in evidence against them upon their trial, notwithstanding such promise or threat.

Whereupon the said Joseph Tancock saith as follows: 'I have nothing to say.'

his
Joseph X Tancock
mark

The said Mary Prouse saith as follows:
'I have nothing more to say than that I am not guilty I never touched Baker. I was stood close by them when they falled on the ground. I never touched Baker at all. I was pulling off Tancock from him.'

her
Mary X Prouse
mark

Taken before me
  Sylvanus Fox

PRO, HO 27/172 Criminal Register

Joseph Tancock   Offence: Manslaughter   Sentence: 4 months hard labour
Mary Prouse   Offence: Manslaughter   Acquitted

THE OLD BAILEY AND CENTRAL CRIMINAL COURT

Middlesex was never covered by an Assize Circuit, the Old Bailey Sessions acted as the equivalent. Sessions were held every month and were separated into two divisions:

i Cases of those living in and accused of committing crimes in the City of London;

ii Other cases for the County of Middlesex (excluding London).

The Old Bailey Court Proceedings were printed and bound into volumes. Copies of these are deposited at the Public Record Office, London, Class PCOM 1 and at the Guildhall Library, London.

Original manuscript material for the Old Bailey Sessions is held in two repositories:

i The Corporation of London Record Office which holds material for those tried by City Juries.

ii The Greater London Record Office which holds all material relating to cases tried by the Middlesex Juries.

It should be noted that the printed sessions referred to above are detailed accounts of the trials and include depositions by witnesses; they usually give the age of the accused if found guilty. They do not, however, include the full indictment. For the family historian an indictment is usually the key document because it invariably gives the place of residence of the prisoner, a record of which is not always found elsewhere in the proceedings.

Indictments for the period 1834 to 1957 are found in PRO, Class CRIM 4, and

Calendars of Indictments which can be used as a reference to the indictments are found in PRO, Class CRIM 5.

From 1834 the Old Bailey was known as the Central Criminal Court when its jurisdiction was extended to parts of Essex, Kent and Surrey.

PRO, Class CRIM 1 also contains original depositions of cases tried at the Central Criminal Court of which the following types of cases are preserved: murder, sedition, treason, riot, conspiracy to effect political changes and other trials of historic interest. Pardons are also included. This class also consists of a 2 per cent random sample of depositions of less interest.

The following is a selection of cases from these records:

PRO, PCOM 1/1
Old Bailey Sessions   First Session, 2nd December 1801

Nicholas Piriole was indicted for stealing on the 29th of October, ten pounds weight of preserved apricots, value 50s, one hundred pounds weight of carraways, value 30s, two pounds weight of apple jelly, value 8s, twelve pounds of sugar, value 6s, a wooden box, value 1s, twelve sheets of foil, value 6s, twelve jars, value 12d, and twelve gallipots, value 6d, the property of Martha Hoffman, widow, Charles Godfrey Hoffman, and James Rix Hoffman.
(The case was opened by Mr Knowlys)

James Rix Hoffman sworn. Examined by Mr Const.
Q. 'What is the firm of your house?'
A. 'Martha Hoffman, widow, Charles Godfrey Hoffman, and myself; we are confectioners, in Bishopsgate Street; the prisoner was our servant. About three days before the 29th of October, I missed some preserved apricots from two pans; we suspected the prisoner, and had master-keys made to his boxes. On the evening of the 27th, I examined the boxes, and found two bladders containing preserved apricots.'
Q. 'Are bladders the common mode of keeping them?'
A. 'No; about a quarter past eight in the evening I concealed myself; we had placed Mr Holdsworth outside the door where he was to wait for a signal, when he was to stop the prisoner. I saw the prisoner take the bladders one by one out of the box and put them in his pocket. After that I saw him return them into the box again. I should suppose they were too large for his pockets. The next day about twelve o'clock, I examined his boxes and found the bladders reduced in size and in the corner of the same box, I found a brown paper containing preserved apricots. In the evening I concealed myself as before and saw the prisoner take the bladders out of the box and put them in his pockets. Mr Holdsworth was outside the door; my brother gave him the signal and he brought the prisoner in and searched him. He fell on his knees and begged for God's sake we would save his life and he would confess his guilt. Upon his finding that would not do, he fell flat upon his face, kissed our feet and begged we would save his life, and he would confess everything. I made answer that his conduct had been too infamous for him to expect any mercy; there were two bladders containing preserved apricots found upon him.'

Cross-examined by Mr Gurney.
Q. 'I presume the skill that he had used in your house would have enabled him to make up goods of this sort at his own lodgings?'
A. 'I don't know that he did.'

Q. 'Of course you don't mean to swear to preserved apricots?'
A. 'No.'

Mr Charles Godfrey Hoffman and Mr Philip Holdsworth corroborated the testimony of the last witness.

The prisoner being a Frenchman, made his defence by means of an interpreter, as follows:

'I bought these apricots of a person at different times; his name is Joseph Fondiere, he lives in the Little Minories; he had been to my house in Lemon Street, Tabernacle Walk several times particularly one evening when I bought twelve pounds of apricots of him, which he was to bring me the next morning; and, as I was going to my work the next morning I met him in Bishopsgate Churchyard with the apricots in two bladders; he said he was in a hurry and could not carry them to my house; he gave them to me and I took them to Mr Hoffman's house and put them in my box, not thinking there was any danger in it. I intended to take them all home in the evening but meeting with a friend in the day, with whom I was to go and sup, I only took a part of them and that I might not give my master any room to suspect I took them out of the bladder and put them into a brown paper, and on the 29th of October I took the rest away thinking there was no harm in so doing. Mr Charles Hoffman came into the shop and asked me some questions about some ornaments for the Lord Mayor's day and upon quitting the house I was stopped by the City Marshall and brought back, and when I was brought back I was very much frightened and did not know what I said.'

The prisoner called four witnesses who gave him a good character.

GUILTY, aged 44

Transported for seven years.

London Jury, before Mr Recorder

PRO, PCOM 1/1
Old Bailey Sessions   Third Session, 17 February 1802

William Whittick and Sophia Bennet were indicted for feloniously stealing on the 27th of January, two gowns, value 15s, two shirts, value 10s, an apron, value 6d, a waistcoat, value 2s, a shift, value 6d and a handkerchief, value 6d the property of Mary Southall, spinster.

Mary Southall sworn.

'I am a single woman. On Monday the 25th of January I lost the things mentioned in the indictment from my lodgings at the Coal-hole Tavern, in the Strand. They were in my bed-room in a large chest. I missed them on Wednesday the 27th, I put them in the chest on the 25th; I saw one of my gowns on Wednesday at a pawnbroker's in the Strand. I went there because I thought they might be pledged.'

Q. 'Do you know the prisoners or either of them?'
A. 'Yes, I had seen them about the house, I saw them at the house together. I found a shirt the same day in a box in the prisoner's apartment, No. 10, Marygold Court in the Strand. The prisoners were both at home; I went with the officers who had a search warrant.'

Q. 'How do you know when the things were lost?'
A. 'I put them in the chest after six o'clock.'

Cross-examined by Mr Knowlys.
Q. 'You never found more than two of the articles, a gown and a shirt?'
A. 'No.'

William Blackman sworn.
'I am a patrol and constable. I have a shirt which I found at No. 10 Marygold Court. I had a search warrant and forced the door open.'
Q. 'Do you know in whose apartment you found it?'
A. 'The prisoner's; they cohabited together two or three years; they were in the room at the time I went to execute the search warrant. I came to a box and asked whose it was, the prisoner Whittick said "it is mine." I asked whose cloaths they were in the box, he said "they are mine." I asked whose shirt it was he said, "it is mine." There was a coat, waistcoat and breeches, his wearing apparel in the box; this shirt was along with them. I took the shirt out and shewed the prosecutrix; she said it was her property. I asked Bennet where the duplicate[1] of the gown was and she told me it was under the leaf of the card-table between the green baize which I took, (produces it). There were three or four more duplicates with it. I went there and found it; I kept the duplicate, I have it now.'

Cross-examined by Mr Knowlys.
Q. 'She shewed the duplicates readily?'
A. 'She was at the Brown-bear.'
Q. 'You did not find it yourself; she told you where it was?'
A. 'She did, before the Magistrate.'
Q. 'Do you mean to say she said so when she had the duplicate, or before the Magistrate?'
A. 'Before I had the duplicate.'
Q. 'There was no concealment at all?'
A. 'No.'
Q. 'There was no difficulty in finding her; the pawnbroker knew her?'
A. 'Yes' (Produces the shirt).

James Cook sworn.
'I keep the Coal-hole in the Strand. Mary Southall lodged at my house. The prisoner Whittick was at my house on the 25th of January, in the evening, at the club. The club room has a small room detached off, where there is a large chest; he was there sometime among the rest of his acquaintance and companions.'
Q. 'They were all members of a club at your house?'
A. 'Yes; he stopped there about an hour and a half. They went away two or three at a time. On Wednesday morning the prosecutrix, who kept her things unlocked in that chest went to the chest and missed them. On the lid of this large chest I put a bedstead, a mahogany side-board upon that for the purpose of securing the property because I had no lock on the chest. It must be a strong arm to lift the lid up and take away the things. After the company had gone the prosecutrix slept in that small room that night. On Tuesday morning the door was locked, and kept locked the whole of that day. On Tuesday night she slept there; on Wednesday morning she missed these things and made enquiry of the pawnbroker. I was present when she found it at the pawnbroker's.'
Q. 'Is the pawnbroker's man here?'
A. 'Yes; Bennet told the Magistrate at Bow Street she had the gown and shirt given to

---

[1] A *duplicate* was the ticket of receipt for pawned goods.

her by a man at the top of Fountain Court. The shirt Whittick claimed as his, at their lodgings in Marygold Court. I was present.'

Cross-examined by Mr Knowlys.
Q. 'I believe you invited this man to come to your club that night?'
A. 'No.'
Q. 'Did you give some tickets to distribute?'
A. 'I do not think I did.'
Q. 'Upon your oath, did you not give him tickets to distribute and bring persons to your club?'
A. 'I am not certain; I think I did not for that night.'
Q. 'Did you not frequently?'
A. 'No I have never seen him above three or four times at furthest.'
Q. 'You had given him tickets to distribute?'
A. 'Yes I did it when I was a little acquainted with him.'
Q. 'You will not swear you did not give him tickets that night?'
A. 'I did not that night.'
Q. 'Will you swear it?'
A. 'I don't think I did; I cannot be positive.'

Thomas Roberts sworn.
'I am a servant to a pawnbroker, Mr Salked, 423 Strand. I have the gown.' (producing it). 'It was pledged by the prisoner Sophia Bennet on the 6th of January, about ten in the morning. She gave in her name and place of abode, No. 10 Marygold Court. I knew her before for some time; I lent her eight shillings upon it. She had been in the habit of pledging things at our shop for a considerable time.'

Cross-examined by Mr Knowlys.
Q. 'You have known this woman some time as a person who pledged things?'
A. 'Yes.'
Q. 'Had you any reason to suspect her as to honesty?'
A. 'I never heard any thing dishonest of her.'
Q. 'This she did in her own name and place of abode?'
A. 'Yes.'
Q. 'You gave some information about her lodgings?'
A. 'Yes.'

Court.
Q. 'Do you know the man she lived with?'
A. 'No.'

The property was identified by the prosecutrix.

The prisoner Whittick left his defence to his Counsel and called two witnesses who gave him a good character.
The prisoner Bennet was not put upon her defence.

Both NOT GUILTY
Second Middlesex Jury before Mr Justice Le Blanc.

PRO, PCOM 1/1
Old Bailey Sessions   Seventh Session, 15th September 1802

Thomas Porter was indicted for breaking and entering the dwelling house of Samuel Brady, no person therein, about the hour of eleven in the forenoon of the 31st of August, and feloniously stealing a feather bed, value 40s, a blanket, value 2s, two sheets, value 2s, and a counterpane, value 10s, the property of the said Samuel.

Thomas Burland sworn.

Q. 'Do you know the house of Samuel Brady?'
A. 'Yes, in King of Prussia Walk, Hoxton Fields.'
Q. 'Do you live near him?'
A. 'Yes, very near.'
Q. 'Do you know what parish it is?'
A. 'In St. Leonard's, Shoreditch.'
Q. 'Do you recollect being near that house about the end of August?'
A. 'On Tuesday, the 31st of August, about eleven in the forenoon, I was in my own privy where I had a view of the door of Mr Brady's house; I saw the prisoner go in at the front door.'
Q. 'Did you know him before?'
A. 'No but I am sure he is the man, he went in at the front door, he had an instrument in his hand which I saw him very plainly move; the door opened and he went in.'
Q. 'Was any body with him?'
A. 'There was another in company but he did not go into the house.'
Q. 'Was the door shut afterwards?'
A. 'Yes as soon as I saw him go in, I called to my man that was at work for me in the shed and told him to bring a stick and follow me immediately, for there was a thief gone into Mr Brady's house. I immediately ran and called upon Fitzgeorge as I went along. I desired Fitzgeorge to go round to the back door and sent my man to watch upon the wall even with the front of the house and I kept the front door myself. I had alarmed all the neighbourhood.'
Q. 'Did you try the door to see if it was fast?'
A. 'Yes, and it was fast.'
Q. 'That was the door at which the man had gone in?'
A. 'Yes I might wait five or six, or ten minutes for any thing I know, or somewhere thereabouts; people came about, but nobody would believe there was any body in the house. My man was impatient, he jumped down from the wall and looked through the key-hole. I immediately looked through the key-hole and saw a man. I desired one of the people to fetch an axe and I would break the door open in a minute and immediately upon that the door was opened from within. The prisoner forced himself against me and tried to force me backwards. My man immediately assisted me and we took him. Fitzgeorge and I searched the house; I left the prisoner in custody of my man.'
Q. 'What did you observe?'
A. 'I observed the bed thrown off the bedstead on to the floor.'
Q. 'Was that in the upper chamber?'
A. 'In the one pair of stairs room; the sheets and blankets were on the floor, on the right hand, by the side of the bedstead.'
Q. 'Were they loose upon the floor?'
A. 'All except the bolster and one blanket, and a matrass which were on the bedstead.'
Q. 'Were they folded up at all?'
A. 'No, loose in a heap; then we took the prisoner to Worship Street. I saw him searched and there were found upon him two picklock keys and an iron crow [bar], one of the keys had a double end.'

Q. 'Where were they?'
A. 'They were in his breeches pocket, between the breeches and the lining; one key and the crow [bar] were on one side and the other key on the other side.'

Cross-examined by Mr Courthorpe.
Q. 'These things appeared thrown down in such a way that the person last up might have thrown them there?'
A. 'I cannot say.'
Q. 'You had not previously locked the door?'
A. 'No I had not.'

Sophia Gregory sworn.
Q. 'Do you live with Mr Brady?'
A. 'Yes.'
Q. 'Do you remember the last day of August going out?'
A. 'Yes.'
Q. 'Are you servant with him?'
A. 'Yes.'
Q. 'What time in the morning did you go out?'
A. 'At nine o'clock.'
Q. 'Who did you leave at home?'
A. 'Nobody.'
Q. 'Which door of the house did you go out at?'
A. 'The front door.'
Q. 'When you were gone out what did you do at the door?'
A. 'I locked it and took the key with me.'
Q. 'Is there one bed-room, or two, up one pair of stairs?'
A. 'Two, but only one bed.'
Q. 'Had that bed been slept in the night before?'
A. 'Yes.'
Q. 'Had you done any thing to the bed before you went out?'
A. 'Yes I made the bed up for my young master to go to bed.'
Q. 'What is your master?'
A. 'A tea dealer. I came home about half past twelve.'
Q. 'How did you find the door?'
A. 'I found it locked as I had left it, and I went in.'
Q. 'In what state did you find the house?'
A. 'I found bed and bedding thrown upon the floor.'
Q. 'Was that the bed you made up in the morning?'
A. 'Yes.'
Q. 'Did you find many people about your master's house?'
A. 'No. I found one blanket folded upon a matrass.'
Q. 'Do you know whether your master had come home since you went out at nine in the morning?'
A. 'I am sure he had not.'
Q. 'Had he a key of your house?'
A. 'No.'
Q. 'How soon after that had you any information of what had happened?'
A. 'Before I got home.'
Q. 'Are you at all a judge of the value of that bed?'
A. 'I don't know.'
Q. 'Was it a good feather bed?'
A. 'Yes.'

Q. 'How were the blankets?'
A. 'Very good.'
Q. 'How many blankets were upon the floor?'
A. 'Three, and two sheets.'

Cross-examined by Mr Courthorpe.
Q. 'You were not with your master all morning?'
A. 'No.'
Q. 'Where was your master?'
A. 'In town; my mistress was with him.'
Q. 'Then, of your Knowledge, you cannot tell whether he had been home or not?'
A. 'They and the children were at St. Mary Axe.'
Q. 'That is not such a distance but that, from nine to twelve, they might have been to the house?'
A. 'No, that could not be because I had the key.'
Q. 'But they might have been in the house by other means?'
A. 'No.'

Court.
Q. 'Where does your master carry on his business?'
A. 'In St. Mary Axe.'
Q. 'Is his son in the business?'
A. 'Yes.'
Q. 'What time did they go out?'
A. 'About half past eight.'
Q. 'And what time do they generally come home?'
A. 'Not till the evening.'
Q. 'They are not there in the daytime?'
A. 'No, they are not.'

William Gray sworn.
Q. 'Are you servant to Burland?'
A. 'Yes.'
Q. 'Did you go at the desire of your master?'
A. 'Yes.'
Q. 'Do you remember your master calling for something to break open the door?'
A. 'My master placed me upon the wall; I would not believe there was any body in the premises and got off the wall, looked through the key-hole, and saw a man stooping down, and doing something to his shoe, but what I cannot tell. I was coming to the wall again. I heard my master call for a large axe and immediately saw the door open, and my master got hold of the prisoner. I immediately laid hold of him and held him while my master and Fitzgeorge went into the house.'
Q. 'Did you see him searched?'
A. 'Yes.'
Q. 'You did not go into the house?'
A. 'No.'
Q. 'Was your master and Fitzgeorge the first persons that went into the house?'
A. 'Yes.'

Fitzgeorge sworn.
Q. 'You were called upon by Burland to go to his house?'
A. 'Yes.'

Q. 'Did you see the door open, and any person come out of it?'
A. 'When Burland gave me the alarm I went down the passage, knowing the premises in order to secure the back part; Mr Brady has a house there.'
Q. 'Speak of the house where the wife lived.'
A. 'The house that the prisoner went into is not the house Mrs Brady lived in; there is a party-wall between the two houses; it is now Mr Brady's.'
Q. 'How long has he had it in his possession for the use of his own family?'
A. 'I cannot say; I think, as near as I can recollect, five or six months. I am not certain; it adjoins to his own garden and the green-house extends from Mr Brady's house to this little house adjacent. I went with another man, a baker, and fixed him upon the wall while I went over into Mr Morris's garden, and just as I was jumping over the fence the man had unlocked the door and came out.'
Q. 'Did you see who the man was that came out?'
A. 'I did.'
Q. 'Who was it?'
A. 'The prisoner, Thomas Porter, I was the first that went into the house with Burland after the prisoner was secured.'
Q. 'Did you, or Burland first go up stairs to the bed-room?'
A. 'We all three went up together, as near as could be. I found the clothes and the bed on the floor, except the pillow, which laid upon the matrass with a blanket folded up.'
Q. 'Did you see the prisoner searched?'
A. 'No; I left Mrs Marsom, and other people, to take care of the house till somebody came back.'
Q. 'Can you form any judgment of the whole of these things?'
A. 'The three blankets were worth at least a guinea and a half, and I would not make the bed under ten pounds.'
Q. 'What is the age of young Mr Brady?'
A. 'I cannot tell his age.'
Q. 'The father and mother never slept in the house?'
A. 'Never.'
Q. 'The young man is four or five and twenty is he not?'
A. 'I don't know, I was there when Harper and Burland came back with a key, which opened the door very easy.'

Samuel Harper sworn.
Q. 'You are an officer?'
A. 'Yes.'
Q. 'Did you search the prisoner?'
A. 'Yes; in one thigh of his breeches I found this crow [bar] and this key, and in the back part of the other thigh I found this key (producing them), which opened the door as well as any key in London, and the lock was a good way in. It took greatest part of the key, they are picklock keys.'

Court to Gregory.
Q. 'How long has this house adjoining to your master's green-house, been occupied by your master's family?'
A. 'I cannot say.'
Q. 'How long have you been servant to him?'
A. 'Fifteen months.'
Q. 'Was it then used by your master?'
A. 'No.'
Q. 'How long before this happened had it been used by him?'
A. 'I cannot say.'

Q.   'A month, or two months?'
A.   'More than that.'
Q.   'What use has been made of it?'
A.   'My young master sleeps there at nights.'
Q.   'What age is your young master?'
A.   'About five and twenty.'
Q.   'Where did he eat and have his diet?'
A.   'In St. Mary Axe.'
Q.   'Did he use to come home to sup?'
A.   'Yes, he supped at my master's house.'
Q.   'And went to this house to sleep?'
A.   'Yes.'
Q.   'And you went to this house and looked after the bed, as a servant of the father?'
A.   'Yes.'
Q.   'Where did your young master sleep before your master took that house into his possession.'
A.   'He slept then at St. Mary Axe.'
Q.   'How came he not to sleep at the other house in King Prussia Row?'
A.   'There was not room enough.'

Cross-examined by Mr Courthorpe.
Q.   'I believe the father and son are partners?'
A.   'Yes.'
Fitzgeorge. 'No, they are not partners, the father is here.'

Samuel Brady was called, but being a Quaker refused to be sworn.

Q.   To Gregory.
      'Do you know any thing of your master's business, whether they are partners or not?'
A.   'No.'

The prisoner left his defence to his Counsel and called two witnesses who gave him a good character.

GUILTY, DEATH,   aged 26
Second Middlesex Jury, before Mr Justice Le Blanc.

PRO, CRIM 1/41
The Murder of Frances Maud Smart Gregory

Depositions taken at Inquest on the body of the above at Richmond on the first day of March 1895.

Names of Witnesses	Epitome of Evidence Given	Page
Adams, John	On 21st February this witness was told by Walker he had found the body. Adams took the body to the Mortuary.	2
Burrage, Sarah	On 25th January Amy Gregory came to lodge with Burrage and brought baby. Stayed until 12th February. Speaks as to condition of child and habits of the mother.	9
French, Ann	Gregory lodged with French from 12th Feby to 21st Feby. Speaks to Gregory leaving the house with deceased on 20th February and returning later without baby.	13
French, James William	Identified the body and confirms the statement of his wife Ann French.	16
Gardiner, Matthew	Doctor who examined body and made postmortem. States cause of death.	4
Hawkins, Thomas	Arrested Mrs Amy Gregory and tells what statement she made.	19
Jones, Frances	Nurse at Workhouse. Speaks as to the birth of deceased and condition of child.	7
Preston, Isobel	Nurse at Workhouse. Speaks as to state of child when leaving the House on 24th Jan.	8
Priest, Mary	On 22nd February Mrs Gregory brought this witness the deceased child's clothing and gave them to her.	18
Pugsley, William	Police Inspector. Charged Mrs Gregory. Tells what statement she made.	21
Walker, William	On 21st February found deceased's body in Old Deer Park Richmond and informed Constable Adams.	1

[contd]

Names of Witnesses	Epitome of Evidence Given	Page
Williams, Charlotte	Had the care of deceased from the 30th Jan. to 10th February. Speaks as to the mother and condition of child.	11
VERDICT of the JURY	Wilful murder against Amy Gregory	23

A. Braxton Hicks.
Coroner for Surrey

page 1

Information of witnesses severally taken and acknowledged on behalf of our Sovereign Lady the Queen, touching the death of Frances Maud Smart Gregory at the House known as the Vestry Hall in the parish of Richmond on Friday the first day of March 1896 before ATHELSTAN BRAXTON HICKS, Esquire, one of Her Majesty's Coroners for the said County, on view of the Body of the said Person then and there lying dead.

William Walker on oath deposes:
I am a coach builder's smith and live at 8 Market Place, Hounslow. On the 21st February last I was going along the towing path about 20 minutes to 7 a.m., going to work, when about 150 yards from the new Lock footbridge I saw the body, now lying dead at the mortuary, laying on some ice in the Old Deer Park about 2 yards from the fence. I found a police constable and told him what I had seen and then I left to go to my work.

[signed] William Walker

page 2

John Adams on oath deposes:
I am a Metropolitan Police Constable 52 V.R. stationed at Richmond and on the 21st February I was on duty in the Askell Lane when last witness came up and gave me some information and in consequence I proceeded along the towing path looking into the Old Deer Park on the Haha, and there saw the body of the child half way between the Lock footbridge and the Railway bridge, on the ice, laying face downwards.

I examined the body. It was that of a female child with no clothing on. An old pocket handkerchief (produced) was tied round her neck. It was very wet. It was tied with one knot and twisted twice round the neck of the child.

The handkerchief was slightly scorched in one corner. I then conveyed the body to the police station and Dr Gardiner was called and after he examined it I took it to the Richmond Mortuary accompanied by the Coroner's Officer and that body is the one the jury have now viewed.

[signed] John Adams

page 4

Matthew Gardiner on oath deposes:
I am a Registered Medical Practitioner and acting Divisional Surgeon of Police at Richmond. On Thursday 21st February I examined the dead body of this female child at

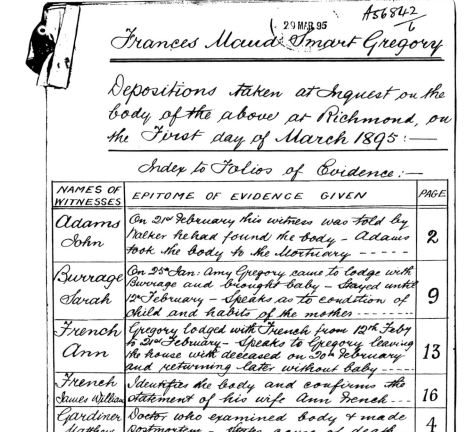

Frances Maud Smart Gregory

29 MAR 95   A56842/6

Depositions taken at Inquest on the body of the above at Richmond, on the First day of March 1895:—

Index to Folios of Evidence:—

NAMES OF WITNESSES	EPITOME OF EVIDENCE GIVEN	PAGE
Adams John	On 21st February this witness was told by Walker he had found the body – Adams took the body to the Mortuary -----	2
Burrage Sarah	On 25th Jan: Amy Gregory came to lodge with Burrage and brought baby – Stayed until 12th February – Speaks as to condition of child and habits of the mother -------	9
French Ann	Gregory lodged with French from 12th Feby to 21st February – Speaks to Gregory leaving the house with deceased on 20th February and returning later without baby -----	13
French James William	Identifies the body and confirms the statement of his wife Ann French ---	16
Gardiner Matthew	Doctor who examined body & made Postmortem – States cause of death...	4
Hawkins Thomas	Arrested Mrs Amy Gregory and tells what statement she made --------	19
Jones Frances	Nurse at Workhouse – Speaks as to the birth of deceased & condition of child	7
Preston Isobel	Nurse at Workhouse – Speaks as to state of child when leaving the House on 24th Jan: ---	8
Priest Mary	On 22nd February Mrs Gregory brought this witness the deceased childs clothing and gave them to her -------	18
Pugsley William	Police Inspector. Charged Mrs Gregory Tells what statement she made.	21

(INDEX)   (CONTINUED OVER)

Index of Evidence for the case of Amy Gregory, 1895 (PRO, CRIM 1/41)

the police station. The body was naked with the exception of a handkerchief wound twice tightly round the neck and knotted. From the external appearance I gave the opinion that the child had lived at least a month and probably longer and that its death was due to suffocation by strangling.

On Friday 22nd February I performed a postmortem. The body weighed $5\frac{1}{2}$ lbs and was $19\frac{1}{2}$ inches long, the hair of the scalp well developed. The cord entirely gone and the navel quite healed. The hands were clenched, the eyes wide open, the tongue prominent between the gums and deeply congested. On the left side of the face were two abraided wounds which had been caused either during life or immediately after death. There were two broad bands round the neck separated at places by a little ridge of skin. The neck was squeezed in all round. The body was emaciated. Dissection proved that the fat that ought to be under the skin was almost entirely absent and that the marks round the neck had been caused during life, probably. Internally all the organs of the body were healthy.

The venous system throughout was congested. This was noticed more particularly in the head. The right side of the heart was filled with blood, the left empty. The stomach was small, quite empty and quite healthy. The intestines were destitute of food. Nothing else of note was found. I am of opinion that the child was healthy at birth; that it had lived quite a month and probably longer. That it had been starved. That death was due to suffocation by strangulation, presumably by the handkerchief.

[signed] M. Gardiner MB

page 7

Frances Jones on oath deposes:

I am a nurse at the Richmond Workhouse.

I recognize Mrs Gregory now in Court as a person who came into the Workhouse in the name of Amy Smart. She came there to be confined and she was confined and delivered of a female child on 31st December. In my opinion it was a healthy full time child and she remained under my care for eight days and then handed over to nurse Preston. It was a healthy child then and the mother was feeding it at the breast.

[signed] Frances Jones

page 8

Isabel Preston on oath deposes:

I am a nurse at the Richmond Workhouse. I recognize Mrs Gregory now in Court as that of a person I knew as Amy Smart in the Workhouse.

Amy Smart and her child were under my care from the 7th January to 24th January when she left with the child. She was at that time nursing the child and it appeared quite healthy. The woman was admitted to the Workhouse on 12th December 1894 and entered her name as Amy Smart, a single woman. The child was registered as Frances Maud Smart, and daughter of Amy Smart, single woman and domestic servant.

[signed] Isabel Preston

page 9

Sarah Burrage on oath deposes:

I am the wife of Frederick Burrage a Lath render and live at 57, Alexander Road, Richmond.

On 25th January Mrs Gregory came to me about 10.30 p.m. with a baby and gave her name as Sharp and asked me if I knew where she could get a furnished room. I told her I thought she would not get one as it was late. I took the baby then and it was very cold and hungry. I gave the baby some food. I put her up for the night as she said she would otherwise have to walk the streets. That was Friday 25th January. The baby remained with me from the Friday to the Wednesday 30th January and the mother remained till Tuesday 12th February. She gave me to understand she was working at the Steam Laundry. On the 30th January a Mrs Williams took charge of the baby because the mother went to work. When Mrs Gregory left me on 12th February she told me she was going to Jocelyn Road. As she had not paid me I told her she must find rooms somewhere else. That was the last I saw of her.

her
Sarah X Burrage
mark

witness [signed] J.W. Burrowes
Coroner's Clerk

page 11

Charlotte Williams on oath deposes:

I am the wife of James Williams a sawyer and live at 2, St. Georges Place, Mortlake Road, Richmond.

Mrs Gregory sent for me on 29th January and I saw her at Mrs Burrage's house on that day. I saw Mrs Gregory who is now in Court and we spoke as to taking the baby to nurse. I asked her if she could not get any support from the father and she said no and that she would like me to take it as cheaply as I could and agreed to pay me 5/– per week. She brought the baby to me on the 30th January. I had charge of the child till the 10th February and on that day I took it back to the mother as I had had no payment from her. I left the child with her. It was healthy and a very strong child then. I have seen the body of the child at the Mortuary and identify that as the body of Mrs Gregory's child.

[signed] Charlotte Williams

page 13

Ann French on oath deposes:

I am the wife of James William French a plumber and live at 25, Raleigh Road, Richmond.

Mrs Gregory came to me on a Tuesday night, 12th February and knocked at my door with a baby and asked me if I had got a bed. The baby was sleeping alright. It was at 11.30 p.m. and I gave her a bed. She got up next day and went out. She was out during the daytime and told me she went to the Steam Laundry. She took the baby out every morning and brought it back at night. She told me Mrs Williams took care of the child. Baby was only fed three times in my house but the mother told me she gave it the breast. The mother appeared to be a sober woman but did not appear to think much of the child. She told me to call her Ann and I asked her where her husband was and she said he was away. She did not pay anything. On Wednesday 20th February about 8.45 p.m. I heard the baby being hushed by the mother as she left the house. She returned about 10.15 p.m. I saw her and she came into the kitchen. She had no baby with her then. I asked her where the baby was and she said she had taken it to a Mrs Whitrod. She said it would be better cared for. She said she had supper there and left the baby with her. On Thursday 21st she got up and went out. She seemed more lively then. On Friday 22nd she left about half past 10 as she told me, to go to work but she never returned. I saw the clothes which the child wore. The clothes now here shewn to me are similar to what the child was wearing and I recognize them as far as I know to be the same.

[signed] Ann French

page 18

Mary Priest on oath deposes:

I am the wife of Henry James Priest a General labourer and I live at 18, Garden Row, Mortlake.

I used to know Mrs Gregory now in Court. I knew her as Mrs Gregory and I knew her husband. I heard they were not living together 15 months ago. She told me so. I do not know what she was doing for a living. She had two children by her husband and they are with his mother. I saw her on the 25th January (Friday). I understood she slept with her mother the night after she came out of the Workhouse, (on the 24th). She asked me for lodgings and I told her I could not lodge her. I have seen her between that time and Sunday last two or three times. She told me she was working at the Steam Laundry. On Friday last 22nd February she came to my house between 10.30 a.m. and 10.45 a.m. She handed me some baby clothes now produced. She told me she had intended to give them to Mrs Whitrod but she said to me 'You can have them.' She stopped till 7 p.m. and we went out together and she said she was going to the Steam Laundry. On Saturday 23rd February she came to my house again at 6.15 or 6.30 a.m. I was in bed then and she asked me if I was going to get up. I got up and we chatted and she stopped till about 2 p.m. and then left saying she was going to meet the father of the child at 8 o'clock to take the money to Mrs Whitrod.

[signed] Mary Priest

page 19

Thomas Hawkins on oath deposes:

I am a Police Sergeant, Criminal Investigation Department stationed at Richmond.

From information I received on the 24th February about 11.15 p.m., I went to 23, Springfield Terrace, Sandycombe Road, Richmond, and went into a front parlour and there saw Mrs Gregory in bed. I told her I was a Police Officer and should have to arrest her for the wilful murder of her child. I cautioned her, 'This is a serious charge and you need not say anything unless you like but what you do say will be used in evidence for or against you.' She said 'My child is in Richmond.' After some hesitation she then said 'How did you find it out, I wish I had went some miles away.' She was taken in a cab to the police station and there detained and charged the next day. When charged Inspector Pugsley was present.

[signed] Thomas Hawkins

page 21

William Pugsley on oath deposes:

I am Local Inspector Metropolitan Police, 'V' Division.

I was informed of this occurrence and came to Richmond on the 25th ultimo where I saw the prisoner who was charged with felonious and of malice aforethought murder of her own child. She replied 'I did not murder my child, it died of starvation, my milk went away through worry. I had no money to get food and no work.' She was charged before the Magistrates and remanded. She gave her name as Amy Gregory and said she was a married woman living apart from her husband, and formerly was a domestic servant. And

Whereas Amy Gregory was, at the Central Criminal Court, on the twenty seventh day of March, 1895, convicted of Wilful Murder, and sentenced to Death:

We, in consideration of some circumstances humbly represented unto Us, are Graciously pleased to extend Our Grace and Mercy unto the said Amy Gregory, and to grant unto her Our Pardon for the crime of which she stands convicted on Condition that she be kept in Penal Servitude for Life:

Our Will and Pleasure therefore is that you do give the necessary directions accordingly And for so doing this shall be your Warrant Given at Our Court at St. James's the eleventh day of April 1895 in the 58th Year of Our Reign

To Our Trusty and Well-beloved Our Justices of the Central Criminal Court, The High Sheriff of the County of Surrey, The Governor of Our Prison at Newgate, and all others whom it may concern.

By Her Majesty's Command
W. H. Asquith

Amy Gregory's Pardon (PRO, CRIM 1/582)

her age she gave as 23 years. I have reason to believe from enquiries made that she has been in very poor circumstances.

[signed] Wm Pugsley

Verdict of the Jury
Wilful Murder against Amy Gregory

Should the woman be convicted the Coroner's Jury wish to recommend her to his merciful consideration of the Court.
Taken and Acknowledged before
me this 1st day of March 1895.

[signed] Athelstan Braxton Hicks
Coroner for Surrey

PRO, CRIM 1/582

Whereas Amy Gregory was at the Central Criminal Court, on the twenty seventh day of March 1895 convicted of Wilful Murder and sentenced to Death:
    We in consideration of some circumstances humbly represented unto Us are Graciously pleased to extend Our Grace and Mercy unto the said Amy Gregory and to grant unto her Our Pardon for the crime of which she so stands convicted on Condition that she be kept in Penal Servitude for Life.
    Our Will and Pleasure therefore is that you do give the necessary directions accordingly. And for so doing this shall be your Warrant. Given at Our Court at St. James's the eleventh day of April 1895 in the 58th Year of Our Reign.

To Our Trusty and Well-
beloved Our Justices of the
Central Criminal Court, The
High Sheriff of the County of   } By Her Majesty's Command.
Surrey, The Governor of Our
Prison at Newgate, and all
others whom it may concern.

THE PALATINATE COURTS

The counties of Cheshire, Durham and Lancashire were know as Palatinates. Until 1830 the Assize equivalent for Cheshire was the Palatinate Court of Chester, sometimes also referred to as the Chester Assizes. The Palatinate Court of Chester was abolished in 1830 and Cheshire was then covered by the North and South Wales Assize Circuit.

Durham had its own Palatinate Court (sometimes also referred to as the Durham Assizes) which continued until 1876 when Durham was included in the newly created North Eastern Assize Circuit.

Lancashire also had its own Palatinate Court known as the Palatinate Court of Lancaster (sometimes also referred to as the Lancashire Assizes). This court also continued until 1876 when Lancashire was included in the Northern Assize Circuit.

All records of Palatinate Courts are held by the Public Record Office, Chancery Lane, London. The following are some examples of the records of these courts:

PRO, CHES 24/192/6
Joseph Rogers alias Wallis charged with stealing a silver watch
Pallatinate Court of Chester, Summer 1830

Cheshire to wit. The Jurors for Our Lord the King upon their Oaths present that Joseph Rogers late of the parish of Bunbury in the County of Chester, Labourer otherwise called Joseph Wallis on the twenty first day of June in the eleventh year of the Reign of our late Sovereign Lord George the Fourth [1830] by the Grace of God King of the United Kingdom of Great Britain and Ireland Defender of the Faith with force of arms at the parish aforesaid in the county aforesaid one silver watch of the value of twenty shillings and one other watch of the value of twenty shillings of the goods and chattels of John Eborall from the person of the said John Eborall then and their feloniously did steal and carry away against the form of the statute in such case made and provided and against the peace of our Sovereign Lord the late King his crown and dignity. And the Jurors aforesaid upon their Oaths do further present that heretofore to wit at the Sessions of Chester held at Chester in the County of Chester in the Common Hall of Pleas of the said county on Monday the twelfth day of April in the fifth year of the Reign of our late Sovereign Lord George the Fourth [1824] the Honourable Charles Warren the said Lord the late King's Justice of Chester and the Honourable Thomas Jervis the said late Lord the King's other Justice of the said county, the said Joseph Rogers otherwise called Joseph Wallis by the name and description of Joseph Wallace otherwise called Joseph Rogers was then and there convicted of Felony and which said conviction is still in full force. . . .

Pleaded not Guilty
Jurors say Guilty

Witnesses: John Eborall
             Chas. Hollowood
             Mary Lovatt
             Jas. Hodgkinson Beckett

PRO, HO 27/39, Criminal Register

John Rogers   Verdict: Guilty   Sentence: 14 years Transportation

PRO, DURH 18/1
Thomas Johnson charged with sedition

Palatinate Court of Durham, 2 March 1857, at Durham

Rex	Endeavouring to
V	seduce soldiers
Johnson	from their
	allegiance

Borough of Sunderland

The examination of John Kenny, private in the 9th Regiment of Foot, John Blanchfield, corporal in the said Regiment, Richard Danby, colour sergeant in the same Regiment, William Banbury, quarter master of the said Regiment, Duncan Munro Bethune, major of the said Regiment and all now quartered in Sunderland Barracks and Robert Gifford of East Cross Street, Bishop Wearmont, Superintendent of Police at Sunderland taken on oath the thirteenth day of December 1858, at the Police Court in Bishopwearmouth, in the said Borough before the undersigned, George Smith Ranson, Henry Tanner and John Lindsay, Esquires, three of Her Majesty's Justices of the Peace in and for the said Borough, in the presence and hearing of Thomas Johnson late of the parish of Sunderland in the County of Durham, labourer, who is charged this day before us for that he the said Thomas Johnson on the twenty third day of December 1857, at the parish of Sunderland in the said Borough, did feloniously maliciously and advisedly endeavour to seduce divers persons serving in Her Majesty's land forces from their duty and allegiance to Her Majesty.

John Kenny sworn saith: I am a private in Her Majesty's 9th Regiment of Foot now stationed at the barracks in Sunderland aforesaid where I am residing. On the night of Wednesday the 23rd December instant I was in the Low Street of Sunderland the prisoner met me and handed me a letter. Prisoner said to me 'You are to give it to any one of your corporals.' I said to him 'Will it matter about any corporal?' and the prisoner answered 'No.' The letter which prisoner handed to me was sealed, but not addressed to any one. Shortly after receiving the letter from the prisoner I went to Barracks and handed the letter to Corporal John Blanchfield. On Thursday evening I got a letter from Mr Gifford, Superintendent of the Sunderland Police Force with instructions to go to Sunderland Moor and hand it to the person who had given me the letter which I afterwards handed to Corporal Blanchfield. Accordingly at 6 o'clock I proceeded to Sunderland Moor, met the prisoner and gave him the letter which Mr Gifford had placed in my hands, and the prisoner was shortly afterwards seized by the police and taken into custody.

[signed] John Kenny

John Blanchfield sworn saith: I am a corporal of the 9th Regiment of Foot and am resident at the Barracks, Sunderland. On Wednesday evening the 23rd December instant, private John Kenny placed in my hands the letter now produced marked 'A', it was sealed, but not addressed to any one. I opened the letter and read the contents and the following are extracts from the letter.

'Soldiers! the day, the very hour has arrived, at which your Country must become a republic or go back to a despotism, and I have every reason to believe that all people sincerely desire a complete change of government but through the damnable policy of those German Bastards and titled Tyrants they are setting class against class and man against man, and cannot attain their liberty without your example and assistance. Your example, that shall fire the rest of the army, arouse all the people, and set your Country at once and for ever free. Is there not something nobler in the bare idea of such a thing than throwing away your time and life to a government that has sold the liberties of Europe, as it has sold the rights of its own poor and oppressed citizens, your lives, and relations? . . . I now take upon myself that responsibility, and make the following proposals to you. Tomorrow night at ten o'clock I will be at the Barracks where you shall disarm and secure your officers, appoint others from the ranks, and follow me from the Barracks up High Street proclaiming a republic and calling the citizens to arms . . . tomorrow night I will walk in the front of the Sailors' Home on the Moor, from six until nine awaiting your answer to this appeal.'

I afterwards handed this letter to Colour Sergeant Richard Danby.

[signed] J. Blanchfield

Richard Danby sworn saith: I am colour sergeant of the 9th Regiment of Foot and now resident at the Barracks Sunderland. On Wednesday evening last about a $\frac{1}{4}$ past 9 o'clock the witness John Blanchfield came to me with a letter unsealed which he handed to me, the letter marked 'A' now produced is the same letter. After reading the letter I acquainted the Sergeant Major and went with him to the Commanding Officer's quarters and handed the letter to the Quarter Master of our Regiment.

[signed] R. Danby
Col. Sgt. 9 Foot

William Banbury sworn saith: I am Quarter Master of the 9th Regiment of Foot and am now resident at the Barracks Sunderland. On Wednesday evening last the Sergeant Major accompanied by Colour Sergeant Richard Danby came to me and the letter now produced marked 'A' was handed to me by the Sergeant Major in the presence of Danby. Next morning I handed the letter to Major Bethune.

[signed] William Danbury
Qr Master 9 Foot

Duncan Munro Bethune sworn saith: I am Major of the 9th Regiment of Foot and Commanding Officer of that regiment now stationed at the Barracks Sunderland where I am residing. The letter produced marked 'A' was handed to me by William Banbury on Thursday last.

I called upon the Mayor of this Borough with the letter which was handed to Mr Gifford the same day.

[signed] D.M. Bethune
Major 9 Regt
Comdg 1st Battn

Robert Gifford sworn saith: I am superintendent of Police at Sunderland and reside at East Cross Street Sunderland. I produce the letter marked 'A' which was handed to me by the Mayor in the presence of Major Bethune on the morning of Thursday the 24th December. On the evening of the same day I placed a note in the hands of private Kenny which I now produce, I gave Kenny instructions to place it in the hands of the man who had given the letter (marked 'A') on the previous night. I followed Kenny to the Moor in front of the Sailors' Home (Kenny being in uniform). I saw the prisoner walking in front of the Sailors' Home. I saw the prisoner and Kenny meet. They appeared to be in conversation for a few minutes when Kenny left him. Prisoner turned round and was walking towards the Sailors' Home. Kenny gave me some information in consequence of which I gave a signal to some of my men whom I had stationed near and they immediately arrested the prisoner. I ran up at the same moment and found prisoner struggling with my men who were endeavouring to take something out of his hand, and by force I took from his hand the letter which I had placed in the hands of Kenny a short time previously. The prisoner was taken to the barracks and searched. Whilst there I asked him his name, he said William Barter. He said he belonged to New York, that he had belonged to a ship called the *Reliance* in which he came down from London by the run. I asked prisoner if he resided in the Home and what the number of his room, he said, 'No. 25 here's the key but you'll find nothing there'. I said to him, 'why did you make that remark'. Prisoner replied, 'I see I have gone too far, I shall answer no more questions.' I then had him conveyed to the Central Police Station where he was examined by Mr Francis Surgeon. I produced the letter marked 'A' to the prisoner and said to him do you know any thing about this, he replied 'I can't tell till I see it.' I handed him the letter he looked at it and said, 'yes that's my handwriting.' I said to prisoner, 'In carrying out this mad scheme what would you have done with the Officers after you had secured them, surely you would not have murdered them.' He replied, 'Yes I would if they had resisted.' He added there would have been no necessity for it as the men would have been with me. I am not positive whether the prisoner said 'as the men would have been with me' or, 'If the men were with me.' It might have been the latter. Prisoner subsequently gave the name of Thomas Johnson.

[signed] Robert Gifford

The said Thomas Johnson, the before-named prisoner, stands charged before us the undersigned Justices of the Peace, this thirtieth day of December in the year of our Lord 1858 at the Police Court in Bishopwearmouth in the said Borough, for that he, the said Thomas Johnson on the twenty third day of January 1858, at the parish of Sunderland in the said Borough, did feloniously maliciously and advisedly endeavour to seduce divers persons serving in Her Majesty's Land Forces from their duty and allegiance to Her Majesty. And the said charge being now read over to the said Thomas Johnson and the witnesses for the prosecution being severally examined in his presence, the said Thomas Johnson is now addressed by me as follows:
'Having heard the evidence, do you wish to say anything in answer to the charge? You are not obliged to say anything, unless you desire to do so, but whatever you say will be taken

STATEMENT OF THE ACCUSED.

David Thomas   stands charged before

Durham (to wit.) the undersigned, ~~one~~ *two* of Her Majesty's Justices of the Peace in and for the County of Durham this *fifth* day of *November* in the year of our Lord, one thousand eight hundred and sixty *Six* for that he the said *David Thomas* on the *Second* day of *November* at the Township of *Ecomb* in the County aforesaid, did *together with divers other persons to the number of Ten and more unlawfully and riotously assemble to disturb the public peace and did then and there make a great riot and disturbance to the terror and alarm of Her Majesty's Subjects there being*

and the said Charge being read to the said *David Thomas* and the Witnesses for the prosecution *Thomas Williamson, Daniel Jones, Henry Hudson, Ellen Hope, William Askew, James Jordison and Joseph Mattress,*

being severally examined in *his* presence, the said *David Thomas* is now addressed by me as follows :—" Having heard the evidence, do you wish to say anything, in answer to the charge ? You are not obliged to say anything unless you desire to do so, but whatever you say will be taken down in writing and may be given in evidence against you, upon your trial, and you are also clearly to understand, that you have nothing to hope from any promise of favour, and nothing to fear from any threat, which may have been holden out to you, to induce you to make any admission or confession of your guilt, but that whatever you shall now say may be given in evidence against you upon your trial, notwithstanding such promise or threat."

Whereupon the said *David Thomas* saith as follows :—

No.

Taken before us at Bishop auckland the day and year first above mentioned

Mark of   ✗   *David Thomas*

Palatinate Court of Durham, 5 November 1866. Statement of David Thomas accused with others of rioting (PRO, DURH 18/1)

down in writing and may be given in evidence against you upon your trial. And you are also clearly to understand that you have nothing to hope from any promise of favour and nothing to fear from any threat which may have been holden out to you, to induce you to make any admission or confession of your guilt, but whatever you shall now say may be given in evidence against you upon your trial, notwithstanding such promise or threat.'

Whereupon the said Thomas Johnson voluntarily, and without oath saith as follows: 'I am guilty of writing that letter not guilty of any offence against this Country or its interests, on the contrary I always have been and will be a good friend.'

[signed] Thomas Johnson

Geo. S. Ranson
H. Tanner
John Lindsay

PRO, HO 27/119, Criminal Register

Thomas Johnson   Verdict: Guilty   Sentence: 1 month Imprisonment

PRO, PL 27/11
Walter Scott charged with rioting

Palatinate Court of Lancaster

Regina v Walter Scott
for rioting on the 13th August 1839

The information of William Holt of Great Bolton in the county of Lancaster, labourer taken upon oath before me one of Her Majesty's Justices for the said county the fourteenth day of March 1840.

Who saith, 'I am a Special Constable for the Borough of Bolton. I was made one during the time of the rioting in August last. About one o'clock in the afternoon of Tuesday the thirteenth day of August last I saw a party of Horse Soldiers conducting the two prisoners Warden and Lloyd on their way towards Manchester. There was a great mob of persons consisting of some hundreds following the chaise in which the two prisoners were. I was standing near the Manchester and Bolton Railway Station. I then went to my dinner to my house in Howel Croft and about half past one o'clock I came down street into the new market place near to the Exchange. At that time a great crowd of persons came running in the direction from the Police Office in Bowkers Row towards the Exchange in New Market Place. When the crowd got into Newport Street opposite the end of the Exchange which fronts New Port Street a man who was leading the crowd shouted "Now lads fire away." The crowd halted and a shower of stones flew from the crowd against the Exchange Room windows. The prisoner Walter Scott was one of the leaders of the crowd and stood within three or four yards from the man who shouted to the crowd to "Fire away." When the crowd halted I saw that the prisoner had several stones in his hands. He was one of the crowd who threw stones at the windows of the Exchange. The crowd then went up Newport Street and turned up Ashburner Street throwing stones at the windows on their road.'

The mark of
X
William Holt

Joseph Heywood of Great Bolton, labourer, says, 'I was standing in Newport Street between one and two o'clock on Tuesday the 13th August last. I saw a crowd of persons and amongst them the prisoner Walter Scott. The crowd were throwing stones at the Exchange windows. I saw the prisoner throw one stone at the windows he then got mixed with the crowd who dispersed in different directions.'

The mark of
X
Joseph Heywood

Edward Thompson of Great Bolton, police sergeant, says, 'I am police officer in Great Bolton. Several months ago I had information of the prisoner Walter Scott being concerned in the riots at Bolton in the month of August last. I have been on the look out for the prisoner for several months back. I have not been able to meet with him until the twelfth of March instant when he was apprehended.'

[signed] Edward Thompson

Francis Loughrin of Great Bolton, police officer, says, 'I had information that the prisoner was in Bolton and on Thursday the twelfth instant I found him in Deansgate coming out of a shop with a book in his hand. He had the book now produced with him and endeavoured to pass it to another man who was with him.'

[signed] Francis Loughrin

George Holt of Great Bolton in the said county, cotton spinner, says, 'the factory I worked at in Bolton was stopped on account of the holiday on Monday the twelfth day of August last. On the morning of Tuesday the thirteenth August I was in the street and betwixt twelve and one o'clock the Military went on the road to Manchester guarding the chaise conveying the prisoners John Warden and George Lloyd to gaol. I saw the crowd throw stones at the Military as they proceeded down Bradshawgate. One of the Military was knocked off his horse. The crowd followed the Military as far as the Railway Station in Bradford Square and then returning to opposite the Police Station in Bowkers Row. There were only two or three soldiers guarding the Police Office and the mob began to throw stones through the windows of the Police Office. I saw the prisoner Walter Scott in the front of the mob. Before the mob threw stones the prisoner said, "now boys fire away, now's your time." Upon this a shower of stones were thrown by the mob through the windows of the Police Office. I saw the prisoner throw several stones through the windows. The prisoner appeared to be a leader of the mob. The stones that were thrown were not picked up at the time they were thrown but the crowd had their pockets filled and appeared to have come supplied. After the stones had been thrown for some minutes a cry was raised, "The soldiers are coming" upon which the mob turned round, ran down the Acres and turned on to the New Market Place.'

The mark of
X
George Holt

William MacLean of Great Bolton, Police Inspector, says, 'The town of Bolton was in a state of riot on the morning of Tuesday the thirteenth day of August last. The riot act was read in the morning the shops were closed and the whole town in a state of disorder.'

[signed] William MacLean

Sworn before me in
presence of the prisoner.

[signed] Robert Heywood

PRO, HO 27/61, Criminal Register

Walter Scott   Verdict: Guilty   Sentence: Discharged on Sureties

THE COURTS OF GREAT SESSIONS OF WALES

In 1543 Wales was divided into twelve counties. In each county sessions were to be held twice yearly and known as the Great Sessions of Wales. (Not to be confused with the County Quarter Sessions which were also held in each county.)

The Great Sessions were the Welsh equivalent of the English Assize Courts and were arranged in four circuits:

1.	Chester[1] Circuit:	Counties of	a. Denbighshire b. Flintshire c. Montgomeryshire
2.	North Wales Circuit:	Counties of	a. Anglesey b. Caernarfonshire c. Merioneth
3.	Brecon Circuit:	Counties of	a. Brecknockshire or Brecon b. Glamorgan c. Radnorshire
4.	Carmarthen Circuit:	Counties of	a. Cardiganshire b. Carmarthenshire c. Pembrokeshire

---

[1] Sessions for Cheshire were not included in this circuit. Cheshire criminals were tried at the Palatinate Court of Chester until 1830, then North Wales Assize Circuit 1830 to 1876 and North Wales Division of Assizes 1876 to 1945. Cheshire also held County Quarter Sessions.

In 1830 the Courts of Great Sessions of Wales were abolished and the newly formed North and South Wales Assize Circuit took jurisdiction over the whole of Wales.

Records of the Great Sessions of Wales are held by the National Library of Wales, Aberystwyth.[2] The criminal records of these courts are listed in Appendix 3. A few related records also survive with Quarter Sessions records in County Record Offices.

The following are selected examples from these records. It should be noted that in many cases the outcome of a trial is not recorded. It has been necessary to refer to the criminal registers at the Public Record Office to ascertain the sentence of the court.

NLW, WALES 4/70/1, Crown Book
John Jones charged with murder by strangulation

Chester Circuit, County of Denbigh, Spring Session 1814

The Jurors for our Lord the King upon their Oaths present That John Jones the younger late of the parish of Ruthin in the County of Denbigh, labourer not having the fear of God before his eyes but being moved and seduced by the instigation of the Devil on the seventeenth day of January in the fifty fourth year of the Reign of our Sovereign Lord George the Third of the United Kingdom of Great Britain and Ireland with force of arms at the parish aforesaid in the County aforesaid in and upon one William Foulkes in the peace of God and our Lord the King then and there being, feloniously and in the fury of his mind did make an Assault and that the said John Jones the younger with a certain neckhandkerchief of the value of six pence which was then and there worn by the said William Foulkes and which was then and there about the neck and throat of him the said William Foulkes then and there feloniously and in the fury of his mind did violently take hold of, twist, pull and tighten and that the said John Jones the younger with the neckhandkerchief aforesaid by means of such taking hold of, twisting, pulling and tightening the said neckhandkerchief of him the said William Foulkes then and there feloniously and in the fury of his mind did choak, suffocate and strangle of which said choaking, suffocating and strangling the said William Foulkes then and there instantly died. And so the Jurors aforesaid upon their oaths aforesaid do say that the said John Jones the younger, the said William Foulkes in manner and form aforesaid feloniously and in the turn of his mind did kill and slay against the peace of our said Lord the King his Crown and Dignity.

Pleads NOT GUILTY

Jury say GUILTY
No true Bill for murder but true Bill for manslaughter

PRO, HO 27/10, Criminal Register

Denbigh, Spring Great Session 1814

John Jones   Manslaughter   3 months imprisonment

---

[2] All records of Welsh courts are written in the English language.

NLW, WALES 4/200/7, Gaol File
Mary Hughes charged with stealing a quantity of flannel

Chester Circuit, County of Montgomery, Spring Session 1818

Mary Hughes aged 28 charged on suspicion of having feloniously stolen, taken and carried away a quantity of flannel, the property of John Titley of the parish of Llangurrig. Committed 12th January 1818 by George Meares, esq.

The Jurors for our Lord the King upon their oath present that Mary Hughes late of the parish of Llangurrig in the County of Montgomery, singlewoman on the twenty third day of December in the fifty eighth year of the Reign of our Sovereign Lord George the Third King of the United Kingdom of Great Britain and Ireland with force and arms in the night time of the same day to wit about the hour of ten of the night at the parish aforesaid in the County aforesaid four yards of woollen cloth called flannel of the value of ten shillings, four yards of other woollen cloth of the value of ten shillings and four yards of flannel of the value of ten shillings of the goods and chattels of one John Titley (the same woollen cloth called flannel, then and there being put and being on tenters for the drying thereof) feloniously did cut steal take and carry away from the said tenters against the form of the statute in such case made and provided and against the peace of our said Lord the King his Crown and Dignity. And the Jurors aforesaid upon their oath do further present that the said Mary Hughes afterwards to wit on the said twenty third day of December in the fifty eighth year of the Reign of our said Lord the King with force and arms at the said parish of Llangurrig in the County of Montgomery aforesaid four yards of other woollen cloth called flannel of the value of ten shillings, four yards of other woollen cloth of the value of ten shillings and four yards of other flannel of the value of ten shillings of the goods and chattels of the said John Titley then and there being found, feloniously did steal take and carry away against the peace of our said Lord the King his Crown and Dignity. And the Jurors aforesaid upon their oath aforesaid do further present that the said Mary Hughes afterwards to wit on the said twenty third day of December in the fifty eighth year of the Reign of our said Lord the King with force and arms at the said parish of Llangurrig in the County of Montgomery aforesaid four yards of woollen cloth called flannel of the value of ten shillings, four yards of other woollen cloth of the value of ten shillings and four yards of other flannel of the value of ten shillings of the goods and chattels of one Thomas Lewis then and there being found feloniously did steal take and carry away against the peace of our said Lord the King his Crown and Dignity.

Felony   Pleads NOT GUILTY
         Jury say GUILTY of stealing but not at night time

PRO, HO 27/16, Criminal Register

Montgomery, Spring Great Session 1818

Mary Hughes   Larceny   7 Years Transportation

NLW, WALES 4/1020/1, Gaol File
Sarah Beddows charged with passing counterfeit money

Chester Circuit, County of Flint, Spring Session 1824

Sarah Beddows late of the parish of Holywell in the County of Flint, Labourer, on the 29th August 4 Geo. IV at the parish aforesaid did utter one piece of false and counterfeit money made and counterfeited to the likeness and similitude of a piece of good lawful and current money and silver coin of this Realm called a shilling unlawfully, unjustly, and deceitfully did utter to one Alice the wife of William Williams.

The Examination of David Hewitt of Holywell in the County of Flint, yeoman taken in writing and on oath the sixteenth day of September 1823. Who on his oath saith that having heard that there was a good deal of bad silver in circulation in the Market in Holywell on the twenty ninth day of August last and that the witness Alice Williams had received a shilling he in consequence went to her and requested to see it. That she delivered the shilling now produced to the examinant at the same time informing him that she had received it on that day in payment for some potatoes from the prisoner Sarah Beddows. That he examined the same and discovered that it was a bad one.

[signed] David Hewitt

The Examination of Alice the wife of William Williams of the parish of Holywell in the County of Flint, Labourer taken in writing and on oath this 16th day of September 1823. Who on her oath saith that she attended the Market at Holywell on Friday the twenty ninth day of August last for the purpose of selling potatoes and other vegetables. That in the course of the morning of that day the Prisoner Sarah Beddows came up to this examinant's standing and asked her to sell a pennyworth of potatoes which she did. That the said Sarah Beddows gave this examinant the shilling now produced to pay for the same and requested her to give her the said Sarah Beddows the change which witness accordingly did and the Prisoner went away. That witness afterwards saw the Prisoner in conversation with the witness Margaret King from whom she understood that the Prisoner had given her some bad silver which had examinant to examine the shilling which she found was counterfeit. That witness gave the shilling which she received from the prisoner to the witness David Hewitt. That she was not aware that it was bad at the time she received it from the Prisoner.

[signed] Alice Williams

The examination of Margaret King wife of William King of the parish of Holywell in the said County, farmer taken in writing and on oath this 16th day of Sept. 1823. Who on her oath saith that she attended the Market at Holywell on Friday the twenty ninth day of August last for the purpose of selling vegetables. That in the course of the morning of that day the prisoner came up to this examinant's cart and asked her to change a shilling which witness refused at the same time telling the Prisoner it was a bad one. That upon this the said Sarah Beddows gave the witness half a crown which witness said she would not change as it was also bad and that she the said Sarah Beddows deserved to be taken up for offering bad money. That the Prisoner upon this observed that she did not know they were bad and requested witness to give her change for a note which she refused. That upon this the said Sarah Beddows requested witness to return her the silver. That witness refused to do so, and again told her she ought to be taken up when the Prisoner immediately went off. That she this examinant afterwards delivered the shilling and half crown in question to the witness Thomas Morris[3] and that the silver now produced and therein to the witness is the same as was given to her by the said Sarah Beddows.

[signed] Margaret King

PRO, HO 27/27, Criminal Register

Flint, Spring Great Session 1824

| Sarah Beddows | Uttering Counterfeit Coin | 6 Months Imprisonment |

---

[3] No examination of Thomas Morris has been found among the papers of this case.

NLW, WALES 4/301/4, Gaol File
Rowland Jones charged with poisoning

North Wales Circuit, County of Merioneth, Spring Session 1766

The Jurors for our Lord the King upon their Oath present that Rowland Jones late of the parish of Llasaintfraid in the said County, yeoman being a person of wicked mind and disposition and maliciously intending to poison Robert Jones of the said parish of Llansaintfraid in the said County, yeoman and Elizabeth his wife, his master and mistress, Catherine their child and Catherine their maid servant on the eight and twentieth day of February in the sixth year of the Reign of our Sovereign Lord George the third now King of Great Britain and so forth, at the parish aforesaid in the County aforesaid, did knowingly, willfully and maliciously put a quantity of arsenick or other poisonous drug (being a deadly poison) into a pot or kettle of flummery which said pot or kettle the said Robert Jones and Elizabeth his wife had then and there immediately before directed the said Rowland Jones to boil in order for the supper of the said Robert Jones, Elizabeth his wife, Catherine their child and Catherine their maid servant and the said Rowland did then and there knowingly willfully and maliciously boil the said arsenick or other poisonous drug in the said pot or kettle of flummery and the same pot or kettle of flummery in which the said arsenick or other poisonous drug was so boiled as aforesaid did immediately afterwards to wit on the same day and year then and there deliver to the said Robert Jones, Elizabeth his wife Catherine their child and Catherine their maid servant to eat and the said Robert Jones, Elizabeth his wife, Catherine their child and Catherne their maid servant not knowing the said arsenick or other poisonous drug to have been put in the said flummery did use the same and eat a quantity thereof wherein the said Arsenick or other poisonous drug had been so boiled as aforesaid whereby the said Robert Jones, Elizabeth his wife, Catherine their child and Catherine their maid servant became variously distempered in their bodies and were in extreme danger of loosing their lives to the great damage of the said Robert Jones, Elizabeth his wife, Catherine their daughter and Catherine their maid servant, to the evil example of all others in the like case offending and against the peace of our said Lord the King, his Crown and Dignity.

GUILTY

To be imprisoned for five years without bail or main prize and at the end of five years to give security for his good behaviour for seven years more, himself in fifty pounds and two Sureties in twenty five pounds each.

NLW, WALES 14/15, Rule Book

North Wales Circuit

Great Session held at Caernarfon Monday 15th August 43 George III [1803].
The Court continued on Wednesday after.

Between Our Sovereign Lord the King on
the Prosecution of John Rasbrook
            and   } For Grand Larceny
David Prichard of Llanllechid, tinker

Whereas the said culprit David Prichard was at this Great Session and General Gaol Delivery indicted, arraigned, tried and convicted for having on the twenty first day of May last past privately and feloniously stolen taken and carried away twelve knives of the value of six shillings of the property of the said Prosecutor John Rasbrook in the shop of the said Prosecutor being. It is ordered that for the said crime he the said David Prichard be from hence conveyed to the Common Gaol the place from whence he came and from thence to the Common Place of Execution in this County and there be hanged by the neck until he be dead.

The same Court:

Between Humphrey Jones, gentleman Plaintiff
        and   }   In Debt
Owen Roberts and Jane his wife, Defendants

Upon the motion of Mr Wyatt it is ordered that the Defendants in this action do withdraw their Plea filed therein and that Judgement do thereupon go against them on the usual Terms.

The same Court:

Between Thomas Holland, merchant, Plaintiff
        and   }   In Debt
Ellis Evans, shopkeeper, Defendant

Upon the Motion of Mr Att^y General upon reading the Petition Schedule and Notice of said Defendant a Prisoner for Debt in the Common Gaol of this County at the Suit of the said Plaintiff charged in Execution on a *Capias ad Satisfactendum* as well for a Debt of Twenty Pounds One Shilling and ninepence as also Nine Pounds and Sixpence Costs of Suit, Upon the said Defendant now taking in Court the Oath appointed for that purpose by the tatute of the Thirty Second Year of the late King George the Second made for the Relief of Debtors with respect to the Imprisonment of their Persons Upon the said Defendant's Assigning all his Real and Personal Estate in manner and for the purpose by the said Statute directed. It is ordered that the said Defendant be charged from the present Confinement upon his complying with the other and further requisitions of the said Statute and paying the incidental Fees.

NLW, WALES 14/15 Rule Book

North Wales Circuit

Merioneth Great Session held at Bala Tuesday 12th April 48 George III [1808]. The Court continued on Friday after.

Between Our Sovereign Lord the King on the Prosecution
of Joseph Kaye, esquire
        and   }   For Felony
William Foulkes, labourer

Whereas the said William Foulkes was at this Great Session and General Gaol Delivery indicted, arraigned and Tried for feloniously knowingly and wittingly and without lawful excuse having in his possession and custody at the parish of Llandrillo in the said County on the twenty seventh day of August last past divers forged and counterfeited bank notes he the said William Foulkes then and there well knowing the same notes to be forged and counterfeited against the form of the Statute in such case made and provided and was upon his Trial convicted of the said crime. It is therefore ordered by this Court that he the said William Foulkes for the said crime of which he hath been so convicted as aforesaid as soon as conveniently may be shall be sent and Transported to such of his Majesty's Colonies or Plantations abroad or beyond the seas as his said Majesty shall hereafter be pleased to order or direct for the term of Fourteen Years. And it is also ordered and directed that Richard Watkin Price esquire, Francis Parry, Rice Anwyl, John Lloyd and Richard Hughes, clerks, five of his Majesty's Justices of the Peace of and for the said County of Merioneth or any two or more of them shall have full power and authority to contract with any person for the performance of the Transportation of him the said William Foulkes as aforesaid and shall take a bond in the Penal Sum of Two Hundred Pounds in the name of the Clerk of the Peace for the said County of Merioneth from such person or persons with whom the said Richard Watkin Price, Francis Parry, Rice Anwyl, John Lloyd and Richard Hughes or any two or more of them shall so contract as aforesaid for the performance of the Transportation of him the said William Foulkes with such condition as is directed by an Act of Parliament passed in the Fourth Year of the Reign of his late Majesty King George the First Intitled 'An Act for the further preventing Robbery, Burglary and other Felonies and for the more effectual Transportation of Felons &c.' And it is further ordered that the Keeper of the Gaol of the said County of Merioneth do deliver the Body of him the said William Foulkes to such person or persons or to his or their Assigns with whom the aforesaid Richard Watkin Price, Francis Parry, Rice Anwyl, John Lloyd and Richard Hughes or any two of them shall so contract as aforesaid. And lastly It is ordered that such Contract so to be made and such Security so to be taken as aforesaid shall be Certified by them the said Richard Watkin Price, Francis Parry, Rice Anwyl, John Lloyd and Richard Hughes or any two or more of them to the next or any other subsequent Great Session and Gaol Delivery to be taken and kept in and for the said County of Merioneth there to be filed and kept amongst the Records of the said Court.

NLW, WALES 4/281/1, Gaol File
Mary Roberts charged with stealing a cloak

North Wales Circuit, County of Caernarfon, Spring Session 1820

The Information and Complaint of Ellin Jones the wife of John Trevor of Brynllys in the parish of Llandegai in the said County, quarryman taken upon oath before me, The Revd. John Hamer, clerk one of his Majesty's Justices of the Peace in and for the said County, the nineteenth day of February in the first year of the Reign of His Majesty KING GEORGE the fourth. Who saith that on the night of Tuesday the fifteenth day of February instant she was at the house of Richard Jones shopkeeper and baker (who is married to her sister) situate at Bangor in the said County and that at the time she went to the said house she had on her a china coloured cloth cloak the property of her said husband. That she took the cloak off and laid it on the stair case in the sd. Richard Jones' house and then went up stairs where she remained about an hour and a half. That during this time some person unknown to her feloniously stole and carried away the said cloak. That she has probable cause to suspect and doth suspect that one Mary Roberts did steal the said cloak and that the same is now concealed in the dwelling house of Lewis Jones, yeoman and John Owen, joiner both of Bangor aforesaid in the said County.

The mark of
X
Ellin Jones

The Examination of Ellin Jones the wife John Trevor of Brynllys in the parish of Llandegai in the said County, quarryman taken upon oath before me John Hamer, clerk, one of his Majesty's Justices of the Peace in and for the said County, the nineteenth day of February in the first year of the Reign of His Majesty KING GEORGE the fourth. Who saith that on the night of Tuesday the fifteenth day of February instant she was at her sister's at the house of Richard Jones in the town of Bangor in the said County having on her at the time she entered the house a blue cloak the property of her said husband. She afterwards took off the cloak and having folded it up she put it on the bannister of the stair case. She afterwards went up stairs to her sister where she remained about an hour and a half when she came down stairs and found her cloak was missing. She immediately enquired of a little girl who was the only person she found below, whether she had seen any thing of the cloak when she replied she had not, but that several persons had passed by the corner of the stair case along the passage to the bake house (which her sister keeps). She never saw her cloak afterwards until she saw it delivered up by Mary Roberts of Bangor at the house of one Lewis Jones, yeoman into the possession of the constable which cloak is now produced and identified to be the cloak which she wore and which she proves to be her husband's property.

The mark of
X
Ellin Jones

John Trevor of Brynllys in the parish of Llandegai in the said County of Caernarfon, quarryman acknowledges himself to be indebted to our Sovereign Lord the King in the sum of twenty pounds upon condition that he the said John Trevor do personally appear at the next General Sessions of the peace to be held for the said County of Caernarfon at the Sessions House, then and there to prefer a Bill of Indictment, and to prosecute the Law with effect, and to give evidence in his Majesty's behalf against Mary Roberts for feloniously taking and stealing one blue coloured cloth cloak the property of the said John Trevor wherewith she stands charged before me James Greenfield esquire one of his Majesty's Justices of the Peace for the said County of Caernarfon. And if the Bill be found a true Bill, and returned so by the Grand Jury, that the said John Trevor do appear in Court and prosecute and give evidence upon that Indictment and do not depart the Court without leave, then this Recognizance to be void or else to remain in full force.

[signed] Jas. Greenfield

The Examination of John Jonathan of Bangor, constable taken on oath before me The Revd. John Hamer, clerk, one of his Majesty's Justices of the Peace in and for the said County this 19th day of February 1820. Who saith that in obedience to a Magistrate's Warrant directed to him he went to the house of Lewis Jones and John Owen yeoman at Bangor this day in search of a cloak the property of John Trevor yeoman which was lately stolen from the dwelling house of Richard Jones of Bangor aforesaid baker and shopkeeper and which said cloak was suspected to be concealed in the dwelling house of the said Lewis Jones and John Owen. That when this Examinant went in to the dwelling house of the said Lewis Jones and John Owen he was accompanied by Ellin the wife of the said John Trevor. That on going in they saw one Mary Roberts spinster to whom this Examinant asked if Lewis Jones was within for that he had a warrant to search the house for John Trevor's cloak which had been stolen from the dwelling house of the said Richard Jones. Mary Roberts upon this became much frightened and a complete tremer seized her and then she said 'John here it is', meaning the cloak and she immediately took it out of a dresser cupboard and gave to this Examinant. Constable then asked Ellin the wife of John Trevor if she could certify the cloak to be her husband's, upon which she immediately said it was his. This Examinant then took Mary Roberts before the Magistrate. This Examinant did not hear Mary Roberts nor did she in his presence at the house say any thing about her intention to return the cloak and this Examinant did not threaten nor offer her any reward if she confessed to stealing the cloak.

[signed] John Jonathan

The Voluntary Confession of Mary Roberts of the parish of Bangor in the said County, spinster taken before me, James Greenfield esquire one of his Majesty's Justices of the Peace in and for the said County the nineteenth day of February in the first year of the Reign of His Majesty KING GEORGE the fourth. Who saith that on the night of Tuesday the fifteenth instant she went into the house of Richard Jones shopkeeper and baker aforesaid and saw a cloak hanging on a nail in the passage and took the loan of it and carried the same away into the house of Lewis Jones of Bangor aforesaid with whom she lived as a servant and put it up in a cupboard in the said dwelling house. That she neither shewed the said cloak or mentioned a word about the same to any body but that she had an intention of taking the same back again.

her
Mary X Roberts
mark

North Wales Circuit, County of Caernarfon. Confession of Mary Roberts, 19 February 1820 (NLW, WALES 4/281/1)

PRO, HO 27/19, Criminal Register

Caernarfon, Spring Great Session 1820

Mary Roberts   Larceny   6 Months Imprisonment

NLW, WALES 28/36, Black Book

Brecon Circuit

Radnorshire
The docket of the Gaol of the Great Sessions held at Presteigne in and for the said County
on Monday the sixth day of April in the year of our Lord 1829.

John Morris, Esquire, Sheriff

Page of Brecon Circuit Black Book, 1829 (NLW, WALES 28/36)

Po se NOT GUILTY by the Jury
Thomas Thomas of Dissirth, labourer otherwise Thomas Pritchard Thomas. For an assault upon one William Phillips. Bail given to appear next Sessions.

Evan Powell of Rhayader, butcher. For an assault upon one David Edwards.

Po se GUILTY by the Jury
John Pugh of Rhulen, labourer. Felony in stealing a goose the property of one John Rice.

NOT APPREHENDED
Jeremiah Beavan of Rhulen, labourer and John Pugh of the same, labourer. Felony and stealing divers pieces of oak and other wood.

Breconshire
The docket of the Gaol of the Great Sessions held at Brecon in and for the said County on Saturday the eleventh day of April in the year of our Lord 1829.

John Parry Wilkins, Esquire, Sheriff

Po se GUILTY by the Jury
John Davies of Llanfrynach, labourer. Felony in stealing one Gelding the property of one Thos. Price.

Po se GUILTY by the Jury
Charles Jones of Talgarth, labourer. Burglary.

GUILTY on the foregoing Indictment
John Davies of Llanfrynach, labourer. Felony in stealing one stone colt the property of one Evan Jones.

NLW, WALES 4/635/4, Gaol File
Hannah Price charged with stealing money, two handkerchiefs, etc.

Brecon Circuit, County of Glamorgan, Autumn Session 1818

Hannah Price, aged 26, committed 27th April 1818 by Thomas Charles, esq., charged on the oath of David Evans of the Town of Cardiff, victualler, Margaret Evans wife of the said David Evans and Mary Holland wife of Jeffreyson Holland, blacksmith, with feloniously stealing, taking and carrying away two pocket handkerchiefs, of the value of one shilling, one leather pocket book of the value of sixpence and one promissory note of the Cardiff Bank for the payment of one guinea, the goods and chattels of the said David Evans and also one gown of the value of ten shillings the goods and chattels of the said Jeffreyson Holland.

The information and complaint of David Evans of the Town of Cardiff in the County of Glamorgan, victualler taken the twenty eighth day of April in the year of our Lord one thousand eight hundred and eighteen. Who on his oath saith that he keeps a Public House in the Town of Cardiff called the Cardiff Boat. That on Thursday the twenty first day of April instant Hannah Price came to examinant's house and inquired if she could have lodgings for a night or two which examinant agreed to let her have. On Friday the twenty fourth instant she inquired of examinant if he knew Mrs Price of Pontypandy. Examinant replied he did not know her but believed there was a person of that name in Cardiff. Hannah Price then said she was her Aunt and that she would go to see her. On the same evening she quitted Examinant's house for an hour or two and then returned. Hannah

Price informed Examinant her Aunt was angry she had not made herself sooner known to her and that she was going to spend the following day with her. On Sunday night the twenty sixth instant Hannah Price went to bed between nine and ten o'clock. Examinant and his wife remained in the kitchen till about twelve o'clock when they went to bed. Examinant's wife having first taken the candle out of Hannah Price's room. About six o'clock on the following morning, Monday, Examinant got up and when Examinant came down stairs he found the street door open. Examinant had bolted the street door when he went to bed. After washing himself Examinant went to a parlour in the house to fetch some money, consisting of County Bank Notes, silver and copper diposited on Saturday in a cupboard in that room. When Examinant placed the money there he locked the cupboard. On putting the key to the key hole however on the Monday morning Examinant found the lock had been forcibly removed from its place and the cupboard was open. Examinant then searched for the money, the silver and copper remained but the notes were gone. Examinant then went to the room occupied by Hannah Price when he found she had quitted it in consequence of which he immediately went in pursuit of her and at last found her about twelve o'clock in a house in the Town of Newport in the County of Monmouth. Examinant asked her when she came there. Hannah Price replied that she had walked there that morning. Examinant said she had treated him very ill for the civility that had been shewn her in Examinant's house. Hannah Price replied she could not help it. Examinant said she could have helped it and ought to have known what she was about. Examinant then asked her where was the money she stole from his house. She replied 'It is here on this table and the book' (meaning a leather pocket book of Examinant's). Examinant desired her to give them to him which she did. The articles given to Examinant by Hannah Price were a leather pocket book, six promissory notes for the sum of one guinea each, four promissory notes for the sum of one pound each, one check for the sum of ten shillings and silver to the value of sixteen shillings. Examinant inquired for the rest (having placed in the cupboard promissory notes to the amount of twenty one pounds and seven shillings). Hannah Price replied she had purchased some clothes with them and had paid some debts she owed at Newport. Examinant then asked her for a red cotton handkerchief she had taken. Hannah Price said 'here it is' and gave it Examinant as well as two other cotton handkerchiefs and a gown which she had on her. The clothes she stated she had purchased were also given to Examinant. She said she did not know the amount of money she had taken. Examinant told her she must come with him to a Justice. She asked if Examinant could not let her go free. He replied no she must go to the Justice. Examinant took her to a Magistrate at Newport and at his desire brought her to Cardiff. Examinant says he is certain the pocket book, two cotton handkerchiefs and one of the promissory notes are his. The latter has *21. 7. 0* on it in Examinant's hand writing being the amount of the notes placed by him in the cupboard. The pocket book is worth six pence and the handkerchiefs six pence each.

[signed] David Evans

The examination of Margaret Evans wife of David Evans of the Town of Cardiff in the County of Glamorgan, victualler taken the twenty eighth day of April in the year of our Lord one thousand eight hundred and eighteen. Who on her oath saith that Hannah Price came to lodge at her husband's house on Tuesday the twenty first day of April. On Sunday night the twenty sixth instant Hannah Price retired to bed about nine o'clock. Previous to Examinants going to bed she took the candle from Hannah Price's room who was then in bed. Two cotton handkerchiefs now produced by Llewellyn David are the property of her husband David Evans who keeps the Cardiff Boat at Cardiff aforesaid. The handkerchiefs are worth six pence a piece.

The mark of
X
Margaret Evans

The examination of Mary Holland the wife of Jeffreyson Holland of Cardiff in the County of Glamorgan, blacksmith, taken the twenty eighth day of April in the year of our Lord one thousand eight hundred and eighteen. Who on her oath saith that a cotton gown now produced by Llewellyn David is the property of her husband Jeffreyson Holland and was sent by Examinant to Hannah Price to be altered. The gown is worth ten shillings.

The mark of
X
Mary Holland

GUILTY of stealing to the value of 25s.

PRO, HO 27/15, Criminal Register

Glamorgan, Autumn Great Session 1818

Hannah Price   Larceny   2 Years Imprisonment

NLW, WALES 4/396/4, Gaol File
Edward Williams charged with arson

Brecon Circuit, County of Brecon, Autumn Session 1821

Edward Williams aged 37 of the parish of St Davids in the County of Brecon carpenter, committed 12th June 1821 by the Rev. Charles Griffiths, bailiff and William Williams, Esq., Alderman of the Borough of Brecon, charged on the oaths of John James and others with having on the thirtieth day of November 1817, wilfully, maliciously and unlawfully set fire to four houses situate and being in Llanvaes Ward in the Borough aforesaid in the possession of the aforesaid Edward Williams, Ann Jones, Howell Jones and Morgan Charles with intent thereby to injure or defraud the said John James, (the owner thereof) then being one of his Majesty's subjects, against the form of the Statute in that case made and provided.

The examination on oath of John James of Baileyglaes in the Borough of Brecon. Who saith that on a Sunday morning in the latter end of the year 1817, four houses, his, deponents property, situate near Hoolhurst in Llanvaes Ward were burnt down. That when deponent went there, there was a great crowd, and among them Edward Williams of Llanvaes Ward aforesaid, carpenter (the prisoner). That the said houses were in the occupation of Ann Jones and Margaret Jones and another person, and that this examinant hath just cause to suspect and doth suspect that the prisoner did wilfully and maliciously set fire to and burn the said dwelling houses.

Sworn 12th June 1821   [signed] John James

The examination on oath of Ann Jones of Llanvaes Ward in the said Borough, widow. Who saith that on a Sunday morning in the beginning of the winter about three years ago the house in the occupation of this deponent, and three houses beside, the property of John James, were burnt down, of which the house in the occupation of the prisoner was one, and was first burned. That on the Saturday night preceding the prisoner (Edward Williams) came home drunk, accompanied as she believes, by his brother David. That the brother desired prisoner to go to bed and the prisoner called to his wife to go to bed, but she answered nothing and went out shutting the door after her. That the prisoner damned his wife for going out and she afterwards heard some person in prisoner's house breaking the furniture and hearing the fire burning fiercely she was much frightened. And at the same time she heard the prisoner say, 'There's a bonfire for the boy to warm himself, what will the butcher do now for his rent'. Witness got up and ran to the street in the front of the houses and saw the fire coming out of the chimney of the prisoner's house. Witness called John Jones the constable and the neighbours who came to the house when the neighbours had put out the fire. This was about midnight. Afterwards they went to bed. As also the prisoner and his children according to the best of her knowledge. That the witness was not able to sleep afterwards that night and about the dawn of day she saw the fire breaking into her room in the thatch and was falling down into her room. Witness then called her daughter and they immediately left the house crying 'hubbub'. That the prisoner had carried the furniture out of his house. That she heard the prisoner say to witness and her daughter 'Damn you, don't make so much noise.'

Sworn 12th June 1821   The mark of
                                                                            X
                                                                        Ann Jones

The examination on oath of Margaret Jones of Llanvaes Ward in the said Borough singlewoman (daughter of the witness Ann Jones). Who saith that on a Sunday morning in the beginning of the winter between three and four years ago the house in which she and her mother lived, and the prisoner (Edward Williams) and two other houses were burned down (the property of John James in Llanvaes Ward). That the night preceding prisoner and his brother David came to prisoner's house, the brother brought him into the house drunk (as she thinks) his brother told him not to abuse his wife but to go to bed. Prisoner then went to bed and called on his wife three times to which she answered nothing but went out. Prisoner then leaped out of bed and said 'God damn you you have locked me in the house, have you?' He then got out of the house and then came in again when witness heard him breaking the furniture and a small table saying, 'What will the Lady do for a little table to drink tea upon again.' She heard a fire and smelt meat cooking on it and heard him say, 'There's a bonfire for the boy to roast his meat, there's the gravy of the Lady's meat going, what will the old butcher do for his rent, he shan't have the furniture of Neddy Rheollaes to make it.' That she could not sleep for the noise of the fire and the smoke so filled their room that they both got up and she and her mother got into the brook before the houses and the first light she saw was a burning chair thrown out before the door. That she saw the fire in prisoner's house as high as the mantle piece and it was coming out in large flames from the chimney. That a quantity of wood was all on fire in the hearth. Her mother said 'Do you mean to burn the houses?' He answered 'No, no.' Witness and her mother cried out 'Hubbub' and the neighbours came (she and her mother went for a constable for fear of prisoner doing further mischief). That the neighbours had put out the fire before their return with John Jones the Constable who came to the light of the houses and said that as he saw no light of fire he would turn back. He went away saying what do you want to disturb people in the night it is fitter to take you up for disturbing people. She being afraid, desired Jones to go with her and her mother to their house, to which he answered that he would not lose his own life to save the life of another. Witness and her mother went by their own house to Howell Jones's who told them that they might venture to go to bed as the fire was all out and the prisoner and his children were in bed. They did so. Her mother and she in separate beds. Witness in the bed next the partition dividing the prisoner's house from theirs. She heard the prisoner say to his son 'did your father beat you to night?' He answered 'Yes.' Prisoner said 'why did he beat you?' Prisoner then said 'let us go to sleep, the boy has done a bad job to night.' Witness then went to sleep. About dawn of day she was awoke by her mother who caught her by the hair of her head and said 'O God the house is on fire over our heads.' Witness says the fire was beginning to fall on the foot of her bed as she was getting up. She ran down with the child in her arms in her shift into the court before the houses, preceded by her mother. The first sight she saw was the prisoner who had carried every thing out of his house into the court. There was nothing downstairs in his house by the best of her knowledge. The bed and the bedclothes were all taken out. The roof of prisoner's house was completely burned. She called 'Hubbub' to the neighbours to come down to save their houses and their furniture as all the houses were on fire. Prisoner said while witness was crying 'Hubbub' 'God damn you, what do you make of all this noise for?' he had a spade in his hand and he said 'if you make any more noise I will knock your brains out with the spade' and he also raised a stone to strike witness, but his brother (David) prevented him crying 'what are you going to do?' and took him away.

Sworn 12th June 1821
The mark of
X
Margaret Jones

The examination on oath of Howell Jones of the said Borough, labourer. Who on oath saith that about midnight on Saturday the thirtieth of November last he heard Ann Jones cry out 'Hubbub'. Witness and his family arose and saw fire in Edward Williams's chimney, he fetched a pole and a ladder to Edward Williams's yard went to the top of the chimney and put the fire out completely to the best of his knowledge and belief. Edward Williams scolded him much for taking the pole to burn it. Witness after putting out the fire attempted to go into the house to see the state of it when Edward Williams warned him not to enter into it.

Sworn 8th December 1817
The mark of
X
Howell Jones

The examination on oath of Martha Powell of the said Borough, widow. Who saith that about midnight on last Saturday week she heard Ann Jones cry 'Hubbub'. That she awoke Howell Jones her son in law who went into Edward Williams's garden (whose chimney was on fire) and went with a ladder and pole to the top to put it out. Witness saw a chair on fire outside the door. She went into Edward Williams's house, the hearth was full of fire as high as the mantle piece. Some sort of wood all on fire. The two children of Edward Williams came down stairs crying. Witness took hold of an old spade and began to draw the fire from the bottom of the hearth on the floor. A neighbour (David) came in and then witness loosed the spade. Edward then came and turned them all out of the house.

Sworn 8th December 1817
The mark of
X
Martha Powell

The examination of Mary Williams the wife of David Williams of the said borough shoemaker who saith that she saw the fire at Edward Williams's house on last Saturday fortnight. Heard Edward Williams say it was no fool of a joke to clean the chimney.

Sworn 8th December 1817
The mark of
X
Mary Williams

The examination on oath of William Bowen of Llanvaes in the said Borough labourer. Who saith that about midnight on Saturday week he was in bed heard the cry of 'Hubbub'. Arose and went out. Saw Howell Jones on the top of Edward Williams's chimney putting out a fire with a fishing pole. Went with a stick and scraped the inside of the chimney. Edward Williams went out to stop Howell to burn the pole and scolded him for burning it.

Sworn 8th December 1817 [signed] William Bowen

PRO, HO 27/21, Criminal Register

Brecon, Autumn Great Session 1821

Edward Williams   Arson   DEATH

NLW, WALES 4/538/1, Gaol File
John Hobby charged with stealing wheat, etc.

Brecon Circuit, County of Radnor, Spring Session 1827

John Hobby of the parish of Llanstephan in the County of Radnor, labourer, aged 76 committed February 15th 1827 by Richard Venable, D.D, charged upon the oath of Richard Williams of the parish of Broynllys in the County of Brecon with having in his possession a bag with a quarter of wheat and divers other articles the property of the said Richard Williams, stolen from the house of the said Richard Williams.

The examination of Richard Williams of Broynllys in the County of Brecon taken this 15th day of February 1827 upon oath who saith: That upon Saturday morning the 9th instant he discovered that his house at Trevithel in Broynllys had been opened by some person throwing the bolt back and upon search he found that the drawer of his dresser in which he kept his money had been broken open by the bolt of the lock being forced back and that two 5 guinea notes of the Brecon Old Bank, a pair of cloth gaiters, his property had been taken out and stolen and that having a suspicion that Thomas Hobby had been concerned in the robbery he upon the 10th instant obtained a warrant to search the houses of John Hobby of Boughwood, father of the said Thomas Hobby and that in company with John Prosser the Constable of Glasbury he went to Boughwood and saw John Hobby dig in his garden and afterwards stamp with his foot on the space where he had dug. That he then went into John Hobby's house and searched his house and found behind the bed in a hole in the wall a pettycoat of flannel which he believed to be his wife's, and upon opening the pettycoat he found a pocket book containing several articles and also a purse, a case of cards, a cap and frils. He proceeded with his search and in a cupboard found some foreign copper coin and on a shelf he found a little lock, and then went into the garden towards the spot where he had seen John Hobby dig and met the Constable carrying a bag containing about 1 peck of wheat. He then took John Hobby into custody. That upon looking at the bag now produced he deposes that the same is his property but cannot say when lost. That upon examining the wheat contained in the bag he verily believes the same is his and was part of what he mowed on the Monday before.

[signed] Richard Williams

John Prosser of Maesgwnyn, yeoman being examined upon oath the 15th day of February 1827 saith: That upon Saturday the 10th of February instant he accompanied Richard Williams of Trevithel to the house of John Hobby. That upon searching the house this examinant proceeded into the garden and in a potatoe hole he found a bag containing a little bag and the little bag containing a peck of wheat which wheat and the bag he delivered to Peter Chaloner from whom he this day received it which he now produces. That the bundle he received from Mr Williams he also delivered to Peter Chaloner from whom he this day received it and now produces it.

[signed] John Prosser

The Deposition of Robert Symes of Broynllys aforesaid, gentleman taken upon oath the 15th day of February 1827, who saith: That learning of the property found at John Hobby's he went to Dr Venables and there saw a purple moroco pocket book containing a pair of steel scissors, one silver gilt bodkin, one steel do, a silk purse with several foreign copper coin and a small ivory stilleto which being now produced to him he deposes to their being the property of his daughter Harriet Symes. He also saw a padlock and being now produced he deposes it to be his property.

[signed] Robt Symes

PRO, HO 27/34, Criminal Register

Radnor, Spring Great Session 1827

John Hobby   Larceny   3 Months Imprisonment

NLW, WALES 4/830/6, Gaol File
David Thomas charged with intent to commit buggery

Carmarthen Circuit, County of Pembroke, Autumn Session 1800

The King on the Prosecution of David Thomas

Town and County of Haverfordwest

The Jurors for our Lord the King upon their oath present that David Thomas (sic) late of the parish of Saint Martin in the said Town and County of Haverfordwest, yeoman, not having the fear of God before his eyes but being moved and seduced by the instigation of the Devil on the twenty first day of June in the forty ninth year of the Reign of our said Lord George the Third, King of the United Kingdom of Great Britain and Ireland with force and arms at the parish aforesaid in the Town and County aforesaid in and upon one David Thomas (sic) in the peace of God and our said Lord the King then and there being did make an assault and him the said David Thomas then and there did beat wound and ill treat so that his life was greatly despaired of and with an intent that most horrid detestable and sodomitical crime (among Christians not to be named) called Buggary with the said David Thomas against the order of nature then and there feloniously, wickedly and devilishly to commit and do to the great displeasure of almighty God to the great damage of the said David Thomas and against the peace of our Sovereign Lord the King His Crown and Dignity. And the Jurors aforesaid upon their Oath aforesaid do further present that the said David Thomas on the said twenty first day of June in the year aforesaid with force of arms at the parish of Saint Martins aforesaid in the Town and County aforesaid and upon the said David Thomas in the peace of God and our Lord the King then and there being did make an assault and him the said David Thomas then and there did beat, wound and ill treat so that his life was greatly despaired of and other wrongs to the said David Thomas then and there did to the great damage of him the said David Thomas and against the peace of our said Lord the King his Crown and Dignity.

[signed] John Touchet

[The sentence of the court has not been found.]

NLW, WALES 4/911/3, Gaol File
James Phillipps charged with stealing four silver watches

Carmarthen Circuit, County of Cardigan, Spring Session 1812

The voluntary Examination of James Phillipps[4] (a prisoner charged upon suspicion of having feloniously taken, stolen and carried away four silver watches sometime in September last the property of Thomas Lewis, John Hughes, Richard Roberts and another person from an outhouse being a room over a coach house at the Devil's Bridge in the County of Cardigan) taken before me John George Philipps, Esq., one of his Majesty's Justices of the Peace in and for the said County of the Borough, the seventh day of December one thousand eight hundred and eleven.

That some time in the later end of the month of September last the prisoner was at the dwelling house of John Thomas an Innkeeper called the Devil's Bridge situate in the County of Cardigan, that he was taken ill there and went up some stairs of an outhouse intending to go to a hay loft but found that there were some beds in the room he got into where servants slept being over head a Coach House at the Devil's Bridge aforesaid. That he saw in that room a small wooden box with the lid or cover of it open that the Prisoner put his hand into the said box and took out of it a small parcel covered with brown paper that he put the said parcel into his pocket and that after he had gone about seven miles from the said Devil's Bridge he opened the said parcel and found it to contain the said four silver watches which were afterwards found upon him when taken up at Carmarthen in the said County of the Borough.

[signed] James Phillipps

PRO, HO 27/8, Criminal Register

Cardigan, Spring Great Session 1812

James Phillipps   Larceny   7 Years Transportation

NLW, WALES 4/765/4
John Abraham charged with fraud

Carmarthen Circuit, County of Carmarthen, Autumn Session 1827

The Jurors for our Lord the King upon their Oaths present that John Abraham late of the parish of Conwyl Elvet in the said county of Carmarthen, labourer on the thirtieth day of August in the eighth year of the Reign of our Sovereign Lord George the Fourth, by the Grace of God of the United Kingdom of Great Britain and Ireland King Defender of the Faith with force and arms at the parish aforesaid in the County aforesaid wilfully knowingly and designedly did falsely pretend to one Elizabeth Evan the wife of one David Evan that he had brought certain sugar and soap in certain boxes which he the said John Abraham had brought to the dwelling house of the said David Evan and that he the said John Abraham would leave the said boxes and the said sugar and soap at the said dwelling house by which said false pretences the said John Abraham did then and there to wit on the same day and year aforesaid at the parish aforesaid in the County aforesaid wilfully knowingly and designedly obtain from the said Elizabeth Evan a large sum of money to wit the sum of twenty six shillings of the proper monies of the said David Evan with intent then and there to cheat and defraud him the said David Evan of the same. Whereas in truth and in fact he the said John Abraham had not brought any sugar and soap in the said boxes. And whereas in truth and in fact the said John Abraham did not leave any sugar or soap at the said dwelling house to the great damage and deception of the said Elizabeth Evan. To the evil example of all others in the like case offending against the Peace of our said Lord the King his Crown and Dignity and also against the

---

[4] Indictment says he was a yeoman of Llanfihangely.

form of the statute in such case made and provided. And the Jurors aforesaid do further present that the said John Abraham on the same day and year aforesaid at the parish aforesaid in the County aforesaid with force and arms did wilfully knowingly designedly and falsely pretend to the said David Evan that he the said John Abraham had brought certain other sugar and soap in certain other boxes which he the said John Abraham had brought to the dwelling house of the said David Evan and that he the said John Abraham would have the said last mentioned boxes and the said last mentioned sugar and soap at the said dwelling house. By which said last mentioned false pretences the said John Abraham did then and there to wit on the same day and year aforesaid at the parish aforesaid in the county aforesaid wilfully knowingly and designedly obtain from the said David Evan a certain other large sum of money to wit the sum of twenty six shillings of the proper monies of the said David Evan with intent then and there to cheat and defraud him the said David Evan of the same. Whereas in truth and in fact he the said John Abraham had not brought certain sugar and soap in the said last mentioned boxes. And whereas in truth and in fact the said John Abraham did not leave any sugar or soap at the said dwelling house to the great damage and deception of the said David Evan to the evil example of all others in the like case offending against the peace of our said Lord the King his Crown and Dignity and also against the form of the Statute in such case made and provided.

PRO, HO 27/33, Criminal Register

Carmarthen, Summer [Autumn] Great Session 1827

John Abraham   Fraud   7 Years Transportation

NLW, WALES 4/765/4, Gaol File
David Griffiths and Joseph Leonard charged with assault on a constable

Carmarthen Circuit, County of Carmarthen, Autumn Session 1827

The Jurors for our Lord the King upon their Oath present that David Griffiths late of the parish of Saint Peter in the County of the Borough of Carmarthen labourer and Joseph Leonard late of the same place labourer on the seventh day of August in the Eighth year of the Reign of our Sovereign Lord George the Fourth by the Grace of God of the United Kingdom of Great Britain and Ireland King Defender of the Faith with force and arms at the parish aforesaid in the County of the Borough aforesaid in and upon one Thomas Thomas then being one of the Constables of the said parish in the said County of the Borough in the peace of God and our said Lord the King and in the due execution of his said office of Constable then and there also being did make an assault and him the said Thomas Thomas in the due execution of his said office then and there being then and there did beat wound and ill treat so that his life was greatly despaired of and other wrongs to the said Thomas Thomas then and there did to the great damage of the said Thomas Thomas and against the Peace of our said Lord the King his Crown and Dignity.

   And the Jurors aforesaid on their Oaths aforesaid do further present that the said David Griffiths and Joseph Leonard on the same day and year aforesaid at the parish aforesaid in the County of the Borough aforesaid with force and arms in and upon the said Thomas Thomas in the peace of God and our said Lord the King then and there being did make another assault on him the said Thomas Thomas then and there did beat and bruise and ill treat and other wrongs to the said Thomas Thomas then and there did to the great damage of the said Thomas Thomas and against the peace of our Lord the King his Crown and Dignity.

[The sentence of the court has not been found.]

NLW, WALES 4/260/6, Gaol File
Mr William John Lewis charged with shooting with intent

North Wales Circuit, County of Anglesey, Autumn Session 1827

The examination of John Bulkeley of the parish of Llangoed in the said County, mariner taken in writing and upon oath this twenty seventh day of April in the year of our Lord 1827. Who saith that he was in a boat with Thomas Williams on the ninth April instant near the quarries in Llangoed when Mr Lewis came down. That Mr Lewis was up on the cliff at a distance from the boat which Examinant cannot tell but he can point out the places where both were. That Mr Lewis was walking to the westward, stopped, and faced towards the boat and him and immediately fired a pistol having his arm in the direction of Examinant but whether his hand was higher or lower than his head Examinant cannot say. Examinant did not observe any whistling noise after the pistol was fired. Examinant has been on board of a man of war upwards six years. Examinant thought that Mr Lewis was aiming at the boat when he fired the pistol.

The mark of
X
John Bulkeley

On the day and year within written the said John Bulkeley further saith that he hath since his last examination measured the space from point to point where Mr Lewis stood when the pistol was fired to the place where according to the opinion of Examinant the edge of the waters then was, and that the same measures two hundred and thirty six feet or thereabouts and that according to the estimation of this Examinant the distance from the water's edge to the boat was about forty five feet.

The mark of
X
John Bulkeley

The examination of Thomas Williams of Gale House in the parish of Llangoed in the County of Anglesey, quarryman taken in writing and upon oath this 24 day of April in the year of our Lord 1827. Who saith that on the 9th day of April instant he went by order of his employer to Mr Lewis's Quarry to fetch some poles which his master said were his property. Mr Clough was the Examinant's Master and claimed the poles as his property. Examinant went to Mr Lewis's Quarries to fetch the poles on the 9th April instant and saw Mr Lewis's labourers at the Quarry. Mr Lewis was not then present. Examinant loosened the poles from the ropes and iron to which they were fastened and ordered his own men to take them to a boat which Examinant had in attendance and they were taken down to the boat accordingly. Examinant then towed them away accordingly and in the boat were the Examinant John Radley, John Buckley, John Parry, Edward Thomas, Richard Thomas, Hugh Owen and Hugh Rowlands. When the boat and the poles were afloat Mr Lewis came down and said something which Examinant did not hear by reason of the noise in the boat. Mr Lewis standing on the grass upon his own land then fired a pistol at this Examinant and his party in the boat who were then distant between 200 and 300 yards. Mr Lewis fired the pistol towards the boat and this Examinant is of opinion that he fired the pistol at Examinant. Examinant immediately upon the pistol being fired heard something like shot slugs or a ball whistling by the Examinant. Examinant did not turn towards the direction where they would have fallen and did not see any thing fall into the sea. Examinant took the poles from Mr Lewis's Quarry against the will of Mr Lewis's quarrymen and had with him at the time a greater force of men than were at Mr Lewis's Quarry. When the shot was fired Radley was taking Examinant's directions and his right hand in the stern of the boat. Mr Lewis was not at the Quarry when Examinant went there first and the Quarry is a quarter to half a mile from Mr Lewis's house and only one shot was fired.

[signed] Thomas Williams

The examination of Francis Broadhead of Beaumaris in the said County, gunsmith taken on oath this 27th day of April 1827 who saith that he fired the pistol now produced loaded with powder and ball against the Castle wall in Beaumaris at the distance of eighty yards and upwards and that the pieces of lead now produced appear to be the balls so fired.

[signed] Francis Broadhead

The examination of Richard Thomas of the parish of Llangoed in the said County taken upon oath this 27th day of April 1827 who saith that he was in a boat with Thomas Williams near Llangoed Quarry on the ninth of April instant when Mr Lewis fired a pistol and thinks he aimed at the boat. Cannot say how far Mr Lewis was from the boat when the pistol was fired.

The mark of the said
X
Richard Thomas

The Examination of Hugh Owen of the parish of Llangoed in the said County of Anglesey taken upon Oath the 27th April 1827. Who saith that he was in the boat with Thomas Williams on the 9th April instant when Mr Lewis fired a pistol and thinks he aimed at the boat. Mr Lewis extended his arm towards the boat and fired immediately. Examinant did not hear a whistling noise after the pistol was fired.

[signed] Hugh Owen

The examination of John Parry of the parish of Penmon in the County of Anglesey, quarry man taken in writing and upon oath this 27th day of April in the year of our Lord one thousand eight hundred and twenty seven. Who saith that on the ninth of April instant Examinant was in a boat with Thomas Williams near the Quarries in Llangoed when Mr Lewis fired a pistol. Examinant thinks that Mr Lewis aimed at the boat. His arm was extended in the direction of the boat. Examinant cannot say how far Mr Lewis was from the boat when he fired the pistol but can point out the places where both were within a few yards. Examinant did not hear a whistling noise after the pistol was fired. Examinant wished to get a shore for fear another shot be fired at the boat.

The mark of the said
X
John Parry

The examination of Edward Thomas of the parish of Llangoed taken upon oath this 27th day of April 1827 who saith that he was in the boat with Thomas Williams on the ninth of April instant when Mr Lewis fired a pistol, and examinant thinks he aimed at the boat his arm being extended in that direction. Examinant did not hear a whistling noise after the pistol was fired. Examinant was put in fear by the manner in which the pistol was fired.

The mark of the said
X
Edward Thomas

The examination of John Hughes of the parish of Llangoed in the said County taken on oath this 27th day of April 1827. Who saith that he was from 40 to 60 roods[5] from Mr Lewis when he fired a pistol on the ninth of April instant. Did not think Mr Lewis aimed at the boat. Thinks Mr Lewis' elbow was on his side when he fired. Is sure Mr Lewis' arm was not extended towards the boat when he fired.

The mark of the said
X
John Hughes

The examination of Richard Roberts of the parish of Penmon in the said County taken upon oath this 27th day of April 1827. Who saith that he was near the above named John Hughes when Mr Lewis fired the pistol on the ninth of April 1827. That Examinant thought Mr Lewis' arm was bent and the pistol elevated when fired.

The mark of the said
X
Richard Roberts

The examination of Hugh Hughes of the parish of Llangoed in the County of Anglesey, labourer taken in writing and upon oath this 24th day of April in the year of our Lord 1827. Who on his oath saith that he is a quarryman in Mr Lewis's Quarry and was present when Thomas Williams came there on the 9th April instant. Thomas Williams came to Mr Lewis's Quarry with 5 or 6 men in the boat and 10 or 12 men on the land and claimed the poles with great violence and afterwards took the same away with force and violence before Mr Lewis came, and took them away down to the boat and towed them away. Mr Lewis came down soon after Thomas Williams took the poles and boat away and stood on the cliff distant from the boat from 140 to 160 yards and the boat afterwards turned towards the shore to fetch a man and when it was distant from the shore from 80 to 100 yards this Examinant being then not more than 3 yards distant from Mr Lewis, Mr Lewis fired the pistol now produced straight up in the air and afterwards Mr Lewis showed the side of the pistol to the people in the boat. There was only one shot fired and Examinant was there the whole time.

[signed] Hugh Hughes

The examination of Robert Roberts of the parish of Llangoed in the County of Anglesey, labourer taken in writing and upon oath this 24 day of April in the year of our Lord 1827. Who saith upon his oath that he is the petty Constable of the parish of Llangoed and was employed by Mr Lewis to protect his property in the Quarry in Llangoed on the 9th April instant. That when Mr Lewis was from 100 to 120 yards from the boat and walking along the Cliff Examinant was from 8 to 12 yards from Mr Lewis. Mr Lewis fired the pistol in the air without stopping and there was no other pistol fired and Examinant was present the whole time. Examinant had been previously taken on as a workman at the Quarry by Mr Lewis.

The mark of the said
X
Robert Roberts

PRO, HO 27/33, Criminal Register

Anglesey, Summer [Autumn] Great Session 1827

| William John Lewis | Shooting with Intent | Not Guilty |

---

[5] A *rood* is a unit of area. The use here is presumably an error for *rod*, which is 16½ feet.

Ang. RO, W/QA/G/993
David Evans charged with stealing two sovereigns

Great Sessions, Court Orders, County of Anglesey

At the Great Session, and General Gaol Delivery of our Sovereign Lord the King, of the County aforesaid holden and made at Beaumaris in and for the said County before Jonathan Raine, Esquire, Justice of our said Lord the King, of his Great Session for the said County, and William Kenrick, Esquire one other Justice, and so forth. Also of the said Lord the King, to deliver the Gaol of the said County of the Prisoners, in the same being. AND also Justices assigned to keep the Peace in the County aforesaid, and to hear and determine divers felonies, trespasses and other misdemeanors in the same County committed on Monday to wit, the sixth day of April in the Tenth year of the Reign of our Sovereign Lord George the Fourth [1829], now KING of the United Kingdom of Great Britain and Ireland, and so forth.

[signed] Wynn Belasyse

Wednesday first Court:

Between our Sovereign Lord the King on the Prosecution of
Thomas Hughes, corndealer
and
David Evans, labourer

For Larceny

Whereas the said David Evans was at this present Great Session and General Gaol Delivery indicted arraigned and tried for feloniously stealing taking and carrying away on the first day of March last past at the parish of Llangeinwen in the said County two pieces called Sovereigns of the current gold of this realm of the value of two pounds of the goods and chattels of the said Prosecutor Thomas Hughes then and there being found upon his trial Guilty thereof. It is therefore ordered by this Court that he the said David Evans for the said Crime be Imprisoned in the Common Gaol of this County for the term of two years and kept to hard labour and at the end thereof that he be discharged and set at liberty.

By the Court

PETTY SESSIONS AND JUVENILE OFFENDERS

Petty Sessions Courts arose out of the increasing amount of work which justices found too much to be dealt with at the County Quarter Sessions Courts. When a magistrate was appointed for a county he was given wide powers, he could, for example, issue summons, grant warrants, take recognizances. Much of his work was carried out at his home and he had no regular clerk. From the beginning of the eighteenth century magistrates began to organize regular divisional meetings called Petty Sessions. These developed at the initiative of the individual magistrates, sometimes being ordered by the Courts of Quarter Sessions. Petty Sessions dealt with all manner of minor cases including the trials of many juvenile offenders.

Under an Act of 1848, 11–12 Vict. c. 43, the Clerks of Justices were ordered to send details of fines imposed at Petty Sessions to the Clerk of the Peace. Under the Criminal Justice Administration Act, 1855, 18–19 Vict. c. 126, and confirmed by the Summary Jurisdiction Act, 1879, 42–43 Vict. c. 49, Justices of Petty Sessions were required to send depositions and case papers to the Clerks of the Peace at subsequent County Quarter Sessions. From 1848 records of Petty Sessions should therefore be found among the County Quarter Sessions papers.

The Juvenile Offenders Act, 1847, 10–11 Vict. c. 28, imposed a responsibility on the justices to make returns of convictions to the County Quarter Sessions. County Quarter Sessions records should therefore include records of juvenile offenders sentenced under this act.

Som. RO, Q/Rc
Sarah Ann Franks, aged 8 years, charged with stealing peppermints
Somerset, Petty Sessions at Wellington, 7 May 1857

In the County of Somerset

Register of the COURT OF SUMMARY JURISDICTION sitting

at Wiveliscombe the sixteenth day of January 1883.

SUMMARY JURISDICTION PART I. FORM A.—(79-1-80.)—London : SHAW & SONS, FETTER LANE.

Number.	Name of Informant or Complainant.	Name of Defendant and Age, if under 16.	Nature of Offence or Matter of Complaint.	Minute of Adjudication.	Justices Adjudicating.
1	2	3	4	5	6
1	George Hennifely	Arthur Victor Pearce	Rackway	Dismissed	Arthur Capel, Henry Grieve Mopesey, James Edward Vardly and Thomas Henry Pecketto Winwood Esquire
2	John Ross	Thomas Hartnell	Drunkenly and refusing to Quit Licensed premises	Convicted. Fined 2/ & costs 3/ in default payment 21 days imprisnt. with hard labour	"
3	Eliza Vicars	do	Threat	Dismissed	"
4	John Ross	Henry Loram	Vagramy (Begging)	Convicted. Sentenced to 21 days hard labour	"
5	Emily Loram	Edwin King	Rackway	Order made for pay't of 9/6 per week from birth of child till [...] above Kof 13 years and 10/ for Midwife and £2.6.3 for costs	" "
6	Wiveliscombe Local Board	Abraham Christopher Lukey	Rentpayt of Govt Order Rate (applic anothr prem Nuisn)	Warrant granted	" "
7	do	Abraham Christopher Lukey and Eldon Nicolay Lukey	do	do	" "
8	John Cridland	Charles Musgrave	Assault	Dismissed	" " "
9	Joe Cridland	Francis Ward	do	Dismissed	" "
10	John Ross	Thomas Cowling	Drunk in licensed on Licensed premises	Convicted. Fined 2/ & costs 6/ in default of payt. 21 days hard labour	"

Arthur Capel.

Be it remembered, that on the seventh day of May in the Year of our Lord one thousand eight hundred and fifty seven at Wellington in the County of Somerset Sarah Ann Franks is convicted before us, the undersigned two of Her Majesty's Justices of the Peace for the said County for that the said Sarah Ann Franks on the twenty eighth day of April in the year aforesaid at the parish of Sampford Arundel in the said County then and there being under the age of sixteen years, to wit, of the age of eight years a tin box containing a quantity of peppermints of the goods and chattels of one John Morgan then and there being found, then and there feloniously did steal take and carry away against the peace of our said Lady the Queen, her Crown and Dignity; And we the said Justices aforesaid, adjudge the said Sarah Ann Franks for her said Offence to be imprisoned in the said County Gaol Taunton in the County aforesaid, for the space of three calendar months.

Given under our Hands and Seals on the day and year and at the place first above mentioned.

[signed] H^y George Moysey
[signed] Saml Dobree

Petty Sessions, Wellington

Som. RO, Q/Rc
Henry Orchard, aged 10 years, charged with stealing a fowl

Somerset, Petty Sessions at Dulverton, 21 November 1866

The Examination of Elizabeth Ann Griffiths of the parish of Kingsbrompton in the County of Somerset, singlewoman and George Broadribb of the parish of Kings-brompton, Police Constable. Taken on Oath this twenty first day of November in the year of our Lord one thousand eight hundred and sixty six at Dulverton, in the County aforesaid, before the undersigned two of Her Majesty's Justices of the Peace, for the said County, in the presence and hearing of Henry Orchard who is charged this day before us for that he the said Henry Orchard a Gipsy Boy aged ten years on the seventeenth day of November one thousand eight hundred and sixty six at Kingsbrompton in the said County of Somerset did feloniously steal one fowl of the value of one shilling and nine pence the property of John Squires of the parish of Kingsbrompton aforesaid.

This Deponent Elizabeth Ann Griffiths on her Oath saith as follows: I am a single woman residing with my Uncle John Squires in the parish of Kingsbrompton. On Saturday the 17th instant the prisoner accompanied by a man came to the house selling tins and clothes pegs. I did not purchase any and they left, the man going through the court first followed by the prisoner. I saw the prisoner take up a fowl the property of my Uncle John Squires. I saw him take up the fowl and turn the head under the wing. I then spoke to him and told him to put down the fowl and he put it down.

[signed] Elizabeth Ann Griffiths

George Broadribb being sworn saith: I am a Police Constable residing in the parish of Kingsbrompton. From information I received on Saturday last I went in pursuit of the prisoner and apprehended him in a field near Hillbridge and charged him with stealing a fowl. He said he knew nothing about it.

[signed] George Broadribb

George Davey, aged ten years; imprisoned for one month with hard labour in Wandsworth Gaol for stealing two tame rabbits (PRO, PCOM 2/290)

The above depositions of Elizabeth Ann Griffiths
and George Broadribb were taken on oath this 21st }
      W.H. Bernard
day of November 1866 at Dulverton in the County }
      Jno. Arthur Locke
of Somerset before us

Be it remembered, that on the twenty first day of November in the Year of our Lord one
thousand eight hundred and sixty six at Dulverton in the County of Somerset, Henry
Orchard a Gipsy Boy aged ten years is convicted before us John Arthur Locke and
William Hawker Bernard two of Her Majesty's Justices of the Peace for the said County
for that he the said Henry Orchard on the seventeenth day of November in the Year
aforesaid, at the parish of Kingsbrompton in the said County then and there being under
the age of sixteen years, to wit, of the age of ten years, did feloniously steal one fowl of
the value of one shilling and nine pence of the Monies, Goods and Chattels of one John
Squire then and there being found, then and there feloniously did steal against the Peace
of our said Lady the Queen, her Crown and Dignity; And we the said John Arthur Locke
and William Hawker Bernard the Justices aforesaid, adjudge the said Henry Orchard for
the said Offence to be imprisoned in the Common Gaol at Taunton and there be kept to
hard labour for the space of fourteen days.

    Given under our Hands and Seals on the day and year and at the place first above
mentioned.

Jno. Arthur Locke
W.H. Bernard

Wilts. RO, A1/260
Robert Parker aged 12 years charged with stealing a toy trumpet

Wiltshire, Petty Sessions at Warminster, 27 January 1872

The examination of Josiah Cross of the parish of Warminster in the said County of Wilts,
Post Office Assistant and Edmund Curtis Manley of the parish of Warminster in the said
County Post Master taken on Oath the 27th day of January 1872 at the Town Hall,
Warminster in the said County aforesaid, before the undersigned, two of Her Majesty's
Justices of the Peace for the said County in the presence and hearing of Robert Parker
who is charged this day before us for that the said Robert Parker being under the age of
sixteen years to wit of the age of twelve years on the twenty third day of January in the
year of our Lord one thousand eight hundred and seventy two at the parish of Warminster
in the said County did feloniously steal take and carry away one toy trumpet of the value
of six pence of the goods and chattels of Edmund Curtis Manley contrary to the Statute in
such case made and provided.

    This deponent the said Josiah Cross on his oath saith as follows: I am an assistant in the
Post Office at Warminster kept by Mr Manley. On Tuesday last the 23rd January 1872 I
was in the Post Office when I saw the prisoner come into the shop he asked me the price
of some masks which were in the window. I saw the prisoner take something from where
he was standing; I could not say what. I called Mr Manley who came into the shop and I
saw the prisoner produce from his pocket the toy trumpet now produced.

[signed] J.D. Cross

Edmund Curtis Manley. I am Post Master at Warminster and keep a shop. On the 23rd
January last from what the last witness told me I charged the prisoner with stealing
something from the shop. He afterwards produced the toy trumpet now produced from
his jacket pocket. He strongly denied stealing anything for some time. The trumpet is
worth 6d.

[signed] Ed. Curtis Manley

The foregoing depositions of Josiah Cross and Edmund Curtis Manley were severally taken on oath at the Town Hall Warminster in the County of Wilts on the twenty seventh day of January one thousand eight hundred and seventy two.

Before us: Nath. Barton

John Smith

And we the said Justices now propose to dispose of the said charge summarily under the provisions of the Juvenile Offenders Act and after the examination of all the witnesses for the prosecution have been completed and before calling upon the said Robert Parker to shew cause why he should not be convicted I the said Nathaniel Barton one of the said Justices did state to the said Robert Parker the charge against him and did say to him 'We shall have to hear what you wish to say in answer to the charge against you, but if you wish the charge to be tried by a Jury you must object now to our deciding upon it at once.' Upon which the said Robert Parker says that he wishes the charge tried and determined by us.

Upon which we having reduced the charge into writing and read the same over to the said Robert Parker we did then ask him whether he was guilty or not guilty of the said charge. Whereupon the said Robert Parker says he is guilty of the said charge.

Sentenced to be once privately whipped out of Gaol by Sergt. Pearce that the number of strokes be twelve and that the whipping be inflicted with a birch rod.

Som. RO, Q/Rc
Henry Badman, aged 13 years, charged with stealing firewood

Somerset, Petty Sessions at Wells, 31 July 1875

City and Borough of Wells in the County of Somerset

Birch used to punish young offenders (Northampton Police Museum)

The Examination of Thomas Salisbury and James Knight taken on Oath this thirty first day of July in the year of our Lord 1875 at the City and Borough of Wells aforesaid, in the County aforesaid, before the undersigned two of Her Majesty's Justices of the Peace, in and for the said City and Borough, in the presence and hearing of Henry Badman for that he the said Henry Badman on the 30th day of July 1875 at the Liberty of Saint Andrew in the said City and Borough, did steal take and carry away a quantity of firewood and slabs of the value of two shillings the property of Messrs Hillier Capes and Hillier.

And this deponent Thomas Salisbury on his oath saith as follows: I am manager of Messrs Hillier Capes and Hillier's brush factory. On Friday the 30th July 1875 the prisoner came to the factory yard to take away sawdust which was given to Mr John Jerrard the Surveyor to the Town Council and which he removed in hand trucks. I met the prisoner between 6 & 7 in the evening in the Market Place wheeling the truck with which he had been previously removing the sawdust. I found the truck was full of firewood and small slabs. The slabs now produced by Police Constable Knight were a portion of those in the truck and I have no doubt they are the property of Messrs Hillier Capes and Hillier.

When I saw the prisoner he was coming from the direction of our factory. The value of the wood is two shillings. I have no doubt the whole of the wood is the property of Messrs Hillier Capes and Hillier. I cautioned the prisoner not to remove any of the firewood in the sawdust but to throw it on a heap of firewood in the factory yard.

When I asked the prisoner what he was going to do with the wood he dropped the trucks and ran away.

[signed] Thos. Salisbury

And this deponent James Knight who on his oath saith: I am a Police Constable of the said City and Borough. On Friday the 30th July 1875 between 6 and 7 in the evening Mr Thomas Salisbury came to the Station & gave information that the prisoner had been stealing wood from Messrs Hillier Capes and Hillier. I went in search of the prisoner; I found him at his father's house upstairs and asked him if he had been at work at the Brush factory. He said he had. I asked him, 'What about that wood you had in the trucks?' He began crying and said 'It was some I picked up round where I was taking up the sawdust. I did not think it any harm.' I took him to the station and charged him with stealing same from Messrs Hillier Capes and Hillier. He said a boy named Stephens helped put some of the wood into the trucks. I took charge of the wood and that now produced is a portion I took from the truck.

[signed] James Knight

Be it remembered, that on the thirty first day of July in the year of our Lord one thousand eight hundred and seventy five at the City and Borough of Wells in the County of Somerset Henry Badman is convicted before us, Albion Andrews and John Gabriel French, Esquires, two of Her Majesty's Justices of the Peace for the said Borough for that he the said Henry Badman on the thirtieth day of July in the year aforesaid, at the Liberty of Saint Andrew in the said City and Borough then and there being under the age of sixteen years, to wit, of the age of thirteen years, did steal take and carry away a quantity of firewood and slabs of the value of two shillings of the monies, goods and chattels of Messrs Hillier Capes and Hillier then and there being found, then and there feloniously did steal take and carry away against the Peace of our said Lady the Queen, her Crown and Dignity; And we the said Justices aforesaid, adjudge the said Henry Badman for his said Offence to be imprisoned in the Gaol at Shepton Mallett in the County of Somerset for the space of fourteen days and that in pursuance of the Reformatory Schools Act 1866

Form X.

123/3 *(5*

Wandsworth Gaol,

County of *Surrey*

25 Jany 18*73*.

PARTICULARS of a Person convicted of a Crime specified in the 20th Section of the Prevention of Crimes Act, 1871.

Name .... *James Leadbetter 4415*

and

Aliases...

Description when liberated.	Age (on discharge)	*11*	Photograph of Prisoner.
	Height..................................	*4 ft 1 ¾*	
	Hair......................................	*Brown*	
	Eyes.....................................	*Brown*	
	Complexion.............................	*Fresh*	
	Where born.............................	*Middlesex*	
	Married or single	*Single*	
	Trade or occupation	*None*	
	Any other distinguishing mark	*Scar on*	

forehead and on right shoulder

[17198.]   E. & S.—20,000.—9/72.

James Leadbeater, aged eleven years, imprisoned for four days with hard labour for stealing celery. He had been previously imprisoned for seven days for stealing a quantity of pears (PRO, PCOM 2/290) we also sentence the said Henry Badman to be sent to the Reformatory School at [blank][1] to be there detained for the period of five years commencing from and after the expiration of the before mentioned period.

Given under our Hands and Seals on the Day and Year and at the place first above mentioned.

H.W. Livett
J.G. French

City and Borough of Wells

Wilts. RO, A1/260
Ellen Berrett aged 13 years charged with stealing a pig's foot

Wiltshire, Petty Sessions at Trowbridge, 26 January 1874

The examination of William Albert Webb of the parish of Trowbridge in the County of Wilts, rating house keeper and James Drake of the same place, police constable, taken on oath this 26 day of January 1874 at Trowbridge in the County aforesaid, before the undersigned, two of Her Majesty's Justices of the Peace for the said County, in the presence and hearing of Ellen Berrett who is charged this day before us for that she the said Ellen Berrett on Saturday the 25th day of January 1874 at the parish of Trowbridge in the County of Wilts did feloniously steal a pig's foot of the value of two pence the goods and chattels of William Albert Webb against the peace of our Lady the Queen.

This deponent William Albert Webb on his oath saith as follows: I keep a Rating House in Trowbridge. The prisoner Ellen Berrett has been in my service as general servant for about three months. On Tuesday morning the 25th January about 10 the prisoner was dressed to go home to Steeple Ashton. She had in her hand the paper bag I now produce. I had previously seen her go with the bag up to the Bakehouse. I asked her what she had in the bag. She said her bonnet and pads. I told her to put them on the table. She did so and with the bonnet and pads she took out the pig's foot I now produce. She said she got it up in the bakehouse. She said she'd never do it any more if I'd let her go home. I refused and sent for a policeman and gave her into Custody. The value of the pig's foot is two pence. It is my property. On two or three occasions I have found some of my property in her possession and I have forgiven her. The prisoner is 13 years of age.

[signed] William Albert Webb

James Drake on his oath saith, I am a Police Constable at Trowbridge. Yesterday morning about 11.30 I took the prisoner into custody. I charged her with stealing the pig's foot. She admitted having done so and said she took it from the Bakehouse.

[signed] James Drake

We adjudge the said Ellen Berrett for her offence to be imprisoned in the Common Gaol at Devizes in the said County and there kept to hard labour for the space of fourteen days. And we also direct . . . at the expiration of her sentence to be sent to some Reformatory School duly certified under the said Acts as we may hereafter, and before the expiration of the said term of Imprisonment . . . and there detained for the period of two years, commencing from the ninth day of February next.

---

[1] The Shepton Mallet Prison Register (Som. RO, Q/AGs 14/4) shows that Henry Badman was removed to Kingswood Reformatory on 14 August 1875.

Wilts. RO, A1/260
Harry Shepperd, Frederick Denning, Jesse White, James Chapman and Albert Bennett, aged from 11 years to 13 years, charged with stealing apples.

Wiltshire, Petty Sessions at Trowbridge, 4 September 1872.

The examination of James Huntley of the parish of Trowbridge in the county of Wiltshire, farmer, taken on oath this fourth day of September in the year of Our Lord one thousand eight hundred and seventy two at Trowbridge in the county aforesaid, before the undersigned, two of Her Majesty's Justices of the Peace for the said county, in the presence and hearing of Harry Shepperd, Frederick Denning, Jesse White, James Chapman and Albert Bennett who are charged this day before us for that they on the eighteenth day of August 1872 at the parish of Trowbridge in the said county then and there being under the age of sixteen years to wit of the ages of 11, 12 and 13 years certain apples of the value of sixpence of the goods and chattels of one James Huntley then and there being found there feloniously did steal take and carry away against the peace of our said Lady the Queen her crown and dignity.

This deponent James Huntley on his oath saith as follows: I am a farmer living at Galley Farm in Trowbridge. I saw the prisoners running away from my orchard on Sunday the 18th August last. I ran after them and caught them. They had some apples in their possession which I have no doubt they took from my orchard. The prisoners now plead guilty to the charge.

[signed] James Huntley

Sworn before us at Trowbridge the day and year first aforesaid.

T. Clark
Wm. Fowler

For their offence to be imprisoned in the Common Gaol at Devizes in the said County for the space of one day and to be once privately whipped in addition to such imprisonment, 12 strokes each with a birch rod.

Ang. RO, WU/1/126
Elizabeth Davies, charged with stealing three pieces of flannel

Anglesey Petty Sessions, 17 September 1874

To the Constable of Beaumaris and the keeper of the Common Gaol at Beaumaris in the said County of Anglesey.

Whereas Elizabeth Davies was this day charged before me the undersigned one of Her Majesty's Justices of the Peace in and for the said County on the oath of Joseph Parry of the parish of Llandysilio in the County of Anglesey and others, for that she the said Elizabeth Davies did, at the parish of Llangeinwen in the County of Anglesey did feloniously steal take and carry away three pieces of flannel of the goods and chattels of Butler against the Peace of our Lady the Queen her Crown and Dignity. And it appears to me to be necessary to remand the said.

These are therefore to command you the said Constable of Beaumaris to take the said Elizabeth Davies, and her safely to convey to the Common Gaol at Beaumaris aforesaid, and there to deliver her to the Keeper thereof, together with this Precept; and I do hereby command you the said keeper of the said Common Gaol to receive the said Elizabeth

William Watts, aged 11 years; stealing 20 ploughshares, one month hard labour, Northampton, 1871 (Northampton Police Museum)

Mary Ann Barber, aged 12 years; stealing a hat and a pair of boots, one month hard labour, Huntingdon, and then 5 years in the reformatory school at Doncaster (Cambridgeshire Constabulary Archives)

Hannah Martin, aged 12 years; stealing 7 shillings and sixpence, 3 months' imprisonment, Northampton, 1870 (Northampton Police Museum)

Charles Henry Edward Twist, aged 13 years; simple larceny, 21 days hard labour, Birmingham, 1871 (PRO, PCOM 2/430)

Davies into your custody in the said Common Gaol and there safely keep her until Thursday next the 17th instant at eleven when I hereby command you to have her at the office of Mr John Rue Roberts at Beaumaris before me or before some other Justice of the Peace for the said County as may there be there to answer further to the said charge and to be further dealt with according to Law unless you shall be otherwise ordered in the meantime.

Given under my Hand and Seal this eleventh day of September in the Year of our Lord one thousand eight hundred and seventy four at Fryaris in the County aforesaid.

Vivian

I hereby Certify that I consent to the within named Elizabeth Davies being Bailed by Recognizance her self in ten pounds and two surities in five pounds each.

Wilts. RO, A1/260
Edmund Dowding charged with stealing dried cut grass

Wiltshire, Petty Sessions at Hindon, 5 September 1855

The examination of William Flower taken on Oath this 5 day of September 1855 before the undersigned, two of Her Majesty's Justices of the Peace for the said County of Wiltshire in the presence and hearing of Edmund Dowding charged this day before us for that he the said Edmund Dowding on the 11th day of August 1855, at the parish of Chilmark in the County of Wilts certain dried grass cut and severed from the land the property of William Flower feloniously did steal, take and carry away, the said grass being of the value of two pence only.

The said William Flower upon his oath saith: I am a Farmer living at Chilmark in this County. I had some sainfoin[2] grass cut in a field of mine adjoining the Turnpike Road on the 11th day of August last. In the evening about half past 6 I saw several waggons passing the Turnpike Road and the person now present, Edmund Dowding near one of the waggons. He went over into my field and took a quantity of the grass (which I now produce) and brought it back to one of the waggons and tied it up at the tail of the waggon where there was a horse tied. The grass he took was worth about two pence.

[signed] William Flower

The before named Edmund Dowding pleaded GUILTY to the foregoing charge.

Sworn before us   Robt. Graves
                                                                          W. Chafyn Grove

We adjudge the said Edmund Dowding for his said offence to be imprisoned in the House of Correction at Fisherton Anger in the said County and there kept to hard labour for the space of ten days.

---

[2] Sainfoin was a clover-like plant grown for cattle feed.

C H A P T E R   10

ASSIZE VOUCHERS, SHERIFFS' CRAVINGS AND PAYMENTS, TREASURY WARRANTS AND MONEY BOOKS

Assize Vouchers contain lists of persons convicted at Assizes. Sheriffs' Cravings are requests by County Sheriffs for the payment by the Treasury for the costs incurred in organizing and conducting court proceedings and in maintaining prisoners in gaol up to the time of their trial. They also include the costs for conveying convicts to prison hulks and for executions. It should also be noted that these 'cravings' applied only to Assizes and not to Quarter Sessions cases. All expenses accrued prior to and during Quarter Sessions trials were paid for out of county funds. Assize Vouchers and Sheriffs' Cravings are found together in PRO, Class E 370 (1714 to 1832). Sheriffs' Cravings are also found in PRO, Class T 64 (1745 to 1785).

Sheriffs' Payments are records of payments actually made to County Sheriffs including justices' expenses, gaol fees, conveying convicts to prison hulks, etc. Sheriffs' Payments are found in PRO, Class T 90 (1733 to 1822) and continue in PRO, Class T 207 (1823 to 1959).

Treasury Warrants contain 'Conviction Money' and are warrants for the payments made by the Treasury to County Sheriffs for expenses incurred in apprehending and convicting criminals. These are written into books and are indexed. References to criminals are indexed under 'Sheriffs' Conviction Money'. Treasury Warrants are found in PRO, Class T 53 (1721 to 1805) and continue in PRO, Class T 54 (1806 to 1827).

It has already been stated that Assize Courts were the courts where serious crimes were tried and minor crimes such as larceny and other petty offences should have been tried at Quarter Sessions. Many historians have been perplexed by the number of petty crimes tried at Assizes and have assumed that it was simply the next most convenient court at which a prisoner could attend. It is, however, reasonable to assume that county justices arranged for as many prisoners as possible to come before the Assize Courts thus alleviating the county of this expense. The following document confirms the official use of these expenses for Assize prisoners only and sheds light on the misuse of these funds and the corrupt behaviour of some gaolers.

PRO, T 207/1
Sheriffs' Payments

Exchequer Seal Office
25th Feb. 1834

State of the Exchequer Allowance for the diet of Assize Convicts with other matters connected therewith.

When a Sheriffs' Bill of Cravings which usually includes the Gaoler's Bill for the diet of a certain class of prisoners, has been duly examined the sum granted under the allocation of the Chancellor of the Exchequer is received by the Under Sheriff, who transmits the allowance for the discharge to the gaoler who in his turn forwards the amount to the Treasurer of the County by whom it had been advanced the preceding year.

It should be kept in mind that this Exchequer Allowance is restricted to Assize Convicts. Criminals before trial and convicts sentenced at Sessions are entirely maintained by the County.

Several Counties defray the whole of the diet charge for all the prisoners and several bear part of the burden for all. Thus the Exchequer payments vary considerably; some Counties as Oxfordshire receiving therefrom at the rate of 1s 2d only, and others, as Staffordshire claiming per week for every Assize convict at the rate of 2s 6d, a liberal but well considered allowance, it having ever been the policy of Government not to aggravate the severity of a Judicial sentence but rather to enable the convict to undergo his merited punishment.

In the following Table is exhibited the Exchequer allowance for Assize convicts in the County of Staffordshire for twelve years ending at Michaelmas 1832:

1821	£77– 2–10	1827	£ 71–12–2
1822	£26–17– 6	1828	£104– 4–4
1823	£25	1829	£ 64– 1–5
1824	£26–12– 1	1830	£ 67–10–1
1825	£15–15	1831	£ 86– 3–7
1826	£65– 4– 7	1832	£ 64–17–6

In few Counties is the Exchequer allowance under the above head of charge so high, and in none is the fluctuation so striking; a circumstance not to be overlooked. For where many prisoners are to be maintained in two or three rooms or wards under one roof their increasing number will but little affect the consumption of certain items involved in their maintenance. Coal is one of these items; and unless the gaoler be permitted in addition to his salary to his share in the diet allowance, the charge for firing ought often to be in the inverse ratio of the number of prisoners committed to his care. In some gaols which are seldom full 3d per week amounting to one tenth of his diet allowance has been deducted for each convict to meet the expense of coal, and the deduction may have been fair enough. But where a prison is large and crowded the charge for firing ought to bear a much lower proportion to the diet allowance. Here it may be asked what becomes of the saving and what ought to become of it in the case supposed. If it would not be wise to permit the gaoler to derive profit direct or indirect from an increase of his prisoners, it would be still more objectionable to grant to the prisoners themselves an increase of comfort to be measured by their increasing numbers. Better on such occasions to apply the presumed saving to some of the incidental expenses of the gaol. The application would still be in accordance with the allowance, and swerve but slightly from the strict line if its appropriate.

Without meaning to cast the smallest imputation on any particular officer the diet charge has in many counties become of late years so large that the subject should undergo a searching examination. It has sometimes happened that a resolution agreed to at a meeting of magistrates in behalf of criminals has been rendered worse than unavailing by the covetousness of the gaoler who has been enriched by the bounty intended for the convicts. When such practices occur the best way is to call on the gaoler for a statement resolving into its component parts the expense of maintaining each prisoner; and should the statement be unsatisfactory a few of the better class of prisoners should be questioned on the points in dispute. The following account was formerly furnished by a gaoler of Lincoln:

3 loaves for each prisoner	0– 1– 0
1 lb of beef without bone	4
Straw and coal about	6
Guarding	8
	2– 6

In this most unfair account the wretched convict received under the head of allowance emphatically termed Sick Allowance, little more than half the sum to which he was strictly entitled, while the gaoler blind in his greediness forgot that in the very word gaoler the duty of 'guarding' his prisoners was implied and in the performance of his duty he ought to have been satisfied with his salary without encroaching on an allowance deemed no more than sufficient to support the convict in health and strength to undergo his sentence.

Upon the whole there is reason to suspect that where some Counties bear the charge in whole or in part of maintaining the Assize Convicts, the gaoler nevertheless receives from the Exchequer the full diet allowance which however ought to be reduced according to the sum paid by the County or withdrawn altogether where the County pays at the rate of 2s 6d per week for each prisoner. For the humanity dictates that the allowance should be sufficient to uphold the strength of the Convicts, prudence suggests that it ought not to be raised so high as to act like a stimulant to crime or to swell the remuneration of the gaoler already in receipt of an adequate salary.

The full diet allowance in question is now granted by the Exchequer to some Counties which thirty or forty years ago received no relief of the kind at the public cost. Warwick for instance, where the gaoler's bill is heaviest of all, drew no diet allowance from the Exchequer previous to the year 1792.

R.B. Adderley

Appendix 4.1 shows that some early Assize records are not extant for some 'circuits'. In particular those studying criminal matters for the counties of Derbyshire, Leicestershire, Lincolnshire, Northamptonshire, Nottinghamshire, Rutland and Warwickshire (Midland Circuit) should note that the earliest surviving records date from 1818. Although the actual proceedings are not reported, Sheriffs' Cravings and the other material outlined in this chapter go some way towards replacing these lost documents.

The following are examples:

PRO, E 370/42, Part 2
Sheriffs' Cravings

A Bill of Cravings from the Gaoler of Nottingham for one year.
Commencing Michaelmas 1787. Richard Stenton Esq. High Sheriff.

Paid for the dieting and maintenance of Paul Hufton convicted of a burglary from the 1st day of Jany 1788 to the 12th day of Feby. the time of his removal for transportation, being six weeks and two days @ 2/6 per week	0	15	0
Lent Assizes held March 13th 1788			
Cloth and cushions matting, workman's labour, candles and halbertmen attending both the Assizes	5	5	0
Joseph Heathcoat convicted of an assault with intent to carnally know and abuse an infant child, fined one shilling and ordered to be whipt at Mansfield and imprisoned in Gaol twelve calendar months. Whipping and guard	0	10	0
Removing the said Joseph Heathcoat to Mansfield to be whipt, being 14 miles @ 1s 0d per mile	0	14	0
Paid for the dieting and maintenance of George Tilley, convicted of Grand Larceny, from the time of his conviction to his escape Oct. 26th 1788 being 32 weeks two days @ 2/6 per week	4	0	0
Paid for the dieting and maintenance of John Launder convicted of Grand Larceny from the time of his conviction to the time of his removal for transportation Nov. 22nd 1788 being 36 weeks 1 day @ 2/6 per week	4	10	0
Paid for the dieting and maintenance of Saml. Cullinbine alias Cullubine, convicted of Grand Larceny, from the time of his conviction to the time of his removal for transportation Novr. 22nd 1788, being 36 weeks 1 day @ 2/6 per week	4	10	0
Lamas Assizes held July 10th 1788			
Paid for dieting and maintenance of Richd Haynes convicted of stealing lead fixed to a building against the Statute from the time of his conviction to the time of his removal for transportation Nov. 22nd 1788 being 19 weeks and 1 day @ 2/6 per week	2	7	6

Paid for the dieting and maintenance of Joseph Markham convicted of Grand Larceny from the time of his conviction to the 1st day of Jany 1789 being 25 weeks @ 2/6 per week		
	3	2	6

Paid for the dieting and maintenance of Joseph Markham convicted of Grand Larceny from the time of his conviction to the 1st day of Jany 1789 being 25 weeks @ 2/6 per week   3   2   6

Paid for the dieting and maintenance of Thomas Johnson convicted of Grand Larceny from the time of his conviction to the 1st day of Jany 1789 being 25 weeks @ 2/6 per week   3   2   6

Paid for the dieting and maintenance of Sarah Cumberland convicted of Grand Larceny from the time of her conviction to the first day of Jany 1789 being 25 weeks @ 2/6 per week   3   2   6

         £31   19   0

PRO, E 370/49
Assize Voucher

Oxfordshire   At the Assizes and General Delivery of the Gaol of our Lord the King holden at Oxford in and for the County of Oxford on Wednesday the seventh day of March in the second year of the reign of our Sovereign Lord George the Fourth [1821] by the Grace of God of the United Kingdom of Great Britain and Ireland, King Defender of the Faith before Sir James Allan Park knight one of the Justices of our said Lord the King of his Court of Common Pleas at Westminster, Sir William Garrow knight, one of the Barons of our said Lord the King of his Court of Exchequer at Westminster and others their Fellows Justices of our said Lord the King assigned to deliver his gaol of the said County of Oxford of the prisoners therein being.

Charles Peers Esquire, Sheriff

GUILTY to be hanged

reprieved	William Bolter	
	and	for burglary
reprieved	John Lee	
reprieved	William Blea	for the like
reprieved	Thomas Woodbridge	
	and	for the like
reprieved	William Dearlove	
reprieved	Richard Grisold	
	and	for sheepstealing
reprieved	John Gregory	
reprieved	Samuel North	
	and	for the like
reprieved	Thomas Drewitt	
reprieved	Richard Rowles	for horse stealing
	Richard Franklin	for an highway robbery
reprieved	George Godfree	for housebreaking
reprieved	Henry Thomas	for the like
reprieved	Charles Turfrey	for stealing a calf

Guilty of Grand Larceny. To be each kept to hard labour in the House of Correction for six kalendar months and on the Monday next before the end of their imprisonment to be each whipped therein & at the end of the six months to be discharged:

Thomas Lewington
Daniel Stephens

Guilty of Grand Larceny. To be kept to hard labour in the House of Correction for three kalendar months and during next week to be once well whipped therein and at the end of their imprisonment to be discharged:

William Larner
Edward Hinder

Guilty of Grand Larceny. To be kept to hard labour in the House of Correction for three kalendar months and then to be discharged:

Joseph Walker

Guilty of Grand Larceny. To be kept to hard labour in the House of Correction for two kalendar months and then to be discharged:

Richard Pearman

Guilty of feloniously and without lawful agence having in their custody forged notes of the Bank of England knowing the same to be forged. To be each transported to parts beyond the seas for the term of fourteen years:

Samuel Butler
Richard Johnson
Jesse Barnes
Lizabeth Montague
Thomas Smith
William Boseley

Guilty of receiving goods knowing the same to have been feloniously stolen. To be transported to parts beyond the seas for fourteen years:

Charlotte Moss

Guilty of Grand Larceny. To be each transported to parts beyond the seas for seven years:

Maria Pratt
William Carter the younger

Guilty of Grand Larceny. To be kept to hard labour in the House of Correction for two years and within that time to be once whipped therein and at the end of his imprisonment to be discharged:

Thomas Knibbs

Guilty of Grand Larceny. To be each kept to hard labour in the House of Correction for twelve kalendar months and then to be discharged:

Edward Morris
William Spicer

Guilty of Grand Larceny. To be each kept to hard labour in the House of Correction for three kalendar months and on the 17 inst. to be whipped therein & at the end of his imprisonment to be discharged:

Thomas Barnes

Guilty of Grand Larceny. To be imprisoned in the Gaol until Saturday next and then to be discharged:

Israel Robins

Guilty of manslaughter. To be imprisoned in the Gaol for six kalendar months and then to be discharged:

Joseph Rainbow

Guilty of manslaughter. To be imprisoned in the Gaol for fourteen days and then to be discharged:

John Owen

Guilty of poaching in the night time. To be imprisoned in the Gaol for one year and then to enter into a recognizance in £40 for good behaviour for two years more and be further imprisoned until such recognizance be entered into:

Joseph Kaile

Guilty of an assault. To be fined one shilling and then discharged:

Thomas White

Guilty of an assault. To be imprisoned in the Gaol for six kalendar months and to enter into recognizances for himself in £80 and two sureties in £40 a piece to keep the peace for one year and to be further imprisoned until such recognizance be entered into:

Francis Padbury

Guilty of an assault. To be imprisoned in the Gaol for six kalendar months and to enter into his own recognizance in £40 to keep the peace for one year and to be further imprisoned until such recognizance be entered into:

Joseph Couling

Not Guilty nor fled; discharged:

Henry Harvey
Nathaniel Gregory
John Webb
James Trinder
George Rook
Ralph Rook

Discharged by proclamation:

Stephen Munt
John Pead
Thomas Moss

Sarah Hardyman
Thomas Stringer
John Stringer
William Edden
John Hardyman
Elizabeth Trotman

Guilty of an assault, to be imprisoned in the gaol for nine kalendar months and to enter into recognizance himself in £40 and 2 sureties in £20 apiece to keep the peace for one year and to be further imprisoned until such recognizance be entered into:

Ewin Sellwood the younger

Guilty of an assault. To be imprisoned in gaol for three kalendar months and enter into his own recognizance in £40 to keep the peace for one year and to be further imprisoned until such recognizance be entered into:

Henry Jessett

Guilty of an assault. To be imprisoned in the gaol for one kalendar month and then be discharged:

William Piper

Guilty of an assault. To be imprisoned in the gaol for three kalendar months and then to be discharged:

George Truman

To be discharged he having in Court entered into his own recognizance to answer a charge at the next assizes:

Benjamin Evans

To be discharged she having entered into a recognizance in Court with sureties to answer a charge of felony at the next assizes:

Elizabeth Dipper

To remain according to their commitments:

William Denry
Robert Hoare
John Tyrrel
John Hornsby
Thomas Horwood
John Robbins
John Bridgewater
David Wiggins
William Peats

To remain according to their sentences at former assizes and Courts of Quarter Sessions for this County:

Edward Breakspear
William Taylor

Christ^r Lipscomb
James Smith
Thomas Bignall
William Shepperd
James Purbrick
Thomas Betts

Ben. Pugh, Deputy Clerk of the Peace

PRO, E 370/42
Assize Voucher

Leicestershire

At the General Delivery of the Gaol of our Lord the King holden at the Castle of Leicester in and for the County of Leicester on Saturday the twenty eighth day of March in the twenty ninth year of the Reign of our Sovereign Lord George the Third [1789] before The Honourable Sir Alexander Thompson, Knight one of the Barons of our Lord the King of his Court of Exchequer and others his fellows Justices.

To be hanged: William Massey for burglary

Reprieved: John Digby for sheepstealing

William Erpes otherwise George Cox John Dickinson otherwise John Ramsdale	Severally convicted of Grand Larceny are severally ordered to be transported beyond the Seas for the Term of Seven years
John Robins	Convicted of Grand Larceny is fined sixpence and ordered to be imprisoned and kept to hard labour in the House of Correction for one year
William Williamson	Convicted of Grand Larceny is ordered to be privately whipped and imprisoned in Gaol for the space of three calendar months

Not Guilty – delivered:

Mary Bampton
Mary Taylor
Ann Palmer
Thomas Gilbert
Thomas Sherwin
Samuel Glover

PRO, E 370/49, Part 3
Sheriffs' Cravings

County of Stafford
Allowance to Assize Transports of 2s/6d per week from
Michaelmas 1822 to Michaelmas 1823

Name	When Convicted	When Delivered on board the Hulks	No. of Weeks Paid	£ s d
	1822	1823		
Sarah Phillips	Summer Assizes	May 13th	42	5 5 –
Dorothy Phillips	do	do	"	5 5 –
William Broadstock	Lent Assizes	April 30th	7	17 6
James Courtney	do	do	"	17 6
John Barrett	do	do	"	17 6
Samuel Taylor	do	do	"	17 6
Oliver Wilkes	do	June 5th	12	1 10 –
John Williams	do	do	"	1 10 –
James Child	do	do	"	1 10 –
Thomas Mills	do	do	"	1 10 –
Charles Hayward	do	do	"	1 10 –
William Bibb	Summer Assizes	Sept 8th	8	1 – –
William Harrison	do	do	"	1 – –
Henry Page	do	do	"	1 – –
William Poyser	do	do	"	1 – –
Thomas Poyser	do	do	"	1 – –
James Meeson	do	do	"	1 – –

James Horden, Esquire   £27 10 0
Sheriff
                                                        ———————
                                                    Thomas Brutton
                                                  Governor County Gaol

PRO, E 370/49, Part 2
Assize Voucher

Sussex

To the High Sheriff of the County of Sussex his Under Sheriff and also to the Keeper of his Majesty's Gaol for the said County and whom else it may concern.

Let the execution of David Eagles who was at the last Special Session of the Delivery of the Gaol of our Lord the King of the County of Sussex holden at Lewis in and for the said County on Monday the twenty third day of December instant of Feloniously disposing of and putting away a forged Bank Note with Intent to defraud the Governor and Company of the Bank of England be Respited until further Order Dated the thirty first day of December 1822.

                                                        R. Graham

PRO, E 370/49, Part 3
Sheriffs' Cravings

Essex

Thomas Cawkwell keeper of Chelmsford Gaol in account with the Undersheriff during the Sheriffalty of John Joliffe Tufnell, Esq., from the 11th February 1823 to the 4th February 1824 both inclusive.

Money paid to Convicts during the above mentioned period as under named at 2/6d per week.

Deborah Lowden convicted Lent Assize 1822 and remained in Gaol from said 11th February till 19th May 1823 when she was delivered on board the Convict Ship off Woolwich.

14 weeks at 2/6   £1–15–0

Ann Layshaw convicted Summer Assize 1822 and remained in Gaol and delivered as last.

14 weeks at 2/6   £1–15–0

Isaac Pryor	All convicted Special Gaol Delivery in December
Thomas Adams	1822 and remained in Gaol till 19th February
Charles Steward	1823 when they were delivered on board the
John Ballard	*Leviathan* at Portsmouth.
Benjamin Cooper	
Thomas Willsmore	9 prisoners, 1 week and 2 days each at 2/6 £1–8–10½
Robert Gray	
William Pryer	
Abraham Parish	

£4–18–10½

etc., etc. carried forward

Very occasionally a detailed report was made, as is shown by the document overleaf.

PRO, T 53/59
Treasury Money Book

Arthur Dowel U.S. [Under Sheriff] Montgomery
An order for paying for £50 dated 14 March 1789 to Catherine Price for apprehending and convicting John Griffiths, David Morris, Edward Evans, Margaret Webster and Evan Jenks of felony, sheepstealing as by certs. signed 14 August 1797, and 12th, 15th and 17th March 1788.
Evan Foulkes gent, U. Sheriff, Hertfordshire
A like Warrant for £50 signed 1st April 1789.
To Richard Mullins *et al* for do John Ward of Felony and Robbery as by cert. dated 5 March 1789.

B. Hotham

PRO, E 370/42

A List of Felons and other Offenders who have been received into the Gaol at Oakham in the County of Rutland between the fourteenth day of February 1788 and the second day of May 1789

No.	When Committed	Name	Descriptions Stature	Com-plexion	Where Born	Single or Married	Profession	By Whom Committed	Crime	When Tried	By Whom	Original Sentence	Present Sentence	When Carried into Execution
1		James Lewin							Grand Larceny	March 4th 1785			Transported 7 yrs	
2		James Young							Horse Stealing	July 8th 1785		To be hanged	Transported 7 yrs	Delivered on board the *Lion* Hulk at Portsmouth
3		William Sherwin							Assault with intent to rob	July 8th 1785		Judgement respited 10th March 1786	Transported 7 yrs	
4		Robt. Brewett							Grand Larceny	March 10th 1786			Transported 7 yrs	16th June 1788
5		Christopher Palmer							Felony	Sept. 20th 1786	At the Gen. Q. Sessions		Transported 3 yrs	
6		William Walker							Sacrilege	July 4th 1788	Mr Baron Thompson		Discharged by Proclamation	
7		John Burnard							Buggary	July 4th 1788	Mr Baron Thompson		Aquitted	
8		Watts Atkins							Buggary	July 4th 1788	Mr Baron Thompson		Discharged by Proclamation	
9		John Barker							Felony and Petty Larceny	Jan. 15th 1789	At the Gen. Q. Sessions		To be imprisoned one month	
10	Nov. 19th 1788	Wm. Weldon	5ft 3in	Dark	Hambledon	Single	Labourer	The Rev. T. Foster	Murder	March 14th 1789	Mr Baron Thompson	To be hanged & their bodies dissected & anatomized	To be hanged – bodies hung in chains	March 16th 1789
11	Nov. 19th 1788	Rd. Weldon alias Dodson	5ft 3in	Dark	Hambledon	Married	Labourer	The Rev. T. Foster	Murder	March 14th 1789	Mr Baron Thompson			March 17th 1789
12	March 13th 1789 Removed from Town Gaol	- - - -				Married	A Gipsy		Horse Stealing	March 14th 1789	Mr Baron Thompson	To be hanged	To be transported	Remains in prison

A more particular account cannot be returned on account of the murder of the Gaoler by Richard Weldon one of the men above mentioned.

William Belgrave Esq.

Sheriff

Edward Allen U.S. [Under Sheriff] of Co. of Brecon
Do for £50 dated and signed as above.
To Wm. Williams Junr. *et al* for do Philip Bevan, Lewis Lewis, Morgan Morgan, Owen
Williams and John Lewis of sheepstealing as by cert. dated 4 April 1788, Geo. Harding
and A. Moysey, and 14 August 1788, Geo. Harding.

Sir Hedworth Williamson Bt. Sheriff of Co. Durham
Do for £40 dated 9 April 1789 and signed above. To George Greensitt *et al* for do
Elizabeth Jones alias Horner of Felony and Burglary as by cert. dated 17 March 1788.

Loughborough

Richard Link, gent, U.S. [Under Sheriff] Co. Surrey
A like Warrant dated 13 May 1789 and pd. Graham Ed. J. Eliot Mornington.
To Robert Lowe *et al* for apprehending and convicting John Sloan, Wm. Sloan, Geo.
Uwins and Wm. Lee of Felony and Robbery as by cert. signed 26 and 27 March.

B. Hotham

PRO, T 64/262
Sheriffs' Cravings

Somersetshire to wit, John Halliday Esq. Sheriff, for the year ending at Michas 1746

20 0 0	Paid for the Judges lodgings and for necessarys for the Judges at Taunton Assizes.	20 0 0
	Paid the like at Bridgwater.	10 0 0
	Paid for lodgings and other necessarys for the Judges' servants at both Assizes.	10 0
5 0 0	Paid for fitting up the Courts for both Assizes and for the hire of chairs, carpets, cushions and other necessarys.	10 0 0
5 0 0	For making an alphabetical list of the names of all persons in the County (there being more than 40 hundred in it) returned as qualified to serve on Jurys.	7 7 0
	For making a book and entering therein the names of persons summoned and serving on Jurys between Party and Party at both Assizes for making them certificates thereof for which no Fee is to be taken of the Juror, and for providing a balloting box for the Jury Tickets and making the Tickets pursuant to the Act of Parliament.	5 5 0
	Paid Mr Trip at Taunton Assizes for a chamber for the Grand Jury to sit and do business in there being none for that purpose but such as the Sheriff hires.	3 0 0
16 0 0	For carrying six prisoners from Ivelchester to Taunton Assizes 40 miles to and from thence under a strong guard being charged with felony and receiving there from the Bridewells 3d more and expences in keeping them 5 days and carrying them back to Ivelchester.	20 0 0
10 0 0	For keeping John Moor and John Bridge from the 31st March under sentence of Death to the 14th of April under a strong guard when they were Executed.	2 0 0

	For erecting Gallows at Ivelchester for their Execution.	5 0 0
	For guards' expences and Execution.	10 10 0
6 0 0	For carrying three prisoners from Ivelchester to Bridgwater being sixteen miles distant under a strong guard charged with felony and receiving there 26 more from the Bridewells and Expences in keeping them 6 days and carrying them back to Ivelchester.	15 0 0
1 0 0	For carrying Dorothy Taylor from Ivelchester to Taunton being convicted of petty larceny and whipping her pursuant to her sentence, cart and other expences.	3 3 0
2 0 0	For carrying Richard Evans and Thomas Berryman from Taunton Assizes to Ivelchester being charged with Seditious or Treasonable words where they were comitted, keeping them there, guards and expences.	6 6 0
1 0 0	For carrying Donald MacCloud a Highlander from Bridgwater to Ivelchester being comitted for speaking Seditious and Treasonable words, keeping him there, guards and expences.	3 3 0
	For fitting up the several courts for holding the several Quarter Sessions in and for the said County and for chairs, carpets, cushions candles and other necessarys.	10 0 0
1 0 0	For publically whipping James Bone being convicted of Petty Larceny according to his sentence, cart and other expences.	2 0 0
1 0 0	For Elizabeth Williams the like	2 0 0
2 0 0	For burning in the hand several prisoners pursuant to their sentences at both Assizes and Quarter Sessions.	5 0 0
5 0 0	For carrying Mary Hamilton (who was taken up for a deceipt, she having ran about the County in man's dress and seduced many young women and married them under that disguise and the Law providing no punishment for a crime of this sort, as a vagrant she was ordered to be publickly whipt) to Taunton and whipping her there pursuant to her sentence from thence to Glastonbury, Wells and Shepton Mallett and for whipping her at each town according to her sentence, carts and expences.	10 0 0
3 0 0	For carrying Moisey John Calway and Francis Wilkins under sentence of death from Ivelchester to Taunton 20 miles from thence to the several places of their Executions where they were hanged in chains viz Calway at Chilston Heathfield being 6 miles from Taunton and Wilkins on Blackdown being 5 miles from Taunton under a strong guard for fear of a rescue which was much expected.	10 0 0
10 0 0	For digging the hole through a hard rock on the summit of the hill and also erecting 2 gibbets for executing them.	8 8 0
	For the two setts of irons to hang them in.	10 10 0
	For executing them and fixing them in the irons.	10 10 0

2 0 0	Paid a Clergyman who attended the criminals under sentence of Death from their Condemnations to their respective executions.	5 5 0
1 0 0	For publickly whipping Thomas Perry convicted of larceny and Mary Thompson according to sentences, carts and other expences.	4 0 0
4 10 0	For dietting and guarding Ambrose Maby, John Harvey, George Laurence and Elizabeth Smith under sentence of Transportation from the 19th February 1745 to the 26th of April 1746 being nine weeks at 2s 6d a week.	4 10 0
3 0 0	For dyet and guarding Rachel Bowen, Richard Mosse, John Pinney, David Rawle, Wm. Cameles als. Masey and Jasper Tottle under sentence of Transportation from the 31st March 1746 to 26th April following when they were Transported. 4 weeks.	3 10 0
2 15 0	For dyet and guarding Wm Hobbs under sentence of death from 31st March 1746 to the 2nd September following; 22 weeks at 2s 6d a week.	2 15 0
5 0 0	For dyetting and guarding Jane Cole, Ann Cracy, Mary Hayman, Elizabeth Miles under sentence of transportation from 2nd September to the 11th November following being 10 weeks at 2s 6d a week.	8 10 0
2 10 0	For dyetting and guarding John Watson and William Hobbs under sentence of transportation from 2nd September 1746 to the 11th November following being 10 weeks at 2s 6d per week.	2 10 0
7 17 6	For dyetting and guarding George Parsons alias Russler, Nicholas Roe, Mary Millard under sentence of Death from 2nd September 1746 to the 27th January following at 2s 6d per week.	7 17 6
10 0 0	For dispersing 50 Acts of Parliament for the Land Tax and writing and sending letters to the Community over the whole County to give notice of the first General Meeting and attending them.	15 0 0
20 0 0	Also for proclaiming and dispersing a bundle of Proclamations for his Majesty's Audit.	6 6 0
	Also for proclaiming and dispersing a bundle of Proclamations for a General Thanksgiving.	6 6 0
	Also for proclaiming and dispersing a bundle of Proclamations for proroguing the Parliament.	6 6 0
	Also for proclaiming and dispersing a bundle of Proclamations for a General Fast.	6 6 0
29 6 2	Paid the Justices of the Peace and their Clerk their wages at the several Sessions held for the said County within the Sheriffalty more than what the fines received at the said Sessions amount unto as by affidafit annext appears.	29 6 8

176 18 8   309 12 8

John Treble, Under Sheriff

Sworn at Bedford Row the
4th day of March 1746 before E. Clive

    Allowed by Mr Baron Clive   260–0–0
    Let this Sheriff be allowed in full of this Bill the sum of one hundred
    seventy six pounds eighteen shillings and eight pence.

H. Pelham
16th March 1746

[The right-hand column lists the expenses claimed; the left-hand column gives the actual amounts paid out by the Treasury.]

PRO, T 64/262
Sheriffs' Cravings

An Account of monies paid, laid out and expended for the use of his present Majesty King George the Third in the Sheriffalty of Sir Barnard Turner knight deceased and Thomas Skinner, Esquire Sheriffs of the City of London and Sheriff of the County of Middlesex from the Feast day of Saint Michael the Archangel in the year of our Lord 1783 to the 15th day of June 1784 and in the Sheriffalty of William Pickett Esq, and the said Thomas Skinner from the said 15th day of June to the Feast day of Saint Michael the Archangel in the year of our Lord 1784 for which they humbly crave an allowance as follows:

Lent Assizes 1784

For conducting Edward Adams to the County of Surry charged with murder for five men and five horses hire, for mans meat, horses meat, care, pains &c, one day at 12s p day each man and horses	3	0 0
Two writs of Habeas Corpus and Order of Court for one	1	6 6
For conducting Henry Snook to Chelmsford charged with horse stealing for five men and five horses hire, for mans meat, horses meat, care, pains &c, three days at 12s p day each man and horses	9	0 0
For conducting William Peters to the County of Surry charged with felony, for five men and five horses hire, for mans meat, horses meat, care, pains &c, one day at 12s p day each man and horse	3	0 0
Two writs of Habeas Corpus and Order of Court for one	1	6 6
For conducting James McMurphy to Maidstone charged with felony, for five men and five horses hire, for mans meat, horses meat, care, pains &c, four days at 12s p day each man and horse	12	0 0
Two writs of Habeas Corpus and Order of Court for one	1	6 6
For conducting Samuel Warren alias Earl to Surry charged with felony, for five men and five horses hire, for mans meat, horses meat, care, pains &c, one day at 12s p day each man and horse	3	0 0
Two writs of Habeas Corpus and Order of Court for one	1	6 6
For conducting John Ansdon to Bedford charged with horse stealing, for five men and five horses hire, for mans meat, horses meat, care, pains &c, five days at 12s p day each man and horse	15	0 0

An Account of monies paid laid out and expended for the use of his present Majesty King George the Third in the Sheriffalty of Sir Barnard Turner Knight deceased and Thomas Skinner Esquire Sheriffs of the City of London and Sheriff of the County of Middlesex from the Feast day of Saint Michael the Archangel in the Year of our Lord 1783 to the 15th day of June 1784 and in the Sheriffalty of William Pickett Esqr and the said Thomas Skinner from the said 15th day of June to the Feast day of Saint Michael the Archangel in the Year of our Lord 1784 for which they humbly Crave an Allowance as follows:

Lent Assizes 1784.

For Conducting Edward Adams to the County of Surry charged with Murder for five Men and five Horses hire for Mans meat Horses meat Care Pains &c one Day at 12s ⅌ Day each Man and Horse is — — — — — —	3 " "
Two Writs of Habeas Corpus and Order of Court for one — — — — — —	1 6 6
For conducting Henry Snook to Chelmsford charged with Horse Stealing for five Men and five Horses hire for mans meat Horse meat Care Pains &c three Days at 12s ⅌ Day each Man and Horse is — — —	9 " "
Two Writs of Habeas Corpus and Order of Court for one — — — — — —	1 6 6
For conducting William Potts to the County of Surry charged with Felony for five Men and five Horses hire for mans Meat Horses meat Care Pains &c one Day at 12s ⅌ Day each Man and Horse is — — — — —	3 " "

Sheriffs' Bill of Cravings for London and Middlesex, 1784 (PRO, T 64/262)

Two writs of Habeas Corpus and Order of Court for one	1 6 6
For conducting Ann Paris to the County of Surry charged with felony, for five men and five horses hire, for mans meat, horses meat, care, pains &c, one day at 12s p day each man and horse	3 0 0
For conducting William Johnson and John Ramsay to the County of Surry charged with robbing on the highway, for ten men and ten horses hire, for mans meat, horses meat, care, pains &c, at 12s p day each man and horse	6 0 0
Two writs of Habeas Corpus and Order of Court for three	2 2 6
For conducting John Shirley to Aylesbury charged with horse stealing, for five men and five horses hire, for mans meat, horses meat, care, pains &c, four days at 12s p day each man and horse	12 0 0
Two writs of Habeas Corpus and Order of Court for one	1 6 6
For conducting Morris Daley to Chelmsford charged with robbing on the highway, for five men and five horses hire, for mans meat, horses meat, care, pains &c, three days at 12s p day each man and horse	9 0 0
Two writs of Habeas Corpus and Order of Court for one	1 6 6
For conducting William Holmes and Elizabeth Brown alias Cave to Chelmsford charged with burglary, for ten men and ten horses hire, for mans meat, horses meat, care, pains &c, three days at 12s p day each man and horse	18 0 0
Two writs of Habeas Corpus and Order of Court for two	1 14 6
For conducting Richard Frasear to Chelmsford charged with robbing on the highway, for five men and five horses hire, for mans meat, horses meat, care, pains &c, three days at 12s p day each man and horse	9 0 0
Two writs of Habeas Corpus and Order of Court for one	1 6 6

etc., etc.

PRO, T 90/163
Sheriffs' Payments

Nottingham to wit, Lancelot Rolleston Esq. Sheriff of the County aforesaid for the year ending at Michaelmas 1781.

25 0 0	For lodgings and other necessary accommodations for the Judges at both Assizes	25 4 0
5 0 0	Fitting up the Courts at do	6 6 0
5 0 0	Fitting ballotting boxes &c and for the Jury at do	6 6 0
5 0 0	Distributing the Land Tax Acts of Parliament	6 6 0
2 10 0	The like Acts appointing Commissioners	6 6 0
2 0 0	Dispersing proclamations for holding the Judges Audit and postage / The like for the meeting of Parliament	3 3 0
2 0 0	The like for a General Fast on 8th Feby 1782	3 3 0

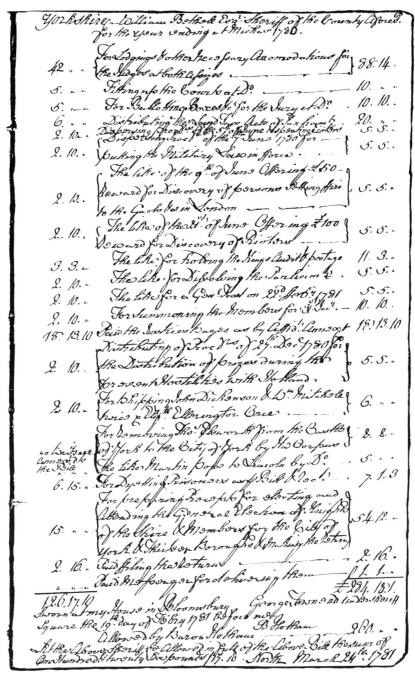

Sheriffs' Payments for Yorkshire, 1780. Includes: £6 for whipping John Dickenson and Wm Mitchell twice and Elizth Ellerington once (PRO, T 90/163)

15	0	For Summoning the members for 31st Jany 1782	3	3	0
15	0	The like for the 21st of Jany proceeding	3	3	0
7 6	11	Paid the Justices Wages as by affidavit annexed	7	6	11
2 0	0	Dispersing proclamations for the distribution of prizes	3	3	0
10	0	{ Dyetting George Bounds alias Brown and Adam Bagshaw from conviction to execution }		10	0
4 0	0	Expences and attending their execution	6	8	0
15	0	{ Dyetting Hannah Boster convicted of house breaking but reprieved – six weeks }		15	0
15	0	The like Richard Cooper convicted of Grand Larceny – 6 weeks		15	0
2 5	0	{ The like Samuel Pearce and John Bates convicted of Grand Larceny from conviction to the time of their being sent to the Thames – 9 weeks }	2	5	0

£65 11 11   £84 2 11

Sworn at my Chambers in Sergeants Inn   Francis Evans, Under Sheriff
the 1st day of Feby 1782 before me

         J. Skynner

Allowed by Lord Chief Baron Skynner £70

Let the above Sheriff be allowed in full the above Bill the sum of sixty five pounds eleven shillings and eleven pence.

                                            North
                                            March 16th 1782

[The right-hand column lists the expenses claimed; the left-hand column gives the actual amounts paid out by the Treasury.]

PRO, T 207/1
Sheriffs' Payments

Sussex, Sir Charles Montolieu Lamb, Baronet, Sheriff of the said County for the year ending at Michaelmas 1829. Also the third or Winter Assizes.

55 0	0	Lodgings &c for Judges at both Assizes	11	6	3
5 0	0	Fitting up the Courts at do and for carpets &c	7	6	3
5 0	0	Balloting box and list of Jurors	5	0	0
2 0	0	Proclamation 10 Decr 1829 proroguing Parliament to 4 Feby 1830	2	0	0
2 0	0	. . . for holding His Majesty's audit	2	0	0
2 0	0	Attending persons to peruse Public Acts	2	0	0
		Fees paid the Judges Officers at Spring Assizes	5	15	6

			Glove Money there being no Execution	5	5	0
			The like fees and Glove Money at the Summer Assizes	11	0	6

see last year	Ingrossing on parchment 4 copies of the estreat roll and delivering the Sheriff's return to the Justices at 4 Quarter Sessions pursuant to the Statute 3 & 4 Geo. 4th and for making a copy on paper with an account of the sums levied sent to the Treasury and for levying and receiving the same the Sheriffs having the additional duty imposed by the inspector of Fines claiming and receiving from the Sheriff the whole money levied without deducting the Sheriff's poundage which was allowed for levying and receiving the same before this Act passed.	5 0 0

Winter Assizes

55	0	0	Lodgings and other accommodations for the Justices &c.	66	18	6
2	10	0	Fitting up the Courts and for providing carpets, candles, etc.	2	10	0
			Fees paid the Judges Officers	5	15	6
5	5	0	Glove Money there being no Execution	5	5	0

88 4 0	Sheriff for the expences of himself, trumpeters, javelin men and attendance during the Assizes 1 day going and 1 day returning being 7 days at the rate of £12 12 0 per day, the Assizes commencing 19 Decr and finishing on the 23 Decr both days inclusive.	88 4 0
44 2 0	Under Sheriff for the expences of himself and G. Palmer and M.H. Palmer, his agents attending the Assizes including also the making out of warrants, selecting Jurors, making pannels and returns to process and other trouble at the rate of £6 6 0 per day for 7 days as above	44 2 0
42 0 0	Paid 8 bailiffs employed in summoning Juries and attending the Assizes at the rate of 15/- per day each during the Assizes being 7 days as above with the 1 day coming and 1 day returning viz, Thomas Ward, William Edwards, Charles Hunt, Charles Knight, W.S. Camp, T.A. Mantoll, T.D. Smith and William Austin	42 0 0

Gaoler's Bill

Dieting Mary Ann Sturt from 3 June 1828 to 4 Feby 1829 being 249 [days]	4 11 7
. . . Thos Hitchins, Geo. Howell, Edward Gates, Peter Daw, William Bennett, John Fishwicke, James Carpenter, from 30 March to 9 April being 10 days each	1 5 0
John Williams, Benj. Povey, Thos. Huggett, John Carpenter, William Jones, John Holder, John Kinnard, James Watson, John Wheeler, William Wheeler, William Martin, Thos. Colbran, Edward Jordan, Richd Nicholl, Geo. Boxall and William Evans (16) from 30 March to the 4 May being 35 days each	10 0 0

John Cuflice Brooker, Geo. Pope, Stephen Colvin, John Moore, William Hunt, William Millo, Robert Robinson, William Wheeler, William Hazelgrove (9) from 24 Aug. to 15 Sept. being 23 days   }   3 13 11

Dieting Geo. Moody, James Mills, Joel Sands, John Elliott and John Simmonds (5) from 24 Aug. to 15 Sept. being 23 days   }   2 1 0

James Stainsbury, Charles Minall, William Hawkins, Edmund Nye, James Fibbins, Charles Boghurst, James Wiston, Robt. Sweeney, Thos. Smith, William Rolf, Daniel Jones and William Haylor (12) from 24 Aug. to 21 Sept. 1829 being 28 days each   }   6 0 0

Caroline Wood from 24 Aug. to 29 Jan. 1830   2 16 5

Edward Richardson, Benj. Smith, James Mitchell, Thos. Whiting, William Frost, Benj. Davis, Wm. C. Vincent, Thos. Akehurst, (8) from 28 Dec. to 4 Jany 1830 being 7 days each at 2/6 per week   }   1 0 0

84 prisoners
for 2806 days
or 400 weeks
& 6 days at
2/6 per week
each is
£50 2 1½
   say £50 2 2

50 2 2   Mary Shelvey and Mary Chester 28 Dec. to 29 Jany 32 days   1 2 10

Henry Holden, Jesse Cominge, Geo. Marchant, William Brazier, Thos. Linden, James Wright, M. McCarthy, James Gray, Joseph Carter, Ben. Terry, George Aytwood, William Wilson, Thomas Marchant, William Freeman, John Snelling, and Moses Stevens (16) from 28 Dec. 1823 to 8 Feby 1830 being 42 days each   }   12 0 0

Charles Hemmington, William Wildish, Wm. Toye, Thomas Elmes, Edward Moon and James Thompson (6) from 28 Dec to 8 Feby 1830. 45 days each   }   4 16 5

Jno. E. Hewlett from 28 Dec 1829 to 15 Feby being 49 [days]   17 6

_____   _____

£358 3 2   £468 13 2
_____   _____

Sworn at Battle in the County of
Sussex the 9 June 1830   T.C. Bellingham, Under Sheriff
                              Before me   Edwin Martin, Under Sheriff
Allowed by Mr Baron Vaughan £468

Let the above Sheriff be allowed in full for this Bill the sum of three hundred and fifty eight pounds three shillings and two pence.

Henry Goulbroin [?]

24 July 1830

[The right-hand column lists the expenses claimed; the left-hand column gives the actual amounts paid out by the Treasury.]

C H A P T E R   11

CRIMINAL LUNATICS

Up until 1800 insane criminals were held in all gaols and no distinction was made between them and other prisoners. By an Act of 1800 felons found insane on arraignment or acquitted by reason of insanity were to be committed to asylums or mad houses. In practice this did not always happen and many of the insane criminals continued to be held in gaols for the following reasons:

1. Those who were insane but committed to gaol before the Act of 1800.
2. Those who became insane after commitment.
3. Those awaiting trial, apparently insane, but not having been certified. (These sometimes waited as much as two years before their trial.)
4. Those who had not been officially recognized as insane upon their trial.
5. Offenders whose maximum sentence for their crime was so short as to gain them nothing by pleading insanity.

The term *Criminal Lunatic* was first officially used by a select committee appointed by the House of Commons in 1807. Criminal lunatics were then described as persons who were in custody as a result of either acquittal by reason of insanity, or of a finding that they were insane on arraignment. The proposals of this committee resulted in the County Asylum Act of 1808 which recommended the building of a separate establishment for criminal lunatics.

The first statutory definition of the term *Criminal Lunatic* was given in the 1860 Act which referred to criminal lunatics as 'Her Majesty's Pleasure Patients'. The term Criminal Lunatic Asylum caused much distress to the families of criminal lunatics and as a result in 1938[1] the terms *Broadmoor* and *Broadmoor Patient* were used. But Broadmoor Patient was something of a misnomer because many of these patients went to other mental hospitals and not to Broadmoor. *Broadmoor Patient* was soon to become an equally distressing term and in 1959 it was agreed that more precise terms were to be used, e.g. *Special Hospital Patient, Hospital Order Patient, Restriction Order Patient*, etc.

---

[1] The Criminal Justice Bill which eventually reached the Statute Book in 1948.

Bethlem Asylum, 1836 (from *Tales About Great Britain and Ireland*, Peter Parley, 1836)

The admission to an asylum, transfer and final release of all patients, including criminal lunatics, is recorded in County Asylum and Hospital Registers, PRO, Class MH 94. These date from 1846. An example of an entry is given in the case of Thomas Hartnell in Chapter 21. These registers are usually annual and record the patients alphabetically.

Under the Criminal Lunatic Act 1884 it was stated that criminal lunatics who were paupers who had served out their sentences and still remained insane were to be transferred to County Lunatic Asylums. The cost of maintenance of each of these lunatics was chargeable to the union or parish where the offender was resident at the time the offender was committed. If, however, it was not clear to what parish the offender rightfully belonged then the following would be the determining guidelines:

Charges would be made on:

a   That parish where the said offence was alleged to have been committed.

or b   If it appears that the offence was alleged to have been committed out of the United Kingdom, to that place in which it appears that such person was first apprehended.

or c   If such person appears to have been so apprehended out of the United Kingdom, to that place in which it appears to the said justices that such person first landed in the United Kingdom.

It is likely, therefore, that further information about a pauper lunatic formerly convicted of a crime will be found among the records of the Poor Law Union as in the case of Thomas Hartnell given in Chapter 21.

PRO, HO 20/13
Bethlem[2] Lunatic Asylum, London

NAME	AGE	CRIME	WHEN AND WHERE ARRAIGNED OR TRIED, WITH VERDICT OF THE JURY	TO WHAT PARISH BELONGS
Hadfield James	44	Shooting at His Majesty	Lord Pelham's Warrant 22 Sept. 1802 Kings Bench Westminster Insanity	Unknown
McKernot Anthony	33	Forgery	Old Bailey Jany 1816 Insanity	Unknown
Newcombe John	64	Stealing a quantity of books	Old Bailey Dec. 1815 Insanity	Unknown
Burgess Martha	22	Felony	At the General Sessions of Gaol Delivery of Newgate for London held on the 3rd April 1816 found guilty	Stated by the prisoner to be St. George in the East, Midx.
Conner George	about 24	Committed for manslaughter Tried for murder	Rochester October 1815 Verdict, not returned being proved to be Insane at the time the offence was committed	Some parish in Ireland
Hodges Rebecca	35	Acquitted of shooting with intent to murder	Warwick Lent Assizes 1809 being found insane by the Jury on her trial, is ordered to remain until His Majesty's Pleasure be known.	Hales Owen, Shropshire
Morley Jonathan	31	Murder Committed 26 April 1813 under a Coroner's Warrant	Indicted at the Assizes held in and for the City of Norwich and County of the same city on the 17 day of Aug. 1813, but having upon his arraignment been found by a Jury lawfully impannelled for that purpose, to be insane he was ordered to be kept in strict custody until His Majesty's Pleasure should be known pursuant to the Statute.	Badwell Ash, near Walsham Le Willows in the County of Suffolk
Horder John	48	Murder	Wells Assizes, Aug. 1802. Acquitted it appearing to the Jury that he was under the influence of insanity when the fact was committed. Let him be kept in strict custody until His Majesty's Pleasure shall be known pursuant to the Statute in that behalf.	Mells
Burrows Elizabeth the wife of Thomas Burrows	38	Murder by administering poison to two of her own children	Stafford Lent Assizes 1815. Acquitted, the Jury having found her insane	Woolstanton near Newcastle under Lyne

[2] Bethlem Asylum was originally founded in 1247 as the Priory of St Mary of Bethlehem. It was therefore also known as Bethlehem Asylum (or Hospital).

CHARACTER AS FAR AS KNOWN PREVIOUS TO COMMITMENT, AND CONDUCT IN GAOL SINCE, WITH ANY OTHER PARTICULARS CONCERNING THE PRISONER'S INSANITY THAT MAY BE CONSIDERED USEFUL TO THOSE WHO ARE TO BE ENTRUSTED WITH THEIR FUTURE SAFE CUSTODY	WHEN REMOVED TO THE CRIMINAL LUNATIC ASYLUM	WHEN DISCHARGED	REMARKS
Furious paroxyoms [sic] at times, but tranquil at present		Dead	
Malicious and Designing	29 Oct 1819	25 Aug 1825	
Quiet and orderly		Discharged	
Her character previous, unknown but as far as it can be collected from herself she has been an idle, drunken abandoned young woman. The character received with her from Newgate, that her behaviour was good, her connection and former course of life suspected. During her confinement at this place her behaviour has occasionally been correct but she early exhibited symptoms of insanity by noisy and unaccountable behaviour during divine service, giving incoherent answers to questions put, riotous and violent conduct, which neither good or severe treatment corrected or controlled, and by sitting up repeatedly all night in the window of her cell in rainy and cold nights singing but taking scarcely any nourishment. It appears that a few months before her first imprisonment she received a severe wound on the head by a blow with a quart pot, was taken to the London Hospital insensible, and where she remained upwards of six weeks to be cured.			Transferred to the Penitentiary Feb. 1819
Offence was committed on board His Majesty's ship *Cumberland* lying in River Medway where it is understood he behaved well until he became Insane. Is now occasionally melancholy, sullen and obstinate.			
Not known before committment to the Gaol and since that time has not shewn the least sign of being insane during confinement, and has been used to wash and mend linen for her fellow prisoners the whole time; is of thin stature but well made, her temper very bad.		Discharged, afterwards convicted for setting fire to her former master's hay ricks and sent to New South Wales.	
Previous to his committment the prisoner was confined in a Lunatic Hospital in Norwich having been placed there by his parish. The keeper of which he wounded with a scythe so as to occasion his death. It is stated that until this count he was considered as less mischievious than the generality of patients and was frequently employed in the yards of the hospital in menial offices. For a few months afterwards his committment he was frequently outragious and coercion was obliged to be used, since however the gaoler has found him manageable with common caution. He dislikes strangers and it will be prudent for those in whose custody he is to be placed, to be very watchful and cautious of him at first, and to be particularly careful of leaving weapons within his reach, with which he might do himself or others mischief. When offended he becomes resentful, sullen and somewhat malicious.			
Being coachman in a gentleman's family his first apparent act of insanity was stopping his horses going home one evening placing his master on the box to drive and himself inside, where he continued until the carriage reached home. Insanity now appeared in all his acts and the father of his wife dreading her perilous situation took her home. Prisoner no sooner discovered what had been done than he loaded a gun and placed himself in a tree under which the father in law usually passed, he very shortly after came by and was shot dead. Prisoner will now relate particulars and laugh at the kicking of the old man when he fell. Once attempted to escape on being told by another prisoner that the gaoler had no right to keep him. He sings and whistles at changes of the moon, at other times is quite harmless, if not disturbed or contradicted.			
Very good character before trial and has behaved orderly and properly during the whole of her imprisonment.			

NAME	AGE	CRIME	WHEN AND WHERE ARRAIGNED OR TRIED, WITH VERDICT OF THE JURY	TO WHAT PARISH BELONGS
Riley Anne	32	Feloniously stealing from the person of Edward Mainwaring on the 2nd October 1817 at Greenwich a silk purse a twenty pound Bank of England note and a guinea together of the value of twenty three pounds three shillings his property	Kent Lent Assizes for the year 1818 at Maidstone. Verdict of the Jury guilty. Sentenced to ten years transportation	Cavan in Ireland
Narroway Thomas	20	Stealing six live pigs	12th Sept. 1821, Old Bailey Sentenced to 7 years transportation	Spitalfields in the County of Middlesex
David John	36	Cutting and maiming his wife	At Cardiff Spring Great Sessions 1822. Acquitted on the grounds of Insanity	Langainer
Bay Elizabeth alias Darby	40	Stealing Plate value 40s & upwards in dwelling house	Special Gaol Delivery at Kingston upon Thames December 1822. Acquitted on account of Insanity at the time of committing the offence	St. Andrew Birmingham
Murphy Sarah	38	Stealing from ye shop of W.R. Vant of Woolwich. linen and other articles value £4.15. Also stealing from the shop of E. Vale 1 pair of boots & 1 pair of shoes value 10s. Also stealing from the auction room of W. Austen at Woolwich 1 writing desk value £1.0.0. Also of stealing from the shop of P. Johnson of Woolwich one piece of pelisse cloth value £1.5. Also stealing from the shop of W. Pike of Woolwich one shawl value 18s.	Summer Assizes at Maidstone 1822. Sentenced to be transported for seven years	Bristol Somersetshire
Raddon John	35	Cutting with intent to Murder his wife	Exeter Castle, Lammas Ass. 1822. Insane by the Visitation of God	Stoke Damerel, Devon
Clifford Amy	40	Charged with having feloniously, wilfully, maliciously and unlawfully struck at and cut Sarah Worger with a Hand Bill with intent to Murder or to do her some grievous bodily harm at Ashford on the 5 October 1823	Maidstone, Dec.ʳ Ass. 1823. Acquitted of Felony but the Jury having found that she was Insane at the time of Committing the Offence and having declared that she was acquitted by them on the grounds of such Insanity ordered to be kept in strict Custody in Gaol until His Majesty's Pleasure shall be Known.	Wye in Kent
Shade Wᵐ etc., etc.	33	Assault and Cutting with an Axe	Old Bailey Session, February 1825. Acquitted on the grounds of Insanity	St Martins in the Fields

CHARACTER AS FAR AS KNOWN PREVIOUS TO COMMITMENT, AND CONDUCT IN GAOL SINCE, WITH ANY OTHER PARTICULARS CONCERNING THE PRISONER'S INSANITY THAT MAY BE CONSIDERED USEFUL TO THOSE WHO ARE TO BE ENTRUSTED WITH THEIR FUTURE SAFE CUSTODY	WHEN REMOVED TO THE CRIMINAL LUNATIC ASYLUM	WHEN DISCHARGED	REMARKS
Character previous to committment not known. Has been for the last twelve month very troublesome running about the ward stripping herself, tearing her clothes and making great noises from morning till night nearly exhausted, frequently in hospital chiefly occasioned by her violent conduct. Has once or twice struck and kicked the Turnkeys. Uses threatening language to the prisoners in the ward and the Turnkeys who have had the charge of her. Thomas Agar Keeper	Anne Riley's bodily state of health has varied during the last year, her mental affliction has been great. At the present moment she may be said to be in good bodily health. J. Whatman Surgeon Thos. Day Surgeon		
Character sent from Newgate. Supposed 1st offence, had a previous good character. Conduct since confined in the penitentiary has been very indifferent. This man for some time there has been somewhat singular in his manners. On the 13th Aug. 22 he was removed into the infirmary with symptoms of insanity, at which time there was an increase action of artirial system, he was bled and restricting applied. In a short time that ceased, he continued deranged. I have been informed that his mother's family as well as herself was subject to fits of insanity and she died in that state a short period after his birth. He is very filthy and obstrepolous. Surgeon J. Pratt	Health when received was good	Discharged to the penitentiary	
His character previous to committment is unknown to me. His conduct while in Gaol has been very strange at times and at this moment I consider him religiously Insane & dangerous. State of bodily health Good. Jnᵒ Woods Governor of the Gaol Cardiff		Died 11 Jan 1837	
No information can be gained as to her conduct previous to commitment. The offence was committed near Guildford Surrey at the time a Fair was holding there, and she was apprehended on the spot. She has been very violent since her commitment to Gaol (2 Oct 22) and two women have been hardly sufficient with the assistance of a straight waistcoat to prevent her from injuring herself. She has been obliged to have a change of linen daily. W. Walker Keeper	Bodily health Good	Died 9 August 1824	
Character previous to commitment represented to have been very good. Her conduct since in gaol very orderly. She has been in a very low melancholy state during the whole time of her confinement. Thos. Agar Keeper	Her general state of bodily health is good. Sluggishness of the bowels the principal point that has required attention. Her case is a decided one of Insanity. She is not violent in her manners, her lucid intervals are not very frequent. James Whetman Surgeon	Discharged 25 March 1829	
Good previous to commitment. Irrational but Inoffensive since commitment. Wᵐ Cole, Acting Keeper Devon County Gaol and Keeper of the Bridewell	Good		
On the Trial it was stated that she had not been of sound mind for a considerable period previous to Commitment, her conduct in Gaol since has been tolerably tranquil but she is at times very irritable and it has been judged necessary to place two Prisoners constantly with her. Thos. Agar, Keeper	Her Bodily health is good J. Whatman, Surgeon	Died 8 Augᵗ 1829	
Before for 3 years in the mad house at Bethnal Green. Easily irritated. Jnᵒ Wontner, Keeper	Good		

Broadmoor Criminal Lunatic Asylum.

Return of Criminal Lunatics.

for the Quarter ending 31st December 1872.

Regr. No.	NAME	Age	Whence and when received	Where and when tried	Crime	Sentence or order of the Court	Present state of — Body	Present state of — Mind	Date of — Removal and whither	Date of — Discharge	Date of — Death	REMARKS
1	Mary Ann Parr	43	Bethlem 27 May 1863	Nottingham 3 March 1853	Murder	Life 1849	Indiff	Unsound				
3	Mary Ann Payne	45	do	Winchester July 1872	Wounding	Acquitted insane	Good	Unsound				
6	Mary Ann Hamilton	47	do	C. C. Court 7 January 1862	Murder	Acquitted insane symptoms	Indiff	Fair, Unsd				
7	Jane Lower	46	do	Lord George Manslaughter 20 July 1860		Acquitted insane symptoms	Indiff	Unsound				
8	Ann Cartlage	47	do	Liverpool December 1858	Murder	Acquitted insane	Good	Unsound				
10	Mary Ann Ogden	36	Bethlem 29 May 1863	C. C. Court July 1859	Murder	Acquitted insane symptoms	Indiff	Establst				
12	Mary McNeile	41	do	C. C. Court January 1856	Murder	Acquitted insane symptoms	Bad	Unsound				
13	Martha Baines	42	do	C. C. Court May 1857	Murder	Acquitted insane symptoms	Good	Fair				

Two pages from Broadmoor Criminal Lunatic Asylum, Female Quarterly Returns, 31 December 1872
(PRO, HO 8/194)

Registers of inmates for Bethlem and Broadmoor Lunatic Asylums are found with prison registers (see Appendix 4.10). In addition detailed accounts have been preserved of criminal lunatic cases in PRO, Class HO 144 and warrants for the movement of criminal lunatics are given in PRO, Class HO 145.

PRO, HO 8/180
Quarterly Prison Returns

Broadmoor Lunatic Asylum, quarter ending 30 June 1869

No. 614	
Name	William Bisgrove
Age	19
Whence and When Received	Taunton, 26 January 1869
Where and When Tried	Taunton, 15 December 1868
Crime	Murder
Sentence or Order of the Court	Life Penal Servitude
Body	Epileptic
Mind	Unsound

[Further details of William Bisgrove are given in Chapter 18.]

PRO, HO 8/198
Quarterly Prison Returns

Broadmoor Lunatic Asylum, quarter ending 31 December 1873

No. 283	
Name	William Bowskill
Age	60
Whence and Where Received	Fisherton, 20 March 1865

[contd]

Where and When Tried	Nottingham, March 1848
Crime	Wounding
Sentence or Order of the Court	Insanity, H.M. Pleasure
Body	Good
Mind	Unsound

No. 799	
Name	Edward Abbott
Age	41
Whence and Where Received	Taunton Gaol, 27 September 1873
Where and When Tried	Wells Assizes, 8 August 1873
Crime	Murder
Sentence or Order of the Court	Death
Body	Good
Mind	Improving

[Further details of Edward Abbott are given on page 185.]

No. 171	
Name	Jane Clarke
Age	53
Whence and Where Received	Essex County Prison, 15 December 1870

Where and When Tried	Assizes Chelmsford, 21 October 1869
Crime	Attempt to Murder
Sentence or Order of the Court	Acquitted, Insane, H.M. Pleasure
Body	Indifferent
Mind	Unsound

PRO, HO 8/180
Quarterly Prison Returns

Broadmoor Lunatic Asylum, quarter ending 30 June 1869

No. 608	
Name	Thomas Douglas
Age	31
Whence and When Received	Millbank, 16 September 1864 Escaped 8 November 1868 Re-admitted 30 November 1868
Where and When Tried	General Court Martial, Corfu, 3 August 1860
Crime	Striking Corporal Oakley
Sentence or Order of the Court	10 years Penal Servitude
Body	Good
Mind	Unsound

PRO, HO 145/1

Warrant for the reception of
Charles Copping into the
County Lunatic Asylum at
Prestwich, Manchester

The Right Honourable Sir William Vernon Harcourt one of Her Majesty's Most Honourable Privy Council and Principal Secretary of State. Whereas, by an Act passed in the 27th and 28th years of Her Majesty's Reign, intitled 'An Act to amend the Act Third and Fourth Victoria, Chapter Fifty-four, for making further Provision for the Confinement and Maintenance of Insane Prisoners,' it is enacted, that if any Person while imprisoned in any Prison or other place of Confinement under any Sentence of Transportation, Penal Servitude or Imprisonment, or under a charge of any Offence, or for not finding Bail for good behaviour or to keep the Peace, or to answer a Criminal Charge, or in consequence of any Summary Conviction, or Order by any Justice of the Peace, or under any other than Civil Process, shall appear to be insane, it shall be lawful, if such Person is confined in a Prison to which Visiting Justices are appointed, for two or more of the Visiting Justices of such Prison, or, if such Person is in any other place of confinement, for two or more Justices of the Peace of the County, City, Borough, or Place in which such place of confinement is situate, or, if such Person is in a Convict Prison, one of the Directors thereof and such Visiting or other Justices or Directors are hereby required to call to their assistance Two Physicians or Surgeons or One Physician and one Surgeon, duly registered as such respectively, under the Provisions of an Act passed in the Session of the Twenty-first and Twenty-second years of Her Majesty's Reign, Chapter Ninety, and to be selected by them for that purpose, and to inquire with their aid as to the Insanity of such Person, and if it shall be duly certified by such Justices or any two of them, and such Physicians or Surgeons, or such Physician and Surgeon, that such Person is insane, One of Her Majesty's Principal Secretaries of State may, upon receipt of such Certificate, if he shall think fit, direct by Warrant under his hand that such Person shall be removed to such Lunatic Asylum, or other proper Receptacle for Insane Persons, as the said Secretary of State may judge proper and appoint. And Whereas it has been Certified to me under the hands of Charles L. Clare and H.J. Leppoe Esquires being two of the Visiting Committee of Her Majesty's Prison at Strangeways, Manchester, and Justices of the County in which such Prison is situated and under the hands of Charles H. Braddon and Charles H. Hitchen surgeons, being Persons authorised as aforesaid that Charles Copping who was at the Sessions of the Peace holden at Manchester in and for the Hundred of Salford on the 9th January 1882 convicted of Housebreaking and sentenced to twelve calendar months hard labour and four years police supervision, has become insane. And whereas the County Lunatic Asylum at Prestwich, Manchester has been recommended to me as a fit and proper Recepticle for the said Lunatic I do hereby in pursuance of the Act of Parliament above recited authorize and direct you to cause the said Charles Copping to be received from the said Prison, to the said Lunatic Asylum, there to remain until further order shall be made herein. And for so doing this shall be your Warrant.

Given at Whitehall the 3rd day of April 1882 in the 45th Year of Her Majesty's Reign.

To the Superintendent   W.V. Harcourt
of the County Lunatic
Asylum Prestwich,
Manchester and all others
whom it may concern.

PRO, HO 144/11
Edward Abbott charged with the murder of his daughter

Western Summer Circuit 1873 [Assizes]

The Queen v Edward Abbott for Murder
Tried before I. Fitzjames Stephen Esq. Q.C. at Wells 13th August

William Thomas Abbott, 18 years old.
My father has a contract for brickwork in Arnolds [Arno's] Vale Cemetery. Five or six men under him. I worked at the cemetery. My father lives in his own house. Mrs Peglar lives next door. We have lived in that house about two years. Change in my father's conduct since he came back to our house from London two months ago. He used to drink before he went to London but not to stay away from his work. Since he came back from London he has been sober but has stayed away from his work. My mother occasionally drank. They lived happily together.

There are three bedrooms up stairs, two back, one front. One of the back rooms larger than the other. There were five of us living at home I and four little ones besides my father and mother. I am the eldest. The next at home was 7, the next 5, and the last Maria 3. Also a baby, all girls. The two sisters of 7 and 5 slept in the front room. Father and mother in big back room, the baby with them. I slept in the small back bedroom with Maria. She slept in my bed.

My father was very fond of her. Early in the morning if she was awake when he went he would take her into his room and play with her. Monday July 7 father went to work in the morning came back to breakfast and was not seen after till Tuesday night. He came home between 10 and 11 p.m. on Tuesday. My mother was then out. I was up. When my father came home he had his supper, I dont recollect his drinking anything. I had my supper with him. My sisters were all abed.

My father did not talk to me much. He seemed strange. He looked rather bad in his face. He looked rather ill, paler than usual. We both went upstairs together. My mother had not come back then. It was 11 when we went to bed. He went to his bedroom. I to mine. He took no notice of Maria that night.

After I was in bed heard my mother come in. The door had been left shut but not bolted for her to come in. I was awake when she came in. I heard her come upstairs. I heard a few angry words between them. She spoke some angry words to him. I did not hear him say anything.

I got out of bed and told her she had better go to bed. I did not see her. She was then in the bedroom with my father. I heard nothing more after that. She slept down stairs I know because she called me from the room down stairs. She said she slept down stairs. My father usually called me at 6. That morning my mother called me at 4, that was by arrangement.

I left Maria asleep in bed. I came back to breakfast. I left the cemetery at 8.30. That was the usual time. The other men had been at work there that morning. My father had not been there before 8.30.

Sometimes he came before breakfast, sometimes not. His business was that of an overlooker. Mother was in the breakfast room when I came back, father not there nor either of my sisters. The little baby was with my mother. I did not go up stairs, I sat to breakfast, I was about half an hour at breakfast. My father did not breakfast with us. He came in and put on his boots while we were at breakfast. I cannot say where he came from, he had cord trousers on, he had stockings on.

He sat down in a chair put his boots on and went out. He told me to look sharp back to work. He was there not many minutes before he went out. He asked my mother to get him a pair of clean stockings before he came back. I observed nothing particular about his

25785

HOME OFFICE
31 OCT
1881
DEPT №

BROADMOOR CRIMINAL LUNATIC ASYLUM,

Crowthorne, Berks,

28th October 1881.

We hereby certify that we have carefully examined a patient in this asylum named Edward Abbott, and have now to report as follows:—

He is at the present time about 49 years of age and is, by occupation, a stone-mason. He was tried at Wells Assizes on the 13th of August, 1873, for the murder of one of his children, aged about three years, and was found guilty, and was sentenced to death. He was subsequently certified to be insane under the provisions of the Act 27 and 28 Victoria, and he was admitted into the Broadmoor Asylum from Taunton Gaol on the 27th of September, 1873.

His history shows that up to the year 1870 he had been a hard-working and industrious man.

Part of a report on Edward Abbott by Dr Orange and Dr Isaac, of Broadmoor, 1881
(PRO, HO 144/11)

dress I did not take much notice. He looked bad, pale still. I observed nothing else in his appearance. I dont think the children had had their breakfast. One of them came in as I went out. That was the eldest of the three younger. After my father went out my mother went out. As I was going out I met her coming out of our next door neighbours. I spoke to her, she went in and I went on back to work, did not see my father till a fortnight after in the hospital. Know nothing about my father's razors. He had a razor, a white handled one. Cannot say whether this is it. He used to keep it in his room where he slept. He kept it high up out of the way. Remember Dewey (P.C.) coming to the house after I was out for somebody else. Showed him the room my father slept in. It was correctly pointed out. This little child was my father's favourite, he brought home sweetmeats for it. My father has been very absent in his manner for some time lately. He has several times gone away and stayed away all night. Dont know of his walking out to the Bull at Chelwood one night. He was in London not long ago. Dont know why he went. He went without saying a word about why he was going. He and my mother were living on very good terms when he went. I believe my mother wrote to the police to make inquiries after him. I have heard of his being found in the Thames. My father was very strange after he came back. He was more absent after he came back than before he went.

Thomas Hale. Landlord of the Phoenix Inn at Knowle.
Prisoner lives half a mile from my Inn. Saw prisoner 9th July between 7 and 8 a.m. in my bar. He called for 3d of rum and drank it, that is half a noggin. After that he had 6d worth in a bottle which he took away with him. It was a small glass bottle like this (produced). He said good morning and off he went. I noticed nothing more than usual in his manner. He was perfectly sober. He was only a few minutes in my house I saw him seldom, perhaps not once a month. When I did see him there was nothing in the least peculiar about him.

Amy Pegler. Married woman, live next door to the Abbotts.
He has not been quite so steady lately. There has been a change since February. He used to be very steady and industrious. Since February he has been away from his home several times. Know nothing of his habits in regard to sobriety. Tuesday July 8th my husband went to Bristol. I went to the Abbotts a little after 11 at night. I saw the son but neither Abbott nor his wife. I can hear something of what goes on in the house but we must listen attentively to hear. After I had gone to sleep I was waked up by a noise like

July 9th   some one falling over a chair. Next morning I saw Mrs Abbott between 7 and 8. I was preparing breakfast and saw her coming in. I went into her house a little before 8.30 saw Mrs Abbott there. None of the children downstairs. I cannot say whether the baby was there or not. I afterwards went and had breakfast with my husband. Observed nothing in Mrs Abbott's dress or manner, saw nothing of Abbott afterwards. Saw Abbott pass our door as if he was going to the cemetery about 8.50.

My husband works at the cemetery, he comes to breakfast at 8.30. When my husband had gone to his work 3 or 4 minutes Mrs Abbott came in to me, she only came to ask me a question. She was there 3 or 4 minutes and took some things away, a hat box and clothes,

July 8th   I believe her husband's. They had been left on Tuesday.

Did not see her son then. I saw her pass out of our yard. Only just time that she could go upstairs with the clothes she came out into the road with the child screaming 'Murder'. She was holding it on her arm. She cried 'Oh my God Murder'. The child was bloody. While Mrs Abbott was in my house she had no blood on her dress. When I saw the child I noticed the blood on the head was beginning to get dry. I believe prisoner was very fond of the child. He was away, I dont exactly know when. A great many people talked about it. His wife inquired for him. I dont exactly know when he came back. Since he came back he has not seemed to attend to his work. He has been away from his home two or three times for a day or two. Cant recollect whether he ever stayed away for a week. He was a quiet inoffensive man as far as I knew. Never heard him make complaint of his head. He was a reserved man.

Q. Did you notice anything peculiar about him?

A. Mr Abbott was always active and very quick in his manner, always a very fond father and good husband. I noticed nothing peculiar or strange about him. Since he came back from London he has been less attentive to his work and has stayed away from his family. His manner otherwise was unchanged.

W.T. Abbott. recalled – further examined.

After my father came back from London he never said anything about his head being bad either to me or others in my presence. My mother used to put vinegar pads to my father's head. He said his head pained him. The pads were put on his forehead. She did it before he went to London. Sometimes she would do it in a morning when he woke up after a drop of beer. Sometimes she did it when he had not been drinking. I cant say how often it was done. Done generally in the morning.

Jane Blackmore. Wife of Frederic Blackmore.

Live at Knowle. Cannot say how far I live from his house. My house is in sight of his and to the back.

Wednesday July 9th I was in my garden I heard Mrs Abbott scream 'My child is dead, my child is dead.' I passed into the road and met her with the baby lying across her arms. The child was smothered in blood. It looked to me as if the blood was then running. Some of the blood was dry. Cannot say whether the child was then dead. It opened its eyes twice when its mother screamed. Mrs Abbott was in the house sitting on a chair. I stayed with her till the Surgeon came. I have known Abbott 10 months. Never spoke to either of them till Mr Abbott went to London. She was in a great way about it. People talked about his going to London.

Alexander Carr. MRCS at Knowle.

9th July last went to Abbott's house soon after 9. Saw the mother sitting in a low chair in the back kitchen. Child on her knees. The child throat was cut and that killed the child. The child could not live a moment after. It could not have opened its eyes after but a motion of the mother's arm might have made it look as if the eyes moved. The body was becoming stiff and the extremities were cold when I saw it. I should think the child must have been dead half an hour. I went into the back bedroom in the house, the larger of the two back bedrooms. I saw the ordinary furniture of the room the bed clothes of the bed were bloody and the pillow. The razor might have given the cut. I never to my knowledge saw the prisoner before. No special experience in dealing with persons of unsound mind. I know about sanity and insanity as part of my general reading and experience. If a man left his home very strangely without motive and if having previously attended to his work he systematically neglected it, and was out at night being a married man that would not alone show that he was insane but coupled with other circumstances it might lead to that conclusion. If a man apparently with absence of motive cut the throat of a favourite child of three years old that would have to be taken into consideration in determining his sanity. If a man tried to commit suicide afterwards it would not in my opinion tend to show that he was insane. People may commit suicide without being insane. Motiveless murder followed by attempted suicide would be evidence of insanity. Repeated attempts to commit suicide are evidence of insanity. A marked change in habits of life is evidence of brain disease. If I was asked about a man whose habits had altered for the worse in a remarkable way I should fear even if there were no other symptoms that there was disease of the brain. I assume the absence of other explanations independent of health in testing the sanity of a man as to any particular act my first question would be what was his motive. If a woman advanced in life began to use obscene language I should regard it as a matter to be inquired into at any rate with reference to her sanity.

John Trott. Engineer in Mill.
Have known the prisoner five or six years so as to say good morning to him.
9th July I heard screams went to the house and Mrs Abbott with the child in her arms. Remained 10 minutes sent for police and doctor and after doctor came fetched the police. We went in search of Abbott. We went up stairs to the back rooms, looked round but did not make a thorough search, found nothing with which the child's throat could have been cut. We went to a wood half a mile off. It is on the right from the house to the cemetery which it adjoins. It adjoins both cemeteries. The General and the Roman Catholic Cemetery. I went back to the house and then to the cemetery. Saw prisoner over the wall reclining against a tombstone. I got over the wall. His neck was covered with blood, I said 'what made you do it?' He could not speak though he tried. I asked where was the instrument, he pointed to a tool house. I found this razor (produced) and gave it to Chivers. There was blood in the toolhouse in three separate pools. He was very pale owing to loss of blood.

John Charles Blackmore. Son of Mrs Blackmore, 11 years old.
Remember hearing of the child being killed. Saw Mr Abbott just before 9. I saw him go towards the cemetery from the direction of his own house. I saw him come out of his house. He walked sharpish and soon got out of my sight. I cannot hardly tell but I think he was afterwards running.

Philip Cars. Lives near Bristol.
Saw prisoner Wednesday 9th July going along near the cemetery between 9 and 10, he was walking quick. Foxwell's orchard adjoins the cemetery.

George Henry Hawkins.
I am in employ of prisoner in his cemetery. He was out at work in the cemetery on July 7th. Did not see him on the 8th. Whilst at work for the last 2 or 3 months he worked hard the time as usual. He was a kind-hearted man, could not be better. He was not so regular in his attendance lately. Sometimes he came only once or twice a week to the cemetery. He has been irregular for perhaps 9 months. He was sometimes worse and sometimes better.
(repeats Trott's evidence)
He was a very quiet and inoffensive man, he went to London very strangely. He had six men. He worked the same as any one of us. He had occasionally other work besides the cemetery, sometimes he did. We wondered where he was when he was away. He was away several times a week lately. He had to superintend our work. He knew when it was not done right. The only difference I noticed about him was his stopping away.

James Chivers. P.C. Bristol.
Apprehended prisoner at R.C. Cemetery. Trott gave me the razor which I produce. Prisoner's house is half a mile out of the City of Bristol.

Christian Davy. P.C. at Knowle.
9th Inst. called to prisoner's at 9.30. Found Mrs Abbott and child down stairs. His house is in the County of Somerset. I went into the large back bedroom. Bed covered with blood in middle part. Searched for weapon but could find none. Spots (not warm) from right side of staircase to where Mrs Abbott was sitting. On a subsequent search after prisoner

had been taken to hospital found a small bottle produced before which smelt of rum on the dressing table near the looking glass and window at the foot of the bedstead. I charged him afterwards and he made no reply relating to the charge. There was no cork in the bottle. It smelt of rum at the time but the smell went off afterwards. I did not cork the bottle for two or three days. The few drops are in the bottle now. There was and still is a mark of blood on it.

Thomas Elliott. House Surgeon to Bristol General Hospital.
9th July prisoner brought to the hospital half conscious. Had a wound on the neck near Adam's Apple $2\frac{1}{2}$ inches long, it opened the wind pipe. It was dangerous. I treated it and he recovered. He recovered his consciousness before long. He was in my charge about three weeks. Unconscious probably from shock to nervous system he could have not lost much blood. His conduct betrayed no eccentricity. He did as he was told. During the time he was in the hospital he was rational. I had no reason to suppose from what I observed of him in the hospital that he had anything the matter with his mind.

From my own observation of him I had no reason to doubt he was a sane man. I observed no symptoms in his conduct which indicated insanity. Since his recovery I have spoken to him, I spoke to him July 31st, he had then perfectly recovered. I said 'I suppose the police have told you the charge of which you are accused'.

He said 'Yes'. I said 'It was a very sad affair'. He said 'It was'. I think I mentioned to him about going to London. He said he had frequently since he was a young man thought of committing suicide. (He is now 41).

He said he came home that morning and could not find his best clothes and socks and he went out and got some drink and he was maddened by this, and he thought he would destroy himself.

I said 'I suppose you did not intend to kill the child, but happened to come in your way and you did not know what you were about and killed the child.' He replied it was so. He also said he and his wife had taken to drink and been very unhappy and he had frequently attempted to commit suicide. I asked him if he had any recollection of the events that day. He said he had a dim recollection, a very slight recollection of the whole affair. I did not state this before the Magistrates because I asked Mr O'Donohue whether I should state what he said. He asked if I had cautioned him. I said No. I was asked no further questions. Assuming his previous statements to be true I should take this greatly into consideration in considering whether he was sane. A marked change in habits in life if unexplained would with other things be evidence of insanity.

Repeated attempts at suicide would be evidence of insanity. The destruction of the life of a child to which a parent was more than usually attached would be evidence of insanity if there were no apparent motive. I put these questions in order to discover the state of his mind.

W.T. Abbott. Further evidence.
I have an Aunt called Mary I think on my mother's side. My father had an Aunt called Hollis. I have heard she died in the Wells Lunatic Asylum after being sometime confined there. Lost 3 little brothers and sisters in a very short space of time somewhere about four years ago. That preyed a great deal on my father's mind.

Verdict   Guilty

To   The Right Honorable Robert Lowe
      Secretary of State for the Home Department

13 Redcliff Parade West
Bristol
26th November 1873

Sir,
   A Mr Edward Abbott of this City a master mason was convicted at the Summer Bristol Assize 1873 of murdering his infant daughter about four years of age and was sentenced to be hung but reprieved and is confined in Broadmoor Lunatic Asylum. He was the contractor for building the vaults and graves at the Bristol Cemetery and from the time of his imprisonment to his conviction the work of the Cemetery was carried on by myself and a Mr Padfield of this City (being the principal creditors of Abbott) for which work we have not been fully paid. Upon Abbott's conviction the Cemetery work was relet to another party and upon finally making up an account of work done there remains a balance due of £25 which the Company say they cannot now legally pay over, the same being forfeited to the Crown by Abbott's conviction for murder. May I ask the favor of your informing me if the Crown would forego its claim under the circumstances of the case in consideration of the Creditors being the actual losers and the amount only £25. I shall be thankful for your kindness in furthering the object of my application through the Treasury Solicitor.

I have the honor to be
Sir
Your most obedient and humble servant
Wm. Hutchings

BROADMOOR CRIMINAL LUNATIC ASYLUM
Crowthorne, Berks.
28th October 1881

Reg^r No. 799
Edward Abbott
Admitted 27th Sept. 1873 from Taunton Gaol. Tried at the Wells Assizes 8th August 1873 for the murder of one of his children and sentenced to death, but afterwards reprieved in consequence of being certified to be insane.

The Under Secretary of State for the Home Department, Whitehall

Sir,
I am desired by the Council of Supervision of this asylum to forward to you, for the consideration of Secretary Sir William Vernon Harcourt, a report as to the mental and physical condition of Edward Abbott, a patient.

The papers relating to this case, 28 in number, are returned herewith.

I am,
      Sir,
      Your obedient Servant

Warwick Morehead [?]

BROADMOOR CRIMINAL LUNATIC ASYLUM
Crowthorne, Berks.
28th October 1881

We hereby certify that we have carefully examined a patient in this asylum named Edward Abbott and have now to report as follows:

He is at the present time about 49 years of age and is, by occupation, a stone mason. He was tried at Wells Assizes on the 13th of August 1873 for the murder of one of his children aged about three years, and was found guilty and was sentenced to death. He was subsequently certified to be insane under the provision of the Act 27 and 28 Victoria, and was admitted into the Broadmoor Asylum from Taunton Gaol on the 27th of September 1873.

His history shows that up to the year 1870 he had been a hard working and industrious man. In that year he lost three of his children from diphtheria within a short time of one another. Partly owing to grief at their loss and partly owing to the physical fatigue caused by nursing them during their illness, he then fell into a depressed condition of mind. His appetite and sleep became affected; and, most unwisely he had recourse to drink with the view of relieving his depression. This naturally made matters worse, and, amongst other results, it again lighted up some old mischief in the head which had been caused in his youth by a fall from a scaffold, but which had not troubled him for many years. At last a delusion took possession of his mind that people were trying to kill him, and determined, in order to avoid this fate, to commit suicide. On many occasions he wandered away from home with the intention of drowning himself. Once he threw himself into the Severn, not far from Bristol where he resided; on another occasion he wandered farther and reached London and there threw himself into the Thames, but was rescued by the police. On another occasion, feeling that he required to be taken care of, and not liking to own this to his family he walked from Bristol to Wells with the intention of asking to be taken into the County Asylum, but he did not reach Wells until a late hour in the evening, and he then felt ashamed to make his intended request, so he passed the night in a shed and walked home to Bristol the next day without having carried out his object. Still continuing to be a prey to thoughts of suicide it at last occurred to him that as he had not been successful in his attempts to drown himself he would select another method, and fearing that in case of his death his youngest and favourite child would be left unprovided for, he thought it would be better that she should die with him. He therefore killed her by cutting her throat with a razor, and, at the same time, he attempted to take his own life in the same manner. The wound that he inflicted upon himself, although severe, did not, however, prove fatal.

On his reception into this asylum, in 1873, he was found to be suffering from acute melancholia, from which he gradually recovered, and, for the last four years he has appeared to be sane, being now rational, cheerful, coherent in his conversation, and free from delusion or other indication of insanity.

His conduct has been good, and for the last two years and a half he has worked steadily and well at his trade and he has shown himself quite competent to earn his living.

His wife is very anxious that he should be discharged in order to support her and the surviving children, and, so long as he might remain in his present condition we are of the opinion that he might be at large without danger.

In the event of his being conditionally discharged his wife is quite prepared to promise to give immediate notice if she should ever observe any symptoms indicative of a relapse.

W. Orange MD
John B. Isaac MD

Broadmoor

Edward Abbott

Drs Orange and Isaac certify prisoner's
fitness for conditional discharge.

He was sentenced to death 8 years ago for the murder of his favourite child. He was no
doubt insane at the time and for the last 4 years has shown no symptoms of insanity is
steady and hard working and quite able to earn his living as a mason.
  His insanity does not seem to have been in the main constitutional, but was brought on
by distress of mind and by drinking acting on an old injury to the head by a fall from a
scaffold.
  Dr Orange says his wife will undertake to report any renewal of the symptoms, but she
is stated to be also of intemperate habits. Shall Mr Ommancy be asked whether there is
any one who is willing to give the usual written undertaking in the event of his conditional
discharge?

Yes G.L., N.M.
4 Nov 1881, Sir W.V. Harcourt

Informed the Rev. G.C. Ommancy 14.11.81

To the Right Honourable Sir William Vernon Harcourt
Secretary of State for the Home Department

The petition of the undersigned Mary Jane Abbott, on behalf of her husband, Edward
Abbott, now confined in Broadmoor Criminal Lunatic Asylum, sheweth:
  That on several occasions I have visited my husband and have found him restored to
health mentally and bodily.
  That the Medical Superintendent and other authorities of the asylum speak highly of
his conduct during the time he has been under their care and that my husband is well able
to support himself and is fit to be at liberty.
  That I will undertake and promise that if at any future time there should be any
symptoms indicative of a relapse notice shall at once be given to the proper authorities.
  I therefore, humbly beg that you will recommend to the Crown that clemency be shown
towards him and that he should be set at liberty.

March 17th 1882   [signed] Mary Jane Abbott

                                              Witness G.C. Ommancy MA
                                         Curate of Holy Nativity Church
                                            in the parish of St. John's
                                                Bedminster, Bristol.

Broadmoor Boot and Shoe Manufactory, 1903 (from *Sidelights on Convict Life*, George Griffith, 1903)

Broadmoor Asylum
Berkshire
Feb. 22, 1883

To the Right Honourable Sir William Harcourt, MP
Secretary of State
Whitehall
London

Honourable Sir,

I beg leave to present this humble petition for your consideration. This is my tenth year in Broadmoor Asylum and I have dun all that good conduct and perseverance can do to merit my discharge from here, there as been nothing the matter with my mind for over 6 years and I am fully persuaded that with proper attention there will not be again. My cure was slow but effectual and I have carefully studied the caus effect and cure of the complaint under which I suffered so long. In ignorance wich will place me in a position to detect the first symptoms should it return at eny time in the future and as this place as no terror for me I sincearly promas to surrender my self to the proper authorities at any time I should feal it approach as it dose not come on sudden and I shall allwaz be on my gard and should be only to glad to seek advise in the right direction insted of suffering as I did before. I have a good Trade in my Hands and very Industrous Habits as the meney good jobs I have dun hear will testify and I could earn a good living outside. But as one summer is worth two winters in any Trade it would be a Charity to send me gain in the Spring time if I am to go at all.

Honourable Sir I shall ever be al grateful if I am given one more chance to place my family in a respectable position again and pleas god if I do go from hear it shall be my whole study to live a sober industrous and religous life for the remainder of my days wich force of habit and self denial since I have been hear have trained me for.

So Honourable Sir hoping you will give my case your mercyful consideration
I remain your most
Humble and Obedient Survent

[signed] Edward Abbott

[Edward Abbott was discharged from Broadmoor 'recovered' 30 May 1883 (PRO, MH 94/22). Records of the Bedminster Union record that Sarah J. Abbott was given Indoor Relief *from Michaelmas 1878 to Midsummer 1880 (Som. RO, D/G/Bedminster/72). Fuller details of her relief do not survive.]*

TRANSPORTATION TO AMERICA 1615 TO 1775

In 1597 an Act of Parliament was passed authorizing the banishment of dangerous criminals from the Kingdom. The penalty for returning to this country was the death sentence. This Act was amended by further Acts in 1616, 1718 and 1784. A Privy Council Order of 1615 authorized the removal of criminals to America. Many useful artisans found guilty of criminal offences and who had been given the death sentence were granted reprieves and sent to Virginia. In most cases a condemned prisoner could request that he be transported as an alternative to hanging. Merchants were paid to transport these convicts and on arrival in America each prisoner was sold to the highest bidder. In 1716 Francis March a London merchant was paid £2 by the Treasury for each felon he transported. By 1727 the rate had risen to £5 per head. The merchants made a handsome income from the sale of these convicts on their arrival. Up to £10 a head was paid in the plantations with the added bonus of returning with cargoes of tobacco for sale in England.

Records of criminals sentenced to transportation are to be found in all Criminal Courts and many County Record Offices have *Transportation Bonds*. These are bonds of agreement binding a contractor and the master of a ship to transport a number of named convicts to America.

The Western Circuit of Assizes (covering the counties of Cornwall, Devon, Dorset, Hampshire, Somerset and Wiltshire) maintained a series of Transportation Order Books dating from 1629 to 1819 which list all persons sentenced to transportation at these Assizes. The place and date of trial is given. Among the Treasury Board Papers (PRO, Class T 1) are lists of criminals on board ships, under sentence of transportation. Much time may be needed to locate a particular criminal in these lists but such a search will not only reveal the name of the transportation ship but often give its destination in America. Similar lists are also to be found in Treasury Money Books (PRO, Class T 53). These records are therefore of especial interest to Americans tracing a transported ancestor back to Britain.

Transportation continued to the American Colonies until the War of Independence in 1776 when it has been estimated that about 40,000 convicts had been transported there. Examples of the various records which contain details of convicts sentenced to transportation to America are given in this chapter.

PRO, T 1/378
Home Circuit Lent Assizes, 1757

Hertford	1. Keziah Little to be transported for 7 years

Essex Quarter Sessions	2. Wm. Ballantyne 3. Joseph Green 4. Richard Cole 5. William Probuts 6. John Mead	for 7 years

Kent	7. Elizabeth Smithers 8. Sarah Fisher 9. John Smith 10. Thomas Fowler	
City of Canterbury	11. John Freeman 12. Margaret Winterbottom	seven years
Kent Quarter Sessions	13. Thomas Ticehurst 14. Edward Kidder	
Sussex Rye Quarter Sessions	15. William Pilcher	

Surrey	16. Thomas Dalton 17. Michael Davis 18. William Jones 19. Moses Joseph 20. Andrew Ridge	14 years
	21. William Good 22. William Hornsby	7 years

These are to certify that Mr John Stewart of London, merchant hath contracted for the transportation of the above felons and that the bonds, contracts and other instruments for their transportation are in my custody. Dated the 21st day of July 1757.

Jerome Knapp   Clerk of the Assizes for the said counties

List of convicts sentenced to transportation (PRO, T 1/378)

I do humbly certify that the within named twenty two convicts are those contained for and shipped on board the *Thetis* of which ship I am Master by order of John Stewart of London, merchant, that they may be immediately and effectually transported to some of his Majesty's Colonies or Plantations in America. Given under my hand at Gravesend 29th September 1757.

Jas. Edmonds

PRO, T 1/478/110
Home Circuit

List of convicts ordered to be transported at the Lent Assizes in the Tenth year of the Reign of George the 3rd, 1770. And also at the several Quarter Sessions hereunder mentioned.

Hertfordshire

1.	Thomas Day	Transported for Life
2.	John Day	
3.	Thomas Horner	for 21 years
4.	Silvia Hicks	for 14 years
5.	Rebecca Hicks	
6.	John Abbey	for 7 years

Essex

7.	Alley Solomon	for 14 years
8.	John Inch	for Life
9.	John Hasham	
10.	William Attridge	
11.	George Wood	for 14 years
12.	Prettyman Quanbril	
13.	John Hampil	for 14 years
14.	Henry May	
15.	Peter Paine	
16.	Jonathan Harvey	
17.	Susannah Shelley	
18.	Elizth Middleton	
19.	Ann Inch als. Lee	for 7 years
20.	Henry Evins	
21.	James Biass	
22.	James Thompson	
23.	Shadrake Pride	

Sussex

24.	Richard Peadle als. Read	for 7 years

Michaelmas Q^r Sessions

25.	Henry Kenrick	for 7 years

Surry

26.	William Simmonds	Transported for 14 years
27.	John Brown	
28.	Thomas McGennis	
29.	William Hownsome	

30.	Edward Bennett	for life
31.	John Eldrige	for 14 years
32.	Benjamin Day	for Life
33.	Acteon Greenwell	for 14 years [this entry has been crossed through]
34.	Catherine Kelly	for 7 years
35.	Anthony Jackson	
36.	John Baker	
37.	John Tresler	
38.	James Steward	for 7 years
39.	Richard Adams als. Bandy	
40.	John Pissey	
41.	Christian Anderson	
42.	John Bryan	for 3 years

Kent

43.	John Dixon	for Life
44.	Richard Trott	
45.	Francis Thornally	
46.	John Honey, Junr.	
47.	William Marlow	for 7 years
48.	William Waller	
49.	William Calvert	

Xmas Q\(^r\) Sessions
50.	William Donald	for 7 years

These are to certify all whom it may concern that John Stewart of London, merchant, hath this day contracted with me for the effectual transportation of the above named felons and that the securities for such transportation are in my Custody.
Witness my hand the twentieth day of April 1770.

Jerome Knapp,
Clerk of the Assizes
for the said counties

I do humbly certify that the above list contains the names of the convicts from Hertfordshire, Essex, Sussex, Surry and Kent which have been shipped on board the *Thornton* of which ship I am Master in order to their being immediately and effectively transported to some of His Majesty's Colonies or Plantations in America.

London 23rd April 1770
Dougal M\(^c\)Dougal

PRO, T 53/38

A true list of all the prisoners taken from the Counties of Hertford, Essex, Kent, Surry and Bucks and shipped on board the Dorsetshire, *William Loney commander for Virginia which were ship\(^d\) by Mr Jonathan Forward of London, merchant December the 25th, 1736.*

Hertford
1. William Clapham
2. William Hicks

Essex
3.	Thomas Parker als. Knight
4.	Barn^d Macquire
5.	John Thredgall
6.	Eliz. Edwick
7.	William Woodbourne
8.	John Sutton
9.	Robert Simpson
10.	Thos. Vere
11.	Jane Kelly
12.	Nathl Hardy
13.	Henry Hughes
14.	John Jones

Kent
15.	John Johnson
16.	Lawrence Mainy
17.	Richd Morse

Surry
18.	Saml Jollop
19.	Thos. Edwards
20.	Saml Jones
21.	Fra^s Cockran
22.	James Grainger
23.	Robt Graham als. Grimes
24.	Ann Bennett als. Bennell
25.	Mary Jones
26.	Edm^d Welch
27.	Eliz. Hills
28.	Phillis Travers
29.	Martha Porter

Bucks
30.	Thos. Chaplin

I humbly certify to whom it may concern that the prisoners above named being in number 30 are received by me on board the *Dorsetshire* from the keeper of the several Gaols above mentioned by order of Mr Jona^n Forward of London, merchant, to be effectually transported to Virginia, as witness my hand the 25th Dec. 1736.

Witness   W. Loney
Tho. Hodgson
James Forward

I humbly certify that Jona^n Forward of London, merchant, hath given security for the effectual transportation of the within named 29 felons from the counties of Hertford, Essex, Kent and Surry and that the said security remains in my hands.
Dated this 8th of Jany 1736

Ri. Michell
Clerk of the Assizes for the above named counties

I humbly certify that Jona^n Forward of London, merchant, hath given security for the effectual transportation of the within named Thos. Chaplin from the county of Bucks and that the s^d security remains in my hands.
Dated the 10th day of Jany 1736

R. Jenyns,
Clerk of the Assizes for the above said county

Som. RO, Q/SCt/1
Agreement of George Buck of Bideford to transport felons to America, 1735

Know all men by these Presents that George Buck of Bideford in the County of Devon Esq. am held and firmly bound to William Ring, Clerk of the Peace for the County of Somerset in Three hundred and ninety pounds of lawful money of Great Britain to be paid to the said William Ring and his successors. To which payment well and truly to be made I bind my self my Heires Executors and Administrators firmly by these presents sealed with my seal dated the Twenty Ninth day of Jany in the ninth year of the reign of our Sovereign Lord George the Second by the Grace of God of Great Britain France and Ireland King Defender of the faith and so forth and in the year of our Lord one thousand seven hundred and thirty five.

Whereas at the Assizes and General Gaol Delivery held at the City of Wells in and for the County of Somerset on Tuesday the twelfth day of August in the ninth year of the Reign of our Lord George the Second King of Great Britain and James Roberts, John Hearst, William Gray, John Francis, Robert Cook and Sarah Pearce were convicted of diverse felonies and entitled to the benefit of Clergy and ordered and adjudged to be transported to some of his Majesty's Colonies and Plantations in America for a Term of Seven years. And Whereas at the general Quarter Sessions of the Peace held at the Castle at Taunton in and for the said County on Tuesday the seventh day of October in the said ninth year of the Reign of our Sovereign Lord the King George the second Richard Elliott, Elizabeth Andley, William Puggesly, Richard Tucker, Edward Barnstable, Philip Rutter and Amy his wife were severally convicted of Felonies and entitled to the benefit of Clergy and ordered and adjudged by the said Court to be transported to some of his Majesty's Colonies and Plantations in America for the Term of seven years according to an Act of Parliament made the fourth year of the Reign of his late Majesty King George entitled an Act for the further preventing Robbery, Burglary other Felonies and for the more effectul Transportation of Felons and unlawful Exporters of wool and for declaring the Law upon some points relating to Pirates. And Whereas the said Courts in Pursuance of another Act of Parliament made in the Sixth Year of the Reign of his said late Majesty entitled an Act for the further preventing Robbery, Burglary and other Felonies and for the more effectul Transportation of Felons did nominate and appoint Sir John Trevelian Baronet, William Earle Esquire, Seargant at Law, Thomas Carew Esquire, George Speke Esquire, Joseph Holton Esq., Edward Dike Esq., and Adam Martin Esq., seven of his Majesty's Justices of the Peace of and for the said County of Somerset or any two of them to contract with any person or persons for the Further Performance of the Transportation of the said Offenders and to order and take care that such Contractor or Contractors do give sufficient Security to be taken by Bond in the Name of the Clerk of the Peace of the said County that he or they will transport or cause to be transported effectually the said Offenders conveyed to him or them by such Contract to some of his Majesty's Colonies and Plantations in America according to the direction of the said recited Acts. And Whereas the said George Speke Adair and Adam Martin have contracted with George Buck of Bideford in the County of Devon, Esq. for the effectual Transportation of the said Felons to Maryland or to some other of his Majesty's Colonies and Plantations in America for the Terms aforesaid. Now the Condition of this obligation is such that if the above bounded George Buck or his assigns do and shall within six months from the day of the date hereof transport or cause to be transported effectually the said James Roberts, John Hearst, William Gray, John Francis, Robert Cook, Sarah Pearce, Richard Elliott, Elizabeth Andley, William Puggesly, Richard Tucker, Edward Barnstable, Philip Rutter and Amy his wife to Maryland or some other of his Majesty's Colonies and Plantations in America. And do and shall procure an Authentick Certificate from the Governor or chief custom house officer of the Port or place where such offenders shall be landed in Maryland or some other of his Majesty's Colonies and Plantations in America of their respective landing there (death and the casualties of the sea excepted) And shall by any wilful default of him or his assigns suffer the said offenders or any or either of them to return from the Place where he or they are so landed as aforesaid to any part of Great Britain or Ireland for and during the said recited terms of seven years. Or if the said George Buck his heirs executors or administrators do and shall pay or cause to be paid unto the above named William King or his successors the sum of thirty pounds of lawful British money for each and every of them the said James Roberts, John Hearst, William Gray, John Francis, Robert Cook, Sarah Pearce, Richard Elliott, Elizabeth Andley, William Puggesly, Richard Tucker, Edward Barnstable, Philip Rutter and Amy his wife whom he the said George Buck or his assigns shall not transport or cause to be transported to Maryland or some other of his Majesty's Colonies and Plantations in America within six months next ensuing or whom he shall wilfully suffer to return to any port or place of Great Britain or Ireland during the said terms for which they were ordered to be transported as aforesaid then this Obligation to be void or else to be in full Force.

Sealed and delivered being first   G. Buck
duly stamped in the presence of us
    Edward Clothier
    Willm Strange

TRANSPORTATION TO AUSTRALIA, 1787 TO 1868

With America's Declaration of Independence in 1776 she was no longer a British Colony and transportation of convicts ceased. This resulted in serious over-crowding of the gaols in Britain, and in August 1776 as a 'temporary expedient' disused warships, no longer seaworthy, were moored in the Thames at Woolwich to house the convicts sentenced to transportation. These were known as *prison hulks*. Prison hulks were later used at other ports around the south coast, at Chatham, Sheerness, Portsmouth and Plymouth. It was not long before these, too, became overcrowded and much concern was voiced about the dreadful living conditions the convicts had to suffer. Parliament considered re-introducing transportation, this time to Africa, but Africa was found to be unsuitable. Eventually the Government decided to estabish a penal colony in New South Wales and the 'First Fleet' set sail 13 May 1787 carrying 586 male and 192 female convicts with free settlers, marine guard and naval personnel. This fleet arrived in January 1788 and at Sydney Cove formally declared New South Wales a British Colony on 26 January.

The Home Office was often petitioned by the dependents of criminals who had been sentenced to transportation, pleading for clemency. Even those sentenced to the minimum of five years transportation were unlikely to return home to Britain at the end of their sentence. Many convicts, particularly men, had families to support; without them wives and children became paupers. These dependents therefore petitioned the authorities in an attempt to have the sentence reduced. Others requested that the sentence be carried out in a prison in Britain; thus a convict was readily able to return to his family at the end of his term of imprisonment. There are tens of thousands of these petitions in the

Public Record Office; there is little evidence to show that many of these petitions were effective. Most appear to have been filed away without further action though some have been through the procedure of enquiring as to the convicts' behaviour in prison or on a prison hulk. This is evident by annotations such as, 'connections in prison bad'.

Researchers should note that not all those criminals given a transportation sentence were actually transported. Many, particularly those with a seven year sentence or less often served out their time in Britain in *penal servitude* (imprisonment with hard labour).

Transportation continued to Australia until 1868 when it has been estimated that about 162,000 convicts, men, women and many children, had been transported there.

Records of convicts transported to Australia, often giving the ship they sailed in, are to be found in various classes of records at the Public Record Office. These are listed in Appendix 4.12. Examples of these documents are given in this chapter. The wealth of documents giving further details of convicts before and after their arrival in Australia is covered in the author's book *Bound for Australia* published by Phillimore, 1987.

PRO, HO 31/1

Orders in Council 1782 to 1794 (containing lists of convicts for transportation)

Order in Council, 22nd December 1786
List of Female Convicts to be Transported beyond the Seas

Seven years	Elizabeth Lee alias Lees	Tried in February Sessions 1785 for London
Seven years	Dorothy Handland	do February Sessions 1786
Seven years	Ann Davis	do April Sessions 1786
Seven years	Martha Baker ⎫	do August Sessions 1786
Seven years	Ann Smith ⎭	
Seven years	Mary wife of John Carroll	do October Sessions 1786
Seven years	Elizabeth Hipsley ⎫	Tried in February Sessions 1785 for Middlesex
Seven years	Mary Morton ⎭	
Seven years	Ann Fowles ⎫	do April Sessions 1785
Seven years	Mary Pele ⎭	
Seven years	Ann George	do May Sessions 1785
Seven years	Jane Jackson	do June Sessions 1785
Seven years	Elizabeth Dalton ⎫	
Seven years	Jane Creek ⎪	
Seven years	Jane Langley ⎬	do September Sessions 1785
Seven years	Mary Finn ⎭	
Seven years	Maria Hamilton ⎫	
Seven years	Charlotte Sprigmore ⎬	do October Sessions 1785
Seven years	Mary Harrison ⎭	
Seven years	Mary Williams	do February Sessions 1786

[contd]

List of Female Convicts sentenced to be Transported beyond the Seas for the Terms in their several Sentences mentioned

Seven Years	Elizabeth Lee alias Lees	Tried in February Session 1785 for London
Seven Years	Dorothy Handland	Do. February Session 1786.
Seven Years	Ann Davis	Do. April Session 1786.
Seven Years	Martha Baker	Do. August Session 1786.
Seven Years	Ann Smith	
Seven Years	Mary, Wife of John Carroll	Do. October Session 1786.
Seven Years	Elizabeth Hipsley	Tried in February Sessions 1785 for Middlesex.
Seven Years	Mary Morton	
Seven Years	Ann Fowles	Do. April Session 1785.
Seven Years	Mary Pitt	
Seven Years	Ann George	Do. May Session 1785.
Seven Years	Jane Jackson	Do. June Session 1785.
Seven Years	Elizabeth Dallow	
Seven Years	Jane Creek	Do. September Sessions 1785.
Seven Years	Jane Langley	
Seven Years	Mary Finn	
Seven Years	Maria Hamilton	
Seven Years	Charlotte Sprigmore	Do. October Sessions 1785.
Seven Years	Mary Harrison	
Seven Years	Mary Williams	Do. February Sessions 1786.
Seven Years	Mary Parker	
Seven Years	Mary Dikes	
Seven Years	Elizabeth Cole	Do. April Sessions 1786.
Seven Years	Mary Johnson	
Seven Years	Elizabeth Lee	
Seven Years	Ann Dutton	
Seven Years	Mary Burn	

List of female convicts sentenced to transportation (PRO, HO 13/1)

Seven years	Mary Parker	
Seven years	Mary Dikes	
Seven years	Elizabeth Cole	
Seven years	Mary Johnson	do April Sessions 1786
Seven years	Elizabeth Lee	
Seven years	Ann Dutton	
Seven years	Marg^t Bunn	

PRO, HO 11/1

A List of Persons Transported as Criminals to New South Wales in the Gorgon *in the Month of February 1791 specifying the term for which each Person is Transported and the Date and Place of the Conviction.*

Names	Where Convicted	When	Term
Thomas Massey	Chester Great Sessions	3 September 1789	Life
Isaac Crosby	Chester Great Sessions	3 September 1789	7 years
John Crosby	Chester Great Sessions	3 September 1789	7 years
Charles Cavenah	Cumberland Assizes	14 August 1789	7 years
John Jones	Lancaster Quarter Sessions	16 October 1788	7 years
Henry Carter	Lancaster Quarter Sessions	22 January 1789	7 years
John Lee	Lancaster Quarter Sessions	22 January 1789	7 years
Thomas Wade	Lancaster Quarter Sessions	14 July 1789	7 years
Richard Shuttleworth	Lancaster Quarter Sessions	12 October 1789	7 years
Michael Lee	Middlesex Gaol Delivery	25 February 1789	7 years
James Cam	Norfolk Assizes	12 March 1790	Life
Royal James King	Norfolk Assizes	12 March 1790	Life
James Clarke	Salop Assizes	21 March 1789	7 years
Thomas Hill	Surrey Quarter Sessions	18 February 1789	7 years
Cornelius Caine	Surrey Assizes	3 August 1789	7 years
John Benn	Wilts Assizes	5 June 1788	7 years
William Rous	Wilts Assizes	5 June 1788	7 years
Samuel Marchment	Wilts Quarter Sessions	13 January 1789	7 years
John Cable	Wilts Assizes	7 March 1789	7 years
Thomas Moss	Wilts Assizes	7 March 1789	Life
William Smith	Wilts Assizes	25 July 1789	7 years
Michael Fishlock	Wilts Assizes	25 July 1789	7 years
John Holmes	York (City of) Assizes	21 July 1787	7 years

[contd]

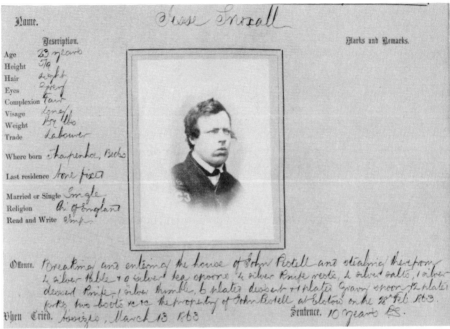

Two pages from Bedford Gaol register showing Jesse Snoxall and David Cooper who were transported to Australia. Rarely are photographs found of transported convicts (Beds. RO, QGV 10/4)

Names	Where Convicted	When	Term
Thomas Harrison	York (East Riding) Quarter Sessions	7 October 1788	7 years
Jasper Whitaker	York (Liberty of Cawood, Wistow and Otley) Quarter Sessions	8 October 1788	7 years
Arthur Robinson	York Assizes	14 March 1789	Life
James Mills	York Assizes	14 March 1789	7 years
Richard Thompson	York Assizes	14 March 1789	7 years
Charles Wright	York (West Riding) Quarter Sessions	16 July 1789	7 years
Joseph King	York Assizes	25 July 1789	7 years
George Allen	York Assizes	25 July 1789	7 years

PRO, HO 17/65

PETITION

Henry Holland aged 23
Notts Lent Assizes, March 1834
Gaoler's Report – Character Moderate
            Connexions not respectable on board the *Fortitude*

Letter to Thomas Houldsworth, Esq., MP
        Salopian Coffee House
        Charing Cross
        London

My dear Sir,
    A poor woman has brought the inclosed to me and has requested me to send it to you for presentation to Lord Melbourn. I think from circumstances which have come to my knowledge since the lad was convicted that he was not a thief, but only employed by an old hand. Will you be so kind as present this petition and with many thanks believe me,
                        Very sincerely yours
Sutton   Edward Unwin
July, 7th 1834

                            To the Right Honourable Lord
                            Viscount Melbourne, his
                            Majesty's Secretary of State
                            for the Home Department

The Humble Petition of us the undersigned Inhabitants of Mansfield in the County of Nottingham. Sheweth that at the Assizes holden for this County in March last, Henry Holland was convicted of stealing a horse belonging to Mr Waterhouse of Oldcoats, and was Sentenced to Transportation for life, and now on board the Ship *Fortitude* at Chatham.

That the Convict who is twenty three years of age, a native of this town, and whose general character we have the means of knowing, was never charged with any Crime before the one for which he is now suffering the penalty of the Law.

That his Father died some time since, leaving a widow, the Convict, and three other Children and, with the exception of the guilt of the unhappy Convict, the Family has always been industrious and strictly honest.

Your Petitioners do therefore Most Humbly and earnestly hope that your Lordship will deem the Convict as deserving of being recommended to His Most Gracious Majesty for a mitigation of his Sentence.

And your Petitioners will as in Duty Bound ever Pray

Thomas Waterhouse, the Prosecutor, Joseph Barratt, Gentleman Farmer, Henery Holland land servant with me six years and a half and I always found him a Steady Industrious youth.

[signatures]   Thos. Greenwood
               Thomas White
               Joseph Godley
               George Marriott
               Geo. Dobb
               John Woolley
               Jos^h Chadwin
               John Fowler
               John Withers
               Stephen Simpson
               James Moore Snr.
               George Pye

I hereby Certify that the above are the signatures of persons of Credit in this parish.
               Thos. L. Gushan[?] Vicar of Mansfield   July 6th, 1834
               W. Parker, Wesleyan Minister
               J. Andrews   ⎫
               T. Kirkland   ⎬ Church Wardens
               Thomas Savage   ⎫
               Richd Girdler ⎬ Overseers

I have reason to believe that the offence for which Henry Holland was convicted was a first offence and that his Character as given by the Prosecutor and Joseph Barratt was as it is stated by them.
                         Edward Unwin
                         The Convicting Magistrate

                                             Salopian Coffee House
                                             July, 8th 1834
My Lord,
    I have received this morning the petition signed by several of the inhabitants of Mansfield in favour of Henry Holland, who was convicted at the Assizes for the County of Nottingham of Horse Stealing and sentenced to Transportation for Life. I also send the remarks of the Magistrate who committed him.
              I have the honor to be
              My Lord
                 Your Lordship's
                 Most obedient Servant
                 Thomas Houldsworth
To Lord Viscount Melbourne

Mansfield
September 3rd 1834

My Lord,

I hope your Lordship will excuse the liberty I have taken of again writing to you respecting my son Henry Holland, now under sentence of transportation. O my Lord if it be possible save my child from going abroad. This was his first offence, and consider his youth. Could you see the letter of penitence he has wrought to me his afflicted mother, I believe you would as far as you could consistently with your situation shew mercy. Day and night has my tears flowed and prayers been offered to God for his being kept from going abroad. I was left with 5 children and all of them except this unfortunate youth I have brought up, and they are a credit to Society. O pity my situation and spare my child, spare my child.

My Lord I am
Your Lordship's Humble
Servant
[signed] Esther Holland

[This petition was ineffective; Henry Holland was transferred to the Bengal Merchant *which sailed for New South Wales on 27 September 1834 (PRO, HO 8/41 and HO 11/9).]*

PRO, HO 17/64

PETITION
Susan Wood aged 32
Kent Qr. Sessions at Maidstone July 1833
Stealing shoes, 7 years transportation
Gaoler's report – Character not known
Married, 4 children

Petition of Alexander Wood in behalf of his Wife Susan Wood, convicted at the last July Sessions at Maidstone in the County of Kent.

To the Right Honorable the Secretary of
State for the Home Department

Your Petitioner having plunged into the deepest affliction from a crime committed by his Wife Susan Wood now a convict in Maidstone Gaol against the Laws of her Country for having pawned goods intrusted to your Petitioner's care, in the moment of extreme distress when a Family of 4 small children aged 2 years, 4 years, 6 years and 8 years was in a state of absolute starvation and your Petitioner labouring under severe illness these circumstances drove your Petitioner's Wife, Susan Wood (now far advanced in pregnancy) in an unguarded moment to commit the Act to supply Food for her starving and destitute Family and for which she deeply and sincerely repents and which has subjected her to the severest suffering of her being torn from her infant family to undergo the penalty of 7 years Transportation.

Your Petitioner most humbly submits his distressing case to Your Lordship's most merciful consideration to be pleased to mitigate the Term of imprisonment and to restore your petitioner's Wife Susan Wood to her distressed Family and disconsolate Husband. Your Petitioner trusting that this being her first offence and committed under such peculiar and distressing circumstances, your Lordship may deem her case one entitled to Your Lordship's feeling and most merciful recommendation and restore a Wife and

Mother to her lost unhappy and distressed Family and Your Petitioner will in duty bound
ever pray.

Testimonials to Character
[signed] Chas. Stokes
[signed] Geo. Taylor   Prosecutors

[The following signatures also appear on the document:]

N.H. Almond
W. Greene
Thos. Bowen
Jn° Tick
Jane Johnson
Rich. Baxter
Wm. Newsom
H.I. Cummings
John Smith
John Esterford
Jn° Deer
Wm. Johnson
Jn. Beavis, Blackheath

John Watson, Blackheath
John Willis
Sam¹ Whittle, Blackheath
James Price, Blackheath
Stephen Price
Peter Stepney, Blackheath
H. North
Thomas Fountain
Wm. Wise
D. Smith
Frances Perkins
Henry Leach
Rich. Wild
William Perkins who is one of the Jurymen
William Fenel Palmer one of the Jurymen
Edward Parker foreman of the Jury which
                    convicted the prisoner
William Garratt
Edwd. Challis
Wm. Challis
S Larkan
Barʳ Sly
T. Dicks
Thomas Jean

We certify that Susan Wood's behaviour in prison has been particularly quiet and orderly
and to all appearances she is truly sorry for her crime.
    John Wiater   Chaplain of the Gaol
    Thomas Agar   Keeper

County Gaol
Maidstone
29th Oct. 1833

Sir,
    I beg to acknowledge the receipt of the Order for the removal of Susan Wood a
Convict under Sentence of Transportation for seven years to the Penitentiary at
Millbank. Since the return was forwarded, viz:- on the 10 of September last she was
delivered of a Male Child which is still alive. I shall therefore feel obliged by your
informing me if it is requisite that the Order should direct the admission of the Child also
as it must of necessity accompany the Prisoner its Mother for nurture.
                    I have the honor to be Sir,
                    Your most obedient
                    Humble Servant
                    Thomas Agar,   Keeper

J.H. Capper, Esq.

County Gaol
Maidstone
6th August 1836

My Lord,

I beg to state to your Lordship that Susan Wood a Convict now in this Gaol was tried at Midsummer Sessions 1833, and sentenced to Transportation for seven years and on the 26th of October following an Order was received to remove her to the Penitentiary at Millbank, but she having been delivered of a Child in the Gaol, a subsequent Order was received not to remove her till the Child was disposed of. The Prisoner having had no means of disposing of the Child, is consequently remaining in the Gaol. Should Your Lordship think proper to recommend her to the Royal Mercy, I further beg to add the Chaplain and Governor of the Prison represent that she has conducted herself with strict propriety during the whole period of her Imprisonment.

I have the honor to be,
My Lord,
Your most obedient and humble Servant
Manham   Visiting Justice

To,   The Right Honorable
The Secretary of State
Home Department

FREE PARDONED 26 Oct. 1836

PRISON REGISTERS AND PRISON HULK RECORDS

Registers of prisoners for many prisons in England and Wales are held at the Public Record Office, the Prison Service, County Record Offices and other local repositories.

The survival of these registers is somewhat random, some counties have good collections covering all the prisons which existed in the nineteenth century. Regrettably other counties have no known surviving prison registers. The information recorded in these registers varies from county to county. Some are very detailed giving not only the name and date and place of conviction of a prisoner, but also a detailed description of him. The obvious reason for such records was the means by which an escaped prisoner could be positively identified. Marks such as scars and tattoos were often recorded. The height, colour of hair and eyes was often noted, and the general build of a prisoner, if at all was described as slender or middling or stout. In rare instances the weight of a prisoner has been found. Often the place of residence of a prisoner is recorded, and very occasionally his place of birth.

The Habitual Criminals Act 1869 required that a register of all persons convicted of crime in England (Wales is not quoted) with 'evidence of identity' should be kept in London by the Commissioner of Police for the Metropolis. The expense for this was to be paid by the Treasury. The words 'evidence of identity' were construed by some to mean a photographic likeness as is shown by the following abstract dated 9 February 1870 from a Surrey Quarter Sessions Order Book[1];

---

[1] Sur. RO, QS2/1/83.

It being considered necessary with a view of establishing the means of complete identification of Criminals convicted of Offences coming within the meaning of the first Schedule of the Habitual Criminals Act 1869 that the Commissioner of Police of the Metropolis should be furnished with a Photographic Likeness of all such Offenders I am directed by Mr Secretary Bruce to request that you will move the Court of Quarter Sessions of the County of Surrey to take such measures as may be necessary for enabling the Governor of any Prison within that jurisdiction to transmit to the Commissioner of Police with the periodical returns already ordered to be supplied a photograph of each prisoner of the class referred to. Provision is made by the sixth Section of the Act for defraying any expenses incurred which Mr Bruce apprehends are not likely to be great in carrying this arrangement into effect.

We therefore find that some prison registers contain not only a physical description of the inmates but also a photograph of each prisoner. Regrettably the survival of such early photograph albums is rare.

Most male convicts, prior to transportation, were held on board prison hulks (disused ships moored at Plymouth, Portsmouth, Sheerness, Chatham and in the Thames at Woolwich). Before being transported these convicts were used to build various government establishments on shore. Except for the *Dunkirk* at Plymouth (1784 to 1791) prison hulks were never used to hold female convicts. Some convicts died on the hulks and others served out their sentences in England and were never actually transported.

Prison hulks were maintained by private contractors who were also responsible for the maintenance and care of the convicts held on board. The cost of keeping these convicts in food and clothing was paid by the Treasury and for this reason records of prison hulks can often be found among Treasury records. In order to claim payment by the Treasury the overseers of the hulks had to send in quarterly returns listing all convicts on board giving such details as age, place of conviction and date when transferred to another hulk, or sent on board a ship for transportation to Australia. Some convicts were transported to Bermuda or Gibraltar where they were also held on prison hulks. All prison hulk records are held by the Public Record Office.

The following examples of entries from prison registers and prison hulk records show the varying detail they contain. It is noted from Appendix 4.10 that there are two coterminous series of prison registers for Millbank and Pentonville. The reason for this is uncertain but it is probable that the PCOM series was kept and maintained by the prisons and the HO series recorded for Home Office use. There is a variation between these two series, the information in each supplementing the other. It is important for the researcher to refer to both and not assume that entries in each are identical. The following two entries show the differences between these registers.

PRISON REGISTERS

PRO, PCOM 2/23
Millbank Prison Register

Number		5062
Name		Thomas Groves
Size		[not entered]
Colour of Hair		Dk. Brown
Complexion		Pale
Eyes		Hazel
Marks (if any)		2 scars on right side of face. Scar on back of neck. Scar inside right leg.
State of Health		[not entered]
Age		13
Married or Single and No. of Children		Single
Read or Write		Imp [imperfect]
Religion		[not entered]
Trade or Profession		None
Convicted	When	2 January 1845
	Where	Maidstone Quarter Sessions
Specific Description of Crime		Stealing Wearing Apparel
Sentence		7 years
Received	When	17 January 1845
	From	Maidstone Gaol

Character Received with Prisoner	Once for being disorderly
When Removed and Whither	25 February 1845, Parkhurst Prison

PRO, HO 24/2
Millbank Prison Male Register

Register No.	5062
Name	Thomas Groves
Age	13
Married or Single and No. of Children	Single
Read or Write	Imp [imperfect]
Trade or Profession	Labourer
When and Where Convicted	2nd January 1845, Maidstone Sessions
Specific Description of Crime	Stealing Wearing Apparel
Sentence	Seven years
When and Whence Received	17th January 1845, Maidstone Gaol
Information Received Respecting Prisoner	Is supposed to have lived in crime about five years. Once imprisoned for having lodged in an outhouse. Was left when an infant at the door of a house in Whitechapel.
When Removed and Whither	25th February 1845 to Parkhurst Prison

The following confirms Thomas Groves' arrival at Parkhurst:

PRO, HO 24/15

Parkhurst Prison for Juvenile Offenders

Received		25 February 1845
From What Gaol		Millbank
Name		Thomas Groves
Age		13
Crime		Stealing wearing apparel
Convicted	Where	Maidstone Sessions
	When	2nd January 1845
Sentence		7 years
Married or Single		Single
Read or Write		Imp [imperfect]
Trade		Labourer
Substance of Gaoler's Report of Character		Once disorderly bad
Discharged	When	3 August 1849
	Where	Van Diemans Land

PRO, PCOM 2/59

Parkhurst Prison for Juvenile Offenders

No.	678
Name	Jabez Bolter
Age	13
Height	4′ 6″
Hair	Light

Eyes	Grey
Complexion, Visage, Appearance, Marks, &c	Fair and oval, slightly freckled, both hands much covered with worts.
Where Born	Trowbridge, Wilts
Last Place of Abode	Trowbridge
Name and Residence of Parents or Next of Kin	Mother, Elizabeth Bolter, Factory, Trowbridge
Trade	Errand Boy
Read or Write	Read imp [imperfect]
Religion	Protestant
Health	Good
Specific Description of Crime	Stealing a set of Harness
Committed	Date	28 September 1850
	Place	Devizes Prison
Conviction	Date	15 October 1850
	Place	Malbro' Sessions
[Blank]	7 [years]
Period Passed in Separate Confinement	Salisbury 1 month Millbank Prison 1 mo [month] 26 days
Character and Conduct Received with the Prisoner	Once convicted, Salisbury very good. Millbank Prison good.
Reception	Date	16 January 1851
	Place	Millbank Prison
Date and Mode of Disposal	15 January 1854, by License No. 1104

PRO, PCOM 2/350

Oxford Castle [Prison], Prisoners' Description Book

Date	2 April 1851
Name	James Ward
Age	74
Instruction	N
Height	5' 6"
Complexion	Sallow
Hair	Grey
Eyes	D. Grey
Married or Single	Married
Children	Eleven
Trade	Shoemaker
Place of Abode	Fristock [?]
By Whom Committed	B.J. Whippy, Esq.
Crime	Assault
Sentence	[blank]
When Discharged	[blank]

PRO, PCOM 2/206

Newgate Prison, Register of Prisoners

Name	William Lees
Age	33

Height	5′ 6″
Description	fresh [complexion] brown [hair] light hazel [eyes] stoutish [build] Hackney Road [address] hairdresser [trade]
When brought into Custody	26th November 1839
By Whom Committed	J. Hardwick, Esq.
Offence Charged with	For the wilful murder of Elizabeth his wife
When Tried	29th November
Before Whom	Baron Parke
Verdict	Guilty
Sentence	Death
How Disposed of	16th December, Executed

PRO, PCOM 2/343

Newcastle on Tyne Prison, Nominal Register

Number	197
When Received	1 December 1859
Name	Charles Muis
Age	11
Read or Write	No
Trade or Profession	Labourer
Place from Whence Brought	Newcastle upon Tyne

[contd]

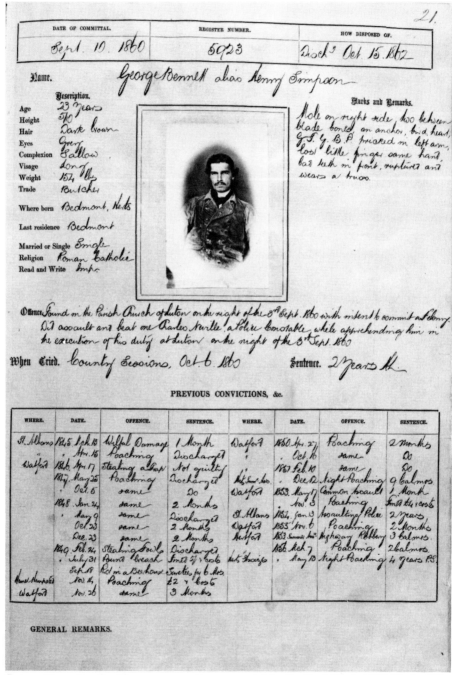

George Bennett, alias Simpson, assault on a constable. Bedford Gaol, 1860 (Beds. RO, QGV 10/4)

By Whom Committed	C.E. Ellisan, Esq.
Offence	Juvenile Offenders Act
Sentence	Committed to House of Correction to be once privately whipped 8 stripes with a birch.
Protestant	✓
Dissenter	
Roman Catholic	
When Executed or Discharged, or Where Removed. If Executed, E. If Discharged, D. If Removed. R.	D [Discharged] after receiving 8 stripes with a birch
Conduct in Prison	Good

PRO, PCOM 2/369

Portland Prison, described as 'General Records'; actually a prison register

Reg. No.	8930	
Name	George Beasley, brickmaker	
When and Whence Received	12th April 1859, Pentonville Prison. Arrived 1 class	
Information as to Age, Education, &c.	Age	34
	Married	Married, 3 children
	Progress at School	Good
	Religion	Protestant
	Wife	Frances Beasley Glosser [?] Street Birmingham
Date and Place of Conviction	16th Dec. 1857	

[contd]

Crime and Sentence	Warwick Winter Assizes
	Stealing lead fixed to a building after a previous conviction.
	4 years P.S. [Penal Servitude]

Previous Convictions	Warwick Lent Assizes '48, Aiding and Abbetting in a manslaughter.
	1 cal. month H.C. [House of Correction] [with] H.L. [Hard Labour]
	27th Oct. '53 Assault 6 weeks
	Worcester Easter Sessions 1855. Stealing fowls. 1 year H.L. [Hard Labour]
	Sept. 1857 Assault and Wilful Damage. 2 cal. months.

Period of Detention and Conduct in Other Prisons, Remarks as to Character	Months Days
	Warwick from 16th Dec. '57 Warwick till 1st Sept. '58 } 8 16 Good
	Millbank from 2nd Sept. '58 Millbank till 17th Oct. '58 } 1 16 Good
	P'ville from 18th Oct. '58 P'ville till 11th April '59 } 5 25 Good
	Portland from 12th April '59 Portland till 16th March '61 } 23 5 Exemplary
	Total 3 years 3 months

General Remarks, Removal, &c	2nd Stage Due 16th Dec. 1859
	3rd Stage Due 16th Dec. 1860

Disposal	Discharged by License 16th March 1861

PRO, PCOM 2/425

Worcester Prison, Register of Convicts

Name	Moses Heathcock
Age	41

Thomas Jenkins, refusing to enter into a recognizance. Bedford Gaol, 1863 (Beds. RO, QGV 10/4)

Height	4′ 6$\frac{3}{4}$″
Weight[2]	10 stone 12 lbs on admission 10 stone 2 lbs on discharge
Complexion	Fresh
Hair	Light Brown
Eyes	D. grey
Visage	Oval
Where born and last residence	Oldswinford, Lye

[2] It is rare to find the weight of a prisoner recorded.

[contd]

Trade or Occupation	Labourer
Married or Single	Widower
Instruction	R [read]
Religion	C.E.
Particular Marks	Nose large, several pockmarks on *do* and upper lip and chin, cut mark end of chin, flesh mole each shoulder, 2 *do* rt. side neck. Cut mark right leg. Proportionate
For What Offence Committed	Assaulting and beating his child age 6 years at Lye
When for Trial or Period of Sentence	One calendar month H.L. [Hard Labour]
Date of Admission	12th September 1874
State of Health on Admission	Good
Whether fit for Hard Labour	Yes
Whether fit for Separate Confinement	Yes
If free from Illness and fit for Removal or Discharge	Yes
Date of Discharge	10th October 1874

PRO, KB 32/23

Millbank Prison

Return of Convicts by the Governor of Millbank Penitentiary in the County of Middlesex in conformity with Act 56 Geo 3rd Cap 63 Sec 38.

Sworn 23rd January 1826

Name	John Bratt
Offence	Felony

The Court before Whom Convicted	General Qr. Sess, Old Bailey, 3rd June 1824
The Sentence of the Court	Transported for 7 years
Age	18
Bodily State	Good
Behaviour	Good

PRO, HO 23/13

Somerset County Gaol [Taunton]

Register Number	690
Name	Charles Hurtley alias Joseph Giles or Henry Palmer or Thomas Jones
Age	34
Married or Single	Married
Number of Children	2
Read or Write	both
Trade or Profession	labourer
When and Where Convicted	5th September 1864 Surrey Sessions
Specific Description of Crime	Stealing a watch from the person after a previous conviction for felony.
Sentence	10 years
When and Whence Received	27 September 1864 Horsemonger Lane Gaol [Surrey]

[contd]

Photographs of prisoners gaoled for stealing, Northampton Gaol, 1871. *From top, left to right*: Elizabeth Wade, Elizabeth Buck, John Hillyer, Ann Spencer, Daniel Bartlett, Thomas Garlick alias Thomas Westley (Northampton Police Museum)

Information Received Respecting Prisoner	Before sentenced to be transported. 1849, Jan 25, Stealing 4/-. 1 month. 1849, Aug. 17. Assault. 14 days or pay 10/- 1850, Aug. 6 Stealing from the person, 3 months. 1851, Feb. Surrey Sessions, stealing from the person. 4 months. 1853 July, Middx Sessions. Stealing from the person. 7 yrs transportation. 1857 Jan. Surrey Sessions. Attempted to Steal from the person. 12 months.

Dor. RO, NG/PRI/A2
Dorchester Prison Register

Number	30
Date	26 September 1809
By Whom Committed	Lodged in gaol for safety
When Brought to Prison	26 September
Name	Fearman le Pinn
Parish	Boulounge [France]
Trade	Carpenter
Family or Condition	Single
Age	28
Size	5′ 4″
Hair	Lt. Brown
Complexion	Fair
Eyes	Grey
Marks	Affected with Fistula [ulcers]

[contd]

Crimes	French Prisoner of War escaped from Dartmoor Gaol
Before Whom Tried	—
When Tried	—
Event of Trial	—
Sentence	—
Remissions	—
Began Work	—
How Employed	—
Left Off Work	—
How Maintained	County
Behaviour	Orderly
When Discharged	12 October 1809
No. Referred to former Committment	—
No. Referred to Prisoner's Reg.	—
Remarks	Taken off by Sgt. Morris and party of 2nd Somerset Militia to Dartmoor

CAMBRIDGE BOROUGH GAOL,

5th August 1876.

PARTICULARS of a Person convicted of a Crime specified in the 20th Section of the "Prevention of Crimes Act, 1871."

Photograph of Prisoner.

Name and Aliases .... Sophia Miller

Age on discharge 57

Height 4ft 10½in

Hair .... Grey

Eyes .... Hazel

Complexion .... Dark

Where born .... Essex

Married or Single .... Widow

Trade or Occupation .... Charwoman

Distinguishing marks ....

Previous Convictions.*

Date to be liberated ....

If the liberation is on licence, date when sentence will expire ......

Intended residence after liberation ... Green Street Cambridge

Summary Convictions.—Dates, nature of offences, and places where convicted. ....

Trials by Jury.—Dates, nature of offences, and places where convicted. ....

Names of police officers, prison warders or others who can identify and prove convictions ....

Any other particulars as to antecedents, associates, &c. ....

Address at time of apprehension ... Cambridge

Whether summarily disposed of or tried by a Jury .... Summarily

Place and date of conviction .... Cambridge ... July 25 1876

Offence for which convicted .... Larceny (2 Charges)

Term of imprisonment ....

If sentenced to Police Supervision—term.

* State whether such convictions were, or were not, proved at last trial by Jury.

Sophia Miller, 2 charges of larceny, 14 days hard labour for each offence, Cambridge Gaol, 1876 (PRO, PCOM 2/300)

Photographs of prisoners in Pentonville Prison, 1882. *From top, left to right*: H 1067, John Shaw, forgery; H 1068 Henry Swinnerton, wounding with intent; H 1070, Arthur Hackett, rape; H 1071, D. Cartwright, rape; H 1072, Charles Rowley, rape; H 1073, John Powell, arson; H 1074, Sampson Waldron, shooting with intent; H 1075, George Moore, rape; H 1077, James Murphy (further details not found). PRO, PCOM 2/103

BIRMINGHAM BOROUGH PRISON,

COUNTY OF WARWICK.

2ᵈ September 187*1*

PARTICULARS of a Person convicted of an offence specified in the First Schedule of
Habitual Criminals Act, 1869, and who will be liberated from this Gaol within
seven days from the date hereof, either on expiration of sentence, or Licence from
Secretary of State.

Name ... ...   *52 Sarah Davis*

and

Aliases ... ...   *Ann Davis*

PHOTOGRAPH OF PRISONER.

Age (on discharge)... ... ...   *20 Years*

Height *5   0*

Hair... ... ...   *Black*

Eyes... ... ...   *Brown*

Complexion ... ...   *Dark*

Where Born... ... ...

Married or Single ... ...   *Single*

Trade or Occupation ... ...   *No Trade*

Any other distinguishing mark *Scars on forehead*
on nose and near right Eye

Address at time of apprehension *12 Ct Bartholomew St Birm*

Whether summarily disposed of or tried by Jury ...   *Tried by Jury*

Place and date of conviction *Borough Sessions 11th January 1871*

Offence for which convicted *Larceny from the Person*

Sentence ... ...   *8 Calendar Months H.L.*

Sarah Davis, larceny. Birmingham Borough Prison, 1871 (PRO, PCOM 2/430)

PRO, PCOM 2/404
Register of Habitual Criminals

Office Register No.	C 5938
Name and Alias	BOWSKILL Mary alias CLARKE
Age	38
Height	5' 4"
Hair	dk. brown
Eyes	br.
Face	dk.
Trade or occupation	—
Prison from which Liberated and date of Liberation	Wakefield 17–11–64
Offence for Which Convicted	larceny simple
Sentence	6 months
Supervision	—
Intended Residence after Liberated	Sheffield
Marks and Remarks	Scar on neck

The following is a transcript of the first page of the earliest discovered list of convicts on the first two prison hulks:[3]

---

[3] All historical literature quotes the *Censor* and *Justitia* as being the first hulks at Woolwich. At the time of going to press the author discovered a list of convicts on board the *Tayloe* in December 1777 (PRO, T1/521).

TREASURY BOARD PAPERS

PRO, T 1/539 Part 2

Report of convicts ordered to hard labour and now on board the Censor *and* Justitia *Hulks from 6th January 1778 to 11th February 1778.*

No.	Name	Age	Date of the Order of Court and Where From	Term Ordered for Labour	
1	John Palmer	24	Middlesex 7th August 1776	3 years	
2	Daniel Daniels	20		3	
3	John Goss	15	London 23rd August 1776	3	
4	Thomas Oliver	22		3	
5	William Reynolds	22		3	Pardoned
6	Jeffrey Ashman	16	Hicks Hall 22nd July 1776		
7	John Hodgkinson	45		3	
8	Patrick Cockrell	40		3	
9	Robert Fludge	18		3	
10	John Jenkins	25	Guildford 29th August 1776	3	
11	John Pool	19		3	Pardoned
12	John Hall	18		3	
13	John M\^{c\}Neal	24	Chelmsford 29th August 1776	10	Pardoned
14	Richard Hatch	21		10	
15	Owen Povey	25	Horsham 29th August 1776	10	
16	Silas Wadman	26	Sarum 29th July 1776	3	
17	Samuel Shoare	19		3	
18	Thomas Collins	35	Bridgewater 16th August 1776	3	
19	John Wrightson	18	York 29th July 1776	4	
20	James Fum	20		4	
21	James Middleton	28		5	
22	William Gifford	23	Devon 12th September 1776	3	
23	John Horton	30	Hicks Hall 18th September 1776	3	
24	William Ellis	23		3	
25	Michael Dulphy	34		5	
26	Richard Mayes	20	Norfolk 18th September 1776	3	
27	John Buchanan	32	Westmoreland 16th October 1776	3	
28	John Wilson	27	Lancaster 17th August 1776	3	
29	Robert Robinson	23	Nottingham 16th October 1776	3	
30	Edward Fines	41	Westminster 31st October 1776	3	
31	James Burch	14		3	
32	John Sram	20		3	
33	Mandle Woolfe	19		3	
34	John Smith	19	London 28th October 1776	3	
35	Levy Solomons	–		3	
36	Tho. Rowney alias Rowley			3	
37	William Clark	22	Middlesex 8th October 1776	3	
38	John Davis etc., etc.	20		3	

Total 369
Pardoned 9
Died on board the *Censor* 4
Died on board the *Justitia* 7
Now on board 349

of which there are on the *Justitia*   118
On board the *Censor*   231
As per Return to the Secretary of State   349

Received since the above return was made out:
From Chester   1
From Maidstone   5
From Morpeth   2

The convicts in the within return have been since the last report constantly employed when health and weather permitted, in raising gravel from Barking and Woolwich Shoals, in wheeling the same to cover and raise the surface of the ground and contiguous to a new Proof Butt of a large extent which they are now erecting, and in making a wide and deep entrenchment round the additional part of the Warren, under the direction of the Board of Ordnance.

I have much satisfaction in saying that the ships are now very healthy, every means in my power has been, and shall be, used to promote so desirable an end having ever considered the same as a principal object of my duty.

Duncan Campbell

PRO, T 1/680

Report of the Convicts under Sentence of Transportation removed from sundry Gaols by Command of His Majesty on board the Lion *Hulk at Portsmouth from 12th Jany to the 12th April 1790.*

Number	128
Name	Robert Silver[4]
Age	35
When and Where Convicted	Reading Quarter Sessions 17 April 1787
Sentence	Colonies 7 years

The Convicts have been employed when health and weather permitted by instructions from Mr Duncan Campbell and in compliance with the desire of His Grace The Duke of Richmond, Master General of the Ordnance, in alterations and improvements making on the Weevil lines near Gosport and in other occasional works under the direction of the Engineers appointed to superintend the Fortifications at that place.

---

[4] Full details of Robert Silver's offence and court case are given in Chapter 4.

PRO, T 38/329

An Account of Sick Convicts belonging to the Retribution *Hulk sent to and from the* Savage *hospital ship from the 1st July to the 30th September 1811 inclusive.*

Entry	Name	When Died	When Discharged	Days Victualled
1811 July 1st	Joseph Stallard			92
	Timothy Boswell			92
	Richd. Morgan			92
	Daniel Aldridge			92
	Stephen Harvey		July 18th	18
	Wm. Clark			92
	John Green			92
	Ralp^h Heathcote			92
	Thomas Wilson			92
	John Mason			92
	John Brewston		Sept 24th	86
	Edward Simons			92
	John Alsher			92
	Henry Streder			92
	James Williams			92
	John Conway		Aug. 6th	37
	Joseph Towers		July 18th	18
	Watkin Roberts		July 11th	11
	John Smart			92
	Wm. Foultes		July 2nd	2
	John Brown		July 11th	11
	Richard Cole		July 16th	16
	James Buchanan	30th Sept		92
	Benjn. Guillim		July 1st	1
July 2nd	Thomas White		July 27th	26
July 3rd	Patrick Brown		July 19th	17
July 7th	George Stanley		——	86
July 12th	John Rack		July 30th	19
July 12th	John Colston		——	81
July 12th	Isaac Bowers		Sept 1st	52
July 14th	Geo. Thorne		July 20th	7
July 16th	Edward Jones		July 31st	16
July 21st	Thomas Price	July 21st		1
July 25th	Henry Price		Aug. 16th	26
July 30th	John Goodwin		Aug. 13th	15
July 30th	Thos. Myery etc., etc.		——	63

PRISON HULK RECORDS

PRO, ADM 6/418
Cumberland *prison hulk*

No.		1469
Name		Joseph Clayton alias Cary
Age		21
Offence		Stealing an ass
Conviction	When	27 June 1831
	Where	Nottingham
Sentence		7 years
Character from Gaoler		Character bad. Been convicted before. Connexions indifferent
[blank]		N.S.W. 21 April 1832 per *Clyde*
Where Born	Town	Nottingham
	County	Nottingham
Hair		Dark brown
Eyes		Black
Eye Brows and lashes		Dark
Nose		Com[5]
Mouth		Com
Complexion		Dark
Visage		Round

[5] *Common*, in this context presumably meaning average.

Make	Stout
Married or Single	Single
Height	5' 5½"
Read or Write	Neither
Trade or Profession	Sweep
Remarks	On his breast *Do not dispute a Thief if he steal to satisfy his soul when hungry.* Printed right hand *GRN* a star *JCN.* Ring on the 1st, 2nd and 4th fingers. Back of the left hand Rope and Anchor. Ring on the 2nd and 3rd finger and other marks on both arms.
Address	Parents live at 17 Clare Street, Nottingham.

PRO, PCOM 2/131

Defence *prison hulk*

Register Number	557
Name	Dennis Trenfield
Age	54
Married or Single Number of Children	M 1
Read or Write	Sup [superior]
Trade or Occupation	Attorney at Law
Crime, date and place of conviction	Forgery, 31 March 1858 Gloucester Ass.
Sentence	10 P.S. [10 years penal servitude]
Date and Place of Committal	29 March 1858, Winchcombe

[contd]

Places and Periods of Separate Confinement	where	Millbank
	months	4.20
Total of Separate Confinement		4.20
Character and Conduct of Prisoner since Conviction		Gaol Good Millbank Good Not Classed from Sep.
Residence of Convict's Family or Next of Kin		Wife Elizabeth Trenfield Mr John Trenfield, solicitor, Chipping Sodbury
Information relative to Prisoner's Conviction and Character		No previous convictions Complexion fresh Hair grey Eyes grey Height 5′ 10″ Tall and stout and respectable looking
Religion		C.E.
Dates of Reception in different prisons		Millbank 29 April 1858 Lewes 18 Sept. 1858
Final Disposal		Dartmoor, 13 July 1859
Remarks		Right side of neck severely injured from pistol shot attempting self destruction.

PRO, HO 8/74

Leviathan *prison hulk, Quarterly Returns*

Number		947
Name		Edward Russel
Age		14
Offence		Stealing 20 lbs Lead
Convicted	Where	Taunton
	When	28 March 1842
Sentence		7 years
Remarks		Parkhurst 14 November 1842

Number		7334
Name		John Whately
Age		24
Offence		Stealing fowls
Convicted	Where	Birmingham
	When	29 June 1841
Sentence		7 years
Remarks		Died 10 December [1842]

PRO, T 38/329

Retribution *Prison Hulk Quarterly Returns*

An Account of the Convicts Victualled on board the *Retribution* Hulk off Woolwich from July 1st to the 30th of September 1811 inclusive.

No.	Entry	From Whence	Name	P DD D or E	When	No. of Days Victualled	Jackets	Waistcoats	Breeches	Stockings	Shirts	Handkerchiefs	Shoes	Hats	Beds	Blankets	Irons
1	July 1st	Newgate	Wm. Williams			92											
2		Northampton	Timothy Boswell			92			1		1						
3		Gloster	John Ferrity			92		1	1	1							
4		Ipswich	Benj. W. Gunn	P	27th Sept.	89	1		1	1	1						
5		Lancaster	Abm. Bradsley	D	11th Aug.	42			1	1	1	1	1	1			
6		Canterbury	Wm. Andrews			92											
7		do	Arth. Hubbard			92	1				1						
8		Newgate	Danl Sutherland	D	12th Sept.	74	1	1	1	1	1	1	1	1			
9		do	Jno. Mason als. Morton			92	1			1		1					
10		Surry	N. Mittobriffer			92				1			1				
11		Newgate	Jos. Asland			92	1		1		1	1		1			
12		do	Thos. Harris			92					1						
13		do	Jas. Reed			92					1		1				
14		do	Jno. Arnold			92					1		1				

No.	Place	Name											
15	do	Ephm. Furmidge	92	1					1		1		1
16	do	Robt. Harrison	92						1		1		
17	Chatham	Jas. Bentley	92					1					
18	Newgate	Jno. Williams	92					1					
19	do	Jno. Murphy	92	1			1	1		1		1	1
20	do	M. als. Js. Husband	92	1	1			1		1		1	
21	do	Jos. Towers	92					1					
22	Lincoln	Thos. Booth	92	1		1	1	1	1	1		1	1
23	do	Jonᵗʰⁿ Fletcher	92		1		1	1	1	1		1	
24	Ailsbury	Danˡ Rowe	92						1				
25	Newgate	Edwᵈ Gardner	92	1	1	1	1	1	1	1		1	1
26	do	Wm Taylor	92					1		1			
27	do	Jno. Keene	92		1	1	1	1	1	1		1	1
28	Surry	Jas. Bartlett	92					1		1			1
29	Isle of Ely	Jno. Johnson	92						1	1		1	1
30	Gloster	Jno. Hathway	92			1		1		1		1	
31	do	Chas. Ballinger	92			1		1		1			
32	Reading	Wm. Rogers	92					1		1			1

P   Pardoned
DD Discharged dead
D   Discharged
E   Escaped

etc., etc.

PRO, HO 9/12

Ganymede *prison hulk*

No.	Prisoner's Name	Age	Crime	Convicted		Sentence
				Where	When	
	Received from the Gaol at Saffron Walden 30th Oct. 1837					
4611	James Lucas	17	Stg. 6 Napkins	Saffron Walden	6 July 1837	7 years
	Received from the Gaol at Oxford 30th Oct. 1837					
4612	William Guy	37	Stg. a shawl	Oxford	16 Oct. 1837	7 years
4613	Henry Harrison	33	Stg. a gander	Oxford	16 Oct. 1837	7 years
	Received from the Gaol at Oakam 31st Oct. 1837					
4614	Robert Seaton	35	Stg. a watch	Oakam	19 Oct. 1837	7 years
	Received from the Gaol at Gt. Stukeley 31st Oct. 1837					
4615	Thomas Barlow	19	Stg. a silk handerchief from the person	Huntingdon	16 Oct. 1837	7 years
	Received from the Gaol at Derby 1st Nov. 1837					
4616	William Petts	21	Burglary	Derby	25 July 1837	7 years
4617	Jeffery Watson	47	Sheepstealing	Derby	17 Oct. 1837	15 years
4618	William Fisher	41	Housebreaking	Derby	17 Oct. 1837	Life
4619	John Horman	20	Robbery	Derby	17 Oct. 1837	7 years
	Received from the Gaol at Gloucester 1st Nov. 1837					
4623	Robert Saunders	40	Housebreaking	Gloucester	17 Oct. 1837	15 years
4624	Allan Keene	18	Stg. in a dwelling House	Gloucester	17 Oct. 1837	10 years
4625	John Smith	30	Stg. Brushes	Gloucester	17 Oct. 1837	7 years
	Received from the Gaol at Worcester 16th Oct. 1837					
4628	John Willis	26	Stg. 4 Elm Boards	Worcester	16 Oct. 1837	7 years
4629	James Soley	23	Embezzlement	Worcester	16 Oct. 1837	14 years
	Received from the Gaol at Hertford 1st Nov. 1837					
4630	William Strattan etc., etc.	25	Housebreaking	Hertford	16 Oct. 1837	14 years

Married or Single	Read or Write	Trade	Gaoler's Report	How Disposed of
Single	Read	Hawker	4 times in prison before for poaching and theft	V.D. Land per *Coromandel* 15 June 1838
Single	Both	Labourer	Char. and Conn^{ns} Bad. Transported before	N.S. Wales per *Lord Lyndock* 28 Mar. 1838
Wife 3 chil.	Both	Gardener	2nd conviction. Char. and conn^{ns} Bad	V.D. Land per *Coromandel* 15 June 1838
Single	Both	Labourer	Twice convicted before. Char. and conn^{ns} Bad	N.S. Wales per *Theresa* 29 Sept 1838
Single	Neither	Hawker & fidler	Char. and conn^{ns} Bad	V.D. Land per *Coromandel* 15 June 1838
Wife 1 child	Neither	Labourer	Not known	N.S. Wales per *Lord Lyndock* 28 Mar. 1838
Wife	Read	Labourer	Not known	N.S. Wales per *Lord Lyndock* 28 Mar. 1838
Wife 8 chil.	Both	Labourer	2nd conviction. Is a very bad char. A notorious housebreaker. Conn^{ns} bad.	N.S. Wales per *Lord Lyndock* 28 Mar. 1838
Single	Both	Cutler	Not known	N.S. Wales per *Lord Lyndock* 28 Mar. 1838
Wife 1 child	Read	Labourer	Char. Bad. Convicted before. Conn^{ns} disreputable	N.S. Wales per *Lord Lyndock* 28 Mar. 1838
Single	Both	Gent^s. Servant	Bad habits. Good disposition	N.S. Wales per *Lord Lyndock* 28 Mar. 1838
Single	Read	Gent^s. Servant and Hawker	Character Bad	V.D. Land per *Coromandel* 15 June 1838
Wife 1 child	Read	Labourer & Brewer	2nd conviction. Char. Bad. Conn^{ns} poor but respectable	V.D. Land per *Coromandel* 15 June 1838
Single	Both	Butcher	Capitally convicted before. Char. Bad. Industrious conn^{ns}. Poor but respectable	N.S. Wales per *Lord Lyndock* 28 Mar. 1838
Single	Neither	Labourer	3rd conviction. Char. Bad. Conn^{ns} indifferent	N.S. Wales per *Lord Lyndock* 28 Mar. 1838

PRO, HO 7/3

Coromandel *Convict Hulk at Bermuda*

Whence and When Received	No. on *Dolphin's* Book	Name	Age	Offence	Where and When Convicted
Dolphin	2520	Jos. Gardiner	23	Stlg from the person	Bedford 26th July 1827
	2568	Wm. Yeatman	25	House brkg.	Aylesbury 23rd July 1827
	2569	Wm. Mendy	30	Horse stlg.	Aylesbury 23rd July 1827
	2570	Thos. King	27	Stlg. Calf	Aylesbury 23rd July 1827
	2571	Jos. King	31	do	Aylesbury 23rd July 1827
	2572	Job Cock	20	Burglary	Aylesbury 23rd July 1827
	2573	Jos. Bedford	26	Burglary	Aylesbury 23rd July 1827
	2580	Wm. Breffitt	48	Horse Stlg.	Old Bailey 12th July 1827
	2581	Jas. Taylor	16	[6]Ly. in a dwg hse	Old Bailey 12th July 1827
	2582	Jno. Byford Smith	21	Burglary	Old Bailey 12th July 1827
	2583	Jno. Wright	20	Burglary	Old Bailey 12th July 1827
	2584	Jos. Wells	18	Burglary	Old Bailey 12th July 1827
	2585	Thos. Wilson	17	Highway Robbery	Old Bailey 12th July 1827
	2586	Jno. Haggerty	16	Highway Robbery	Old Bailey 12th July 1827
	2587	Jno. Williams	20	Highway Robbery	Old Bailey 12th July 1827
	2588	Jas. Brekin etc., etc.	18	Ly. in a dwg hse	Old Bailey 12th July 1827

[6] Larceny.

Sentence	Character		Married or Single	Trade	How Disposed of
	From Gaoler	From *Dolphin*			
Life	In custody before for stealing wood Orderly in Gaol	Orderly	Single	Labourer	Died 20 Jany. 1828
Life	Not known	Orderly	Single	Labourer	
Life	Not known	Orderly	Wife & child	Labourer	
Life	Not known	Orderly	Wife & 3 chil.	Labourer	
Life	Not known	Orderly	Wife & 4 chil.	Labourer	Died 8 March 1829
Life	Not known	Orderly	Single	Labourer	
Life	Not known	Orderly	Single	Labourer	
Life	Here before very orderly	Orderly	Wife & 7 chil.	Labourer	
Life	Here before very orderly	Orderly	Single	Labourer	
Life	Here before very orderly	Orderly	Single	Labourer	
Life	Orderly in Prison	Orderly	Single	Labourer	
Life	Orderly in Prison	Orderly	Single	Labourer	
Life	Orderly in prison	Orderly	Single	Labourer	
Life	Orderly in Prison	Orderly	Single	Dyer	
Life	Orderly in Prison	Orderly	Single	Mariner	Transferred to *Dromedary* 3 July 1828
Life	Orderly in Prison	Orderly	Single	Wire-maker	

PRISON BOOKS AND JOURNALS

In addition to the prison registers of criminals given in Chapter 14 further prison material survives in both the Public Record Office and County Record Offices. This includes Governors' Journals, Surgeons' Orders, Visitors' Books, Chaplains' Journals, Judges' Orders, Pardons, and Letter Books. These can shed much light on the everyday affairs of the gaols and often refer to individual prisoners.

Som. RO, Q/AG (W) 1/1
Wilton Gaol, Taunton

A letter [undated] written into the Gaol Return Book (1809 to 1815)

Dear Sir,

Doctor Blake on the 7th instant by an entry in the Magistrate's Visiting Book ordered me in my next report to you to notice particularly the case of Richard Gibbs who was committed by him to my custody on the 16th Sept last as a deserter from the first Regt. of Royal Scots on his own confession on the 27th of the same month unfortunately met with a severe accident on having scalded his foot from boiling water just on a wound which he met with some years ago as he say in the East Indies. Two or three days after his committal Mr Richardson called at the Gaol to take his examination allowing that some mistake has been made in the Report to the War Office at which time I observed that it would be as well to notice in the second Report about to be made the accident that had befallen him which would prevent his being removed for some time. He has quite got the better of the scald but the wound still continue very bad and I give you Sir an direct a copy of the entry made by Mr Liddon in his book, Richard Gibbs has a forel ulser on the enstep of the right foot. I see no probability of it getting well enough to enable him to join his Regiment. Without some application is made to the War Office I fear Sir it is not unlikely that he will remain with me for life if he is to remain till his wound is perfectly recovered, I therefore must Sir the very great inconvenience and annoyance will be got rid of by a timely report of his case to the War Office. I have Sir to return you many thanks for your very condescending and kind advice confirmed in your favour of the 9th instant and which it shall be always my duty to indeavour to revue in the discharges of my duties, Doctor Blake approve very much of your directions respecting the mangle which I have no doubt to be able fully to carry into execution by the sessions; it is already got considerable forward. Nott says there are thirty mangles of his work at Bath. The store for the laundery I shall get fixt Monday, Mr Dollard is getting on perty nice. I have had a letter from Mr Price concerning the locks and iron gate and he say that I shall have them in a fortnight time.

I am your humble serv^t

Alex^r Gane, Keeper.

PRO, PCOM 2/442

Lancaster Prison, Governor's Journal

22nd June 1816

Robert Lyall complained that John Jackson had struck him a violent blow in the face last evening without any provocation. Jackson had nothing to urge in his defence save drunkeness; this excuse of course could not be tolerated. Locked up Jackson in the strong room.

Clarkson complained that John Mort instead of sweeping up the room with the brush given him for that purpose had dipped it in water and then put it up the chimney and after that daubed the floor with it. In this situation I found the room although Clarkson had given him a mop and bucket to wash the room several hours before. When I entered the room he was whistling and singing. I asked him why he had not cleaned the room. Said he was not well. Asked him what was the matter. Said he had the rheumatism. I informed him he should have no more victuals until he cleaned it. He insolently told me he could do without, and I had better take a bit of bread from him he now had and he never wished to see my face again. I told him I would conquer him before he left the prison. He said much which I did not hear and then began to whistle and sing setting me at defiance.

I am sorry the degree of separation from his fellow prisoners this man has undergone seems only to have increased his audacity. I shall therefore remove him into the solitary cells and try the effect of perfect solitude. I think a more hardened wretch I never had to deal with. At present Mort and Lee can talk to each other and I am afraid only encourage each other to continue in this refractory state. I must of necessity persevere otherwise my authority will be set at nought.

23rd June 1816

Removed Mort into the third solitary cell during the day and into the first at night. Mort refused to go to the cell until I told him I would make him. Told me he would let me know what he was locked up for before a week was over. He would have a magistrate up or he would make all the town hear by calling out murder. Told him these threats would not prevent me persevering. Told him whenever I came to see him I should see a man. I fancy by this expression he meant he would not submit. In the evening he told Clarkson and Peter that cross measures would never conquer him.

24th June 1816

Received information that the female prisoners in the High Room intended to escape. Halliswell left her own room, Dungeon Towers, and was gone to bed to Margaret Pollitt. Removed Halliwell and Pollitt into cell No. 1.

25th June 1816

Searched all the prisoners in the High Room. Found concealed upon Susan Brown a pair of tongs, a smoothing iron, three case knives, a fork, a flint and steel and candles made of weft and fat. Implements intended to escape with. Called Sarah Halliwell into the office and questioned her on this subject. When she confessed all the plot said she was not informed of it until yesterday and Pollitt and Brown were the principals. The plan was to cut a hole through the roof and then let themselves down by their blankets. I really think the plan laid is practicable. Have therefore removed all the convicts under sentence of transportation from this part of the prison and put in their place the elderly women. Put Susan Brown in irons as an example to the rest having no vacant cell and as I must of necessity punish some I think it better to select her having the implements before mentioned upon her.

Visited all the prisoners' rooms, wards, &c., also the workshops and attended the locking up. Visited Mort and Lee still obstinate, found Mort singing. Refuses to carry his chamber pot into his cell and makes water against the door.

26th June 1816

Thomas Clarkson and Thomas Pennington set off with the under written transports for the Hulks at Portmouth and Sheerness.

William Duncan			Willm. Gribbin	
Joseph Green			John Green	
Mich. Mar	Sheerness		Robert Roberts	Portsmouth
Jas. Ogden			and	
			Peter Shavlock	

PRO, PCOM 2/140
Westminster Penitentiary Burials, Millbank

Burials in the Burial Ground of the Penitentiary, Millbank, in the parish of St John the Evangelist, Westminster, in the County of Middlesex.

Name	Abode	When Buried	Age	By Whom the Ceremony was Performed
Ann Stubbs	A Convict in the Penitentiary	2nd April 1817	26	Samuel Bennett Chaplain
Jane Smith	A Convict in the Penitentiary	19	10th April 1817	Samuel Bennett Chaplain
Thomas Penny	Late a Turnkey in the Pen^y and formerly resident at Margate in Kent	16th April 1817	41	Samuel Bennett Chaplain
Mary Wells	A Convict in the Penitentiary	6th Nov. 1817	19	Samuel Bennett Chaplain

Name	Abode	When Buried	Age	By Whom the Ceremony was Performed
Henry Scott	A Convict in the Penitentiary	27th Dec. 1817	14	Samuel Bennett Chaplain
Catherine Winter	A Convict in the Penitentiary	21st Feb. 1818	23	Samuel Bennett Chaplain
Mary Ann Ruffitt	A Convict in the Penitentiary	31st May 1818	28	Samuel Bennett Chaplain
Robert Swinton	A Convict in the Penitentiary	4th June 1818	15	Samuel Bennett Chaplain
Robert Hiron	An inmate in the Porter's Lodge at the Pen^y Millbank	5th Dec. 1818	79	Samuel Bennett Chaplain
William Masters Nichols	A Convict in the Pen^y and late a clerk in the House of Mortlock & Co., bankers, Cambridge	9th April 1819	21	Samuel Bennett Chaplain
Mary Pate	A Convict in the Penitentiary	28th April 1819	28	Samuel Bennett Chaplain
John Smith	Formerly of Park Lane, Middx and late a Patrole in Pen^y Millbank	30th July 1819	42	The Rev. Isaac Mann, Rector of Kingston, Jamaica
Harriet Funnell	A Convict in the Penitentiary	23rd Jan. 1820	15	Samuel Bennett Chaplain
Elizabeth Stubbs etc., etc.	A Convict in the Penitentiary	16th March 1820	30	Samuel Bennett Chaplain

PRO, PCOM 2/349

Oxford Prison, Gaoler's Journal

23 April 1825

William Kurn a prisoner under sentence of imprisonment for three years endeavoured to make his escape by letting himself down by a rope from the top of the Old Tower but was seen by a person in the employ of Mr Hall who gave an alarm and he was secured. I have found it necessary to place him in irons and confine him in Yard No. 4 as a further means of security.

27 March 1827

Removed the following convicts to the *Leviathan* Hulk lying in Portsmouth Harbour pursuant to their sentences of transportation for seven years each.
Viz:-   Thomas Hammerstone, Solomon Oliver, Joshua Oliver, John Gardner, William Barrett, James Hull (desperate character), Joseph Nutt, Richard Wright, and William Carrick.

PRO, PCOM 2/160

Newgate Prison, Chaplain's, Surgeon's and Sheriff's Visits and Inspections

16 December 1839

Monday   Execution of William Lees for the murder of his wife Sarah Lees

I reached the gaol this morning about ½ past 6, proceeded immediately to the ward where the unhappy convict Lees has been confined ever since his committal. He declared that he was glad to see me. I reminded him that fatal morning had at length arrived and that he had only an hour and half to live. I then asked him whether the prospect of death under such ignominious circumstances did not alarm him. He replied 'No'. Death had no terror to him as far as the body was concerned; it was indeed awful to enter eternity, but he hoped Christ would pardon him all his sins, especially this last wicked act of killing his wife unprepared as she must have been to leave the world. His ground of hope that he should be forgiven his iniquities he stated to be that Christ had come into the world to save such worthless, wretched sinners as himself. From the time I left him last night until near 2 this morning he informed me that he had been writing letters to his mother, brother, sister, the Sheriff and myself. The letter addressed to me I immediately put in my pocket and the other letters the Sheriff had promised to deliver to his relatives. After he ceased writing he employed another hour in reading the Bible and repeating that part of Jesus's manual of devotion appropriated to a condemned malifactor and then retired about 3 o'clock. His demeanor this morning was remarkably calm and collected. His spirit seemed impressed with the solemnity of the thought that there was only a step between him and death. After prayer, reading the 51st Psalm and commenting thereon during which he made some very appropriate applications of the words of David to his own case, the sacrament was administered, Mr Sheriff Whalton joining with us in partaking of the sacred elements. Lees appeared to engage in the solemnity with understanding and feeling. A little before 8 Mr Sheriff Evans the Under Sheriff, Mr Commissioner Harvey with the executioner arrived. He walked to the scaffold with a firm and steady step, evidently engaged in prayer. The bolt was quickly withdrawn and the soul of the unhappy man entered into the presence of that Judge, who alone can search the heart and decide whether the poor culprit's profession of penitence and faith were sincere or not.

James Carver M.A.

1824

January 6 Confined William Coleman, a Felon in Ward N° 3, to his room, for fighting with John Ellson a Pris.' in the same class =

7 W.'' Coleman having expressed sorrow for his offence and promised to conduct himself well in future, is restored to his liberty, as usual!

7 John Ellson having been guilty of gross misconduct in fighting with the above named W.'' Coleman, and also by threatening to strike me, I laid the circumstances of the case before Fra.' Ireland Esq.' one of the Visiting Justices, who order'd "that the" "said John Ellson be confined in a Solitary Cell" "for four days and to be kept on bread & water"

9th John Ellson having acknowledged his fault and promised not to offend again, is returned to his work =

10th   State of the Gaol

1.st Hard. For Trial at the Sessions   8
2.nd For Trial at the Assizes   16
3.d For Poaching 25. Felony 10 =   35
4.th Boys for Trial at the Assizes   3
5.th Misdemeanors. Convicted   20
6.th For the Sessions (Misdemeanors)   22
     Spike Had (Bankrupt)   1
     Female for Imprisonment   1
     Debtors   9
                                                      115

                    Tho.' Dilly
                         , Gov.''

Entry from Oxford Prison Gaoler's Journal, 1824 (PRO, PCOM 2/349)

Powys RO, Brecon Q/AG

Brecon County Gaol, Chaplain's Journal

June 15th 1842

Read prayers in the Chapel.
Visited J. Williams in the Infirmary. His illness seems to arise from grief. His wife was buried a few days previously to his committal.
Saw and admonished James Brute before his discharge.

June 18th

Visited the Gaol Department and conversed with each apart from the other prisoners. Read and conversed with Jonathan Williams in the Infirmary and with the Debtors.

June 27th

Visited Wm. Hargest in the Infirmary. Read to the Prisoners in the Gaol Department. Admonished William Humphreys before he was discharged.

June 29th

Read to the prisoners in the Gaol Department, to Wm. Hargest in the Infirmary and admonished Sarah Saunders before her discharge.

June 30th

Visited Rees Protheroe in Solitary Confinement, Wm. Hargest in the Infirmary, and the Gaol Department.

July 1st

Visited Wm. Hargest in the Infirmary. Read to the Prisoners in the House of Correction, also to the Military Prisoners in Solitary Confinement. Admonished Abel Prosser previous to his discharge. The masons working in the Prison were the cause why the Prisoners were not taken into the Chapel this week.

August 4th

Visited the Infirmary and conversed with several of the prisoners apart. Admonished J. Williams prior to his discharge.

Morgan Jones
Chaplain

PRO, PCOM 2/96

Pentonville Prison, Visitors' Order Book

27th Aug. 1847

The Governor is requested to give the necessary orders for sending on board the ship *Marion* the effects, money, and outfit of the prisoners to be embarked as exiles in that ship, together with the extras which have been ordered for use during the voyage. The money to be paid to the Surgeon Superintendent and his receipt taken for the same. The several articles are to be accompanied with the proper invoice in duplicate. The one to be left with the Surgeon Superintendent, the other with the receipt of that officer to be returned.

B.H. [B. Hawkins]

2nd September 1847

The modelling tools belonging to the Establishment used by Reg^r No. 1095 [George Hill] valued at 7/6 and being of little or no further use to the Establishment are allowed to be taken away by him when he embarks in the ship *Marion*.

PRO, PCOM 2/392

Reading Prison, Entry Book of Pardons

Whereas David Saunders was on the 11th day of November 1848 committed to the Gaol at Reading for three months for non-payment of a penalty of £5 and Costs imposed upon him for an Offence against the Game Laws. We in consideration of some circumstances humbly represented unto us are graciously pleased to extend Our Grace and Mercy unto him, and to grant him Our Pardon for the Offence for which he so stands Committed as aforesaid on Condition that he be imprisoned and kept to hard labour for two calendar months, to be computed from the date of his committal. Our Will and Pleasure is, that you do give the necessary directions accordingly. And for so doing this shall be your Warrant. Given at Our Court of St. James's the 28th day of December 1848 in the Twelfth Year of Our Reign.

To Our Trusty and Wellbeloved   By Her Majesty's Command
The Keeper of the Gaol at
Reading in the County of Berks
and all others whom it may concern.   G.G.

PRO, PCOM 2/354

Portland Prison, Governor's Journal

13th Septr. 1849
Thursday

The prisoners employed as usual, except from 1 to 3 p.m occupied in a general change of hulks. Reported for irregularity and disposed of as in Report Book and Misconduct Book, Regr. No. *753, 244, 299, 357*. Also the following prisoners received here on the 11th instant, who were guilty of the following outrageous conduct. Prisoner No. *891* T. Warburton finding that he was going to be reported by Principal Warder Stein for an offence, assaulted him, and on the Deputy Governor's ordering him to close confinement several prisoners who had been at the hulks with the above named man rushed in a violent manner to the palisade of the yard and endeavoured to force it. On my being sent for I found these men very much excited and wanting to see me. Accordingly two of them No. *897* T. Atkins and *895* M. Brittain were passed successively through the door of the palisade and having stated what they had to say (which merely amounted to a kind of intended justification of their previous violence) they were passed back and a third brought out who was immediately pointed out to me as one who had struck Assistant Warder Bond in the face because he required him to perform more work (stonebreaking) than he was doing. The prisoner No. *891* J. Gallavin [?] said at once that he had struck the officer, and on my ordering him off to close confinement he hesitated and drew back. The two officers standing by him took hold of him to take him away when he appealed to me to desire them to take their hands off him and he would go quietly. To shew him that there was no wish to treat him harshly I said 'very well then take your hands off him', and the moment they did so he struck at me but the blow only reached me lightly on the face. The two officers then secured him and immediately the other prisoners inside the palisade tried to force the wicket of it to come to his assistance. There being 65 men in this yard and only 5 officers present and the whole of the other prisoners being on the point of coming in from labour I sent for the military guard to assist in quelling the disturbance, and went to assist Principal Warders Bowerie [?] and Warren who were struggling with the prisoners that were trying to force the wicket. Before it could be closed these officers were severely kicked and beaten by the prisoners inside. The whole of those taking an active part in this violence being, as far as I could ascertain at the time, men who had formerly been at some of the Hulks and were removed to separate confinement for misconduct. Their names are *892* T. Thorpe, *894* J. Oneill, *895* M. Brittaine, *896* S. Hayes, *897* T. Atkins, *898* S.J. Riggs and *899* F. Haynes. I could not ascertain that the other prisoners in the yard (all of whom had arrived from Pentonville with these men on the 11th) had taken any part in the disturbance. The military guard having promptly come up and been drawn up opposite the palisade ready to act, I went into the yard with several officers (who had come in with the working parties) and sent all the prisoners off to their cells by wards.

The two who had previously been sent to the separate cells as before mentioned appeared so much in the character of ringleaders that I judged it better not to send the others into their hearing and according directed them to remain for the present, unless they were troublesome, in their own cells. The main body of the prisoners had come in from the works while these matters were going on but had gone off quickly to their different halls; and the working prisoners who had been stationed for different reasons in the separate cells were moved down to the halls to be out of hearing of the mutinous and gross language shouted to each other by the men in close confinement. It was evident from this language that these hulks men had come from separate confinement to a state of association with an intention of resisting the prison authorities and discipline as they had done before at the hulks, and that after the arrival of another lot of similar characters on the 14th from Pentonville, they intended to renew their violence.

I greatly fear that the presence of these notoriously bad characters from the hulks will prove most injurious to the discipline of this establishment, which has hitherto been so far successful as to render it practicable to take outside the prison walls several hundred convicts, (even to a distance from the prison) provided with heavy hammers and tools of all kinds (in ground most favourable for concealment and escape), under the charge of unarmed officers aided by a very few unsupported sentries. To enforce from them a fair amount of labour conducted generally in a cheerful manner to move them to and from their distant ground with order and quickness and so send them back to their cells with little fear of their breaking any established rules or shewing disrespect to their officers. All this is so different from the general conduct of prisoners at the hulks that it appears impossible to introduce into this prison a number of the notorious ringleaders from those establishments without the greatest risk or even certainty of contamination and injury to the discipline especially as there is here in fact no sufficient means of separating such characters and at the same time making them labour on the Public Works. I have also to observe that one of these men has been convicted since 1842, his sentence being only for 10 years and that his presence in this establishment is in opposition to the terms of the 'notice' which specifies a convict's detention in this country to be only for one half the period of his sentence, a circumstance which will doubtless be made use of by these discontented men to throw doubt on the intention of carrying the terms of these 'notices' into effect, and unsettle the minds of the prisoners who are anxiously looking forward to going abroad with tickets of leave as a reward for good conduct.

I did not attend morning prayers today having been kept up till a late hour by office business last night.

Som. RO, Q/AGw 11/1

Wilton Gaol, Taunton. Letter Book of General Correspondence

H.M. Gaol Taunton
7th April 1851

Sir,

An order was received on the 25th Dated 21st February last for the removal of James Jones a convict in this Gaol under sentence of Transportation, to the Prison at Millbank, but the Prisoner having made some important statements relative to a number of burglaries committed in the neighbourhood and a person having been apprehended and committed for trial, and Jones's evidence being deemed necessary, an application was made to the Sec'y of State for his being detained until the Assizes, and the Sec'y of State directed that the prisoner should be detained in the Gaol until after the next Assizes. The prisoner has given his evidence and the party charged, convicted and transported, I shall therefore feel greatly obliged by your informing me if I can now remove Jones under the original order a calendar month having expired since the receipt of it.

I have to apologize for so frequently troubling you but we are now desirous of the prisoner's removal.

G. Everisit Esq.,
Home Office,
London

I am Sir,
Your most obedient and obliged servant
James Gane

Som. RO, Q/AGw 11/1

Wilton Gaol, Taunton. Letter Book of General Correspondence

Somerset County Gaol
Taunton
5th May 1852

Henry House
Thomas Dyer
    alias Wilson
William Davis
Walter Gardner
Chas Matthews
George Wilkins
Hy. Duckham
Jas. Wingate
Geo. Cox
Wm. Merrick
Step. Wiltshire
John Neale
John Dallimore
Jas. Hewett
John White
John Langley
Wm. Addley

Sir,

In reply to Mr Waddington's letter of the 1st inst. the male convicts named in the margin under sentence of Transportation are reported as between 18 and 50 years of age in sound mental and bodily health and in every respect fit to undergo the discipline of separate confinement.

They comprise the whole of the convicts named in the return forwarded on the 15th day of April last with the exception of Henry Norris who is reported by the Surgeon as unfit for discipline of separate confinement.

We are Sir,
Your Ob^t Servants
Charles J. Helyar
Noel Welman
Visiting Justices

To
  The Right Hon'ble
  Sec^y of State
  Home Department

Som. RO, Q/AGw 11/1

Wilton Gaol, Taunton. Letter Book of General Correspondence

Taunton
14th March 1853

Dear Sir,

Rex v Modley and others

I am at all times most anxious to anticipate the wishes of the Magistrates and should also be much pleased to oblige you but from circumstances that formerly took place here I am assured both the Magistrates and yourself would prefer adopting the strictly legal course this I believe would be unless Jane Jones enter into recognizance either to take her deposition here releasing the prisoner for that purpose after taking the principle evidence or obtain an Habeas which could at once be done from the Clerk of the Western Circuit to bring Jane Jones before the Magistrate the expense being part of the expense of Prosecution to be allowed by the Court and paid by the Government.

I fear that the latter part of Section 20, 11 and 12 Vic. C 42 (Jervis' Act) enacting that if after the Commitment of a Prosecution or Witness in default of Recognizance the Justice shall not commit an accused party it is lawful by order (Form P 2) to discharge such witness, will not meet the case. Whatever the Magistrates' wishes or your advice may be I shall be ready to adopt, in any event you will see the Prisoner being in custody of the Sheriff. There is one of the Gaolers should convey her.

The poor creature has been cleansed and every consideration shown her consistant with the fact that she is only here as a witness.

Yours Truly,
Wm. Oakley
Governor

V. Prance, Esq.

PRO, PCOM 2/293

Bedford Gaol, Governor's Journal

Tuesday 16th August 1853

During the past week I have made a minute examination of the pews occupied by the prisoners when assembled in Chapel and regret to state that the result of my examination is very unsatisfactory. The whole of the pews are more or less defaced with disgusting characters and writings and I am led to suppose that this work is chiefly executed by the prisoners when assembled in Chapel for school instruction. I beg to recommend that the Chapel pews be painted which can be done by the prisoners, after which I propose having a relay of numbers which will I trust materially assist me in detecting these abuses.

PRO, PCOM 2/293

Bedford Gaol, Governor's Journal

24 March 1854

Government Convict Cannon was reported by Warder Main for insubordination. I enquired into the case and found it necessary to remove Cannon from association and no longer to work at the shoemaking, and placed him alone under the charge of another officer.

As soon as Cannon was aware of this he assumed an air of defiance towards me, folded his arms, then threw his cap on the floor and refused to leave the office. When he found I was resolved to remove him by force he at least consented to withdraw. But as soon as he got into the corridor he threatened what he would do to the first officer that approached him, expressing regret that he was not so strong now, as he had been. Allowing his temper to get the upper hand of him in a spirit of revenge he ran with his head two distinct times full bolt against the wall which caused him to rebound again. This man is of an extraordinary mind and when enraged to the pitch that he was this afternoon there is no knowing the consequences. He requires great care and caution and I think a great deal more may be done with him by child like treatment than harsher means. But at the same time I think that he should be made to submit to authority when not misplaced. I have not subjected this man to any punishment, nor deprivation other than I have described, nor do I intend doing so as he expressed regret half an hour afterwards for his past conduct, and appeared deeply affected for what he had done.

PRO, PCOM 2/293

Bedford Gaol, Governor's Journal

5 March 1855

By order of the Secretary of State
Lucy Sharman discharged from this prison on the 31st October last and who has since been in Huntingdon Gaol, is here again, she has been in this and other gaols 15 times for wilful and malicious damage in and out of the Workhouse. She is considered by some to be of unsound mind. If she is found to be so I would respectfully suggest that immediate steps be taken to effect her removal to an Institution better suited to treat her case. Certainly a prison does not appear to me to be the place for her. She scarcely ever enters the prison but it is found necessary to have recourse to stringent measures with her.

Sharman and another girl named Johnson both ragged, dirty and saucy were taken before the Boro Magistrate on Wednesday last for disorderly conduct in the streets of Bedford and were repremanded and discharged. Scarcely had an hour elapsed before they were both again apprehended in the town for breaking windows and committed to prison for twenty days Hard Labour. On Saturday last Sharman refused and did no work and was yesterday placed on bread and water 48 hours. When her food was given to her she threw it at the Officer (Nicholls) and this morning she has broken one by one, 36 squares of glass in the cell she occupied. I have placed her under restraint for the assault she made on the officer and have deferred the subject of the damage for the consideration of the Visiting Justices. It is only recently since she was ordered 14 days confinement by the Visiting Justices for assaulting the Prison Officers and destruction to the prison property. Indeed she scarcely or never enters the prison but what the good order and discipline is in some degree materially disturbed by her. At times no female can behave better than she does.

PRO, PCOM 2/426

Chatham Prison, Governor's Journal

Monday 7 September 1857

Labouring parties the same as usual. Inspected and visited the whole of the Prison.
I saw the Prisoners desirous of seeing the Governor.
Reported for misconduct:-

1000	Henry Skinner	1 day B & W[1]
135[2]	John Stone	3 Days B & W
129[2]	James Hindley	2 days B & W
124	Thomas Allport	3 days B & W, 1 month separate cell
527	Joseph Rainsley	1 day B & W
565	Joseph Laverack	1 day B & W

M. Bullin Governor

PRO, PCOM 2/159

Wormwood Scrubs Prison, Governor's Orders

Shaving Prisoners

Ordered:-   That no prisoner should be allowed to shave himself. He must be shaved by an officer, or, by another prisoner in the presence of the officer. With regard to prisoners for trial or under remand GREAT CARE must be taken by the officer that the appearance of the prisoner be not altered by such shaving.

E.J. Jonas
Governor
24th September 1860

PRO, PCOM 2/395

Reading Gaol, Judge's Orders

Berkshire [21 December 1864]

At the General Sessions of the delivery of the Gaol of our Lady the Queen holden at Reading in and for the County of Berks on Wednesday the twenty-first day of December in the twenty-eighth year of the reign of our Sovereign Lady Victoria by the grace of God of the United Kingdom of Great Britain and Ireland, Queen, Defender of the Faith, and in the year of our Lord one thousand eight hundred and sixty-four before Sir John Barnard Byles knight, one of the Justices of our said Lady the Queen of Her Court of Common Pleas and others, Justices of our said Lady the Queen, assigned to deliver her Gaol of the said County of Berks of the prisoners therein being:-

George Kent	12 years	Convicted of felony
George Parkinson		Are severally ordered to be kept in
James Maynard	7 years	Penal Servitude for the period set
Joseph Haines		against their respective names.
Michael Morley	5 years	
Sarah Bartlett	18 cal. mos.	Convicted of felony and misdemeanor.
John Dandridge	1 year	Are severally ordered to be imprisoned
Thomas May		and kept to hard labor in the House of
James Slark	9 cal. mos.	Correction at Reading for the periods
Josiah Saunders	6 cal. mos.	set against their respective names.
Eliza Chick	3 cal. mos.	

[1] Bread and water.

[2] A cross check has been made against the prison register, PRO, PCOM 2/1, and the following discrepancies found:

No. *735*   John Henry Stone
No. *129*   James Pinkley

Hannah Church   Committed on a charge of felony.
Removed to a Lunatic Asylum by order of the Secretary of State.

John Exall   Bill not found.
Is delivered by Proclamation.   Discharged

Amelia Stead
John Grimsdale
Athalia Watts
Charles Ilsley   Are acquitted and discharged
John Ilsley
William Metcalf
Edwin Fennell

Jesse Oakley   Acquitted of felony on the ground of Insanity. Is ordered to be kept in strict custody in Gaol until Her Majesty's pleasure respecting him shall be known.

> By the Court
> James Hemp, Dep. Clerk of Assize

Sur. RO, QS 5/4 (part)

*Horsemonger Lane Gaol, Surrey. Surgeon's Order Book,
Thomas H. Waterworth, MD*

The following are abstracts:

17 May 1867	Ordered Richard Penno into the Infirmary
24 May	Ordered to his Class
19 May 1867	Ordered Eliza Jewett into the Infirmary
20 May	Sent to the Workhouse by order of the Magistrate upon my certificate
27 May 1867	Ordered William Watson a debtor into the Infirmary
3 June	Died. Jury returned a verdict that he died a natural death
28 January 1868	Ordered Edward Potter into the Infirmary
5 February	Ordered to Wandsworth
17 February 1868	Ordered Richard Lee into the Infirmary
22 February	Discharged
18 April 1868	Ordered Paul Raby into the Infirmary
13 May	Sent to Millbank
26 December 1868	Ordered Francis Pearce, a debtor, into the Infirmary
	Refused to be admitted
9 August 1869	Ordered John Cusack into the Infirmary
25 November	Sent to Newgate Prison

12 January 1870	Ordered Daniel Dexter into the Infirmary
22 January	Discharged from Police Court for attempt at suicide
1 March 1870	Ordered Henry Dare into the Infirmary
1 March	Discharged on bail
31 March 1870	Ordered James Turner into the Infirmary
2 April	Acquitted at the Sessions
5 July 1870	Ordered Edward Leake into the Infirmary
18 August	Discharged out of custody by order of Magistrates
17 July 1871	William Davies sent to the Infirmary by my order
18 August	Removed to Pentonville
12 October 1871	William King, debtor ordered into the Infirmary
9 November	Sent to the Lunatic Asylum by his friends
23 February 1872	Ordered Edward Connor into the Infirmary
[blank]	Tried at the Sessions
29 August 1872	Ordered James Rogers into the Infirmary
4 September	Sent to Broadmoor Asylum
22 January 1873	Alfred Johnson ordered into the Infirmary
5 February	Sent to Wandsworth House of Correction
4 March 1874	George Mitchell into the Infirmary
16 March	Escorted to his ship from Police Court
1 May 1875	William Dudley into the Infirmary
5 May	Tried at the Sessions – Acquitted
9 November 1876	Isaac Wm. Hill into the Infirmary
February	Discharged by Secretary of State
11 November 1876	Emma Edwards into the Infirmary
12 November	Died from accident by burning
26 November 1877	James Ward (Rheumatism) ordered into the Infirmary
9 January 1878	Died in the Infirmary
1 December 1877	Frank Willmott (Paralysis) ordered into the Infirmary
5 January 1878	Died in the Infirmary
10 March 1878	Thomas Testro (Venereal) ordered into the Infirmary
22 March	Classed in *C* Ward. 5 years Penal from the Sessions

PRO, PCOM 2/95

Pentonville Prison, Visitors' Observations

9th May 1884

I have visited every part of the prison today and seen a very considerable number of the prisoners. Every thing as far as I could judge seemed to be in good order. I note that the deaf and dumb boy who has spent the whole time of his incarceration here, is now on the eve of departure. He looks well and healthy and seems to have made considerable progress in his education. I examined some of his school work and think his treatment reflects credit on those who have had charge of him. I had some lengthened conversation with two prisoners in their own cells quite alone. They were both men of superior education and of a very different class. I took some pains to question them quite in a friendly manner as to prison life generally and after four years experience of these establishments I think this is perhaps the most useful employment of one's time in them. The first of these prisoners has been a surgeon in Birmingham. He was now under sentence of penal servitude for life for causing death by procuring abortion and although of good address and superior education, evidently an old rascal. He was however very frank and open with me. He had been four years in penal servitude and therefore had had experience of 'public works life', as well as separate confinement. He said he thought there was very little if any fault to find with their treatment generally, and that the men who complain generally did so to cause trouble and to create a little mild excitement for themselves, and that the men who complained most loudly of the diet were those whose dinner at home consisted of a red herring. For all my conversation, though I encouraged him to talk, I could elicit no complaint at all worth recording.

The other man was perhaps the most painful case it is possible to come across in a convict prison. He is a star class prisoner named Weaver. He had been 34 years Secretary to the Society for the Propagation of the Gospel, and his record shows him to have led an exemplary life till his downfall. He had of course no prison experience, and had only been in separate confinement for four months in this prison. During the whole of that period he bore witness to universal kind treatment to himself and the other prisoners under his observation. He had no complaint of any sort or kind to make and only seemed to dread the unknown conditions of his next stage. He told me that the only difficulty he experienced was occasionally to have to keep off the pertinaceous efforts of some other prisoners to talk to him in Chapel and at exercise. Considering the difference between his former position and his present one he seemed wonderfully cheerful and talked readily. The only shadow of a complaint I could elicit from him was that he would like to have rather more intellectual books, and more time to read them.

I commend these observations to my colleagues (the other visitors) as a proof of the value to be attached to convicts' complaints, an enormous number of which I have often had myself to listen to.

I cordially endorse Lord Charles Beresford's remarks as to the inadvisability of employing separate confinement men on public duty.

Fyfe

PRO, PCOM 2/95

Pentonville Prison, Visitors' Observations

4th June 1884

We have this day visited the prison and devoted nearly three hours to an inspection of the infirmary, some of the workshops, a number of the prisoners in their cells, conversing especially with the whole of the prisoners confined in the punishment cells.

In the case of a prisoner named Carter we found, after a prolonged interview, that notwithstanding his vague complaints against the officials generally, and the prison discipline altogether, that he was a very head-strong, self-willed man, and had really no justification for his complaints.

In another case a prisoner named Duffy desired to be removed to another prison as, he alleged that the master shoe-maker was 'down on him'. We found, however, after a very long conversation that Duffy was the victim of a vile and ungovernable temper, admitting as a matter of fact, that he had on one occasion persisted in whistling loudly in defiance of the Governor. On another, on leaving the room after being tried for a former offence, had struck the warder, for which he was flogged; and on a third occasion when for some irregularity he was ordered to 'fall out' on parade, admitted looking for a brick with which to 'give the warder a doing', but as he further confessed, luckily for the warder 'he could'nt find one'.

In the case of another prisoner who had recently been sent back to penal servitude in consequence of robbery, for which he had been sentenced to eighteen months hard labour, his only request was to be allowed to follow the Roman Catholic faith, but he admitted having declared himself a Protestant when originally convicted.

We also talked with other prisoners, none of whom had any complaints whatever to make, but who expressed satisfaction at their treatment.

We are strong of opinion that in cases similar to that of a prisoner named Bolton, with whom we conversed, who had confessed to being a murderer, (but which he subsequently repudiated) solely with the object, as he stated, to change temporarily his confinement, that some punishment should follow such wanton lying and serious deception.

We think also that a prisoner on being asked his religious persuasion should be warned, that as obviously he must know to what sect he belonged he would be made to follow the one he declared for during the term of his imprisonment. If however, this course should be deemed undesirable the prisoner should be informed that if it is subsequently found he had told a lie and wished to change, it would involve a certain punishment, which in our opinion ought to follow.

Everything about the prison was conducted with good order and discipline.

George Shipton
C.J. Drummond

CAPTIONS, TRANSFER PAPERS AND LICENCES

CAPTIONS

A detailed record was kept of all government prisoners (convicts). On conviction the Court wrote out a Caption (Order of Court) which named the convict and gave details of his crime and sentence.

TRANSFER PAPERS

These are the official documents which authorize and record the removal of a convict from one government prison to another. They contain a full record of the convict's time in prison together with any previous sentences. Details of any misconduct is recorded together with punishments. His physical description is also given together with the name and address of his next of kin.

LICENCES

In October 1853 a system of licences was introduced by which those convicts of good behaviour could be allowed out on parole and were expected to maintain a respectable way of life. Failure to do so would result in them being returned to prison. The tabulations on pages 26 and 27 summarize the numbers of convicts, both male and female, who were granted licences from their introduction to the middle of 1861. Also given are the numbers of those whose licences were revoked and those who were reconvicted for another offence. Licences were usually endorsed on existing Captions and/or Transfer Papers.

SWANSEA GAOL.

PARTICULARS to accompany the Caption of the undermentioned Convict on his removal to *Millbank Prison*

Name .... *George Smith*

Age .... *30.*

Married or Single, and Number of Children .... } *Is married and has one child (by a former wife.)*

Read, Write, General Intelligence .. *R.W. imp:- general intelligence good.*

Trade or Occupation .... *Engine Driver.*

Crime .... *Robbery with violence*

Sentence .... *Seven years transportation*

Date and Place of Conviction ...... *2nd March 1850, at Swansea.*

Date and Place of Committal ...... *17 December 1849, at Cardiff.*

Places and Periods of Confinement since last Conviction .... } *Swansea Gaol. 5 mos:-14 days. Stirling Castle 1 yr-9 mos —*

Number of Months in Separate Confinement, if any, since Committal } *Five weeks. Millbank 7 Months 11 days.*

Character and Conduct of Convict since Conviction .... } *Generally good. Millbank Good. "Stirling Castle" 2 time Good / Stirling Castle Good, Shorncliff Good*

Residence of Convict's Family or next of Kin .... } *Pontypool. Monmouthshire.*

Information relative to former Convictions, whether previously transported, Convict's Character, and General Remarks .... } *Cannot ascertain that he has been previously convicted; but his general character was bad. lived with his wife in a notorious brothel. She is now here - a Convict*

Religion .... *Protestant*

Health .... *Good.*

William Cox Governor,
of the Common Gaol at Swansea.

Dated _____

NOTE.—This Return is to be filled up and signed by the Governor of the Prison from whence the Convict is received into a Government Prison, and dated on the day when so received.

Dates of all removals and receptions to be endorsed.

Page from a Licence granted to George Smith, convicted 2 March 1850 at Swansea (PRO, PCOM 3/3)

Captions, Transfer Papers and Licences are held by the Public Record Office and are listed in Appendix 4.3.

PRO, PCOM 3/1
Licence No. 23 William Young

Somerset

These are to Certify that At the General Quarter Sessions of the Peace of our Lady the Queen, held at the City of Wells in and for the County of Somerset on Tuesday, the twenty sixth Day of March in the thirteenth Year of the Reign of our Sovereign Lady VICTORIA, by the Grace of God of the United Kingdom of Great Britain and Ireland, Queen, Defender of the Faith, and in the Year of our Lord 1850 before William Miles, Charles Aaron Moody, Esquires, Chairmen, and others their Companions, Justices of our said Lady the Queen, assigned to keep the Peace of our said Lady the Queen, in and for the County of Somerset aforesaid, and also to hear and determine divers Felonies, Trespasses and other Misdemeanors committed in the same County.

William Young was convicted of Larceny after a former conviction for Felony and was thereupon ordered and adjudged by the Court to be transported beyond the Seas for Seven years.

Given under my hand this twenty eighth day of March in the year of our Lord one thousand eight hundred and fifty.

Edwin Lovell
Clerk of the Peace

This is a true Copy of the Original Caption and order of Court containing the Sentence, by Virtue of which the above named Convict is in my Custody, in Attestation whereof I hereunto Subscribe my Name.

James Gane
Governor

Name	William Young
Licence	No. 23
Complexion	Fresh
Hair	Light
Eyes	Grey

[contd]

Height	5 feet 2½ inches
Scars, cuts, moles, marks &c on body and limbs	Round full face Feet flat
Description	Moderately stout

Received at Wakefield 2 May 1850
Removed from Wakefield 13 March 1851
Received at Portland Prison from Wakefield 14 March 1851
Received at *York* Hulk from Portland 20 May 1852
Removed to Portsmouth Prison 13 May 1853 from *Stirling Castle* Hulk
Portsmouth Prison 13 May 1853

Licenced 19 Oct. 1853

Name	William Young
Age	18 years
Married or Single, and number of children	Single
Read, Write, General, Intelligence	Read imp., moderate intelligence and very slightly informed on religious subjects
Trade or Occupation	Labourer
Crime	Stealing a tame rabbit the property of William Stag Hilborn, &c, previous conviction.
Sentence	Seven years
Date and Place of Conviction	26 March 1850 Somerton Somerset
Places and Periods of Confinement since last Conviction	County Gaol Wilton Taunton one month. *Stirling Castle* Hulk 11 mo. 23 days.

Number of months in Separate Confinement if any since Committal	one month Wakefield 10 months Portland Prison 13 months and 6 days Wakefield open and pleasing a little steadiness desirable, Conduct Good. Portland Good *Stirling Castle* Good
Residence of Convicts Family or next of Kin	Mother Fanny Young living at Somerton, Somerset.
Information relative to former Conviction, Whether previously transported, Convicts Character, and General Remarks.	Convicted of burglary Lent Assizes 1845 – 6 months H.L. [hard labour]. Once for Larceny – Once for assault, bad in every respect from a child.
Religion	Protestant
Health	Good
	James Gane Governor of County Gaol of Somerset dated 30 April 1850

[It should be noted that the above was signed by James Gane a month after the prisoner's conviction and while he was still in Wilton Gaol where he had been held for trial, the next of kin (his mother) being resident then in Somerton. Obviously information relating to his confinement in other gaols was added later.]

PRO, PCOM 5/32
Transfer Papers Edward Hughes

NAME AND ALIASES	Edward Hughes
Age	28
Married or Single and number of children	Single
Trade or occupation	Green Grocer
Crime (with Particulars)	Larceny after a previous conviction of felony

[contd]

Date and Place of Commital	29 April 1858, York
Date and Place of Conviction	5 July 1858, York Session
Sentence	10 years Penal Servitude
Information as to Previous convictions and character	10 July 1850 York Assize, Robbery from the person, 7 yrs, transportation. 1856 Leeds Boro Sess. St'g a pair of trousers, 12 cal. mos. H.L. [hard labour] 26 March 1858, York City, St'g money from the person 1 mo. H.L. under the Criminal Justice Act. 21 Nov. 1849, Leeds, Assault, 7 days or pay 18/- 28 Dec. 1849, Leeds, Assault, 1 cal. mo. or pay 50/6 30 Jan. 1850 Leeds, Felony, Examination, discharged. 20 Jan. 1853 Leeds, Assault 1 cal. mo. or pay 40/-
Name of Residence of family or next of kin	Mother, Mary Hughes, No, 8, Cornhill, Leeds.
Read Write	Imperfect
Religion (any subsequent change to be noted here, with dates)	Ch. of England

Description

Complexion	Fair
Hair	Dark Brown
Height	5 feet 4 inches
Description of Person Peculiar Marks, &c on Body or Limbs	Deformed left hand, Little finger right hand crooked at the end.

Page from a Licence granted to Margaret Smith, alias Styles, discharged 25 March 1856 at Warwick (PRO, PCOM 4/3)

Transfer from Date of Committal

PRISON	DATE	REGISTER NUMBER WHILE THERE	DESCRIPTION OF CONFINEMENT	GENERAL CHARACTER AND CONDUCT	PROGRESS AT SCHOOL	PRISON TRADE
Received at York City Prison Removed to Millbank	4 Aug. 1858		Association	Good		
Received at Millbank Removed to Lewes	4 Aug. 1858 5 Mar. 1859		Sep	Good	Satis.	Tailor
Received at Lewes Removed to Dartmoor	5 Mar. 1859 17 May 1859	661	P.W.[1]	Indiff.		Labour
Received at Dartmoor	18 May 1859	5203	P.W.	Very Bad	Little	Labour

[1] Probably means Petty Officer's Wing.

[contd]

PRISON	DATE	REGISTER NUMBER WHILE THERE	DESCRIPTION OF CONFINEMENT	GENERAL CHARACTER AND CONDUCT	PROGRESS AT SCHOOL	PRISON TRADE
Removed to Millbank	7 Aug. 1862					
Received at Millbank	8 Aug. 1862		Sep.			
Removed to Pentonville	8 Aug. 1862					
Received at Pentonville	8 Aug. 1862	1038	Sep	Good	1st Class	Mat Maker
Removed to Dartmoor	24 June 1863					
Received at Dartmoor	25 June 1863	7183	P.W.	Very Bad	Instructed When rec'd	Labour
Removed to Pentonville	18 Nov. 1867					
Received at Pentonville	19 Nov. 1867	5089	Separate			
Removed to Millbank	30 June 1868	for discharge on Expiration of Sentence on 4 July 1868				

Pentonville

Abstract of Entries in the Misconduct Book

No. 1038			
NAME	Edward Hughes. To Dartmoor 24 June 1863		
PRISON	DATE	OFFENCE FOR WHICH REPORTED	REMARKS
Pentonville	1863 2 March	Receiving a communication at Chapel	Admonished
	13 June	Continually laughing and talking at exercise after being cautioned, and calling the officer a liar on leaving Governor's Office	Exercise in Round Yard and 3 days on bread and water. Dark cell and forfeit badges
	All remission lost		
	2nd class: 1st class due 13 Sept. 1863		

Dartmoor
Register No. and Name 7183 *Edward Hughes*

DATE	DATE OF CONVICTION AND NATURE OF MISCONDUCT	PUNISHMENT	FORFEITURE RECOMMENDED BY GOVERNOR	DIRECTORS APPROVAL
1864 22 Jan.	Leaving his cell without permission and insolence to an officer	Red. to 2nd class for 3 ms.	10 days 23–1–64	M. Gambier 25–1–64
12 Feb.	Talking in his cell and insolence	Red. to 3rd class	10 days 18–2–64	M. Gambier 17–2–64
3 May	Making use of improper language	48 hours B&W[2] and 12 days on reduced diet	7 days 9–5–64	M. Gambier 10–5–64
3 May	Insolence to the Governor also for having an extra handkerchief in his possession and a piece of black lead pencil			
13 June	Combining with others in refusing to work on the turf bog	To go on B&W until he resumes work, to be deprived of Sunday exercise, School, and Chapel	Forfeit 126 days	
15 June	Insolence when told to make up his bed and leave off talking while under punishment			
18 June	Using insubordinate language while under punishment	9 days pun. diet in C.C.[3] and placed in Penal Class for 6 mos. All remission suspended and all gratuity forfeited.	Forfeit 28 days	
25 June	Insolent and insubordinate conduct when visited by the Assistant Chaplain			
30 July	Loud talking and shouting in the Sep. Cells while under punishment	Sentenced by Director to 7 days B&W C.C.		

[contd]

[2] Bread and water.
[3] Close confinement.

DATE	DATE OF CONVICTION AND NATURE OF MISCONDUCT	PUNISHMENT	FORFEITURE RECOM-MENDED BY GOVERNOR	DIRECTORS APPROVAL
19 Aug.	Shouting to his fellow prisoners in the Sep. Cells and commenting on his punishment by the Director			
15 Sept.	Having concealed inside the lining of his hat 9 leaves abstracted from books issued to him while undergoing penal class punishment			
1865 25 Feb.	Having some picked Oakum in his cell when searched		Forfeit 18 marks	
12 April	Talking in a loud manner in his cell and using impatient language when unlocked		Forfeit 42 marks	
15 July	Impertinence to an officer		Forfeit 42 marks	
18 Aug.	Persisting in talking in his cell and insolence to an officer	48 hours B&W Class red. 2 mos	Forfeit 42 marks	
28 Dec.	Disobedience of orders	3 days B&W Class red. 3 mos	Forfeit 84 marks	
1866 1 Feb.	Making frivolous appeals against the Governor's decision on two reports	Sentenced by Director to 3 days B&W		

Dartmoor
Record of Prison Offences of 7183 Convict – Edward Hughes

| DATE | OFFENCE | CLOSE CON-FINEMENT ON PUNISHMENT DIET [days] | PUNISHMENT AWARDED | | ADDITIONAL PUNISHMENT | FORFEIT FOR REMISSION |
| | | | REDUCED TO | | | |
			CLASS	PERIOD CALCU-LATED IN MARKS		MARKS
1866						
1 Feb.	Making frivolous appeals against the Governor's decisions in two reports	3				
15 May	Leaving his cell and going into another cell and taking there-from some bread	3	2	720		84
27 July	Bringing some young turnip plants into the prison		3	240		42
4 Sept.	Improper conduct during school hours	3 in the dark cell	3	720		84
8 Sept.	Having thread in his possession	1	3	240		24
17 Oct.	Leaving his cell and landing in a very dirty state				Admonished	
18 Oct.	Insolence to an officer	1	3	240		24
1867						
1 July	Gross insolence to officer	3	2	480		84
13 July	Fighting and refusing to desist	3	3	240		84
17 July	Insolence to an officer	3	3	720		84
12 Aug.	Insolence on being searched	3	3	480		84

Lewes	2 reports
Dartmoor	14 reports – All remissions forfeited
Pentonville	2 reports
Dartmoor	17 reports

Dartmoor

STATEMENT respecting a convict recommended for removal from Public Works to separate confinement, or to be retained in separate confinement beyond the ordinary period of misconduct. 8 July 1864.

Proposed to be retained in DARTMOOR PRISON.

Register No. Name, and age	7183 Edward Hughes, 28
Offence for which convicted	Robbery from the person
Date and Place of last Conviction	5 July 1858, York Sessions
and number of previous Convictions	5 Previous convictions (1850 7 yrs. trans.)
Sentence	10 years penal servitude.

Periods of confinement since conviction

PRISONS OR HULKS	YEARS	MONTHS	DAYS	CHARACTER AND REMARKS
York		1		G.
Millbank		7	1	G.
Lewes		2	12	Ind.
Dartmoor	3	2	20	V.B. removed to Millbank in Penal Class
Millbank		10	16	G.
Dartmoor	1		13	Very Bad.

Governor's report on cause of removal:

Refusing with others to work on 13th June and subsequent bad conduct when under confinement in the cells for that offence.

Suggestion of the director as to forfeiture of services:

To undergo punishment of nine days on punishment diet in close confinement and to be placed in the penal class for six months. All remission is suspended and to forfeit all gratuity.

M. Gambier – Director

Pentonville

Special remarks as to conduct, health, &c:

If this prisoner remains without report until within a year of the full sentence he may be brought forward for licence.

W. Fagan 7–5–66

If he remains clear of report from this date till June he may be included for licence in July.

W. Fagan 10–1–67

Dartmoor

WROTE LAST LETTER   5–9–67
RECEIVED LAST LETTER   18–9–67
VISITED   Nil

Licence returned to Home Office see letter attached [the letter does not survive]. This prisoner is removed to complete his time in a close prison, Millbank.

Elliot Salter 18–11–67

FINAL DISPOSAL. Discharged on expiration of sentence.

HOME OFFICE WARRANTS AND CORRESPONDENCE

These records are to be found in the Public Record Office dating from 1782 in Classes HO 13, HO 15 and HO 147. It should be noted that although Class HO 13 continues to 1871 the warrants recorded in this class finish in 1849. The remainder of this class contains related correspondence only. Warrants continue from 1850 in Class HO 15 up to 1886. From 1887 warrants are found in Class HO 147. These warrants include pardons, reprieves and transfer of convicts to the army and navy. They also record details of licences granted (see also Chapters 16 and 18).

Warrants for the death sentence are not included in these; the whereabouts of such records is unknown.

PRO, HO 13/1

John Brown, Pardon on Condition
of Serving in the Army or Navy

George R.

Whereas John Brown was at the last Assizes for Our County of York tried and convicted of stealing cattle and received sentence of Death for the same. And whereas some favourable circumstances have been humbly represented unto Us inducing Us to extend Our Royal Grace and Mercy unto him and to grant him Our Pardon on condition of his entering and continuing to serve Us in Our Land or Sea Service. Our Will and Pleasure therefore is that you cause him the said John Brown to be delivered over to such person or persons as shall be duly authorized to receive him for the purpose aforesaid and that he be inserted on the condition aforesaid in Our first next General Pardon that shall come out for the Northern Circuit. And for so doing this shall be your Warrant.

Given at Our Court at St. James's the 16th day of December 1782 in the twenty third year of Our Reign.

To Our Trusty and Wellbeloved   By His Majesty's Command
Our Justices of Assizes for   Tho. Townshend
the Northern Circuit, The High
Sheriff of Our County of York,
The Keeper of the Gaol at York
and all others whom it may concern.

PRO, HO 13/4

James Livesay
Free Pardon

George R.

Whereas James Livesay was at a Court of Oyer & Terminer & General Gaol Delivery held at Lynn on the tenth day of October 1785 convicted of Grand Larceny & received sentence of transportation for the same and whereas some favorable circumstances have been humbly represented unto us in his behalf, inducing us to extend our Grace & Mercy unto him & grant him our Free Pardon for his said crime. Our will & Pleasure therefore is, that you cause him the said James Livesay to be forthwith discharged out of Custody & that he be inserted for his said Crime in our first & next General Pardon that shall come out for the Norfolk Circuit without any Condition whatsoever. And for so doing this shall be your Warrant. Given at Our Court at St. James's the thirteenth day of December 1786 in the twenty seventh year of Our Reign.

To our Trusty and Wellbeloved   By His Majesty's Command
Our Justices of Assize for   Sydney
the Norfolk Circuit, the Mayor
& Recorder of Lynn & all
others whom it may concern.

PRO, HO 13/4

Overcrowded state of York Gaol

Richard Fenton Esq.   Whitehall
Clerk of the Peace   23rd Oct. 1786
for the West Riding
of the County of York

Sir,
      I have received the representation of the Magistrates of the West Riding of the County of York relative to the crowded state of the Gaol at York.
      I am very sorry that it is not in my power to comply with the desire of the Magistrates by the immediate removal of the said convicts, as the hulks in the River Thames under the direction of Mr. Campbell are at present so crowded, that any addition to their number would most likely produce diseases, which, situated as they are, would be attended with the most alarming consequences. I expect however that most of the people now confined in the Hulks, will, in the course of a fortnight, be sent abroad and as soon as that is effected, directions will be given for the removal of all the male convicts now in York Gaol under sentence of Transportation.
      If there should be any females amongst the convicts now under that sentence at York, I wish you to transmit to me a list of their names, in order that proper directions may be

sent to the Sheriff for their removal to the *Dunkirk* at Plymouth, and as one of the ships intended to proceed to the New Settlement will be ordered to call there on her way down the Channel for such females as are to be sent abroad, provision shall be made for their passage. I must at the same time inform you that it will be necessary that any female convicts who may be sent to Plymouth, should arrive by the first week in the ensuing month, for should their removal be longer delayed the ship appointed for their conveyance will most likely have left that port, and in such case the convicts must be taken back to York as the *Dunkirk* will be discharged.

I am
Sydney

PRO, HO 13/4

Removal of female prisoners from Ilchester Gaol to the Dunkirk *Hulk at Plymouth*

Whitehall
21st Novr 1786

Mary Phillips
Ann Combes
Ann Carey
Mary Bond
Jane Poole

Sir,
His Majesty having been pleased to give directions that five female convicts now under sentence of transportation in Ilchester Gaol, and whose names are mentioned in the margin, should be removed on board the ship *Dunkirk* at Plymouth and be committed to the charge of Mr Henry Bradley, overseer of the convicts on board the said ship; I am commanded to signify to you The King's Pleasure that you do forthwith cause the said convicts, if upon being examined by an experienced Surgeon they shall be found free from any putrid or infectious distemper, to be removed on board the said ship, where they are to remain until their sentences can be carried into execution, or be otherwise disposed of according to Law.

I am
Sydney

High Sheriff of the
County of Somerset

[The Dunkirk *was the only prison hulk used for women.]*

PRO, HO 13/10

Reduction of death sentence to three years hard labour

George R.

Ann Collishaw
Pardon

Whereas Ann wife of Samuel Collishaw was at the last Lent Assizes held at the town of Nottingham tried & convicted of shoplifting & received sentence of Death for the same, and whereas some favorable circumstances have been humbly represented unto us in her behalf inducing us to extend Our Grace and Mercy unto her, and to grant her our Pardon for her said crime, on condition of her being imprisoned & kept to hard labour in the house of correction for the said County for the term of three years. Our Will & Pleasure therefore is, that you give the necessary directions accordingly and that she be inserted for her said crime on the said condition in Our first next General Pardon that shall come out for the Midland Circuit And for so doing this shall be your Warrant. Given at Our Court at St. James's the fourth day of April 1795 in the thirty fifth year of Our Reign.

To Our Trusty and welbeloved Our   By His Majesty's Command
Justices of Assize for the Midland   Portland
Circuit, The High Sheriff of Our
County of Nottingham, and all others
whom it may concern.

PRO, HO 13/10

Pardon on condition of joining the army

George R.

John Bishop
Pardon

Whereas John Bishop is now in Shepton Mallett Gaol under sentence of two years imprisonment we in consideration of some favorable circumstances humbly represented unto us in his behalf are graciously pleased to extend our Grace and Mercy unto him and to grant him our pardon for the crime of which he stands convicted on condition of his enlisting and continuing to serve as a soldier in our forty third Regiment of foot until duly discharged therefrom. Our Will and Pleasure therefore is that upon his enlisting to serve us as a soldier as aforesaid he be forthwith delivered over to such person or persons as shall be duly authorized to receive him for that purpose and for so doing this shall be your Warrant. Given at Our Court at St. James's the twenty first day of April 1796 in the thirty sixth year of Our Reign.

To our trusty and welbeloved our   By His Majesty's Command
Justices of Assize for the Western   Portland
Circuit, the High Sheriff of our
County of Somerset & all others
whom it may concern.

PRO, HO 13/17

Reduction of death sentence to transportation for life

John Burroughs
Pardon

George R.

Whereas John Burroughs was at a Session holden at the Old Bailey in September last tried and convicted of uttering a draft for the payment of money knowing the same to be forged and had sentence of Death passed upon him for the same, We in consideration of some favorable circumstances recently represented unto us in his behalf are graciously pleased to extend Our Grace and Mercy unto him and to Grant him Our Pardon for his said Crime on Condition of his being Transported to the Eastern Coast of New South Wales or some one or other of the Islands adjacent for and during the term of his natural life; our Will and Pleasure therefore is that you give the necessary directions accordingly and that he be inserted for his said Crime on the said Condition in Our first and next General Pardon that shall come out for the poor convicts in Newgate. And for so doing this shall be your Warrant. Given at Our Court at St. James's the 17 day of Decr 1815 in the 46 year of Our Reign.

To Our Trusty and Welbeloved Our   By His Majesty's Command
Justices of Gaol Delivery for   Hawkesbury
the City of London & County of
Middlesex, the Sheriffs of the
said City & County and all others
it may concern.

PRO, HO 15/5

Thomas Pain Edginton
License to be at Large

Order of a License to a Convict made under   Whitehall
the Statute 16th & 17th Vict C 99 S 9   20 Feb 1854

Her Majesty is graciously pleased to grant to Thomas Pain Edginton who was convicted of Forgery at the Assizes holden for the County of Oxford on the 14th day of July 1852 and was then and there sentenced to be transported beyond the seas for the Term of Ten Years and is now confined in the Portland Prison. Her Royal License to be at large in the United Kingdom from the day of his liberation under this order during the remaining portion of his said Term of Transportation unless it shall please Her Majesty sooner to revoke or alter such License. And Her Majesty hereby Orders that the said Thomas Pain Edginton be set at liberty within thirty days from the date of this Order.

Given under my hand and Seal
Palmerston

Warrant for the removal of William Cownley to Worcester Lunatic Asylum
(PRO, HO 15/5)

Licences for the release of prisoners from Stirling Castle, 20 February 1854

No.	Name of Convict	Convicted		Offence	Sentence in Years
		Where	When		
29243	John Buffery	Worcester Q.S.	1 July 1850	Larceny	7
9010	John Bendall	Hants Assizes	11 July 1846	Highway R.	15
2778	Peter Burns	Aberdeen C.C.I.	28 Sept 1848	Fraud	7
9009	Geo. Barnard	C.C.Ct.[1]	27 Nov 1848	Utt^g base coin	10
9011	Peter Caldicott alias Gallier	Stafford Q.S.	18 Jul^y 1850	St^g beef	7
27711	Willm Crawford	Abingdon Ass.	27 Feb 1850	Rec^g stolen Gds	7
1834	Richd Farley	Worcester Ass	17 July 1846	Forging a will	15
9012	John Gardner	Portsmouth	8 Jan 1849	St^g a lamb	10
34819	Jas Savage	E. Retford	8 July 1850	St^g from person	7
9013	Alfred Nunn	C.C.Ct.	18 Dec 1848	Housebreaking	10
3313	Thos. H^y Palmer	Stafford	5 Jan 1852	Obt^g M^y by F^e Pret.	7
25229	Edwd Smart	C.C.Ct.	29 Jan 1849	Rob^y with Viol.	10
9014	Jas. Sutton	Newcastle Q.S.	9 July 1850	Fraud	7
34211	Alex^r Watson	Portsmouth	22 July 1850	Larceny	10
9015	Thos. Walker	Spilsby Q.S.	9 Jan. 1849	Larceny	10
27828	Luke Speakman Ashworth	Liverpool Ass	21 March 1850	Forgery	10

PRO, HO 15/5

Thomas Dumpleton, and others, Conditional Pardons

Whereas the following persons are now under sentence of transportation in the Convict Establishment at Gibraltar they having been convicted of Felony at the times and places hereafter mentioned:

Thomas Dumpleton	at Bedford in July 1851
Edward Cook	at Gloucester in March 1850
George Barker	at Ipswich in July 1847
George Ross	at Perth in September 1849
Owen McGovern	at Maidstone in March 1848
John O'Hara	at Barbadoes in December 1848
Frederick Hole	at Bath in October 1849
Daniel Gibson	at Aberdeen in September 1849
James McLacklan	at Glasgow in September 1849
Thomas Pickering	at Beverley in October 1849
Thomas Townsend	at Gloucester in January 1850
John C. Keys	at Exeter in September 1849

[1] Central Criminal Court (Old Bailey).

William Rodwell	at Leicester in July 1849
Benjamen Treloar	at Exeter in July 1849
Joseph Townsend and	at Northampton in July 1849
Frederick Townsend	
William McDonald	at Kirton in July 1849
James Clayton	at Leicester in July 1849
John Aldersey	at Chester in August 1849
Nathaniel Wright	at Chester in August 1849
Obadiah John Heathcotte	at Chester in August 1849
Robert Eades	at Gloucester in August 1849
Peter Devine	at Liverpool in August 1849
Charles Simpson	at Worcester in October 1849
Joseph Hill	at York in July 1849
Patrick Bray	at Limerick in July 1849
Samuel Smith	at the C.C.Ct. in June 1848
Keiran Cagan	at Kings County in March 1848
Gaiah Dawson	at Durham in July 1847
John Henry	at Glasgow in April 1847
Thomas Farrant	at Winchester in October 1846
Angus Millam	at Edinburgh in November 1846
Charles W. Clark	at C.C.Ct. in October 1846
Edward Yoxale	at C.C.Ct. in November 1847
John Hill	at York in July 1849
Patrick Brassil	at Clare in January 1849
Andrew Hawthorn	at Armagh in January 1849
Charles Connors	at Kildare in March 1850
John Gibbs	at Bath in October 1849

We in consideration &c, &c, and to grant Our Pardon for the crimes of which they severally stand convicted, to each and every of them, who in the opinion of Our Governor of Gibraltar shall not have been guilty of serious misconduct subsequently to their recommendation to mercy, on condition that they be provided with a passage on board any ship or vessel proceeding from Gibraltar and that they do not return thereto, during the residue of their respective sentences. Our Will and Pleasure therefore is that upon being provided with such passage, you cause each and every of them the said Thomas Dumpleton, Edward Cooke, ... who in the opinion of Our said Governor of Gibraltar shall not have been guilty of serious misconduct since the time of their recommendation to Mercy as aforesaid, to be discharged out of custody and embarked on board such ship or vessel in which a passage shall have been provided for them as aforesaid, and that upon being so embarked this Our Pardon shall have all the effect of a Free Pardon, and that for so doing this shall be your Warrant. Given at Our Court of St. James's the fourth day of August 1854 in the eighteenth year of Our Reign.

To The Governor of Our Garrison   By Her Majesty's Command
of Gibraltar, The Overseer of the   Palmerston
Convict Establishment at Gibraltar,
and all others whom it may concern.

OTHER HOME OFFICE DOCUMENTS RECORDING CRIMINALS

Many classes of Home Office records contain references to criminal matters. Those of most interest to the family historian, which include references to individual criminals, are contained in the following:

PRO, Class HO 12	Criminal Papers (Old Series), 1849 to 1871. Letters, memorials and other papers relating to criminal matters. (A subject index to HO 12 is given in HO 14.)
PRO, Class HO 20	Prison Correspondence and Papers. In-letters, 1820 to 1843. Original In-letters and reports as to the administration of prisons and their inmates.
PRO, Class HO 21	Prisons – Entry Books, Series I, 1812 to 1884. Out-letters and instructions to Governors and Inspectors of Government Prisons.
PRO, Class HO 22	Prisons – Entry Books, Series II, 1849 to 1909. Similar to HO 21, to inspectors and the officials of County Prisons.
PRO, Class HO 45	Correspondence and Papers. Registered Papers, 1841 to 1909. Original letters and papers which have been selected for preservation.

Examples from the above records are given in this chapter. Other PRO classes which may contain material of interest are:

HO 42   Original Letters 1820 to 1861.
HO 44   Correspondence 1820 to 1861.
HO 144   Supplementary Registered Papers 1868 to 1947. Papers on Criminals
          and certain other subjects.

CRIMINAL PAPERS

PRO, HO 12/1/5

Guildhall
10th July 1849

Sir,
    I am directed by the Committee of Aldermen to inform you that two persons under sentence of Transportation at present confined in Newgate, are so refractory and incorrigible that the greatest injury is done to the discipline of the Prison by their conduct, and considerable danger created to the officers of the Establishment so that their immediate removal is essentially necessary; and I am requested to press the matter for your earliest attention.

    Their names are Impey and Jeffries. James Impey is now under sentence for 15 years transportation having been before sentenced to a like punishment for 7 years. And Mark Jeffries is now sentenced to transportation for life having been before sentenced to 15 years transportation.

I am, Sir
Your obedient Servant
Henry Alworth Merewether

The Right Honourable
Sir George Grey, Bt.

Removed to Millbank 14 July 1849.
They are the two convicts who
have recently been prosecuted
for assaulting officers of the
hulks and Millbank Prison.

PRISON CORRESPONDENCE

PRO, HO 20/13

Elizabeth Saunders
Remission

George R.

Whereas Elizabeth Saunders was in January Sessions holden at the Old Bailey in the year 1781 convicted of perjury and sentenced to be imprisoned in Wood Street Compter for three years for the same. And whereas some favourable circumstances have been humbly represented unto us in her behalf inducing us to extend Our Grace and Mercy unto her and to remit her such part of the said imprisonment as remains yet to be undergone and performed. Our Will and Pleasure therefore is that you cause her the said Elizabeth Saunders to be forthwith discharged out of custody. And for so doing this shall be your

7329

Guildhall
10th July 1849

Sir,
    I am directed by the Committee of —
Aldermen to inform you that two persons under sentence of
Transportation at present confined in —
Newgate, are so refractory and incorrigible
that the greatest injury is done to —
the discipline of the Prison by their
conduct, and considerable danger created
to the Officers of the Establishment so that
their immediate removal is essentially
necessary; and I am requested to press
the matter for your earliest attention

    Their names are Impey and Jeffries.
James Impey is now under sentence
for 15 years Transportation having been
before sentenced to a like punishment
for 7 years. — And Mark Jeffries is
now sentenced to Transportation for
Life having been before sentenced
to 15 years Transportation

                I am, Sir,
                Your obedient Servant
            Wm. Ashworth Merewether

The Right Honorable
Sir Geo.e Grey Bt.
&c &c

Letter dated 10 July 1849 stating that James Impey and Mark Jeffries are refractory and incorrigible (PRO, HO 12/1/5)

warrant. Given at our Court at St. James's the 31st day of January 1783 in the twenty third year of Our Reign.

To Our Trusty and Wellbeloved	By His Majesty's Command
James Adair Esq. Recorder of	Thomas Townshend
Our City of London, The Sheriff	
of Our said City and County of	
Middlesex and all others whom	
it may concern.	

PRO, HO 20/13

Thomas Clithero and others
Remission

George R.

Whereas the following persons were severally tried and convicted at the times and places undermentioned and were severally sentenced to hard labour on the River Thames, viz:- Thomas Clithero convicted in Surry 17th March 1779 for four years for grand larceny, Abraham Hyams convicted at Maidstone 29th March 1779 for four years, a capital respite, Robert Perry convicted at New Sarum 4th March 1780 for three years for felony, Joseph Barnard otherwise Barnett, convicted at Bristol 20th March 1780 for three years for grand larceny, Benjamin Wyke otherwise Wykes convicted at Nottingham 9th March 1780 for three years for grand larceny, Joseph Blew convicted at Warwick 18th March 1780 for three years for grand larceny, John Harris convicted at the Old Bailey 10th July 1779 for four years, a capital respite, and William Million convicted at the Old Bailey 10th May 1780 for three years for grand larceny. And whereas Our Justices of Our Court of Kings Bench have recommended them as fit objects of Our Mercy We in consideration thereof and also of the punishment which they have already suffered for their past offences and of the signs they have shewn of reformation are hereby pleased to remit that part of their sentence which remains yet to be undergone. Our Will and Pleasure therefore is that you take due notice hereof and give the necessary directions that they the said Thomas Clithero, Abraham Hyams, Robert Perry, Joseph Barnard otherwise Barnett, Benjamin Wyke otherwise Wykes, Joseph Blew, John Harris and William Million be forthwith discharged out of custody and that you do provide them with such decent clothing at the time of their discharge as in your judgement they may deserve. And for so doing this shall be your Warrant. Given at Our Court at St. James's the 5th day of February 1783, in the twenty third year of Our Reign.

To Our Trusty and Welbeloved	By His Majesty's Command
Duncan Campbell, Esq.,	Tho. Townshend
Superintendent of the	
convicts on the River Thames	

PRO, HO 20/13

Duncan Campbell Esq.	Whitehall
Overseer of Convicts	August 24th 1783

Sir,
 Mr Rose late secretary of the Treasury having as appears by his letter of the 3rd of January last, agreed with you by direction of the Lords Commissioners of that board for the hire of a Hulk as a temporary place of confinement for such convicts under sentence of transportation to North America as their Lordships may allow, to be committed to your custody, and for their clothing and maintenance, as well as for a proper guard to

prevent their escape, and to preserve order and regularity among them, until some method can be adopted for sending them to the places of their destination. And having lately received very pressing representations from the several counties stating the necessity of some temporary relief to prevent epidemical distempers which from the crowded state of the gaols in the said counties as well as in London, there is every reason to apprehend. It is now become essentially necessary that the same measure should be again pursued, and as you have signified to me that you are willing to agree to receive 200 male convicts on the same terms as you entered into with Mr Rose, I am to desire you will receive that number on board, and keep them in safe custody until means can be found for sending them to North America for which service you will be paid in the same manner as was before done by the Treasury, and be borne harmless by me for the non-performance of the contract which must of necessity be entered into by you before the convicts can be committed to your custody by the several Courts.

I am,
North

PRISONS – ENTRY BOOKS

PRO, HO 21/1

The Inspectors of Millbank Prison   Whitehall
13th Nov. 1848

Gentlemen,
I have received and laid before Secretary Sir George Grey your letter of the 11th instant and I am desired to inform you that from the recent reports which he has received from Millbank Prison he trusts that he shall soon be justified in considering the prison as free from the cholera when the usual course may be resumed with regard to the reception and disposal of the prisoners. But as several cases of cholera have recently occured in the prison he does not think it would be right immediately and without some interval, to remove the order of temporary suspension which he thought it his duty to issue, of all orders of admission to the prison. With regard to the disposal of the prisoners, the only immediate available outlet consists of the 20 cells vacant at Pentonville which he had desired to be filled from Millbank, but as he was informed by Dr Ferguson, one of the Pentonville Commissioners, and a very eminent medical authority, that he considered it under present circumstances, unsafe that this direction should be carried into effect. Sir George Grey has desired that these vacancies in Pentonville shall be filled up by the selection of twenty convicts from Newgate who would otherwise have to be removed to Millbank.
A certain number of convicts are shortly to be removed from Pentonville and Wakefield prisons, and on their removal taking place Sir George Grey will consider with reference to the then existing circumstances, which vacancies thus to be created in these prisons shall be filled by the removal of convicts to them from Millbank or from any other prison, but it would be premature at present to decide this question.
I am to request with reference to the return enclosed in your letter of the number of prisoners now in Millbank Prison, with the respective periods of their imprisonment, that you will state, for Sir George Grey's information, which any peculiar circumstances have occasioned the unusually long detention of those in the earlier columns of that return. I am further to request that as it appears from Dr Bailey's letter that he considers those prisoners who have been so long detained in Millbank fit for removal to Reformatory Prisons, or to Convict Establishments. You will transmit to me a list of such of these prisoners if any, as being under sentence of transportation for a term not exceeding seven

years and having been already twelve months in prison under sentence, you consider fit for removal with Tickets of Leave to New South Wales and Van Diemans Land.

I am
G. Cornewall Lewis

PRO, HO 21/1

Richard Robins, Esq.   Whitehall
Tavistock   15th Nov. 1848

Sir,
    Secretary Sir George Grey having caused enquiry to be made into the statements contained in the memorial which accompanied your letter of the 17th ult. regarding the disposal of the clothing of William Lewis, and John Skelly who have been recently discharged from Millbank Prison, and the amount of money supplied to them on their release. I am desired to acquaint you that it is reported to him by the Inspectors of that Prison that upon the reception of prisoners into Millbank Prison their clothing is carefully packed up into separate bundles and labelled with the convict's name. It is then valued by the steward of the prison, and the contractor, who engages to purchase the entire quantity, and the amount for which the clothing is sold is credited to the convicts in the prisoners' ledger and paid to them on their discharge from the prison.
    The great proportion of the clothing in which convicts are received is little better than rags and of so offensive a description that it would be quite impossible to adopt any other course than the one pursued, which leads to a speedy riddance of it.
    Every prisoner on his leaving the prison is furnished on the morning of his discharge with an entire new suit of what are called *liberty clothes* similar in material and make to what is ordinarily worn by the laboring classes.
    William Lewis and John Skelly on their discharge from Millbank were treated precisely the same as all other prisoners under similar circumstances. An officer conducted them to the Railway Station, paid their fare to Exeter 16s/2d each, a further sum of 8s/- each was given them to convey them to Tavistock about 30 miles distant and 5s/- each was paid them in addition for personal expenses, making the sum of £1.10.4 paid to each convict. They also received a complete suit of new clothing comprising coat, waistcoat, trousers, shirt, stockings, shoes and cap, superior in quality to what is generally worn by the laboring classes, to which they belong. The clothes in which they were received were of so little value as to bring no more than 6d, which was paid to them on their discharge.
    It appears to Sir George Grey that this report furnishes a very different view of the case of these two men from that stated in their memorial.

I am
G. Cornewall Lewis

PRO, HO 21/1

The Inspectors of Millbank Prison   Whitehall
                                                              17th November 1848

Gentlemen,
    It being proposed that 50 convicts now undergoing probationary confinement in the House of Correction at Wakefield, shall be removed from thence to the Convict Prison at Portland on Wednesday the 22nd inst., I am desired by Secretary Sir Geo. Grey to desire you will cause four Officers appointed to Portland, and now serving at Millbank, to be sent to Wakefield, on the previous day, and that you will direct the remaining Portland Officers serving at Millbank to meet the prisoners who will leave Wakefield on

Wednesday the 22nd inst., by the mail train at 8.30 p.m. at Euston Square, and accompany them in omnibuses to the Waterloo Station, with a view to their removal on Thursday the 23rd inst., by the 8.20 a.m. train to Gosport, from whence they will be conveyed by steam vessel to Portland.

I am further to request that you will confer with Lieut. Col. Jebb as to the general arrangements which it may be necessary to adopt in connexion with the removal of these convicts.

I am to add that directions have been given for the removal of 14 convicts from Pentonville Prison by the same conveyance to the same destination, and that they will be at the Waterloo Station at the appointed time.

I am
G. Cornewall Lewis

PRO, HO 21/5

The Visiting Magistrates of the Court   Whitehall
Wakefield Prison   20 Jany. 1849

Gentlemen,

I am desired by Secy. Sir Geo. Grey to acqt. you that he has recd. from Mr Hill the Prison Inspector of the District, a letter containing some suggestions arising out of a recent inspection of the Convict Department of Wakefield Prison, to two of which Sir Geo. Grey wishes to call your attention.

Mr Hill states, 'some time before my last visit to Wakefield Prison, instructions, I was informed, to bring into association, without reference to their different characters, or various degrees of moral improvement, all those prisoners who were about to be removed to Portland Island; and I consequently found a considerable number of these prisoners at work together, but the Chaplain stated that three of them were of such bad character that they were likely to do the others irreparable injury, and I therefore recommended the Governor to withdraw these three prisoners which he did'. The following is the Chaplain's statement on this subject:-

'During the last fortnight fifty prisoners, preparatory to being removed to the New Prison in Portland Island have been associated. The prisoners however, being of different grades of conduct and character, the association must, I fear, have been injurious, especially at first, when three prisoners of the very lowest grade were mixed with them. If these three prisoners whose names are John Hatton, Robt. Holder, and Henry Jones are allowed to associate with others, and better disposed prisoners on their arrival in Portland Island, I shd. apprehend the worst results, and that very much of our past labor will have been thrown away. I quite approve of the principle of gradual association but I think that there should be no fixed period for withdrawing prisoners from their separate cells; that it should be made to depend on the character and conduct of each individual prisoner, and that it is of great importance that in the associated party no one shd. be permitted to enter who is likely to exercise a bad influence upon the others'.

Upon this point I am to state Sir George Grey's opinion that although it is necessary that the separate confinement of the Convicts shd. be relaxed before their removal from the prison, this relaxation ought to be carried into effect with proper caution, so as to prevent the bad consequences likely to result from the unchecked association of the convicts irrespective of their individual characters, and he trusts that in future occasions it may be found practicable to make such arrangements as will obviate the evils adverted to by Mr Hill. Mr Hill further says, 'The present mode in which the Government Convicts at Wakefield are paid for affords but little motive to those who have the immediate management of the Prison, and who are therefore in the best position for acting to reduce the Cost of the Convicts, either by measures of economy, or by endeavouring to render their work more profitable; inasmuch as the gain to the Prison remains the same wh'n the convicts are expensive or otherwise. By adopting another principle for the Contract, viz, that of paying a certain sum per head to include all charges, as is the case with the convicts of Leeds, I am satisfied that a considerable saving might be effected to Government and a considerable increase also obtained to the remuneration desired from the Convicts by the County. Several Offices are at present multiplied without any advantage, and much additional trouble and expence are created by the necessity of keeping the departments wholly distinct. The following statement was made by the Governor:-

'I am of opinion that the management of the Prison could be greatly simplified, the disbursements materially lessened, and the produce of the labour considerably increased if the two Departments of the Prison were united, instead of having a separate staff of Officers and separate Hospitals for each. As a sample of the saving which might be effected I may mention that there was, for a considerable time, a separate Clerk for the Convict Department, but that on his being dismissed for misconduct and inefficiency, I united his duties with those of the two Clerks in the West Riding Department, with an increase to the salary of each of £15 a year. This increase was, in my opinion more than equivalent for the increased amount of labour, nevertheless a saving was effected by the arrangement of £60 a year, the salary of the other Clerk having been £90 a year. In fact the two Clerks agreed to take the additional duty for nothing, so slight did it appear to them, but the Magistrates thought it right that some increase shd. be made to their Salaries for it. This alteration has not only been beneficial in a pecuniary point of view, but by its tendency to simplify the management has afforded relief in other ways, and especially to myself, in the general direction of the Prison.

For some time I was so harassed by the labor and vexation arising from the necessity of keeping the two Departments distinct at all points, and from the jealousies between the two Corps of Officers, as to become unwell and to be compelled for a time to leave the Prison in order to recruit my strength, and though things work much more smoothly, the labor of management is much greater than it wd be if the division were done away with. The Superintendent of Work in the West Riding Department (Mr Dewhurst) is a very efficient Officer, far more so than the Superintendent in the Convict Department (Mr Parker), and I am satisfied that the work of the Convicts wo^d be much more productive if Mr Dewhurst's Superintendence extended to the whole. I have for example compared the profits arising from a given number of mat makers among the Convicts and I find that the West Riding mat makers produce more by one quarter than the Convict mat makers, altho the difference ought to be on the other side, seeing that the Convicts remain much longer than the generality of prisoners from the West Riding.'

I have ascertained that the Visiting Justices have no objection to the plan of Government paying a certain sum per head, to include all expences, but their Chairman wishes that the offer on the subject sh^d emanate from Government.

Upon the point Sir Geo. Grey will be happy to receive from the Visiting Justices any observations wch. they may be disposed to make.

It is right however that I sh^d state that if the proposition of paying a fixed sum per head should be adopted, that Sum must be calculated with reference to the actual cost of the Convict Department of the Prison, and that the amount agreed upon should be subject to revision from time to time in order that it may be regulated according to the price of provisions, to the scale of Dietary for the time being and to other circumstances affecting the cost of the maintenance of Convicts.

I am,
H. Waddington

PRISONS – ENTRY BOOKS

PRO, HO 22/3

Whitehall
22 Jany 1851

Sir,

The accompanying parchment certificate of discharge from the Royal Artillery of Walter Spence a Military convict lately brought from Bermuda to this country in the transport *Diligence* having been forwarded to this Department by the Board of Ordnance. I am ordered by Sec. Sir George Grey to transmit the same to you in order that it may be delivered up to the prisoner who is now confined in the Millbank Prison, on the expiration of his sentence.

I am,
H. Waddington

Col. Jebb.

PRO, HO 22/3

Whitehall
23 Jany 1851

Sir,

With reference to Captain O'Brien's letter of the 16th ultimo recommending convicts for removal from the Millbank Prison to the Philanthropic Farm School at Redhill. I am directed by Secy Sir George Grey to acquaint you that it appears by a communication which has been received from the Rev. Sydney Turner that the Committee of the above mentioned Society are willing to receive into their institution 7 of the 9 boys recommended for admission, but declines to receive James Moore and Thomas Williams in consequence of the first mentioned prisoner having been discharged from the Institution on the 17 June last as incorrigible and the last mentioned boy having absconded from the School in Jany 1850. Under these circumstances Sir George Grey has thought it right that the convicts Moore and Williams should be sent to Parkhurst, and I herewith forward you orders for their removal and reception in that Establishment.

I am,
H. Waddington

Col. Jebb

CORRESPONDENCE

PRO, HO 45/9347/25166

Robert Sweet and William Bisgrove sentenced to death for murder

Judges Lodgings
Maidstone
Sunday August 2nd. 1868

Sir,

I beg to address you in deference to the case of Robert Sweet and William Bisgrove prisoners now under sentence of death in Taunton Gaol.

The prisoners were tried before me on Monday and Tuesday last at the recent Assizes for the County of Somerset, for the murder of George Cornish. They were both defended by Counsel. Sweet by Counsel of his own selection, and Bisgrove by Mr Saunders who undertook his defence at my request.

Though the evidence was consistent with the notion that the murder was committed by one of the prisoners, with the cognizance and assistance of the other, still taking into consideration the motives suggested for the perpetration of the offence, whether revenge or the hope of plunder, it seemed to me that in all human probability the murder was the act of one man. The Jury were strictly charged that if they thought that one only of the prisoners was guilty, but were unable to say which of the two was guilty, it was their duty to acquit both.

They found a verdict of guilty against both the prisoners, a verdict which was not satisfactory to me, so far as concerned the prisoner Sweet.

On the morning subsequent to the trial, I received information from the Governor of the Gaol at Taunton, that the prisoner Bisgrove had confessed that he alone had committed the murder and had stated that Sweet the other prisoner had in no way been privy to it. This information was given to me just as I was leaving Taunton on my way to Maidstone to proceed with the business of the Winter Assize here.

The following morning in London on my way to Maidstone I received an enclosure from the Governor of the Gaol at Taunton which I now forward for your consideration. It contains the following documents:

1st   An original letter from the Governor of Taunton Gaol to myself.
2nd   Copy of a letter from the prisoner Bisgrove to his brother.
3rd   Statement or confession of the prisoner Bisgrove.

I also enclose a copy of my notes and the depositions taken before the Magistrates. Having taken into consideration the fact that the murder on the evidence as presented at the trial seemed to be the work of one man that the prisoner Bisgrove, whilst by his confession he implicates himself exculpates Sweet, and having carefully considered the evidence by which the prosecution sought to fix Sweet. I consider it my duty humbly to recommend that a free pardon should be granted to Robert Sweet. I also enclose an extract from the *Times* newspaper of the 17th December which contains a short, but substantially correct account with regard to the confession.

I have the honour to remain
Sir
To the Right Honble   Your obedient servant
H.A. Bruce   W.T. Channell

Times *17 December 1868*

Winter Assizes
Western Circuit
Taunton December 16th
(Before Mr Baron Channel)

The Wells Murder

In consequence of the great excitement created relative to this murder, we have taken more than ordinary pains to make inquiries and we are now enabled to state that Bisgrove has said that he was very anxious yesterday, when in court to state the real facts, but he had not courage to do so. After his condemnation yesterday he requested that an independent minister might attend him. Mr Oakley, the Governor, who although a strict disciplinarian, is well known to everyone as the kindest of men to prisoners, immediately acceded to his request, and a rev. gentleman at once went to the gaol. Bisgrove, after having been engaged in prayer said that on the night in question, being quite intoxicated, he lay down near Cornish; he awoke, and he had an impulse, not from any feeling of revenge, or with any intention of robbery, to kill the man. He got up in a semi-drunken state, and went to the brook, and there he took up a stone; he carried it to the spot where

Cornish was lying and threw the stone upon his head, and that blow killed Cornish. No one was with him. Having made this statement he appeared comfortable. This now shows that the evidence of the woman Drew was substantially correct, although at the time it appeared to be most improbable, and all the circumstances led to a supposition that Sweet was the murderer. We are very glad in such a case to be able to elucidate the matter.

Taunton
25 December 1868

Sir,
    I take the liberty of forwarding to you the enclosed extract from the 'Bristol Daily Press' relating to the Wells murder.

  I do not know the writer and I am not connected in any way with the matter referred to but I thought it right that your attention should be respectfully called to the state of the convict Bisgrove's mind with a view to a medical enquiry if you so approve.

I merely write as one of the public.

I have the honor to be

The Right Honorable
Her Majesty's Sec^y of State,
Home Department

Sir,
Your very obedient servant
John Taunton

The Wells Murder
To the Editors of the Western Daily Press

Gentlemen, I have read the letter of 'Medicas', and your own remarks on 'The Wells Murder', in your issue of this day, with no common satisfaction. That Bisgrove is, or rather was, to all intents and purposes insane and irresponsible when he committed the rash and dreadful act for which he is convicted is, in my judgement, most certain and to this effect I had occasion yesterday to declare myself. 'Medicas' has, as you are aware, given four distinct and conclusive reasons why Bisgrove should be held to have been insane, and therefore irresponsible in a degree, at the time the murder was committed. An additional indication of impaired mind (lunacy) remains, as I conceive, to be considered; it is this – Bisgrove made, I believe, no attempt to make good his escape. Like the mad 'Earl Ferrers', and like the late 'G.V. Townley', he (Bisgrove) remained by his victim. This is a highly important fact, and one well known to medical men as constituting in itself a very strong presumption in favour of the existence of insanity in him or her charged with crime. I cannot well doubt that antecedents or personal history (and, probably, the parentage) of Bisgrove would go far to demonstrate the existence in him a long standing, though perhaps a latent, disorder of the brain and nervous system, for the epileptic seizures to which he declared subject are but the external signs or evidences of internal permanent and structural degenerations – the peculiarity of such seizures being that they occur only in paroxysms, like neuralgia, whooping cough, ague, and other diseases. I agree with 'Medicas' that to hang Bisgrove, would be both useless and inhuman. However, of this there can be no doubt, the only place of safety for the poor fellow is the County Asylum. I may add that during my long connection with the large asylums at Hanwell and Colney Hatch, Middlesex, I had the medical charge of some hundreds of epileptic patients, and I cannot but consider all such as occasionally, and more or less insane, and therefore irresponsible – using this word in its common acceptance and as applied to the insane charged with crime.

Your obedient servant
James Geo. Davey M.D.

Northwoods, near Bristol
Dec. 22, 1868

Somerset Prison
Taunton
16th Dec 1868

William Bisgrove a convict under sentence of Death for murder says, I desire to state:-
I done the murder. I went to the river and picked up the stone. I brought it over and throw'd it on the man's head. I picked three pence out of his pocket. Sweet had nothing to do with it. I dont know that he know I done it I never said nothing to him or he to me. I cant say if he see me done it but he never help did it. I throw'd the stone back over the river over the hedge just where I told the Policeman. I should not like for Sweet to have to suffer for me. I was very worse for beer. I had been all day drinking I went with the woman but I dont believe she knew anything about it. When I laid down near the man the woman said I would not lay down there for a gold watch. After I laid down I went to sleep. When I waked up I was going away but something seemed to tell me I must murder that man and then I went over to the river and found the stone and brought it over on my head and I thrown it down on the man's head. I believe it was twice or three times which I am not prepared to say but it was more than once I throw it on his head. I throwed the stone away. I turned round and stood there something come into my mind to see if he had any money about him I went round and put my hand in his pocket and found three pence. I stood there a bit, it was not long. I cant say how long. I looked on the man. While I looked on the man the policeman came and looked over the gate.

Whatever made me do it I cant think. It was not for money. I had no thought of money. I cant think why I done it.

The mark of
X
William Bisgrove

Taken before me
  Wm. Oakley
  Governor Somerset County Prison
  Taunton

Witness
  Henry Berry
  Dep. Gov[r]

Taunton Prison
16th Decr 1868

My Dear Brother,
    I am sorry to state that I am sentenced to death, I am also sorry to tell you it was a parcel of lies I told you in Shepton Mallet Prison. I am guilty and am sorry to own it. I would like you my dear brother to have my clothes that are at Charlton. I desire that Isaac may have my watch but if you think proper you can keep it. I am not sure that I gave my Bible to Elizabeth Jones but I would like you to have it if possible and keep it for my sake, also to get the hair that is at Isaac Jones's and keep it. I would like to see any of you if you can come to see me, tell Hannah if she cannot I shall never see her again in this world but we shall meet again in heaven. Read this letter to my mother and tell her not to fret as I shall meet her again in the next world. I hope you will all forgive me for disgracing you but sincerely hope you will all meet it as firmly as you can trusting in God for his support. I am pretty well in health considering the position and place I occupy. My kind love to my mother, to yourself, Sarah Ann & the child, to Hannah, to Isaac & Elizabeth Jones and to James Wilcombe & his wife. Tell them all if they cannot come to see me to write to me.

Beginning of a letter from William Bisgrove to his brother stating that he is sentenced to death (PRO, HO 45/9347)

You yourself write back as soon as ever you can and let me know how my Mother takes this unfortunate affair.

I remain
Your Aff^t, but unfortunate Brother
William Bisgrove

Wm. Stevens, Schoolmaster, Taunton Prison

Jesus said 'I am the resurrection and the life; he that believeth in me though he were dead, yet shall he live, and whosoever liveth and believeth in me he shall never die.
John XI–25–26

In my Father's house are many mansions, I go to prepare a place for you. I will come again and receive you unto myself, that where I am there may he be also.

John XIV–2–3

To the Right Honourable H.A. Bruce
Secretary of State for the Home Department

The humble petition of the undersigned minister and inhabitants of the parish of Fivehead in the county of Somerset most earnestly, respectfully and solemnly prayeth.

That the sentence of Death passed on William Bisgrove for the murder of the late George Cornish may not be carried into effect. For as much as it appeared on the trial of the said William Bisgrove that he had been for some time subject to fits your petitioners humbly submit that persons subject to fits when recovering from the same are often under delusive impressions and in such a state of agitation that they are not considered responsible for their actions. That many persons have destroyed life whilst in a state of temporary disorder of the brain and have not been subjected to the extreme penalty of the law. That under certain disorders of the brain persons suffering from them are irresistably impelled to destroy life. That the course of intemperance and gross immorality in which William Bisgrove had been indulging had probably occasioned or excited some overpowering delusion and produced an irresistable impulse to destroy the life of George Cornish under which the convict hastened to kill him and as soon as the deed was done he became conscious and was again in his senses. Your petitioners humbly pray considering the full confession he has now made of his being the cause of the death of the deceased, and his earnest desire that Sweet should not suffer on his account and that this indicates a good and honourable feeling, and that on the trial no evidence was given of any malice or ill will or even of previous acquaintance of William Bisgrove with George Cornish. That sentence of Death may not be carried into effect.

That the convict may be subjected to such other penalty as to Her Gracious Majesty may seem fitting. And your petitioners will ever pray.

Richard William Lambert, vicar of Fivehead
William Henry Richardson

George Barnard	Joseph Parsons	John Gridley
Robert Hillard	Thomas Gillard	Josiah Fryer
Philip Meade	Eli Stodgell	Mich. Game [?]
Wm. Mead	Wm. Stuckey	Henry Stodgel
Lewis Meade	Vincent Stuckey	
H. John Thomas	Joshua Corpe	
Alfred Dinham	Susan Corpe	Fivehead nr Taunton
Henry Dinham	Samuel Gridley	December 22nd 1868

Somerset County Prison
Taunton
24th December 1868

Sir,

In reply to Letter signed 'A.F.O. Liddell' dated yesterday and received this day in reference to the Convict William Bisgrove under sentence of Death in this Prison.

The surgeon having entered in his Journal a recommendation that the Convict should be visited by Dr Woodforde a competent medical practitioner (experienced as a proprietor of Lunatic Asylums) I direct that the Convict should be visited by Dr

Woodforde accordingly and herewith annex a joint report from Dr Woodforde and the Surgeon of this Prison.

I am Sir,
Your obedient Servant
Henry Badcock
Visiting Justice

The Rt. Honble
The Home Secretary
Home Office
London

Somerset County Prison
Taunton
December 24th 1868

We have this day seen and examined William Bisgrove under sentence of death in this Prison. We learn from him that about three years since while at work in a Coal Pit at Radstock, Somerset, he was frightened by one of his fellow laborers, who concealed himself in one of the passages of the Coal Pit, and suddenly jumped out as Bisgrove passed by. This caused Bisgrove to fall in an epileptic fit, and he has been subject to these fits at intervals ever since in consequence of which he was obliged to discontinue working at the Colliery.

The usual result of epileptic fits is to weaken the intellect, and we have no doubt that at the time of the fright a strong mental impression was produced on him, independently of the epileptic fit, from which his mind has never recovered.

Bisgrove informs us that he has on several occasions witnessed fatal accidents from falling of stones from the roof of the workings in the Coal Pit, by which he has been greatly shocked. From his own statement as to what he felt and did at the time of the murder we have no doubt that he was at the time subject to an uncontrollable homicidal impulse.

Fras Henry Woodforde M.D.
Proprietor of Amberd House
Private Asylum

Henry Liddon, Surgeon
to the Somerset County Prison

Somerset County Prison
Taunton
16th January 1869

Sir,
    We enclose certificate of insanity of the Prisoner William Bisgrove, and as imprisonment is believed to aggravate his condition we recommend his removal as early as possible to the Broadmoor Asylum he having on two occasions attempted suicide.

    We propose to make an order on the Poor Law Union in which the Parish of his settlement is situate, or on default of ascertaining the same, on the County of Somerset for his maintenance under 3 & 4 Vic. cap 54.

We are Sir
Your obedient Servants

The Rt Honble
The Secretary of State
Home Office
London

William Allen
H. Bethune Patton
Visiting Justices

To Her Majesty's Principal Secretary
of State for The Home Department

Whereas William Bisgrove aged 19 years stated to be of the parish of Wookey Somerset, a prisoner in Her Majesty's Prison at Taunton in the County of Somerset convicted of murder at the Assizes held at Taunton on the 11th day of December 1868 and No. 7 in the Calendar of such Assize sentenced to Death, commuted to Penal Servitude for the term of his natural life appearing to be of unsound mind.

    We The Reverend William Jeffery Allen, Clerk and Henry Bethune Patton two of Her Majesty's Justices of the Peace for the said County with the aid of Francis Henry Woodforde of Pitminster in the said County, Esquire, Physician and Henry Liddon of Taunton, Surgeon have enquired as to the Insanity of the said William Bisgrove and do Certify that the said William Bisgrove is Insane.

Dated this sixteenth day of January 1869

William Allen
H. Bethune Patton   } Visiting Justices
F.H. Woodforde M.D.
Henry Liddon Surgeon

THE RECORDS OF THE DIRECTOR OF PUBLIC PROSECUTIONS

Before 1879 no single authority was charged with the general supervision of criminal prosecutions. The Home Office, in addition to its general responsibility for the administration and enforcement of criminal law, gave advice on prosecutions to the police forces and magistrates' clerks and gave directions to the Treasury Solicitor to institute proceedings in important cases, notably those involving political crimes. The Treasury Solicitor and the Attorney General were also able to institute proceedings. Public prosecutors were employed in certain of the lower courts and four Treasury Counsels were employed by the Treasury Solicitor in the Central Criminal Court. Public Prosecutors were also employed by a number of Clerks of the Peace and certain large police authorities maintained salaried prosecuting solicitors. Thus many persons representing various authorities acted as public prosecutors.

In 1879 the office of Director of Public Prosecutions was established by the Prosecution of Offences Act, 42–43 Vict. c. 22. The Director and Assistant Directors are appointed by the Home Secretary but are responsible directly to the Attorney General. Certain types of offence e.g. sedition and treason, can only be prosecuted by the Director of Public Prosecutions or with his consent. Transcripts of proceedings of selected criminal trials of special interest have been preserved by the Director of Public Prosecutions. These, in the Public Record Office Class DPP 4 cover the period 1846 to 1931. As these date from more than thirty years before the appointment of the first Director of Public

Prosecutions records of the early cases must have been inherited from another government department. Further case papers dating from 1889 are to be found in Class DPP1.

The following is a small part of the transcript of the trial of Robert Pate who was accused of an assault on Queen Victoria. This material covers a total of 305 pages of which the following is taken from 11 pages.

PRO, DPP 4/3

The Trial of Robert Pate, Charged with Unlawfully Striking the Person of our Lady the Queen with an Offensive Weapon.

The Queen versus Robert Pate

Proceedings on the Trial of this Indictment at the Central Criminal Court, Old Bailey before The Hon. Mr Baron Alderson, The Hon. Mr Justice Patteson and The Hon. Mr Justice Talfourd, Thursday 11 July 1850.

The prisoner was arraigned and pleaded 'Not Guilty'.

The following Jurymen answered to their names:-

Henry Brasted	Francis Bint
Thomas Baldock	George Ward
Thomas Chapman	Andrew Larkan
Joseph Herris	George Law
George Boulton	William York
Charles Childs	William Mayo Allen

The Jury were sworn

MR. ATTORNEY GENERAL

'May it please your Lordships, Gentlemen of the jury. It has been my misfortune upon several occasions since I have had the honor of filling the office which I now hold, to appear here as public prosecutor to conduct cases of serious importance. This at all times as you will readily believe, is a most painful duty, but I can assure you with perfect sincerity that upon no occasion in my public office or in my professional experience have I appeared under feelings of deeper regret than upon the present occasion the object of the attack made by the prisoner at the Bar on a Lady who deserving not only our Loyalty and attachment and affection and is therefore calculated to create deep interest in our minds upon this occasion but the fact of the prisoner being a Gentleman of education, a man who has borne Her Majesty's Commission, aggravates the case in my judgement and well warrants me in imploring you before you enter into a consideration of this case to dismiss from your minds everything that you may have heard or read upon the subject, to endeavor if you can, to apply your judgements in this case with the same calmness and coolness that you would apply to a transaction of the most ordinary description, and to direct your attention solely to the evidence which will be adduced before you and direction which you will receive from their Lordships who now preside upon the bench.

I should exceed my duty upon this occasion if I were to dilate upon the motives or conduct of the prisoner or to endeavor to divert your attention by entering upon general topics. My duty as public prosecutor is merely to state to you in detail a general outline of the evidence to enable you to follow the testimony of the witnesses and impartially to

The Queen

versus

Robert Pate

} Proceedings on the Trial of this Indictment at the Central Criminal Court Old Bailey before The Hon: Mr Baron Alderson The Hon: Mr Justices Patteson & The Hon: Mr Justice Talfourd Thursday 11 July. 1850.

The prisoner was araigned and pleaded "Not Guilty"

The following Jurymen answered to their names

Henry Brashetts	Francis Birt
Thomas Baldock	George Ward
Thomas Chapman	Andrew Larkan
Joseph Ferris	George Law
George Bonestong	William York
Charles Childs	William Mayo Alleng

The Jury were Sworn

Mr Attorney General

May it please your Ladship Gentlemen of the Jury It has been my misfortune upon several occasions since

Cover page of the proceedings of the trial of Robert Pate (PRO, DPP 4/3)

arrive at a just conclusion and unhappily the facts of the case are short are plain and to be told in a few words.

The prisoner at the Bar was the son of a Gentleman of high respectibility and station, a Gentleman who had filled the office of High Sheriff of his County, in the neighborhood of Wisbeach where he resides. The prisoner himself has held the Commission of Her Majesty as Cornet and Lieutenant in the 10th Hussars. He has for some time retired from the Army and lived in comparative privacy in London, a life I believe of great regularity. On Thursday the 27th of June last about the hour of six or a little after Her Majesty left the Royal Palace in an open carriage accompanied by the usual attendants and with the Royal children for the purpose of paying a visit at Cambridge House. She arrived there about a quarter or twenty minutes past six o'clock and driving into the Gate to make her general enquiry it was not unnatural to suppose that that took place which of course the curiosity and attachment of Her Subjects would lead you to expect would be the case, a Crowd was attracted round the Gate of Cambridge House for the purpose of seeing Her Majesty leave that place. Amongst them the prisoner at the Bar was a bystander. As Her Majesty came from the gates at a slow pace or the carriage I believe stopped for the purpose of clearing away the crowd or making a turn for Piccadilly, the prisoner stepped forward and with a cane which he then held in his hand struck Her Majesty upon the forehead a blow of some violence which drew blood, caused a considerable swelling and bled for some time after the arrival of Her Majesty at the palace. Sir James Clark was sent for, some application was made and with her usual self possession, and presence of mind Her Majesty being desirous of satisfying Her Subjects that nothing serious had occured to endanger her comfort or her life, appeared in public that evening, as you know, to the universal satisfaction of Her Subjects who had cause of congratulation that she had received comparatively a very slight injury.

Now those are the circumstances of the case, they are short and will be proved to you by one or two witnesses. I believe my learned Friend cannot make them a subject of dispute or endeavor to raise a doubt upon your mind as to the guilt of the prisoner at the Bar. It is not for me, nor, forgive me for saying, is it within your province, as Jurors to speculate as to the motives which may actuate persons who violate the laws of their country. Motives might be suggested for the conduct of various persons which it would be imprudent and certainly indiscreet to enter upon in public discression but above all nobody can for a moment be allowed to say in a Court of Justice that the absence of motive and the unaccountable nature of the act which is charged against him are to be any foundation whatever for immunity from punishment, what ground therefore can be suggested by my learned Friend as an excuse for the act with which the prisoner stands charged? I have heard it rumoured (upon that it will not be my duty now to say a single word) that this Gentleman or the friends of this Gentleman propose to endeavor to establish before you that he is not accountable for his actions. You will forgive me for saying that it is of the most extreme importance that questions of that description should be decided after the most temperate consideration and be governed by the strictest rules of law. It is not to be endured that persons should endeavor to establish any immunity from punishment in consequence of their guilt by endeavoring idly and without the most substantial grounds to set up that they are not responsible for their actions. It would not be becoming of me now to advert to the governing principles by which you must be actuated if that question be submitted for your consideration. My learned Friend if he is in a condition to establish that will of course with the direction which governs his acts, endeavor to lay down before you those rules which will actuate your conduct and to apply his evidence to those rules. If he cannot do so successfully I am sure the public is safe in his hands that he will not endeavor to mislead you by any endeavor to pervert the ends of justice, in this or in any other case and I am certain that whatever may be the result you will be guided by the directions of my Lord to arrive at a safe and just conclusion which will be satisfactory to the Public.'

Witnesses for the prosecution were:

1. Colonel The Honourable Charles Grey, Equerry to Her Majesty
2. Mr Robert Renwick, Sergeant Footman
3. Mr James Silver, Sergeant of the *A* Division of Police
4. Mr Samuel Cowling, bookseller at Norwich Court, Fetter Lane (amongst the crowd waiting to see Her Majesty)
5. Sir James Clark, Bart, M.D. Physician to Her Majesty

Witnesses for the defence were:

1. Colonel John Vandeleur, Lieutenant Colonel of the 10th Hussars at the time Robert Pate joined the regiment
2. Captain Edmund Frith, Captain 10th Hussars
3. Captain Sir Thomas Munro, Bart, Captain 10th Hussars
4. Corporal Thomas Venn, Corporal 10th Hussars
5. Sergeant George Pitt, Sergeant 10th Hussars
6. Thomas Martin, Trumpeter 10th Hussars
7. Mr Robert Francis Pate, father of the prisoner
8. Charles Dodman formerly of the 10th Hussars
9. William Baker Lee, driver of a hansom cab who often drove Robert Pate
10. Mr Charles Mason, keeps livery stables in Dyson's Yard, Park Lane
11. Mr James Startin, surgeon living in Saville Row
12. George Fearon Gardiner, beadle at Burlington Arcade
13. Mr John Squire, Inspector of the Metropolitan Police
14. John Mulling, gate keeper at Buckhill Gate, Kensington Gardens
15. Theo. O'Gormon Mahon, M.P.
16. The Rev. Charles Driscoll of 60 Sloane Street
17. Dr John Conolly, physician of the Hanwell Lunatic Asylum
18. Dr. Edward Thomas Monro

[All the witnesses for the defence indicated that Robert Pate was of unsound mind. It was clear that while in the army he had been held in high esteem by his fellow officers. Apparently his favourite Newfoundland dog and three valuable horses had been bitten by a rabid dog which drove them mad and were, therefore, subsequently destroyed. This had caused Robert Pate to become mentally unbalanced. The jury took three hours and forty-five minutes to reach the verdict of GUILTY.*]*

Sentence

MR BARON ALDERSON

'Robert Pate the Jury have found you guilty after a long and patient investigation and there can be no reasonable doubt that they have come to the right conclusion. At the same time it is quite obvious from the evidence which has been given that you are a person of very eccentric habits, in some degree varying perhaps because God has been pleased to visit you with some degree of mental affliction and therefore much to be pitied in that respect. But the offence of which you have been guilty is a very serious and important one. You have been guilty of striking a female which for a soldier is a very shocking thing, but when one considers that that female is the Sovereign of this Country, one entitled to the respect of all her Subjects by reason of her virtues and by reason of her exalted position, that which in an ordinary case would be a grievous offence becomes in your case a very heinous and serious offence. How could it happen that you a soldier of the Country should insult one whom all the Country love, venerate and respect, one who adds to the dignity of Her station all the virtues of domestic life, one whom it is our pleasure to obey and our satisfaction to love? This is the person upon whom you have thought fit to inflict a blow disgraceful under any circumstances, peculiarly disgraceful under yours . . . . . .

Considering who you are, considering the station of life which you have filled, considering the respectability of those with whom you are connected, it is not the intention of the Court to inflict upon you, as they might do, the disgraceful punishment of whipping because one has a degree of respect towards you even in your miserable and unfortunate condition, one would not wish to add so grievous and heavy a disgrace to your family by ignoble punishment of which I have referred. One has some respect for you though you have had no respect for others. Nevertheless it is the duty of the Court to impose upon you as long a sentence as they can to prevent you from doing mischief in future. I would fair believe that you were not master of your own understanding because I would fair believe that it is the privilege and boast of this Country that no one but a madman would attack the most gracious Sovereign of this Country. I believe it is as great a proof of insanity as it is possible for a person to give. At the same time I think the Jury have done right in finding that you are not irresponsible by reason of that insanity.

The Sentence therefore of the Court, taking all the matter into consideration, taking into consideration the duty which we have to protect the Sovereign by every measure in our power by the longest period of time for which we can subject you to restraint, is that you be transported for Seven Years.'

When arrested Robert Pate was held at Newgate Prison and was returned there after his trial. The day after his sentence he was transferred to Millbank Prison, Westminster.

The Newgate prison register (PRO, PCOM 2/212) describes him as a gentleman, fair-haired with broad face, grey eyes and slender build. The Millbank prison register (PRO, PCOM 2/31) also states that he was single, aged thirty years and could read and write well. He had no previous convictions. His address was given as Wisbeach, Cambridgeshire, and he was recorded as a protestant.

On the 5 August 1850 he was transferred to the ship *William Jardine* then recorded as bound for Australia. (This ship sailed to Hobart, Tasmania.)

The Army List for 1846 shows that he was then a lieutenant in the 10th (the Prince of Wales' own) Royal Regiment of (Light) Dragoons.

CHAPTER 20

BANKRUPTS AND DEBTORS

Although, legally, bankrupts and debtors were not criminals, they did suffer imprisonment and most found themselves confined in county gaols with convicted criminals of all classes. In London, however, there were prisons used solely for bankrupts and debtors.

It was not until the Bankruptcy Act of 1861 (24 & 25 Vict. c 134) that bankrupts and debtors were no longer to suffer imprisonment, the exception to this being those persons found guilty of debt by fraudulent means. On 1 November 1861 most imprisoned debtors were set free.

The following are examples from the various classes of documents in the Public Record Office which contain details of bankrupts and debtors.

PRO, B1/24

Friday the Twenty first day
of December 1750
In the matter of Catherine
Forman and Henry Lang, bankrupts

Whereas Isaac Dias Fernandes otherwise Vianna of London merchant Attorney for and on behalf of Isaac Lopes Pinheiro and Co. of the City of Leghorn [Italy] merchants did on the seventh day of December instant prefer his petition to me shewing that the said Catherine Forman and Henry Lang, the bankrupts on the 11th January 1744 drew two bills of exchange, one for 500 dollars effective and the other for 700 like dollars on Messrs Bruni Bistotto and Winspiase, merchants at Leghorn both which bills were drawn at one usance and made payable to Gabriel Lopes Pinheiro or order for value received of him. That the said two bills after having been indorsed by the said Gabriel Lopes Pinheiro and passed through several hands with other Indorsments were presented to the said Messrs Bruni Bistotto and Winspiase at Leghorn for acceptance. But they refused to accept the same whereupon the said Isaac Lopes Pinheiro and Co. when the said bills became due and were refused to be paid by the said Bruni Bistotto and Co. paid the said bills under protest for the Honour of the said Gabriel Lopes Pinheiro the first Indorsor. That a Commission of Bankruptcy under the Great Seal having on the 14th February 1744 issued against the said Catherine Forman and Henry Lang they were thereupon declared Bankrupts and Robert Bostock since deceased and Lawrence Williams were chosen assignees of the said Bankrupts' estate and effects which was duly assigned to them by the major part of the Commissioners named in the said Commission. That the said Gabriel Lopes Pinheiro in the year 1747 died in Insolvent Circumstances but before his death (to wit) on the 5th November 1746 caused a claim to be entered on the proceedings under the said Commission for the said two bills which charges of protests Commission and Brokeridge amounted together according to the course of the Exchange to the value of £258 – 6 – 10 Sterling in the margin of which claim the said bills were said to be then at Leghorn. That on the 13th November 1746 a dividend of four shillings and six pence in the pound was ordered to be made amongst the said Bankrupts' Creditors who had proved their debts under the said Commission. That by my order of the 4th April last the several claimants under the sd. Commission were to come in and prove their debts before the last day of last Trinity Term or to stand excluded. That in pursuance of the said order and of notice in the London Gazette the major part of the Commissioners named in the said Commission met on the first day of August last to make a further Dividend of the said Bankrupts Estate and Effects. At which time it appeared that the debts proved under the said Commission amounted to £28,455 – 7 – 4 and that there was in the hands of the said Lawrence Williams the only Surviving Assignee of the said Bankrupts' Estate the sum of £2,514 – 12 – 6 and the Commissioners then ordered a further Dividend of one shilling and six pence in the pound to be made amongst the said Bankrupts' Creditors after payment whereof there remained and still remained in the hands of the said Lawrence Williams the sum of £380 – 10 to be divided amongst the said Bankrupts' Creditors besides which there were many considerable debts due to the said Bankrupts' Estate outstanding and unreceived several of which were soon expected to be got in and received. That the petitioner is a Foreigner and as he never read the Gazette and knew nothing of the method of proving the said debt under the said Commission after he received the said two bills from the said Lopes and Co. he frequently applied himself to Mr Conrad Lang the said Henry Lang's the Bankrupts' brother to inform him when it would be a proper time for him to appear and prove the said Debt and the said Henry Lang's brother told him several times not to give himself any concern about it and he would certainly inform the petitioner when and in what manner it would be proper for him to prove the said debt which petitioner relied on his doing but on the petitioner's lawyer applying to the Clerks of the Commission about it he was told the Claim which was made by the said Gabriel Lopes Pinheiro was disallowed and that he was then too late to prove the said Debt. And therefore (and for other reasons therein contained) praying that he might be at Liberty to prove the said Debt before the said Commissioners and that the said Assignee might be ordered to pay the petitioner out of the Estate of the said Bankrupt remaining in his hands the said two dividends of four shillings and six pence and one shilling and six pence in the pound and all future dividends for the same rateably with the Bankrupts' other Creditors the petitioner not desiring to disturb the dividend already made. Whereupon all parties concerned were ordered to attend me on the matter of the said petition. And Councel for the petitioner and for Lawrence Williams the surviving assignee of the said Bankrupts' Estate under the said Commission this day attending accordingly. Upon debate of the matter and hearing the said petition the claim of the petitioners debt entered amongst the Commissioners proceedings under the said Commission and an Affidavit read and what was alledged on both sides I DO ORDER that the petitioner be at Liberty forthwith to go before the major part of the Commissioners named in the said Commission to prove the debt in the said petition mentioned and that he be admitted a Creditor under the said Commission for that he shall so prove and be paid out of the said Bankrupts' estate now remaining in or which shall hereafter come to the hands of the Assignees under the said Commission a dividend or dividends in respect thereof rateable to what hath been already paid to the rest of the Creditors of the said Bankrupts in respect of their debts before any further dividend be made. But so as not to disturb any dividends already made and that in all future dividends the petitioner be paid in respect of the said debt rateably and in equal proportion with the rest of the said Bankrupts and Creditors seeking relief under the said Commission.

Hardwick

PRO, B4/5

Peter Lord King Lord High Chancellor,
Commissions of Bankruptcy awarded against

No. 805 — Robert Whitton of Allen Street in the parish of St. James Clerkenwell in the County of Middx. butcher.

Directed to
Charles Bere and John Derbyshire Birkhead — Esqrs
Amos Callard Joseph Stanwix and Richard Davies — Gents

Test 13th Martii 1726

Ors Stephen Duckett of St. James Clerkenwell aforesaid vintner and Edward Welch of St. Botolphs Aldgate in the City of London Inn holder.

Welland sol[r]

No. 806 — Thomas Dickenson of the parish of St. Paul in Covent Garden in the County of Middx, staymaker.

Directed to
Thomas Vandrey and Joseph Whitehead — Esqrs
William Shaw Tabez Collier and John Yate — Gents

Test 13th Martii 1726

Ors William Lowfield of St. Pauls Church Yard London, hosier.

Boult sol[r]

No. 807 — William Sellecke late of Southwark and since of Westminster in the County of Middx, brewer.

Directed to
Clinton Dowse and William Folkes — Esqrs
Benjamin Whiten Thomas Parker and Henry Barnes — Gents

Test 13th Martii 1726

Ors Anthony Mathews of Hogsdon in the County of Middx., chapman.

Van sol[r]

PRO, B6/48

County Register of Petitions

Gaol	No. of Petition	Name of Prisoner	Trade or Profession	Date of Petition
Stafford	726	Hallsworth Joshua	Ropemaker	12th Sept. 1820
Leicester	727	Underwood Joseph	Frame work knitter	6th Sept. 1820
"	728	Dobney John	Labourer	"
"	729	Repton William	Cordwainer	1st Sept. 1820
"	730	Capp John	Carpenter	"
"	731	Marvin John	Labourer	6th Sept. 1820
"	732	Oldershaw John	Victualler	"
"	733	Crane Thomas	Miller	1st Sept. 1820
"	734	Burrows Henry	Cordwainer/ Publican	"
Northampton	735	Pierce James	Currier	8th Sept. 1820
"	736	Harris John	Carpenter	1st Sept. 1820
Bristol	737	Eshmade Charles	Gent's Butler	14th Sept. 1820
Exeter City	738	Norrish Robert	Grocer	12th Sept. 1820
Exeter St. Thos.	739	Gillard James	Yeoman	21st Aug. 1820
"	740	Marchant James	Yeoman	5th Sept. 1820
Gloucester	741	Lee Enoch	Shopkeeper	24th Aug. 1820
"	742	Matthews Thomas	Saddler	"
"	743	Capelli Peter	Hawker	"
"	744	Collott William	Carrier	"
"	745	King Charles	Baker	"
"	746	Clarke William	Yeoman	"
Appleby	747	Dawson John	Farmer	15th Sept. 1820
"	748	Brockbank Robert	Dealer in Horses and Cattle	"
"	749	Barnett Reginald	Lieut. 40th Regt of Foot	7th Sept. 1820
Lancaster	750	Crighton James	Master Mariner	15th Sept. 1820

Date of Schedule	When Case to be heard	Attorney in the Case	Magistrate's Cert. and when made		Actual Discharge when to take place
15th Sept.	18th Oct.	Wyllie	Intitled	18th Oct.	Forthwith
"	17th Oct.	"	–	–	
"	"	"	–	–	
"	"	"		19th Oct.	Forthwith
"	"	"		"	"
"	"	"		"	"
"	"	"		"	"
"	"	"		"	"
"	"	"		"	"
14th Sept.	19th Oct.	"		"	"
15th Sept.	"	"	to 15th Jan. 1821	24th Oct.	1st Jan. 1821
18th Sept.	16th Oct.	Graham		17th Oct.	Forthwith
12th Sept.	16th Oct.	Wyllie		"	"
9th Sept.	17th Oct.	"	6 months	"	18th March 1821
		"			
14th Sept.	17th Oct.	"		17th Oct.	Forthwith
"	"	"		"	"
"	"	"		"	"
"	"	"		"	"
"	"	"		"	"
"	"	"		"	"
21st Sept.	28th Oct.	Graham		28th Oct.	"
"	"	"		"	"
"	"	"		"	"
23rd Sept.	21st Nov.	"		"	"

PRO, B2/16

Whitecross Street Prison – Gaoler's Returns

The Bankruptcy Act 1861

Return made by Benjamin Constable, Keeper of the Debtors Prison for London and Middlesex, Whitecross Street in the City of London this first day of November 1864 in pursuance of the above Act, of every person now within the walls, rules or Liberties of the said gaol, or prison in custody upon any process whatever for or by reason of any debt, claim or demand whatsoever and not being within any of the exceptions mentioned in Section 104 of The Bankruptcy Act 1861.

Name of Person detained and date of his imprisonment	Weir Charles Sims December 6th 1862
Name and Address of Every Creditor at whose Suit such Prisoner is imprisoned or detained. Nature and Amount of Debt or Demand, or Debts and Demands for which such Prisoner is detained in custody	Ca. Sa.[1] £41–18–6
Whether such prisoner is willing or refuses to petition to Court of Bankruptcy, or is able to do so by reason of poverty	Unwilling
Attorney	John Letts

PRO, B 5/14

Bankruptcy Enrolment Book

At the Rose and Crown Inn at Sudbury
in the County of Suffolk the
thirtieth day of December 1815

John Eley Kemp of Cowlinge in the County of Suffolk, esquire, being sworn and examined on the day and year and at the place above said before the major part of the Commissioners named and authorized in and by a Commission of Bankrupts awarded and issued and now in Prosecution against John Kemp late of Cowlinge in the County of Suffolk, malster dealer and chapman upon his oath saith that about the twelfth of November last he this Deponent and Robert Burleigh parted with the said John Kemp in London who was on his Journey from this Kingdom to France that the reason of the said John Kemp so leaving this Kingdom was in consequence of the extremely depressed state of the times and for the general purpose of facilitating the settlement of his affairs as he

---

[1] Ca. Sa. *Capias Ad Satisfaciedum*. A judicial writ of execution which issues out of the record of a judgement where there is a recovery in the courts at Westminster of debt, damages, etc., and by their writ the Sheriff is commanded to take the body of the defendant in execution, and him safely to keep so that he have his body in Court at the return of the writ, to satisfy the plaintiff his debt and damages (Law Dictionary, Tomlins, London, 1820).

was not able to meet his Creditors and settle their demands that the said John Kemp was at that time indebted to Messrs Bryant of Newmarket in the County of Suffolk, bankers, in a considerable sum of money which he was not able to provide means for payment of, and this deponent believes the reason of the said John Kemp's leaving England was his Inability to settle with his Creditors and a wish to retrieve his affairs that he this deponent is jointly empowered with Robert Burleigh under a certain deed or Letter of Attorney already exhibited under this Commission for the management of the said John Kemp's affairs during his absence that he has received a Letter from the said John Kemp since he left England addressed from Calais on his arrival there but whether the said John Kemp is still in France this deponent does not know.

Capel Lofft
Jas. Borton
Tim^y Holmes

John Eley Kemp

At the Bell Inn, Castle Heddingham
in the County of Essex the
sixteenth day of December 1815

Memorandum. We whose names are hereunder written being the major part of the Commissioners named and authorized in and by the Commission of Bankruptcy awarded and issued and now in Prosecution against John Kemp late of Cowlinge in the County of Suffolk, malster dealer and chapman bearing the date at Westminster the twenty fifth day of November one thousand eight hundred and fifteen having dealt in the said Commission upon good proof before us this day had and taken do find that the said John Kemp became Bankrupt within the true intent and meaning of the some of or one of the Statutes made and now in force Concerning Bankrupts before the date and issuing forth of the said Commission, and we do therefore declare and adjudge the said John Kemp Bankrupt accordingly.

Capel Lofft
Jas. Borton
Tim^y Holmes

PRO, B5/15
Bankruptcy Enrolment Book

At the London Inn and
Talbot Tavern,
Bath Street, Bristol,
Saturday the 1st of June 1799

George Buckmaster Andrews of the City of Bristol clerk to Francis Harris and Samuel Grove of the said City merchants and partners the persons against whom this Commission of Bankrupt now in prosecution hath been issued being sworn and examined at the place and on the day and year above written, before the major part of the Commissioners named and authorized in and by the said Commission upon his Oath saith. That he hath been clerk to the said Francis Harris and Samuel Grove for the space of twenty two months now last past during which time they carried on the trade or business of Merchants trading from this Kingdom to the West Indies, Ireland and divers other places beyond the seas and seeking and endeavouring to get their living thereby as other Merchants usually do.

And this Deponent further saith that upwards of two months ago shortly after the said Samuel Grove's arrival in England whilst he and his said partner Francis Harris and this deponent were together in the Counting House of the said Francis Harris and Samuel Grove situate in Stokes Croft in the said City of Bristol a man was seen coming to the house whom this deponent did not then nor does he at this time know either by name or otherwise but who this deponent hath since been informed and verily believes was a Sheriff's Officer. That upon seeing him the said Francis Harris desired the said Samuel Grove to come out of the Counting House and advised him to go up stairs as this Deponent believes. That they both appeared to be much alarmed particularly the said Samuel Grove. That the said Francis Harris ordered this Deponent to tell the man that neither of them was within and thereupon he the said Francis Harris and the said Samuel Grove left the Counting House with considerable precipitation. And this deponent believes that the said Samuel Grove went up the stairs of the said Francis Harris's house as he had been advised to do by his partners. And this Deponent believes from knowing that the affairs of the said Francis Harris and Samuel Grove were embarrassed on account of some bills of theirs which had been returned that they were under apprehensions of the said persons having a writ against them. That the said person enquired for the said Francis Harris and was told by this Deponent that he was not within altho this Deponent well knew he was within the house at the time. And this Deponent saith that the said Francis Harris and Samuel Grove returned to the Counting House as soon as the man they had been afraid of was gone.

And this Deponent further saith that early in the month of May last on the fourth day of that month as this Deponent verily believes but says he is certain it was several days previous to the eleventh day of the same month as the said Francis Harris and Samuel Grove were in the said Counting House where was likewise this Deponent the said Francis Harris on seeing Mr Arthur Tozer of the said City coming to the house directed this deponent in the presence and hearing of the said Samuel Grove to tell him that they the said Francis Harris and Samuel Grove were not within and both of them immediately quitted the Counting House. That the said Arthur Tozer then came into the said Counting House and enquired for the said Francis Harris and Samuel Grove and was told by this Deponent that neither of them was within agreably to the directions he had received. That the said Samuel Grove having when he went out of the Counting House as aforesaid left his hat behind him this Deponent concealed the same from the view of the said Arthur Tozer. That he has no doubt the said Francis Harris and Samuel Grove so left the said Counting House as last aforesaid in order to avoid the said Arthur Tozer whom this Deponent knew to be a Creditor of the said Francis Harris and Samuel Grove.

[signed] Geo. B. Andrews

At the London and Talbot
Tavern, Bristol, June 1st 1799

Memorandum. That we whose names are hereunder written being the major part of the Commission named and authorized in and by a Commission of Bankrupt awarded and issued against Francis Harris and Samuel Grove of the City of Bristol, merchants and partners having acted in the said Commission upon good proof before us upon oath had and taken do find that the said Francis Harris and Samuel Grove became Bankrupt within the true intent and meaning of some or one of the Statutes made and now in force concerning Bankrupts before the date and suing forth of the said Commission. And we do therefore declare and adjudge them Bankrupts accordingly.

J. Smith
Tho. Morgan
Arth^r Palmer

Fleet Prison, London, a debtors' prison, 1808 (Guildhall Library, City of London)

PRO, PRIS 1/14
Fleet Prison Commitments

No. 6621
15th August 1793, delivered by writ of Superintendent

Mary Dejort on the 15th day of September 1792, was committed there by the Honourable Mr Baron Hotham upon a writ of Habeas Corpus directed to the Sheriff of Middlesex. And by the return it appears that on the 21st day of August 1792 Mary Dejort in the said writ named was taken by the said Sheriff and under his Custody detained by virtue of His Majesty's writ to the said Sheriff directed ret'ble [sic] before the Barons of the King's Exchequer at Westminster on the 6th day of November next to answer The King touching certain articles whereon she is impleaded by an Information lately exhibited against her before the King's said Barons by His Majesty's Attorney General for the forfeitures of the sums of £239 – 5 and £239 – 5 for offences in the said Information Bail for £79 – 15.

J.Carnshaw, Solicitor Ord. for the Customs

PRO, PRIS 4/12
King's Bench Prison Commitment Book

No. 487
John Hawkridge committed 27th March 1790 for want of Bail upon a writ of Habeas Corpus directed to the Sheriff of Yorkshire. And by the return it appears that on the 10th

February 1790 he was taken by the then sheriff by virtue of His Majesty's Writ of Non Omittas Capias issuing out of His Majesty's Court of King's Bench at Westminster and there on Friday next after 8 days after Purification to answer Robert Barclay and John Perkins in a plea of trespass and also to their bill against the said John Hawkridge for £1400 upon promises according to be exhibited. Oath £710, Vincent and Ware, Southwark 21st January 1790. And that he was so taken and detained in the custody of the said Sheriff charged as afforesaid from the said 10th February 1790 to the 8th March 1790 when he was delivered to the now Sheriff of the said County.

Discharged Per Insolvent Act 1794
      N. Grose

PRO, PRIS 6/1
Queen's Bench Prison
Commitment to Strong Room

Queen's Prison
18th May 1847

Mr Champness

    Saith,
      Yesterday afternoon between 3 and 4 o'clock Mr Hastings and myself were playing racquets, a doubt arose as to whether a ball was struck fair or not. Mr Basan and Mr Saunders were sitting a few yards off and I appealed to Mr Basan who thought it was against me. I then appealed to Mr Saunders with whom I had not been on friendly terms, he did not answer but appeared to treat me contemptuously. I then said though not addressed to any person, if ever I ask Mr Saunders a question again he may kiss my backside, or words to that effect. I did not intend him to hear it. Mr Saunders came up to me immediately, and saying 'What did you say?' (I did not answer him). He struck me violently with his fist beneath the ear, he struck at me a second time, I warded off the blow with the racquet which he then seized and taking it to the other end of the yard he broke it in pieces and threw them into the adjoining yard. He resumed his seat on the form having first challenged me to fight which I declined by saying I would not fight with such a blackguard. He renewed the challenge and wished me to take my coat off and as I again declined he arose and struck me again violently on the ribs.
    Mr Hastings, Mr Basan, Mr Saunders and myself were the only persons in the yard at the commencement but Mr Marks and Mr Davis came into the yard while Mr Saunders was breaking the racquet and before the second blow was struck and previously to which I offered to forego making a complaint if he would pay 2/- for the racquet.

[signed] F. Champness

Mr Basan

    Saith,
      I was sitting near, yesterday while Mr Champness and Mr Hastings were playing racquets when a dispute arose and an appeal made to Mr Saunders. He refused to answer but smiled and looked rather supercilliously at Mr Champness, the latter seemed to feel aggrieved and said when next he appealed to Mr Saunders he might kiss his arse. Mr Saunders went towards him and asked if Champness had said he would kick his arse. I heard no reply but Saunders then struck Champness, the latter acted provokingly the other was also excited. Mr S. retired to his seat, Mr Champness flourished his racquet as I suppose in his defence, Mr S. took it away and broke it.

[signed] C. Basan

Examined by Mr Saunders

I heard Mr Champness call Mr Saunders a low bred bone dealer. (Mr Saunders admitted striking the blow also the breakage of the racquet, but contends that he had been provoked by Mr Champness' language to do so). I heard Mr Saunders request Mr Champness to desist in his provocation or that he should be compelled to strike him again.

[signed] C. Basan

Mr Hastings

Saith,
I was playing racquets yesterday with Mr Champness, a dispute as to the game arose. Mr Basan was appealed to, also Mr Saunders. Mr Saunders grinned but did not answer. Mr Champness then said to Mr Saunders when I next appeal to you, you may kiss my arse. Mr Saunders then approached Mr C. and struck him behind the ear. Mr C. raised his racquet to ward off the blows, Mr S. took it from him and broke it in pieces which he threw into the next yard. Mr S. sat down then got up again and struck Mr Champness in the side. There were no foul words used on either side between the first and second blows. There was a 3rd blow. I got between them and said if you strike any one strike me. They then separated.

[signed] Charles Hastings

Examined by Mr Saunders

I heard Mr Saunders call Mr Champness a beer seller, Mr C. then called Saunders a bone seller. Mr Saunders endeavoured to provoke Mr C. to fight and challenged him for £10. I did not hear Mr C. call Mr S. a low bred blackguard or vagabond.

[signed] Charles Hastings

Mr Marks

Saith,
I was in the passage yesterday when a quarrel ensued between Mr Saunders and Mr Champness. I went out and observed the former breaking a racquet. I heard Mr C. call Mr Saunders a blackguard and the other called Mr Champness by similar epithets. I afterwards saw Mr S. strike Mr C. on the side and appeared very desirous of provoking Champness to fight and invited him to take his coat off. I heard the expression on the part of Champness 'low bred bone dealer' but this was after Saunders had struck him.

[signed] Bob Marks

Having maturely considered the aforegoing evidence I am satisfied that both Mr Champness and Mr Saunders have violated a portion of the 35th Rule and I hereby direct that the former be confined in one of the strong rooms for three days (that is to say until Monday next) and the latter to be confined in another of the strong rooms for one week.

Queen's Bench Prison   [signed] J. Hudson
18th May 1849

PRO, PRIS 6/1
Queen's Bench Prison
Commitment to Strong Room

Queen's Prison
16th November 1847

The Rev. J. Bartlett a prisoner saith I was walking up the parade yesterday afternoon
when Mr Hirst addressing himself to me saying 'Do you see that brick', and added 'That
brick is far more honest than you are.' He then called me a rascal in the presence of Mr
Colwell the Chief Turnkey and Matton. There were other expressions which I do not
distinctly recollect.

[signed] J. Bartlett

H. Colwell (Chief Turnkey)

Saith,
   I was sent for by Mr Bartlett yesterday afternoon. I went to him and was told that Mr
Hirst had very much insulted him on the parade. I saw Mr Hirst also near the gate and
heard him say that Mr Bartlett was a villain and the scum of the earth. And pointing to
the brick wall said that is more honest than he is.

[signed] H. Colwell

W. Matton (Lower Turnkey)

Saith,
   While on duty yesterday afternoon Mr Bartlett came to me and requested me to
fetch Mr Colwell saying that Mr Hirst had grossly insulted him. I did so, Mr Colwell came
down. Mr Hirst came to the gate just before this and called Mr Bartlett a damned
shuffling vagabond. Mr B. called my attention to this expression and told me to mind
what he said. When Mr Colwell entered the prison Mr Hirst began with Mr Bartlett again
but I cannot remember the expression. Mr Hirst held up his hand towards Mr B. in a
threatening attitude but said to him I will not touch you. Mr Colwell wished Mr Hirst to
go to his room and he then left. Mr Bartlett said nothing to Mr Hirst in my presence. Mr
Hirst appeared to have been drinking.

[signed] W. Matton

H. Colwell (recalled)

I cannot say whether Mr Hirst had been drinking but he was greatly excited. I requested
Mr Bartlett to go to his room as there were about 30 persons assembled.

Further evidence was given by Margaret Fry, George J. Moor and Mr W. Griffin.

Capt. Hudson after carefully reading over the aforegoing evidence admonished and
cautioned both against any further violation of the rules.

PRO, PRIS 7/9
King's Bench Prison – Discharges 1790

To the Marshal of the Court of King's Bench at Westminster or to his Deputy

Whereas you have in your Custody the body of George Peaceable charged at the several
suits of James Hasselden, and John Bird and James Hasselden. These are to certify you

that common Bails are filed with me for the said Defendant at his said Plaintiff's suit respectively pursuant to two several orders of The Right Honourable Lloyd Lord Kerrison, Lord Chief Justice.

Therefore as to these actions he may be discharged.

Dated the 20th day of May 1790

R. Walter

PRO, PRIS 11/2
Marshalsea Prison Commitments

A List of Debtors brought into Custody and discharged on Wed. June 30, 1813

NAMES	At Whose Suit	Damages [£]	Sums Sworn
Elizabeth Southgate	Elizabeth Lee	17 12 6	17 12 6
Thos. Alley	against James Kilvington & Wm Petty	50 0 0	25 upwards
Richd. Goodyer	against Saml Page returned July 2	50 0 0	18

NAMES	How Discharged	P.F.[2]	R.R.[3]
Edward Holdcraft	Plaintiff's Attorney	10/10[4]	J.S.

A List of Debtors brought into Custody and discharged on Thurs. July 1, 1813

NAMES	At Whose Suit	Damages [£]	Sums Sworn
Edward Darley	against Mary Welcker administratrix of Peter Welcker deceased	200 0 0	52 upwards
Henry Pratt	against Thomas Peake both returned July 2nd	50 0 0	14 4 9

NAMES	How Discharged	P.F.	R.R.
Edward Darley	Plaintiff's Attorney	10/10	J.S.
Sarah Bedwell	Plaintiff's Attorney	10/10	J.S.

[2] Prison fee.

[3] Registrar of Rules who was the officer responsible for the receipt of payments.

[4] Ten Shillings and ten pence.

PRO, PRIS 10/56

Queen's and Fleet Prisons – Discharges

1835 Feby 17th	Philip Burgess	agts agts agts agts agts agts	Walham Wiggins Richard W. Roberts Lewis Jacobs Thos. Douglas Forrest Thomas Roberts Andrew Freeman by order of the Court for the relief of Insolvent Debtors
	Neville Beard sued as Nevill Beard	agts agts	Ann Durrant Harris and another by order of the Court for the relief of Insolvent Debtors William Cutler by Warrant of Plaintiff's Attorney
	James Montgomery Scrymgeour	agts	George Peters by order of the Court for the relief of Insolvent Debtors
Feby 18th	Ronald Price	agts	Anthony Hammond by Judges Order
	Robert Lye	agts	Thomas Harris by order of the Court for the relief of Insolvent Debtors
	Edgar William Dow Remanded 8 months	agts agts agts agts	Philip Abrahams John Turner Billing William Wainwright Joseph Whitbread by Order of the Court for the relief of Insolvent Debtors
Feby 19th	James Greenland etc., etc.	agts	Richard Grant by order of the Court for the relief of Insolvent Debtors

THE CASE STUDY OF THOMAS HARTNELL

The following case study of Thomas Hartnell has been drawn from the many classes of records recording criminals. As he became mentally unbalanced he is also recorded in criminal lunatic records.

Thomas Hartnell was first discovered in the Criminal Registers (PRO, HO 27/172) where he is recorded as being charged at Somerset Assizes at Taunton on 24 March 1875 with 'Assaulting and robbing with violence.' He was found guilty and sentenced to six years penal servitude i.e. imprisonment with hard labour. The Calendar of Prisoners for Taunton Prison (PRO, HO 140/32) shows him as being twenty-two years of age, by trade a miller and unable to read or write. We also find that Robert Greedy, a 52-year-old labourer was charged with him for the same offence. They were committed by J.E. Knollys Esq. of Fitzhead Court. The warrant for their arrest was dated 30 October 1874 and they were 'Received into custody' on 31 October 1874. Their alleged offence is now given in more detail:

Stealing from the person of John Date one silver watch, one knife, eight shillings and eight pence in money and feloniously wounding and beating the said John Date at Wiveliscombe on 28 October 1874.

The verdict records Hartnell as 'Guilty of robbery with violence' and sentenced to six years penal servitude. Greedy was found 'Not guilty of the like'.

No records survive for Taunton Gaol for the time Hartnell and Greedy were held. These would have given a physical description of each of them. The Assize records (PRO, ASSI 25/51/7) repeat the charges and verdicts but additionally record that Hartnell pleaded 'Guilty' and Greedy 'Not guilty'.

The Pentonville Prison Register (PRO, PCOM 2/75) shows that Hartnell was taken there from Taunton Prison on 7 May 1875 again recording his date and place of trial with the sentence of the court. He is again recorded as a miller but additionally we now find that his religion is 'Church of England'. He has now

Thomas Hartnell, photographed in Pentonville Prison, 1875 (PRO, PCOM 2/98)

been registered as number B493. While at Pentonville he was photographed, as were all convicts there. From Pentonville he was transferred to Millbank on 6 January 1876. Under the same 'Register Number' he appears in the Millbank records (PRO, PCOM 2/56) confirming that he had been transferred from Pentonville on 6 January 1876. He is also shown as transferring to Woking Prison on 12 April 1876.

The Woking register (PRO, PCOM 2/144) again as number B493, repeats his trial details again stating his age and trade, but this time it records '12–4–76 Received as a lunatic'. At the end of his six year sentence Hartnell was still certified as 'insane'. On 16 March 1881 he was transferred to Broadmoor. A Home Office Warrant (PRO, HO 15/17) dated 24 February 1881 authorizes his transfer to Broadmoor Criminal Lunatic Asylum and a similar warrant was drawn up for his reception at Broadmoor. It was now the responsibility of his home county to provide for his maintenance. A Home Office warrant (PRO, HO 15/17) dated 4 April 1881 authorized his transfer to the 'Lunatic Asylum for the County of Somerset at Wells'. A similar warrant was drawn up for his reception at Wells.

As pauper lunatics were the responsibility of the county, lists were kept in the Quarter Sessions records as follows:

Somerset Michaelmas Sessions, 18 October 1881 at Wells. 'Names of all Pauper Lunatics in the Asylum at Wells for the County of Somerset on the first day of July 1881'.

This list includes Thomas Hartnell as admitted 11 April 1881.

The records for the Somerset Asylum (now held at Somerset Record Office, Class Q/ALu) contain a large amount of detail about Thomas Hartnell. In addition to that already gleaned from the prison records, the record of him from Broadmoor sent to Wells now also gives his year of birth as 1852, he was single, was 'subject to headaches but has not exhibited violence whilst here. He says he is annoyed at night but cannot say by whom', and 'Does not sleep well, says he drank'. Interestingly he can now 'read and write' yet when arrested in 1875 he was illiterate. He was obviously taught to read and write while in prison.

The Somerset Lunatic Asylum Male Case Book (Som. RO, D/H/men) repeats the already known details but adds that 'he is sober and his general health fair'. His father's address is given as Moor Mills, Lydeard St Lawrence, near Taunton. For the first time we find a physical description of him: 'On admission a young man of powerful build about 5' 8", light hair and light blue eyes. Holds his head down'. It also states, 'Answered questions in a fairly rational style but giggled in a silly manner'.

Another note states that Dr Orange of Broadmoor believed that he 'was probably not right in his mind when he was convicted . . . He said when he found he was sentenced to six years penal servitude his mind completely broke down.'

Much detailed correspondence survives about this man. Because he was a 'pauper' it was the responsibility of the Poor Law Union to which he rightfully belonged by settlement, to provide for his maintenance. A letter from Wells dated 19 April 1881 to the Clerk of the Guardians of the Taunton Union gives details of Thomas Hartnell and requests that the 'Guardians will admit their liability to maintain the Lunatic in the Asylum . . . ' An argument broke out as to whether or not Taunton Union was actually responsible.

William Dunn, Clerk of the Peace at Wells sent Mr W. Dawe on 6 May 1881 to Moor Mills to interview Thomas Hartnell's father and mother. They were absent but a brother of Thomas, Frederick Hartnell was at home. Frederick Hartnell confirmed that Thomas Hartnell 'now in the Lunatic Asylum' was his brother. He also stated that Thomas was 'the lawful son of William and Elizabeth Hartnell who were married in the old church, Wellington' (This statement was not strictly true. William Hartnell had certainly married his current wife Elizabeth Salter at Wellington in 1855 but Thomas was in fact a son by William's previous wife Caroline who had died when Thomas was a child).

Frederick went on to state that his father had rented Moor Mills for about twenty years which is situated in the parish of Brompton Ralph, and his brother Thomas had 'always lived at home up until the time he was taken away'.

Mr Dawe's 'Horse and expenses' amounted to £1–12s. A postal order was sent to him on 21 May 1881.

It was clear from this enquiry that Thomas Hartnell was rightfully settled in the parish of Brompton Ralph which was in the Williton Union (and not the Taunton Union) as Mr Dawe confirmed in his letter of 6 May 1881 to the Clerk of the Peace at Wells. The Guardians of the Williton Union accepted liability for Thomas' maintenance in their letter of 17 May 1881. They evidently sought a way to limit their costs and refused to pay any charges before the date of their letter admitting liability. They were then threatened with an 'Order of Justices' [Court Order] the costs of which they would also have to cover unless they paid the full amount from Thomas Hartnell's entry into the asylum. On 22 August a cheque for £12–18–1 was sent from the Williton Guardians to cover arrears of the maintenance.

The Male Case Book records for Thomas Hartnell:

23 April [1881]	Is quick and well behaved. Health good. Very anxious for his discharge.
16 May	Doing fairly well.
19 May	Application is made for his discharge on probation by his father, by the Rector of Brompton Ralph and by Dr Cordwent the Deputy Coroner for the Western Division of Somerset.
	Quiet and well behaved.
	Might be allowed out on trial as his father guarantees in writing to look after him on 6 months probation.

A questionnaire is included which has been answered and signed by his father William Hartnell. In this William stated that there had never been any insanity in the patient's family. Neither had any member of the family suffered from consumption [tuberculosis], intemperence or fits. He also stated 'If insane which I doubt, it arises from his imprisonment'. He also claimed that Thomas was 'quite sober in habits' [a statement known to be untrue].

In confirmation of Thomas Hartnell's admission to Broadmoor and his removal to the Somerset Asylum, the County Asylum and Hospital Registers[1] (PRO, MH 94/26) were consulted. These show that he was admitted to Broadmoor on 16 March 1881 and transferred 'unrecovered' to the Somerset Asylum on 11 April 1881. He was 'released' from the Somerset Asylum on 7 December 1881.

About a year later on 16 January 1883 at Wiveliscombe Petty Sessions (Som. RO, D/PS/Wiv 1/1) Thomas Hartnell was found guilty of being 'Disorderly and refusing to quit licensed premises.' His sentence was: 'Fined 20/-, costs 3/6; in default of payment 21 days imprisonment with hard labour.' No record survives which records whether he paid the fine or went to prison.

A year later he was in trouble again. This time he was charged with breaking and entering the dwelling house of William Hartnell [his father with whom he had lived!] and stealing one watch, one silver chain and two metal pocket flasks, his [William Hartnell's] property, at Brompton Ralph on 2 March 1884. Of the

---

[1] These commence in 1846.

five witnesses for the prosecution one was Thomas' stepmother Elizabeth Hartnell. In her statement to the court she admitted that her husband William had left her seven or eight months before though she was still in touch with him. She claimed that the stolen items were hers. From the evidence given by the other witnesses it was learnt that Thomas slept on straw in the machine chamber over the mill. [This was a water mill which was demolished many years ago though some of the surrounding walls still stand.] Thomas stated he could find no lodgings elsewhere and his stepmother had apparently banned him from her house. The stolen items were found by PC George Gawler in the machine chamber, the flasks and chain hidden on a beam and the watch in a hole in the wall.

Thomas was found guilty and sentenced to six months with hard labour in Shepton Mallet Prison. The records of Shepton Mallet Prison do not survive for this period but presumably Thomas served out his full sentence.[2] What happened to him after his discharge has yet to be discovered.

The following are detailed transcripts of the documents recording Thomas Hartnell's three offences:

1. **PRO, HO 27/172**
Criminal Register

Somerset Assizes at Taunton 23 March 1875

Thomas Hartnell, Assaulting and robbing with violence
6 years penal servitude

PRO, HO 140/32
Calendars of Prisoners (Taunton)

Somerset Assizes at Taunton 23 March 1875

Number	5
Name	Thomas Hartnell
Age	22
Trade	Miller
Degree of Instruction	N [No, i.e. cannot read or write]

[contd]

---

[2] After going to press the author located two 'lost' prison registers for Shepton Mallet Prison. An entry in one confirmed that Thomas Hartnell was discharged on 8 October 1884 after serving his full sentence.

Number	6
Name	Robert Greedy
Age	52
Trade	Labourer
Degree of Instruction	N [No, i.e. cannot read or write]

Committed by	J.E. Knollys, Esq., Fitzhead Court, and another
Date of Warrant	30th October 1874
When Received into Custody	31st October 1874
Offence	Stealing from the person of John Date one silver watch, one knife, eight shillings & 8d in money and feloniously wounding and beating the said John Date at Wiveliscombe on 28th October 1874
When Tried	24th March 1875
Before	The Hon. Sir G. Pigott
Verdict	No. 5 Guilty of Robbery with Violence No. 6 Not Guilty of the like
Sentence of the Court	No. 5 6 years penal servitude

PRO, ASSI 25/51/7
Western Assize Circuit

Indictment

Thomas Hartnell   pleaded guilty
Robert Greedy   pleaded not guilty
Both of Wiveliscombe co. Somerset on 28 October 1874 upon John Date in fear of his life one knife, one watch and certain money to wit to the amount of eight shillings and eight pence of the said John Date and the said Thomas Hartnell and Robert Greedy immediately before at the time of and immediately after the robbery feloniously did beat, strike and use other personal violence to the said John Date.

Thomas Hartnell   Guilty 6 years P.S.
Robert Greedy   Not guilty

PRO, PCOM 2/75
Pentonville Prison Register

Register Number	B493
Name	Thomas Hartnell
Date of Reception	7th May 1875
Prison from Whence	Taunton
Tried	Taunton Assizes 23 March 1875
Sentence	6 years Penal Servitude
Date of Discharge	6th Jany. 1876
Whither	Millbank
Remarks	Robbery with Violence
Trade	Miller
Religion	C.E. [Church of England]

PRO, PCOM 2/56
Millbank Prison Register

Register Number	B493
Name	Thomas Hartnell
Date of Reception	6–1–76
From What Prison	Pentonville
Date of Discharge	12–4–76
Whither	Woking

PRO, PCOM 2/144
Woking Prison Register

Register Number	B493
Name	Thomas Hartnell
Trade	Miller
Age	22
Received from	Millbank
Date	12–4–76 (Received as a lunatic)
To	Broadmoor 16–3–81
Licence No.	P236/75[3]
Offence	Stealing from the person a watch, etc.
Tried	Taunton Assizes 23–3–75

PRO, HO 15/17
Home Office Warrants

Warrant for the removal of
Thomas Hartnell to the
Broadmoor Criminal Lunatic
Asylum

The Rt. Hon. Sir W.V. Harcourt

Whereas Thomas Hartnell was at the Assizes holden at Taunton in and for the County of Somerset on the 23rd March 1875 convicted of Robbery with Violence and sentenced to 6 yrs P.S. [Penal Servitude] which sentence he is now undergoing in H.M. Convict Prison at Woking. And whereas the said Thomas Hartnell has been duly certified to me to be insane I do hereby order the said Thomas Hartnell to be removed from the said Woking Convict Prison to the said Broadmoor Criminal Lunatic Asylum. Given &c. [sic] 24th February 1881

To the Directors of the Convict Prison,   W.V. Harcourt
the Governor of the Woking Convict
Prison, and all others whom it may
concern.

[Similar warrant for the reception of Thomas Hartnell into Broadmoor.]

[3] No record of this licence has been located.

PRO, HO 15/17

Warrant for the removal of
Thomas Hartnell to the
Lunatic Asylum for the
County of Somerset at Wells

By the Right Honourable Sir William Vernon Harcourt.
Whereas Thomas Hartnell who was convicted at the Assizes holden at Taunton in and for
the County of Somerset on the 23rd day of March 1875 of Robbery with Violence and
sentenced to six years Penal Servitude which sentence expired before such evidence of his
sanity had been given as justified his being discharged. I do direct you to cause the said
Thomas Hartnell to be removed to the Lunatic Asylum for the County of Somerset at
Wells that being in order that he may be henceforth dealt with.
And for so doing this is your Warrant. Given the 4th day of April 1881.

W.V. Harcourt

To the Superintendent of
the Broadmoor Criminal
Lunatic Asylum.

*[Similar reception warrant addressed to the Superintendent of the County Lunatic Asylum
at Wells and all others whom it may concern.]*

Som. RO, Q/SR
Somerset Michaelmas Sessions, 18 October 1881, at Wells

Names of all Pauper Lunatics in
the Asylum at Wells for the
County of Somerset on the first
day of July 1881

Males
Name   Hartnell, Thomas
Date of Admission   11th April 1881

Som. RO, Q/ALu 50

*Particulars with respect to Thomas Hartnell about to be transferred to the Asylum
for the County of Somerset at Wells*

Name	Thomas Hartnell
Year of Birth	1852
Date of Admission into Broadmoor	16th March 1881
Former Occupation	Miller
From whence brought	Woking Convict Prison

[contd]

Married, Single or Widowed	Single
How many children	—
Age of youngest	—
Whether first Attack When previous Attacks occurred Duration of existing Attack	Not known Since 1875
State of bodily health	Subject to headaches
Whether suicidal	No
Whether dangerous to others	Has not exhibited violence whilst here
Supposed cause	Unknown
Chief delusions or Indications of Insanity	Demented – says he is annoyed at night but cannot say by whom. Does not sleep well
Whether subject to Epilepsy	No
Whether of temperate habits	Says he drank
Degree of Education	Can read and write
Religious Persuasion	Church of England
Crime	Robbery with violence
When and where tried	23rd March 1875, Taunton Assizes
Verdict of Jury	Guilty
Sentence or Order of the Court	6 years Penal Servitude
Broadmoor Criminal Lunatic Asylum 11th April 1881	W. Orange M.D. Superintendent

Whitehall
25th March 1881

Gentlemen,

Thomas Hartnell, a Criminal Lunatic, now confined in the Broadmoor Criminal Lunatic Asylum, who was convicted at Taunton on the 23rd day of March 1875 of

Robbery with violence and sentenced to six years penal servitude having become liable, by the expiration of his sentence, to be removed under the provisions of the Criminal Lunatics Act, 1867 to any Lunatic Asylum into which a Justice of the Peace might have directed him to be received in pursuance of the 68th Section of the Lunatic Asylums Act, 1853; I am directed by the Secretary of State for the Home Department to acquaint you that he proposes to issue a Warrant for the removal of the said Thomas Hartnell to the Lunatic Asylum for the County of Somerset, within which County the said Thomas Hartnell was convicted, and to request that you will take such measures as may appear to you to be necessary under the above Statutes for procuring an order for the maintenance of the said Lunatic in the last named Asylum.

The Committee of Visitors of
the Lunatic Asylum for the
County of Somerset, Wells

I am,
Gentlemen,
Your obedient Servant
A.F. O'Liddell

Dear Sir,   19th April 1881

Re Thomas Hartnell

This man was convicted in March 1875 at the Taunton Assizes of robbery with violence at Wiveliscombe and sentenced to 6 years penal servitude.

Subsequently he became insane and was sent to the Broadmoor Criminal Lunatic Asylum where he continued in confinement up to the expiration of his sentence, and on the 11th instant he was removed to the Pauper Lunatic Asylum of the County of Somerset by Warrant of the Home Secretary under the provisions of the Criminal Lunatics Act 1867, Section 6.

The Lunatic at the time of his conviction was said to be 22 years of age and was described in the calendar as a miller, and it will probably be found that about that date he was residing and working with his father, a miller at Moor Mills, Lydeard St. Lawrence, in your Poor Law Union.

I shall be glad to be informed whether your Guardians will admit their liability to maintain the Lunatic in the Asylum; as if so the expense of enquiring into the settlement procurring an Order of Justices may be served to the Union.

The Clerk to the Guardians of
the Taunton Union

I am, Dear Sir
Yours faithfully
William Dunn
Clerk of the Peace

W. Dunn, Esq.
Clerk of the Peace
Wells
Somerset

Union Offices
Taunton
April 28th, 1881

Dear Sir,

Re Thomas Hartnell

You do not give the Board any grounds of settlement in this Union, and it is impossible for them to admit their liability.

If you like my Clerk shall make enquiries, which he can do on the understanding that if the result of that enquiry proves the settlement to be in this Union we will accept.

If not I will give you necessary particulars on which to found an order of adjudication of settlement. In either case you must pay him a reasonable sum for his trouble.

You cannot in any case charge the Union with the expence of investigating the settlement.

> Yours Truly
> H.C. Trenchard
> Clerk

W. Dunn, Esq.   Union Offices
Clerk of the Peace   Taunton
Wells   May 6, 1881
Somerset

Dear Sir,

Thomas Hartnell

I have this day been to Moor Mills in persuance to your letter of the 2nd inst. to Mr H.C. Trenchard.

I send you particulars of what I was informed by which you will see the above belongs to the Williton Union. The father and mother were absent, I therefore saw a brother of the Lunatic.

> Yours obedient
> W. Dawe

Dear Sir,   9th May 1881

re Thomas Hartnell

This man was convicted in March 1875 at the Taunton Assizes of robbery with violence at Wiveliscombe, and sentenced to 6 years penal servitude.

He subsequently became insane and was sent to the Broadmoor Criminal Lunatic Asylum, from whence, on the expiration of his sentence, he was removed to the Pauper Lunatic Asylum of this County by Warrant of the Home Secretary under the provisions of the Criminal Lunatics Act 1867, section 6.

I inclose a statement of the brother of the Lunatic, showing a clear settlement in your Union, and which shall be obliged if you will inform me whether the Guardians will admit their liability. If they do so, the Clerk to the Visitors will merely include the name of the Lunatic in the list of Lunatics chargeable to your Union, and charge in maintenance in the usual way, but otherwise an order of Justices on the Union must be obtained.

The Clerk to the Guardians of   I am, Dear Sir
the Williton Union   Yours faithfully
                                                  William Dunn
                                                  Clerk of the Peace

                                                           Williton,
                                                      near Taunton,
                                                           Somerset
Dear Sir,   17 May 1881

re Thomas Hartnell

The Guardians of this Union admit their liability to maintain this Lunatic, and I enclude that you will instruct the Clerk to the Visitors at Wells accordingly.

W. Dunn, Esq.,   Yours Truly
Clerk of the Peace   W.H. White
Wells   Clerk

18th May 1881

Dear Sir,

re Thomas Hartnell

I enclose you a copy of a letter received from the Clerk to the Guardians of the Williton Union, in reply to mine admitting the liability of the Guardians to maintain this Lunatic.

All that is now required is that you should include the Lunatic's name, and the charge for his maintenance in your usual claim on the Guardians.

I enclose an A/c of out of pocket expenses incurred in inquiring into the settlement which be good enough to remit me.

Yours Truly
William Dunn
Clerk of the Peace

Mr Duke

Appended
Mr Duke called and paid amount
21st May 1881
T.W.M.

Frederick Hartnell states: That Thomas Hartnell now in the Lunatic Asylum is my brother. He is the lawful son of William and Elizabeth Hartnell who were married in the old church, Wellington, and is about 27 years of age. My father has for about 20 years rented Moor Mills, the house and a meadow all situate in the parish of Brompton Ralph. He pays I believe about £25 a year rent, and rates. Mr William Hayman of Nether Stowey is the owner. My brother Thomas always lived at home up to the time he was taken away. May 1881

The Commissioners of Visitors of the
Somerset and Bath Pauper Lunatic Asylum

To Mr Dawe

		£	s	d
1881, May	Paid W. Dawe of Taunton for Journey to Moor Mills, Brompton Ralph, inquiring into the settlement of Thomas Hartnell, a lunatic.	1	1	0
	Ditto Horse and expences		11	0
		£1	12	0

P.O. Postal order sent to Mr Dawe same day 21st May 1881

23rd July 1881

Dear Sir,

re Thomas Hartnell

I understand that y^r Guardians object to pay for the maintenance of this man in the Asylum previous to the 17th May last, the date of your letter to me admitting the liability.

I was certainly under the impression that the Guardians had agreed to pay for the full period for which they would have paid if the order referred to in my letter of the 9th May last had been made and such appears to me still to be the proper interpretation of the matter on having read the two letters together.

The order if made would have been retrospective, under the powers of sect 96 of the 16th and 17th Vict cap 97; sect 103 of which Act provides that where any Guardians would be liable under any provision contained in this Act to have an Order made upon them 'for the payment of any money' such Guardians 'may pay the same without any such order being made'.

I hope to hear from you that the outstanding charges have been paid.

Yours truly
William Dunn

W.H. White, Esq.,
Clerk to Guardians
Williton

16th August 1881

Dear Sir,

re Thomas Hartnell

I wrote you on the 23rd ult° in reference to the charges for the maintenance of the above Lunatic, but have not received any reply.

Please let me know, by return whether your Guardians have ordered payment of the full charges, i.e. from the date of admission of the Lunatic.

Yours truly
William Dunn

W.H. White, Esq.,
Clerk to Guardians
Williton

Williton,
near Taunton,
Somerset
17th August 1881

Dear Sir,

re Thos. Hartnell

In reply to your letter of yesterday.

The Guardians did not consider themselves liable to pay the charges from the date of admission of this Lunatic. They therefore struck the charges out of the account against them and disallowed them.

Yours truly
Wm. H. White
Clerk

W. Dunn, Esq.,
Clerk of Peace
Wells
Somerset

19th August 1881

Dear Sir,

re Thos. Hartnell

The Chairman of the Committee of Visitors of the Asylum requests me to point out that your letter of the 17th inst. is not in accord with the unreserved admission of liability previously given.

Will you be good enough to call the Guardians attention to this, and also to the 96th s. of 16 and 17 Vict c. 97 which clearly states their liability.

The only object in writing you at all was to secure payment of the amount due without the trouble and expence (to your Guardians) of an Order of Justices, and the Committee have no desire to resort to that step now, particularly as the amount is so small.

Yours truly
William Dunn

W.H. White, Esq.,
Clerk to Guardians
Williton

Williton
near Taunton
Somerset
22 August 1881

Dear Sir,

re Thos. Hartnell

The Guardians considered your letter this morning and directed me to send a cheque for the amount due £12–18–1 to the Treasurer of the County Lunatic Asylum which I have done.

Yours truly
W.H. White
Clerk

W. Dunn, Esq.,
Clerk of Peace
Wells

23rd August 1881

Dear Sir,

re Thos. Hartnell

Mr White writes me that the arrears of the maintenance charges have been paid to the Asylum's Treasurer.

I send you on the other side hereof a copy of his letter.

Yours faithfully,
William Dunn

Mr Duke
County Lunatic Asylum
Wells

PRO, MH 94/26
County Asylum and Hospital Registers

No. in Order of Admission	70871
Name	Hartnell, Thomas Pauper/male/C [criminal]
Date of Admission	16 March 1881

[contd]

Asylum	Broadmoor
Discharged	11 April 1881, unrecovered

No. in Order of Admission	72005
Name	Hartnell, Thomas Pauper/male
Date of Admission	11 April 1881
Asylum	Somerset
Discharged	7 December 1881, released

Som. RO, L/A
Somerset Lunatic Asylum Minute Book

Thursday May 19th, 1881
Probation, Thomas Hartnell

Thursday July 21st, 1881

The Clerk reported that one Thomas Hartnell, admitted in this Asylum from Broadmoor
on the 11th April 1881 under Secretary of State's Warrant. His sentence having expired
was found by the Clerk of the Peace to be chargeable to the Williton Union, and that the
Board of Guardians refused to pay for his maintenance for the whole time that he was
detained in the Asylum, but only from the date that they acknowledged their liability.
The Clerk was ordered to consult the Clerk of the Peace on the matter.

Thursday August 18th, 1881

The Chairman reported that he had seen the Clerk of the Peace's Clerk who had
mentioned to him Hartnell's case and said that Mr Dunn would write such a letter to the
Williton Board of Guardians as would secure payment.

Som. RO, D/H/men
Somerset Lunatic Asylum Male Case Book 7

Criminal Transferred from Broadmoor

Name	Thomas Hartnell
Age	29
State	Single

Date of Admission	April 11, 1881
Duration	About 6 years
Education	R & W
Religion	C of E
Occupation	Miller
Habits	Sober
General Health	Fair
Causation	Unknown
Additional Particulars	This patient was sentenced to 6 years penal servitude at Taunton Assizes on March 23, 1875 for robbery with violence
Address of Father	Moor Mills, Lydeard St. Lawrence, nr Taunton

On Admission a young man of powerful build about 5′ 8″, light hair and light blue eyes. Holds his head down. Answered questions in a fairly rational style but giggled in a silly manner. Sent to No. 3.

1881, April 11th. Dr Orange of Broadmoor Asylum writes to say that this patient is a demented man who was probably not altogether right in his mind when he was convicted. The offence charged against him was attempting to steal a watch and assaulting the man to whom it belonged. His own account is that the man had invited him to drink in a public house and that they were intoxicated when the assault occurred. There is no record of his having been previously and his own account is that he worked for his father who is a miller residing at Moor Mills, Lydeard St. Lawrence nr Taunton. He says when he found he was sentenced to six years penal servitude his mind completely broke down. He has not been in Broadmoor very long, but during that time has not shown any violence. He is rambling in his conversation and is inclined to be untidy if not looked after, but otherwise is not a man who will give any unusual trouble.

April 23rd	Is quick and well behaved. Health good. Very anxious for his discharge.
May 16th	Doing fairly well
May 19th	Application is made for his discharge on probation by his father, by the Rector of Brompton Ralph, Wiveliscombe and by Dr Cordwent the Deputy Coroner for the Western Division of Somerset. Quiet and well behaved. Might be allowed out on trial as his father guarantees in writing to look after him on 6 months probation.

Copy

Particulars with respect to Thomas Hartnell, about to be transferred to the Asylum for the County of Somerset, at Wells.

Name	Thomas Hartnell.
Year of Birth	1852
Date of Admission into Broadmoor Asylum	16th March, 1881.
Former Occupation	Miller.
From whence brought	Woking Convict Prison
Married, Single, or Widowed	Single
How many children	—
Age of youngest	—
Whether first Attack	} Not known
When previous Attacks occurred	
Duration of existing Attack	Since 1875
State of bodily health	Subject to head-ache
Whether suicidal	No
Whether dangerous to others	Has not exhibited violence whilst here.
Supposed cause	Unknown
Chief delusions or Indications of Insanity	Demented. Says he is annoyed at night but cannot say by whom. Does not sleep well.
Whether subject to Epilepsy	No.
Whether of temperate habits	Says he drank.
Degree of Education	Can read & write.
Religious Persuasion	Church of England.
Crime	Robbery with violence
When and where tried	23rd March, 1875, Taunton Assizes
Verdict of Jury	Guilty
Sentence, or Order of the Court	6 Years penal servitude

Broadmoor Criminal Lunatic Asylum
11th April 1881

W. Orange M.D.
Superintendent

P.J.O

Part of a report from Broadmoor on Thomas Hartnell
(Som. RO, D/H/Men, Male Case Book 7)

Somerset County Council

Date: April 18, 1881

Please answer, as correctly as possibly, the questions on the other side of the paper [below], and return it at once to the Assistant Medical Officer Mr R.J. Woods.

Name   Thomas Hartnell

1.	Is there any history of insanity in the patient's family?	Answer: No
2.	Has there been in any member of the family:	
	1. Consumption?	Answer: No
	2. Intemperence?	Answer: No
	3. Fits?	Answer: No
3.	Has the patient had lately:	
	1. Any serious illness?	Answer: Not known
	2. Any accident?	Answer: Not known
	3. Any Troubles?	Answer: From confinement
4.	What do you think is the cause of present attack of insanity?	Answer: If insane, which I doubt, it arises from his imprisonment
5.	Can patient read and write?	Answer: Yes
6.	Is patient quite sober in habits?	Answer: Yes
7.	What is the patient's disposition when in health?	Answer: Cheerful and active

[signed] William Hartnell

[Thomas Hartnell was released on 7 December 1881, see page 336.]

2. Som. RO, D/PS/Wiv 1/1

In the County of Somerset
Register of the COURT of SUMMARY JURISDICTION sitting at WIVELISCOMBE the sixteenth day of January 1883 *[See illustration on page 140.]*

[Case] Number	2
Name of Informant or Complainant	John Ross
Name of Defendant	*Thomas Hartnell*
Nature of Offence or Matter of Complaint	Disorderly and refusing to quit licensed premises
Minute of Adjudication	Convicted, fined 20/-, costs 3/6 in default of payment 21 days imprisonment with hard labour.
Justices Adjudicating	Arthur Capel, Henry Gorges Moysey, James Edward Knollys, and Thomas Henry Ricketts Winwood, Esquires.

3. PRO, HO 140/76
Calendars of Prisoners

Somerset Quarter Sessions at Wells 8 April 1884

Number	6
Name	Thomas Hartnell
[Previous Convictions]	23 March 1875, Taunton Assizes, Robbery with Violence. 6 years Penal Servitude. 16 January 1883, Wiveliscombe, Drunkenness and refusing to quit a public house. 21 days Hard Labour or pay fine
Age	30
Trade	Carpenter
Degree of Instruction	Imp[Imperfect]
Name and Address of Convicting Magistrate	Arthur Capel, Esq., Bulland Lodge, Chipstable
Date of Warrant	4 March 1884
When Received into Custody	4 March 1884
Offence as Charged in the Commitment	Breaking and entering the dwelling house of William Hartnell and stealing one watch, one silver chain and two metal pocket flasks, his property, at Brompton Ralph on 2 March 1884
When Tried	9 April 1884
Before Whom Tried	R.H. Paget, Esq., M.P. Cranmore Hall, Shepton Mallet and E.H. Clerk, Esq., Burford, Shepton Mallet
Verdict of the Jury	Guilty of house breaking and stealing, after a former conviction

Particulars of Previous Convictions Charged in the Indictment and Proved in Court	1875, March 23rd, Taunton Assizes Robbery with violence 6 years Penal Servitude
Sentence or Order of the Court	6 calendar months Hard Labour Shepton Mallet [Prison]

Som. RO, Q/SR Easter 1884

Somerset Quarter Sessions 8 April 1884 at Wells

Thomas Hartnell charged with breaking and entering the dwelling house of William Hartnell and stealing one watch, one silver chain and two metal pocket flasks his property, at Brompton Ralph on 2 March 1884.

The examination of Elizabeth Hartnell, Thomas Brice, Henry Hews, George Gawler and John Ross, taken on oath this fourth day of March in the year of our Lord one thousand eight hundred and eighty four at the Police Court, Wiveliscombe, in the County aforesaid, before the undersigned two of Her Majesty's Justices of the Peace in and for the said County in the presence and hearing of Thomas Hartnell of Brompton Ralph in the County of Somerset, who is charged this day before us for that he the said Thomas Hartnell on the second day of March, in the year of our Lord one thousand eight hundred and eighty four at the parish of Brompton Ralph in the said County, feloniously did break and enter the dwelling house of William Hartnell there situate and therein feloniously did steal one watch, one silver chain and two metal pocket flasks the goods and chattels of the said William Hartnell, contrary to the form of the statute in such case made and provided, and against the peace of our Lady the Queen, Her Crown and Dignity.

This deponent the said Elizabeth Hartnell on her oath saith as follows:
'I live at Moor Mills in the parish of Brompton Ralph in the County of Somerset. I am the wife of William Hartnell. I recollect Sunday last the 2nd instant I left my house on that day about twelve o'clock at noon. On leaving the house I examined the doors. They were all fastened up correct. I did not leave any person in the house. I locked the front door and took the key with me. All the doors down stairs were fastened. I returned to my house at five o'clock in the afternoon. On my return I saw the prisoner Thomas Hartnell. He was within a few yards of the front door of my house. He was by the machine house door on the other side of the road. When I unlocked the front door and went in I found the inside of the house was not as I left it. Some of the things had been disturbed. Some bread and cheese which were kept in a cupboard in the kitchen were gone. I then went into the back house and found the door that leads from the back house to the mill open. That door was fastened by a wooden bar propped against it on the back house side of it. This bar was not in the same position as I left it. It could not be moved without some force or being broken. I then went to the door of the Mill which leads into the road. That door was then fastened in the same way as when it was fastened before I left the house. Any one knowing the door and fastening could open it and slip it from the outside. I then came back from the Mill and went up stairs. I looked for my chain and watch and they were gone. I kept them in the case now produced, in the window of my bedroom. I also missed the two flasks now produced. The watch and chain are my property. The flasks now produced are my property. My husband is not now living with me. He left me about seven or eight months ago but I know all about him and he occasionally communicates with me. The prisoner is the son of my husband by a former wife.'

Cross examined by the prisoner. 'I did'nt see you in the house nor any other person near but you.'

Re-examined. 'Mr Hews handed me the two flasks now produced yesterday morning. I brought them to Mr Ross yesterday morning at the Police Station and handed them to him.'

The mark of
X
Elizabeth Hartnell

And this Deponent the said Thomas Brice on his oath saith as follows:

'I am a labourer and I live in one of Mr Bellew's cottages at Oakhampton and I work for him. I recollect Sunday last. I saw the prisoner about two o'clock in the afternoon of that day down by Moor Mills. He spoke to me. He asked me 'Do you want to buy a chain'. I said 'No'. He then produced a chain. The chain now produced by Superintendent Ross is the same. When I gave back the chain to him he wanted three shillings for it. I also saw the flasks now produced which he took out of his pocket and shewed to me.'

The mark of
X
Thomas Brice

And this Deponent the said Henry Hews on his oath saith as follows:

'I am a farmer and live at Moor Mill Farm in the parish of Brompton Ralph. My house is about a gunshot from Moor Mills. I recollect the evening of last Sunday the 2nd instant. I went down to Moor Mills about half past ten o'clock in the evening. When I arrived there I saw there policeman Gawler and another man. I saw the prisoner by the kitchen door of Mrs Hartnell's house. The prisoner sleeps in the machine chamber a room over the mill. I assisted policeman Gawler in searching the room where the prisoner sleeps. I saw Gawler find the two flasks now produced on the beam that goes across the room eight or ten feet above the floor. We left the flasks on the machine. On the next morning I went to Moor Mills and I found the flasks in the same place as I left them the evening before. I brought them to Mrs Hartnell at my house and she identified them and handed them to me. The flasks now produced are the same.'

[signed] Henry Hews

And this deponent the said George Gawler on his oath saith as follows:

'I am a police constable stationed at Wiveliscombe. From instructions I received from Mr Superintendent Ross I went to Moor Mills on the evening of Sunday the 2nd of March inst. in company with the witness Elizabeth Hartnell and a man who works for Mr Bennett. I found the prisoner in the loft over the Mill. The door was bolted on the inside. When he heard me there he opened the door. He asked me 'do you want to see me?' I said 'I do'. I told him 'I want to see what you have in your possession.' He said 'all right, you want to find a watch and chain I suppose.' I searched him but I did not find anything on him then. I saw the mark of the prisoner where he had been lying on some straw there. There was no bed in the room. Afterwards Mr Hews came down. I let Mr Hews have my lamp to hold whilst I got on the machine. I found the two flasks now produced on the beam across the room. I handed them to Mr Hews who said 'I expect they are his own property.' From further enquiries I made I apprehended the prisoner and charged him with stealing a watch from his step mother's dwelling house. He said 'How could any one get in there to steal that?' I said 'Any one could easily get through the Mill door into the kitchen.' He then said 'No one has seen me there.' I then brought him to the Police Station and locked him up. On the following morning (Monday) I went to Moor Mills to the loft where I found the prisoner on the previous night. I then again searched the loft. I found the watch now produced in a hole in the wall and the chain was on the same beam a little distance from where I found the flasks which have been identified by Mrs Hartnell.'

[signed] George Gawler

And this deponent the said John Ross on his oath saith as follows;
'I am Superintendent of Police stationed at Wiveliscombe. On Monday morning the third of the present month the witness Elizabeth Hartnell handed me the two flasks now produced at the Police Station at Wiveliscombe.'

[signed] John Ross

Thomas Hartnell stands charged before the undersigned, two of Her Majesty's Justices of the Peace for the said County of Somerset, this fourth day of March in the year of our Lord one thousand eight hundred and eighty four for that he the said Thomas Hartnell on the second day of March in the year of our Lord one thousand eight hundred and eighty four at the parish of Brompton Ralph in the said County feloniously did break and enter the dwelling house of William Hartnell there situate and therein feloniously did steal one watch, one silver chain and two metal pocket flasks, the goods and chattels of the said William Hartnell, contrary to the form of the Statute in such case made and provided and against the peace of our Lady the Queen her Crown and Dignity, and the said charge being read to the said Thomas Hartnell and the Witnesses for the Prosecution, Elizabeth Hartnell, Thomas Brice, Henry Hews, George Gawler and John Ross being severally examined in his presence, the said Thomas Hartnell is now addressed by us as follows: 'Having heard the evidence, do you wish to say anything in answer to the charge? You are not obliged to say anything unless you desire to do so; but whatever you say will be taken down in writing and may be given in evidence against you upon your Trial. And you are clearly to understand that you have nothing to hope from any promise of favour, and nothing to fear from any threat which may have been holden out to you to induce you to make any admission or confession of your guilt, but whatever you shall now say may be given in evidence against you upon your Trial, notwithstanding such promise or threat.'
Whereupon the said Thomas Hartnell saith as follows:
'They never found anything upon me. I had never been in the house. The house is a chaff house. I was obliged to lie down in this house because no one would lodge me. They throwed all my things out of doors.'

[signed] Thos. Hartnell

Taken before us at Wiveliscombe, in the County aforesaid, on the day and year first above mentioned.

Arthur Capel
C. Lamport

And immediately after obeying the directions of the 18th Section of the Act Eleventh and Twelfth Victoria, Chapter Forty Two, the said Justices of the Peace did demand and require of the said Thomas Hartnell whether he desired to call any witnesses; and thereupon in answer to such demand the said Thomas Hartnell does not call or desire to call any witness.

Verdict   Guilty
Sentence   6 months imprisonment with Hard Labour

BIBLIOGRAPHY

The place of publication is London unless otherwise specified.

Burke, J., *Jowitt's Dictionary of English Law* (2 vols), Sweet & Maxwell, 1977.

Burn, Richard, *The Justice of the Peace* printed by A. Strahan, 1825.

Chadwick, E., *A Description of the Hundred of Salford Assize Courts of County of Lancaster*, Beresford & Havill, Manchester, *c*. 1880.

Cheney, C.R., *Handbook of Dates*, Royal Historical Society, 1970.

Coldham, J., *English Convicts in Colonial America*, vol. 1, Middlesex 1617 to 1775, Polyanthos, New Orleans, 1974.

——, *English Convicts in Colonial America*, vol. 2, London, 1656 to 1775, Polyanthos, New Orleans, 1976.

Colwell, S., 'The Incidence of Bigamy in Nineteenth Century England', *Family History Annual*, ed. M.J. Burchall, 1986.

Fox, K.O., *The Records of the Courts of Great Sessions*, Journal of the Society of Archivists, vol. 3, No. 4, October 1966.

Giuseppi, M.S., *Guide to the Contents of the Public Record Office*, 3 vols, HMSO, 1963 to 1968.

Halsbury, Earl of, *The Laws of England*, 3rd edn., Butterworth, 1964.

Hawkings, D.T., *Bound for Australia*, Phillimore, Chichester, 1987.

Mullins, E.L.C., *Texts and Calendars*, Royal Historical Society, 1958.

[Smith, Thornton], 'The English Convict System', *Cornhill Magazine*, vol. III, pp. 708 to 733, June 1861.

——, 'The Convict Out in the World', *Cornhill Magazine*, vol. IV, pp. 229 to 250, August 1861.

Vincent, B., *Haydn's Dictionary of Dates*, Edward Moxon, 1866.

Wyatt, I., *Transportees from Gloucestershire to Australia, 1783 to 1842*, The Bristol and Gloucestershire Archaeological Society, 1988.

FURTHER READING

Sessions and Assize Records in Print

Anon., *Staffordshire Quarter Sessions Rolls, 1586*, William Salt Archaeological Society, 1927.

Atkinson, J.C., *Yorkshire (North Riding) Quarter Sessions Records, 1605 to 1755* (9 vols), North Riding Record Society, 1884 to 1892.

Axon. E., *Manchester Sessions, 1616 to 1623*, Lancashire and Cheshire Record Society, vol. 42, 1901.

Bates, E.H., *Quarter Sessions Records for Somerset, 1607 to 1625*, Somerset Record Society, vol. 23, 1907.

Bennett, J.H.E. & Dewhurst, J.C., *Cheshire Quarter Sessions, 1559 to 1760*, Lancashire and Cheshire Record Society, vol. 94, 1940.

Bowler, H., *London Sessional Records, 1605 to 1685*, Recusant and Precedent Books of Indictment, Catholic Record Society, vol. 34, 1934.

Burne, S.A.H., *Staffordshire Quarter Sessions Rolls, 1581 to 1589*, William Salt Archaeological Society, 1929.

Cockburn, J.S., *Somerset Assize Orders, 1640 to 1659*, Somerset Record Society, vol. 71, 1971.

Fowle, J.P.M., *Wiltshire Quarter Sessions and Assizes, 1736*, Wiltshire Archaeological Society, vol. 11, 1955.

Gretton, M.S., *Oxfordshire Justices of the Peace (Calendars etc.), 1687 to 1689*, Oxfordshire Record Society, vol. 16, 1934.

Historical Manuscripts Commission, *Huntingdon Quarter Sessions, 1958*.

Jeaffreson, J.C., *Middlesex Indictments, 3 Edward VI to 4 James II*, Middlesex County Record Society, 4 vols, 1886 to 1892.

Jenkinson, H. & Powell, D.L., *Surrey Quarter Sessions Records Order Book, 1659 to 1661, and Sessions Rolls Easter to Midsummer 1661*, Surrey Record Society, vol. 13, 1934.

Johnson, H.C., *Wiltshire, Minutes of Proceedings in Sessions, 1563, 1574 to 1592*, Wiltshire Archaeological and Natural History Society, vol. 4, 1949.

Kimball, E.G., *Lincolnshire Sessions of the Peace, Kesteven and Holland, 1381 to 1396*, Lincoln Record Society, vol. 49, 1955.

——, *Sessions Rolls of Warwickshire and Coventry, 1377 to 1397*, Dugdale Society, vol. 16, 1939.

Lister, J., *Yorkshire, West Riding Sessions Rolls, 1597 to 1602*, Yorkshire Archaeological Society, vol. 3, 1888.

Peyton, S.A., *Minutes of Quarter Sessions, Kesteven, Lincolnshire, 1674 to 1695*, Lincoln Record Society, vol. 25, 1931.

Putnam, B.H., *Yorkshire Sessions of the Peace, 1361 to 1364*, Yorkshire Archaeological Society, vol. 100, 1939.

Redwood, B.C., *West Sussex Quarter Sessions Order Book, 1642 to 1649*, Sussex Record Society, vol. 54, 1954.

Salt, D.H.G., *Staffordshire Quarter Sessions Rolls, 1608 to 1609*, Staffordshire Record Society, 1948 to 1949.

Sillem, R., *Lincolnshire Sessions of the Peace, 1360 to 1375*, Lincoln Record Society, vol. 30, 1936.

Tait, J., *Lancashire Quarter Sessions, 1590 to 1606*, Chetham Society, New Series, vol. 77, 1917.

Wake, J., *Northamptonshire Quarter Sessions Records, 1630, 1657 to 1658*, Northamptonshire Record Society, vol. 1, 1924.

Willis Bund, J.W. *Worcestershire Calendar of the Quarter Sessions Papers, 1591 to 1643*, 2 vols, Worcestershire Historical Society, 1899 to 1900.

Crime, Prisons and Prison Life: Secondary Sources

Adam, H.L., *The Story of Crime*, T. Werner Laurie, c. 1927.

Adshead, J., *Prisons and Prisoners*, Longman, 1845.

Babington, A., *The English Bastille*; *A History of Newgate Gaol and Prison Conditions in Britain, 1188 to 1902*, Macdonald, 1971.

Burford, E.J., *In the Clink*, New English Library, 1977.

Burt, J.T., *Results of the System of Separate Confinement as Administered at Pentonville Prison*, Longman, 1852.

Cadbury, G.S., *Young Offenders*, George Allen & Unwin, 1938.

Cadogen, E., *The Roots of Evil*, John Murray, 1937.

Carlebach, J., *Caring for Children in Trouble*, Routledge & Kegan Paul, 1970.

Carpenter, J.E., *The Life and Work of Mary Carpenter*, Macmillan, 1879.

Carpenter, M., *Reformatory Schools for the Children of the Perishing and Dangerous Classes and for Juvenile Offenders*, C. Gilpin, 1851.

——, *Our Convicts* (2 vols), 1864.

Chesterton, G.L., *Revelations of Prison Life*; *with an Enquiry into Prison Discipline and Secondary Punishment* (2 vols), 1856.

Chichester, The Earl of, *Reports and Observations on the Discipline and Management of Convict Prisons by the late Major General Sir Joshua Jebb*, 1863.

Clay, Rev. W.L., *The Prison Chaplain: A Memoir of the Rev. John Clay*, 1861.

——, *Our Convict System*, Cambridge, 1862.

Cockburn, J.S., *Crime in England 1550 to 1800*, Princeton University Press, New Jersey, 1977.

Collins, P.A.W., *Dickens and Crime*, Macmillan, 1962.

Critchley, T.A., *The Conquest of Violence*, Constable, 1970.

Crofton, Sir Walter, *The Criminal Classes and Their Control. Prison Treatment and its Principles*. Addresses to Social Science Congress, Birmingham, October, 1868.

Dixon, W.H., *The London Prisons*, Jackson and Walford, 1850.

Dorner, J., *Newgate to Tyburn*, Wayland Publishers, 1972.

Du Cane, Major Edmund F., *An Account of the Manner in which Sentences of Penal Servitude are Carried Out in England*, 1872.

Du Cane, Col. Sir Edmund F., *The Punishment and Prevention of Crime*, 1882.

——, *A Description of the Prison of Wormwood Scrubs with an Account of the Circumstances Attending its Erection*, 1887.

Du Cane, Major General Sir Edmund F., 'The Unavoidable Uselessness of Prison Labour', *Nineteenth Century*, XL (July to December), 1896.

Eden Hooper, W., *History of Newgate and the Old Bailey*, Underwood Press, 1935.

Edwards, A., *The Prison System in England and Wales 1878 to 1978*, HMSO, 1978.

Emsley, Clive, *Crime and Society in England, 1750 to 1900*, Longmans, London and New York, 1987.

Field, Rev. John, *The Advantages of the Separate System of Imprisonment as Established in the New County Gaol of Reading with a Description of the Former Prisons and a Detailed Account of the Discipline Now Pursued*, 1846.

Foucault, M., *Discipline and Punish*, Penguin, Harmondsworth, 1977.

Fox, Sir Lionel W., *The English Prison and Borstal System*, Routledge & Kegan Paul, 1952.

Fry, Rev. H.P., *A System of Penal Discipline with a Report on the Treatment of Prisoners in Great Britain and Van Diemans Land*, 1850.

A Gentleman of Chichester, *Genuine History of the Inhuman and Unparalleled Murders of William Galley and Daniel Chater by Fourteen Notorious Smugglers*, William Mason, Chichester, 1749.

Griffiths, Major A.G.F., *Memorials of Millbank and Chapters in Prison History* (2 vols), Chapman & Hall, 1875.

Griffiths, G., *Sidelights on Convict Life*, John Long, 1903.

Haway, J., *Solitude in Imprisonment with Proper Profitable Labour and a Spare Diet, the Most Humane and Effectual Means of Bringing Malefactors who have Forfeited their Lives, or are Subject to Transportation, to a Right Sense of their Condition*, 1776.

Heriques, U.R.Q., 'The Rise and Decline of the Separate System of Prison Discipline', *Past and Present*, February, 1972.

Hill, F., *Crime, Its Amount, Causes and Remedies*, 1853.

Hill, M.D., *Suggestions for the Repression of Crime*, 1857.

Hinde, R.S.E., *The British Penal System, 1773 to 1950*, Duckworth, 1951.

Holford, G.P., *The Convicts' Complaint in 1815, and the Thanks of the Convicts in 1825; or Sketches in Verse of a Hulk in the Former Year, and of the Millbank Penitentiary in the Latter*, 1825.

Horsfall Turner, J., *Wakefield House of Correction*, Privately printed for J. Horsfall Turner by Harrison & Sons, Bingley, 1904.

Howard, D.L., *John Howard, Prison Reformer*, Christopher Johnson, 1958.

——, *The English Prisons, Their Past and Future*, Methuen, 1960.

Howard, John, *The State of the Prisons in England and Wales with Preliminary Observations, and an Account of some Foreign Prisons and Hospitals*, Warrington, 1784.

Howell James, D.E., *A Calendar of the Order Book for Norfolk Sessions, 1650 to 1657*, Norfolk Record Society, vol. 26, 1955.

Jebb, Major J., *Modern Prisons; Their Construction and Ventilation*, 1844.

Johnson, W. Branch, *The English Prison Hulks*, Phillimore, Chichester, 1970.

Judges, A.V., *The Elizabethan Underworld*, Routledge & Kegan Paul, 1965.

Kingsmill, Rev. J., *Chapters on Prisons and Prisoners and the Prevention of Crime*, Longman, 1854.

Klare, J.H., *Changing Concepts of Crime and its Treatment*, Oxford University Press, 1966.

Knipe, W., *Criminal Chronology of York Castle*, C.L. Burdekin, 1868.

Latham, P.M., *An Account of the Disease Lately Prevalent at the General Penitentiary*, 1825.

Laurence, J., *A History of Capital Punishment*, Sampson Low, 1932.

Le Breton, T., *Thoughts on the Defective State of Prisons and Suggestions for their Improvement*, 1822.

Lintot, B., *The Parish Officer*, Printed by E. and R. Nutt, and R. Gosling for Bernard Lintot, 1723.

Mayhew, H. and Binny, J., *The Criminal Prisons of London and Scenes of Prison Life*, Griffin, Bohn & Co., 1862.

McConville, S., *History of English Prison Administration 1750 to 1877*, Routledge & Kegan Paul, 1981.

Measor, C.P., *Criminal Correction*, 1864.

——, *The Utilization of the Criminal*, 1869.

Mynshul, G., *Essays and Characters of a Prison and Prisoners 1618*, republished Edinburgh, 1821.

Neild, J., *The State of the Prisons in England and Wales*, Printed by Nichols, 1812.

Partridge, R., *Broadmoor, A History of Criminal Lunacy and its Problems*, Chatto & Windus, 1953.

Paul, Sir G.O., *A State of Proceedings on the Subject of a Reform of Prisons within the County of Gloucester*, Gloucester, 1783.

Pike, L.O., *A History of Crime in England* (2 vols), Patterson Smith, New Jersey, 1968 (reprint from 1873 to 1876 editions).

Pratt, D., Flintshire. *A Calendar of Sessions Rolls, 1747 to 1752*, Clwyd Record Office, 1982.

Priestley, P., *Victorian Prison Lives*, Methuen, 1985.

Pugh, R.B., *Imprisonment in Medieval England*, Cambridge University Press, 1968.

Radzinowicz, L., *A History of English Criminal Law and its Administration from 1750* (4 vols), Stevens & Sons, 1948.

Ranken, W.B., *English Convicts Before and After their Discharge*, 1863.

Rhodes, A.J., *Dartmoor Prison, 1806 to 1932*, The Bodley Head, 1933.

Robinson, F.W., *A Prison Matron, Female Life in Prison*, 1864.

Rose, G., *Schools for Young Offenders*, Tavistock, 1967.

Rules, Orders and Regulations of the Court of General Quarter Sessions, Somerset, Taunton, 1817.

Russell, Rev. W., 'Statistics of Crime in England and Wales from 1839 to 1843', *Journal of the Statistical Society of London* (1847), vol. X, p. 38.

Salgado, G., *The Elizabethan Underworld*, Dent, 1977.

Shaw, A.G.L., *Convicts and the Colonies*, Faber & Faber, 1966.

Slice, A. van der, 'Elizabethan Houses of Correction', *Journal of Criminal Law and Criminology*, vol. XXVII, p. 45, 1937.

Smith, W., *State of the Gaols in London, Westminster and the Borough of Southwark*, Bew, 1776.

Southerton, P., *The Story of a Prison*, Osprey, Reading, 1975.

Stockdale, E., 'The Bedford Gaol that John Howard Knew', *Bedfordshire Magazine*, Summer, 1973.

——, *A Study of Bedford Prison, 1660 to 1877*, Phillimore, Chichester, 1977.

Such, A., *Remarks on Prison Discipline, and the Model Prison*, 1841.

Surry, N.W., and Thomas, J.H., Portsmouth. *Book of Original Entries, 1731 to 1751*, Portsmouth Record Series, 1976.

Tallack, W., *Peter Bedford, the Spitalfield Philanthropist*, 1865.

Thwaites, W., *A Blue Book, Our Convicts, Their Riots and Their Causes*, 1861.

Ticket-of-Leave Man, *Convict Life, or Revelations Concerning Convicts and Convict Prisons*, 1879.

Tonias, J.J., *Nineteenth Century Crime, Prevention and Punishment*, 1972.

Turner, J.H., *The Annals of Wakefield House of Correction*, Harrison & Sons, Bradford, 1904.

Walker, N. and McCabe, S., *Crime and Insanity in England*, Edinburgh University Press, 1968.

Webb, S. and B., *English Prisons Under Local Government*, Frank Cass, 1963.

Weir, McCook, *Prison Despotism*, The National Pub. Co., 1885.

Whiting, J.R.S., *Prison Reform in Gloucestershire 1776 to 1820*, Phillimore, Chichester, 1975.

Whitmore, R., *Crime and Punishment from old Photographs*, Batsford, 1978.

Willis, A.J., Portsmouth. *Borough Sessions Papers, 1653 to 1688*, Portsmouth Record Series, 1971.

Wines, E.C., *State of the Prisons and Child Saving Institutions*, J. Wilson, Cambridge, Mass., 1880.

Winterton, A., 'Seven Years Penal', *Pearson's Magazine*, vol. XV, Jan. to June 1903.

GLOSSARY

Affidavit   A written statement in the name of a person, called the deponent, by whom it is voluntarily signed and sworn to or affirmed.

Arraignment   To bring a prisoner to court to charge him with the crime against him in the indictment.

Bail   Surety for appearance in court by an accused person.

Benefit (or Privilege) of Clergy   This was exemption from prosecution of clergymen for various crimes and was extended to certain others of the privileged classes both male and female. It was necessary to be literate, proof being the reading of the first few words of the fifty-first psalm in Latin: '*Miserere mei deus . . . .*' Benefit of Clergy was abolished in 1827.

Capias   The term given to several writs directing the sheriff to arrest the persons therein named.

Caption   The formal heading of an indictment, deposition or recognizance, stating before whom the information was found or taken.

Commission of the Peace   Appointment of justices to hold sessions for the keeping of the peace within a specified county.

Commitment   Entrusting to custody before trial.

Convict   A convicted prisoner sentenced to transportation or a period of penal servitude.

Defendant   A person against whom an action is brought.

Deponent   The person who has made a sworn statement, i.e. a deposition or affidavit.

Deposition   A statement made under oath.

Distraint or Distress   Seizure of chattels in order to enforce payment of debt or appearance in court.

Distringas   A writ directed to a sheriff, or other officer commanding him to distrain a man for a debt or for him to appear in court.

Docket or Docquet   Abstract of judgement or warrant.

Estreat   Extract from a record of court.

Examination   The interrogation of a person taken under oath.

Exhibit   Document or item produced in court and referred to in evidence.

Felony   Criminal offence.

Gaol Delivery   Trial of prisoners detained on criminal charges.

Grand Jury   Not fewer than twelve and not more than twenty-three freeholders of a county to hear evidence of the prosecution to decide if there was a case worthy of being tried. The indictment was laid before the Grand Jury under the name of a *Bill*. The witnesses in support of the charge were then examined and if the offence appeared to a majority of the jury to be sufficiently proved, the offender was then put on trial. The *Bill* was then endorsed *True Bill*. If the case was found groundless by the majority then the Bill was endorsed *Ignoramus*, or *Not a True Bill* or *Not Found* and the accused person was then discharged. Grand Juries were abolished by the Administration of Justice Act 1933.

Habeas Corpus   Writ ordering the production in court of a person held in custody.

House of Correction   Originally a place for the punishment of rogues and vagabonds, and disorderly persons.

Indictment or Bill of Indictment   Formal accusation of a crime against a person.

Indictable Offences
  1. Offences of a public nature i.e. riot, affray, assault, etc.
  2. Offences against public decency.
  3. Crimes of evil example.
  4. Practices that tend to endanger the constitution e.g. bribery at elections or seditious pamphlets.
  5. Contempts of the Monarch or Court.
  6. Attempts to corrupt, mislead or pervert public justice.
  7. Fraud or oppression.
  8. Acts against the common good of the public.

Jury   Sworn body of persons (usually twelve) to decide on the issue submitted to the court.

Justice of the Peace   A judge appointed by the Crown to conserve the peace.

Larceny   A felonious and fraudulent taking and carrying away by any person the personal goods of another.

Larceny, Grand   Stealing of goods to above the value of twelve pence (one shilling).

Larceny, Petty or Simple   Stealing of goods to the value of twelve pence or under. Note: The distinction between Grand and Petty Larceny was abolished by the Act of 1827, 7 & 8 Geo. IV c 29.

Mainprize   Appointment of sureties for the appearance in court of a prisoner.

Marshalsea   Office of a marshal entrusted with the care of prisoners.

Misdemeanour   Common Law offence not amounting to a felony.

Nisi Prius   Trial by jury before a single judge either at the High Court or at Assizes.

Nisi Prius *Record*   A commission to the judges at *Nisi Prius* for the trial of a cause, delivered to the officer of the court.

Non Omittas   (That you omit not). A clause inserted in writs of execution directing the sheriff not to omit to execute the writ by reason of any liberty because there were many liberties or districts in which the sheriff had no power to execute process unless he had special authority. Such authority was given by this clause.

Odio et atia   Writ ordering enquiry as to whether a charge of murder has been brought through *hatred and malice*.

Order   Direction or command by a Court of Judicature.

Order in Council   An order made by the King/Queen by and with advice of the Privy Council.

Oyer and Terminer   Commission to justices to *hear and determine* all cases within a specified district.

Penal Servitude   A sentence for a period of hard labour.

Po se (Ponit se super patriam)   Pleaded not guilty and put himself at the mercy of the country (the jury).

Postea   Record of proceedings omitted from a court record or made by reason of subsequent proceedings.

Presentment   Report by jury or peace officer.

Process   The complete course of procedure in a legal action.

Prosecution   A proceeding by way of an indictment in the criminal courts in order to put an offender upon his trial.

Prosecutor   Person charging the accused (usually the person against whom a crime was committed).

Prothonotary or *Protonotary*   Title borne by the chief clerk in various courts.

Recognizance   In common law an obligation or bond before a court. The person bound by it is called the *conusor* or *cognisor*. In criminal law a person who has been found guilty of an offence may be required to enter into a recognizance by which he binds himself to keep the peace and be of good behaviour for a specified period.

Remand   To remand a prisoner in a proceeding before a Justice of the Peace is to adjourn the hearing to a future date and to order that the defendant, unless admitted to bail, be kept in custody in the meantime.

Sentence   A definite judgement pronounced in a criminal proceeding.

Serjeant-at-law   A barrister of superior degree.

Sheriff   The principal agent of the Crown for administrative and financial affairs in a county.

Surety   A pledge of security.

Trespass   A breach of criminal law other than treason or a felony.

Verdict   The decision of a jury on the case tried before it.

Warrant   The document serving as the authority to arrest a person. It is also the authority to make payments, appointments, or transfer prisoners from one prison to another.

APPENDICES

NOTES ON APPENDICES

Appendix 1 outlines the use of the records in locating and identifying a criminal and following him through the various classes of records.

Appendix 2 is the result of an enquiry sent to every county and borough record office in England and Wales. The lists given have been compiled from the returns to these enquiries. This appendix also includes calendars of prisoners and prison records held by other local organizations which have been brought to the attention of the author.

Appendix 3 lists the criminal records of the Courts of Great Sessions of Wales held at the National Library of Wales.

Appendix 4 lists all records held by the Public Record Office which have been found to contain biographical references to criminals with a note on document classification. It also includes sources of bankrupts and debtors.

Appendix 5 gives the records held in Police Archives which are of particular interest to family historians, taken from a survey carried out by Ian Bridgeman and Clive Emsley of the Open University. Other material in this survey but not given in this appendix includes: Coroners' Inquests, Summons Books, Registers of Charges, Warrant Books, Case Books and Registers of Suspicious and Bad Characters. The full listing is available from the Police History Society, Cambridgeshire Constabulary, Huntingdon.

Appendix 6 lists criminal records currently held by the Prison Service. These are not at present available for public search but will in due course be transferred to the Public Record Office or the appropriate county record offices. It should be noted that the Prison Service is unable to answer enquiries or enter into correspondence about these records.

Appendix 7 presents in tabular form a listing of all the criminal courts which had jurisdiction in each historic county in England and Wales. (It does not include Courts of Quarter Sessions which were held in every county.)

Appendix 8 gives a list of all existing prisons in England and Wales which were in use prior to 1900.

Where documents have been identified with their specific piece numbers these have been given in the appendices. Where a series of similar documents has been found the covering range of piece numbers has been given together with the covering dates. It should be noted that in such cases the earliest and latest dates are given but gaps in the series (if any) have not been recorded.

Just before going to press some previously unknown material was discovered and has been added to the appropriate sections. Researchers should not accept these lists as being definitive as additional documents are likely to come to light, particularly among quarter sessions records, which in some record offices have not yet been catalogued in detail.

Much of the material recording the details of criminals and their offences such as court and prison records is considered to be of a sensitive nature and is therefore subject to a hundred years closure period. Other documents such as calendars of prisoners have a seventy-five year closure period.

Since the first draft of this book was prepared several years ago many record offices have changed their location and two others have transferred material to other repositories. At the time of going to press it is believed that the addresses given for the record offices and the material they now hold is up to date. The author will be grateful to receive details of any future changes in record office details as well as details of material known to the reader which is not included in the appendices, for inclusion in any future edition of this book.

APPENDIX 1

USING THE RECORDS

1.1 The Initial Searches

In order to locate a family criminal the following procedure is recommended.

Stage 1 Criminal Registers

A search should be made through the appropriate county registers choosing a period when a family member may have been 'lost'. To be more thorough a wider period could be searched, or, when time allows, a search of the complete series for 'your' county. A note should be made of all names of interest with the accompanying details. (The place of residence of the accused is not given in these registers.) Criminal registers are described in Chapter 2.

Stage 2 Calendars of Prisoners

To obtain further information locate the related calendar of prisoners. Calendars do not give the place of residence of the accused or the place where the crime was committed. The magistrate issuing the warrant, a local dignitary or clergyman, is named. With local knowledge this name will identify the area in which the crime was committed (this may or may not be near the home of the criminal). Further detail of the crime is given and sometimes the age and trade of the accused. His degree of literacy (whether he could read or write) is usually given. Manuscript calendars may also be found pre-dating printed calendars usually written into order books. These and printed calendars can be used as a finding aid for particular criminals as an alternative to the criminal registers. (Printed calendars for many counties survive for a period well before the start of criminal registers.) Calendars of prisoners are described in Chapter 3.

Stage 3 Court Records

Both the criminal register and the calendar of prisoners give the place and date of the trial and whether at Quarter Sessions, Petty Sessions, Assizes, the Great Sessions of Wales, a Palatinate Court or the Old Bailey. The depositions made by witnesses and accused will give a full account of the crime. The indictment is often filed separately from the court proceedings and may be the only document which gives the place of residence of the criminal; the vital piece of information that can identify a person. Records of the various courts are described in Chapters 4 to 8.

It should be noted that the population census returns (for 1841, 1851, 1861, 1871, 1881 and 1891) covered all people in England and Wales including those confined to institutions. Inmates may therefore be found listed in prison census returns and resident staff are also recorded. In many cases (presumably to preserve confidentiality) the initials only of a prisoner are given. All other information will be found, i.e. age, trade, married or single, and place of birth (except in 1841). It is, therefore, possible to identify a person with this information in conjunction with the prison registers. The prison register will also give the place of trial which in turn usually gives the place of residence of the prisoner at the time of his arrest. The sentence of the court may be appended against the name in the pre-trial calendar of prisoners and is often also found with the records of the court proceedings. It should also be recorded in the order book. Post-trial calendars of prisoners also record the sentence. If such records are missing it will be necessary to refer to the criminal register at the Public Record Office but these only date from 1805 (except for Middlesex which dates from 1791). In some cases for periods before the start of the criminal registers it has not been possible to find the sentences for certain criminal proceedings.

Stage 4   Prison Records

Further detail of a criminal is sometimes given in prison registers. In very few instances the place of birth of the prisoner is recorded. Occasionally photographs of prisoners can also be found. Prison registers are described in Chapter 14.

Stage 5   Identifying a Criminal

The place of residence found from court proceedings or the indictment, and the place of birth (if given in the prison register) together with his age (usually recorded in calendars of prisoners and prison registers) will determine if he is a person who fits into your family tree.

Stage 6   Adding Further Details

A picture of the prisoner's time in gaol will be gleaned from the various prison journals: *Governors'*, *Surgeons'* and *Chaplains' Journals*, etc., (see Chapter 15). Transfer from one prison to another for the serious offenders will be found in Home Office Warrants (see Chapter 17). Transfer papers, together with captions and licences for the well behaved to 'Live at Large' give further details of behaviour in prison and add to the recorded detail of convicts. Examples of these are given in Chapter 16. Sheriffs' Cravings and Sheriffs' Payments record the expenses incurred in apprehending and maintaining prisoners in gaol and the costs for setting up and conducting Assize Courts (Quarter Sessions expenses are not included in these). Assize Vouchers and Treasury Warrants also contain similar information of Assize criminals already mentioned, and in cases where Assize records are missing may be the only source of Assize criminals. Sheriffs' Cravings are particularly useful for recording the transfer of a prisoner to a prison hulk after receiving a transportation sentence (see Chapter 10).

1.2   Transportation of Convicts

Transportation of Convicts to America

The Court of Quarter Sessions, the Assize Courts, the Courts of Great Sessions of Wales, the Palatinate Courts and the Old Bailey were all empowered to apply transportation sentences. Having identified a criminal who at one of these courts was so sentenced further detail may be found in the records outlined in Chapter 12. It is of particular interest for Americans to locate the transportation ship and the destination in America to where the criminal was sent to serve out his sentence. Transportation to America ended in 1775.

Transportation of Convicts to Australia

Transportation to Australia began in 1787 and was abandoned in 1868 (see Chapter 13). Convicts were also transported to Bermuda and Gibraltar.

1.3 Criminal Lunatics

Many criminals were certified as insane on arraignment or became mentally unstable after conviction. Many of these criminals were confined in the two government asylums for such offenders: Broadmoor and Bethlem. Some records for these establishments are deposited at the Public Record Office and may reveal further information about the inmates (see Chapter 11).

1.4 Bankrupts and Debtors

Bankrupts and debtors were not legally criminals but until 1861 many of them did suffer imprisonment. The quickest way to locate a debtor is by searching the records of the debtors' prisons and then referring back to the court proceedings (see Chapter 20).

1.5 Newspapers

Newspapers should not be overlooked. Since the publication of the earliest newspapers they have included reports of criminal cases. Sometimes only a list of those convicted with their crime and sentence is given. For the more serious crimes, particularly those involving persons of some eminence, detailed reports may be found. The following case though found at the Public Record Office[1] is in fact gleaned from an unidentified newspaper cutting:

> The reverend James Henry Latrobe Bateman, vicar of Haile, Cumberland was charged and found guilty of 'marrying Robert Little, a minor aged 18 years to Elizabeth Jane Cockburn, a spinster of full age against the consent of the parents of the said Robert Little and without due publication of banns or the production of a certificate of banns.'

The trial took place at the Carlisle October Assizes 1886 and Bateman was given eighteen months hard labour. There followed an outcry about what was generally considered far too harsh a sentence.

> The ways of Magistrates and Judges are past finding out. A day or two ago a clergyman was tried for marrying a man and woman without licence. The marriage was performed in the ordinary manner and there was no objection to the propriety of the match. But the clergyman had not complied with the requirements of the law, and thereby committed a punishable offence. He was sentenced by that great luminary of the Bench, Mr Justice Day, to eighteen months hard labour. Mr Justice Day did not, we believe, say on this occasion, as he had said on several other occasions, that he was sorry he could not add flogging to imprisonment. Contrast this with a case heard yesterday. Two men entered into a conspiracy to play what is called 'the confidence trick' on an intending emigrant. They resorted to subtle means to deprive him of his watch and his purse. They were subsequently arrested. There was no doubt about the facts. The missing articles were found in the prisoners' possession. They were sentenced to three months hard labour and consequently have only to endure one six

[1] PRO, HO 144/470/X12223.

part of the punishment, and not a fiftieth part of the ignomy of the clergyman for marrying without a licence. Why this startling difference? Because in one case Mr Justice Day, who has already won an unenviable reputation for the severity of his sentences, passed sentence; and in the other case the Magistrate at the Marlborough-street Police-court, who is generally actuated by common sense and common humanity, passed sentence.

The enquiry into the case revealed that there was more to this case than had been reported in the press. The mother of Robert Little had stated in court that 'Her son had been more intimate with the prisoner than he should have been.' There were therefore no grounds for remission. 'The prisoner had been more than once cautioned by the mother of the infant not to solemnize the marriage and even so lately as the day before he did solemnize it.' The Bishop of Carlisle had been approached for his views but had refused to comment on the case. The judge when questioned stated that he 'Does not consider the sentence at all excessive' and the accompanying report concludes 'This shows that the prisoner deserves no consideration and is lucky to have escaped proceedings for sodomy.'

A large number of bigamist marriages were detected in the nineteenth century. Stella Colwell has revealed in her researches that from 1805 to 1861, 2,715 persons in England and Wales were charged with bigamy (56 of these were accused of polygamy) and 527 of these were women. Some 170 used aliases of which 43 were women. The Grand Jury found 140 cases to be 'No true bill' and a further 334 were acquitted on trial. Transportation sentences were given to 236 persons of which only 8 were women.

The following was taken from the *Liverpool Daily Post* for 30 July 1887:

Lancashire Assizes, 29 July 1887

A Cool Bigamist

William Hacking (20), stonemason, pleaded guilty to having, at Witton, on the 15th June feloniously married Amelia Knowles, his former wife being then alive.

Mr Blair prosecuted and stated that prisoner was married in July 1884[2] at Darwen, and in June this year he went through the form of marriage with Amelia Knowles. Twelve months after his first marriage prisoner deserted his wife and child and went to live at Blackburn close to where they were living. He must have known perfectly well that his wife and child were in want. The woman whom he married the second time was one whom he had courted before his first marriage. She had refused to cohabit with him unless he went through the form of marriage with her, and she knew he was not supporting his wife and child.

Mr Segar appeared for the defence and stated that the prisoner had been obliged to leave his first wife on account of her mother's behaviour, causing quarrels, and wandered all about the county seeking for work. His wife said she would have nothing more to do with him and she told him he was free to do as he liked.

Mr Blair – 'She denies that'.

Prisoner's brother and brother in law were called to prove this statement, and his lordship said that the only extenuating circumstance was that prisoner's wife knew perfectly well that he was a married man. He had thus not been guilty of the cruel wrong which bigamists frequently inflicted upon women, and which was a very great aggrevation of the crime. Prisoner must go to gaol for nine months.

---

[2] William Hacking married Alice Charnley at Over Darwen, 21 July 1884.

APPENDIX 2

CALENDARS OF PRISONERS, AND PRISON REGISTERS AND JOURNALS IN COUNTY RECORD OFFICES AND OTHER LOCAL REPOSITORIES

2.1   CALENDARS OF PRISONERS

The following is a list of all calendars of prisoners separately catalogued in all the county and borough record offices, and other local repositories in England and Wales. In many counties calendars of prisoners will also be found among Quarter Sessions Rolls and Papers.

2.1.1   England

Bedfordshire

Bedfordshire Record Office
County Hall
Bedford
MK42 9AP

Quarter Sessions	1800 to 1833	ref. QGV 14/1
Quarter Sessions	1809 to 1838	ref. QSC 1
Quarter Sessions	1834 to 1850	ref. QGV 14/2
Quarter Sessions	1840 to 1885	ref. QSC 2/1
Quarter Sessions	1888 to 1907	ref. QSC 2/2
Quarter Sessions	1850 to 1869 }	ref. QGV 14/3
Assizes	1875 to 1881 }	
Assizes	1789 to 1819	ref. QGV 14/4
Assizes	1850 to 1870	ref. QGV 14/5
Assizes	1816 to 1886 }	ref. QSC 3/1
	1889 to 1907 }	
Bedford Borough Sessions	1850 to 1870 }	ref. QGV 16/1
County Prisoners	1869 to 1870 }	
Assizes and Quarter Sessions	1902 }	ref. QSC 3/2
	1905 to 1920 }	

Berkshire

Berkshire Record Office
Shire Hall
Reading
RG2 9XD

Lent Assizes	1755	ref. D/EPb 04
Summer Assizes	1820 to 1822	ref. D/EPb 016
Special Assizes (charges of rioting		
in West Berkshire)	Jan. 1831	ref. Q/SO 14
Sessions and Assizes	1831	ref. D/EF 05
Assizes	1812 to 1813	ref. D/EX 225
Lent Assizes, Reading	1820	ref. D/EX 523/7
Quarter Sessions	1854 to 1933	
Assizes	1854 to 1902	ref. Q/SMc
bound in seven volumes		
Reading Borough Sessions		
Gaol calendars	1854 to 1865	ref. R/Box 517
Gaol calendars	1879 to 1882	ref. R/Box 562

Calendars of prisoners for Oxfordshire held by Berkshire Record Office:

Oxford Summer Assizes	1826	ref. D/EL1 07

For other Berkshire calendars see also Oxfordshire Record Office and Somerset Record Office.

Bristol see Gloucestershire

Buckinghamshire

Buckinghamshire Record Office
County Hall
Aylesbury
HP20 1UA

Quarter Sessions	1827 to 1855	
Quarter Sessions	1889 to 1919	ref. Q/unclass
Assizes	Summer 1836	
Assizes	1783 to 1804	ref. S/2/11

Calendars of prisoners are also filed with Sessions Papers, ref. Q/S from c. 1700 and in Minute Books, 1786 to 1827, ref. Q/SM. For other Buckinghamshire calendars see also Oxfordshire Record Office and Somerset Record Office.

Cambridgeshire

County Record Office
Grammar School Walk
Huntingdon
PE18 6LF

Name Index to Persons Tried }
   before Quarter Sessions as   1660 to 1883   ref. Q/SO/1 to 34
   recorded in Order Books }

Calendars of prisoners are also filed with Sessions Rolls, 1730 to 1958, ref. QS/2A/1 to 83.

Cheshire

Cheshire Record Office
Duke Street
Chester
CH1 1RL

None identified separately but calendars are filed with Quarter Sessions Files, ref. QJF.

Chester City Record Office
Town Hall
Chester
CH1 2HJ

Quarter Sessions   1854 to 1883   ref. DPO/6

Calendars are also filed with Chester City Quarter Sessions Files, ref. QSF.

Cornwall

Cornwall Record Office
County Hall
Truro
Cornwall
TR1 3AY

Launceston	17th century	ref. FS 2/9
Bodmin	1827 to 1828	ref. FS 3/255 to 260
Launceston	17th century	ref. FS 3/551
Bodmin	1746	ref. DDT: 1845
Launceston Assizes, list of } sentences	1817 to 1818	ref. EN 2416, pp. 205 to 209

For other Cornwall calendars see also Somerset Record Office.

Cumberland

Cumbria Record Office
The Castle
Carlisle
Cumbria
CA3 8UR

Quarter Sessions	1830 to 1839	ref. Q/9/1
Quarter Sessions	1839 to 1850	ref. Q/9/2
Quarter Sessions	1850 to 1893	ref. Q/9/3
Quarter Sessions and Assizes	1893 to 1898	ref. Q/9/12

| Quarter Sessions and Assizes | 1899 to 1905 | ref. Q/9/13 |
| Quarter Sessions and Assizes | 1906 to 1917 | ref. Q/9/14 |

For other Cumberland calendars see also Somerset Record Office.

Derbyshire

Derbyshire Record Office
New Street
Matlock
Derbyshire
DE4 3AG

Quarter Sessions
None identified separately but some calendars are filed with Quarter Sessions Records.

Assizes
None identified separately but some calendars are known to be filed with Quarter Sessions Records.

For other Derbyshire calendars see also Somerset Record Office.

Devonshire

Devon Record Office
Castle Street
Exeter
EX4 3PU

Quarter Sessions	1665 to 1963	ref. Q/S 32 to 33
Assizes	1854 to 1919	ref. Devon Q/S 34
Assizes	1791	ref. 63/11/1
Assizes	1803 and 1818	ref. 64/12/29/10
Assizes and Quarter Sessions mixed together	1823 to 1863	ref. ECA book nos. 264, 265, 265a
Assizes and Quarter Sessions mixed together	1801 to 1863	ref. ECA book nos. 267 to 269

For other Devonshire calendars see also Somerset Record Office.

West Devon Record Office
Clare Place
Plymouth
PL4 0JW

Calendars of prisoners for Durham held by West Devon Record Office:

| Durham Assizes | 9 August 1819 | ref. 105/157 |

Dorsetshire

Dorset Record Office
Bridport Road
Dorchester
DT1 1RP

Quarter Sessions	1801 to 1852	ref. QSG/2
Assizes and Quarter Sessions	1854 to 1882	ref. QSG/3
	1882 to 1887	ref. QSG/4
	1887 to 1890	ref. QSG/5
	1891 to 1898	ref. QSG/6
	1899 to 1904	ref. QSG/7
	1905 to 1914	ref. QSG/8
	1915 to 1921	ref. QSG/9
	1922 to 1929	ref. QSG/10
	1930 to 1936	ref. QSG/11
	1937	ref. QSG/12

Post-Trial Calendars		
Assizes and Quarter Sessions	1801 to 1819	ref. 10951A
	1820 to 1833	ref. 10951B
	1824 to 1831	ref. 10952
	1834 to 1846	ref. 10952A
	1801 to 1825	ref. D 423/1

Assizes	1839	ref. KS 2
	1839	ref. 11008
	1729	ref. 11010
	1735	ref. JK 12
	1736	ref. JK 11

Durham

County Record Office
County Hall
Durham
DH1 5UL

Durham Gaol	1824 to 1827	ref. D/X 436/41
Quarter Sessions	1867 to 1966	ref. Q/S/C/1 to 19
Assizes	1880 to 1909	ref. Q/S/C/20 to 22

For other Durham calendars see also West Devon Record Office and Somerset Record Office.

Essex

Essex Record Office
County Hall
Chelmsford
CM1 1LX

Quarter Sessions	1801 to 1816	ref. Q/SMr 1 to 3
Quarter Sessions	1816 to 1842	ref. Q/SMr 1 to 8
Quarter Sessions and Assizes	1860 to 1908	ref. Q/SMc 9 to 14

For other Essex calendars see also Somerset Record Office.

Gloucestershire and Bristol

Gloucestershire
County Record Office
Clarence Row
Gloucester
GL1 3DW

Gaol Calendars	1728 to 1790	ref. Q/SG 1
Gaol Calendars, quarterly lists	1789 to 1878	ref. Q/SG 2
Quarter Sessions	1790 to 1889	ref. Q/SGa 1
Quarter Sessions	1878 to 1889	ref. Q/SGa 2

For other Gloucestershire calendars see also Pembrokeshire Record Office.

Bristol Record Office
'B' Bond Warehouse
Smeaton Road
Bristol

Calendars of prisoners are filed with Bristol Borough Sessions Papers, 1728 to 1889.

Hampshire

Hampshire Record Office
20 Southgate Street
Winchester
SO23 9EF

Quarter Sessions	1868 to 1958	ref. QCP 1 to 6
Assizes	1834 to 1920	no reference

Photocopies of Quarter Sessions calendars, 1788 to 1858, are available on open shelves.

Portsmouth City Record Office
3 Museum Road
Portsmouth
PO1 2LE

Portsmouth Borough Sessions	1842 to 1854	ref. S7/1
	1854 to 1862	ref. S7/2
	1863 to 1870	ref. S7/3
	1871 to 1882	ref. S7/4

For other Hampshire calendars see also Somerset Record Office.

Herefordshire

Hereford Record Office
The Old Barracks
Harold Street
Hereford
HR1 2QX

Quarter Sessions 1849 to 1882 ref. Film Reel No. 13

Some calendars are filed with County Quarter Sessions records for 1802 and 1847 to 1881.

Hertfordshire

None separately catalogued at Hertford Record Office. See Somerset Record Office.

Huntingdonshire

County Record Office
Grammar School Walk
Huntingdon
PE18 6LF

Assizes 1831 to 1832 ref. 163/HCP/2

Calendars for Quarter Sessions are filed with Quarter Sessions Papers, 1790 onwards.

Kent

Kent County Archives Office
County Hall
Maidstone
ME14 1XQ

Quarter Sessions 1627 to 1674 ref. Q/SMc
1702 to 1706

For other Kent calendars see also Somerset Record Office.

Lancashire

Lancashire Record Office
Bow Lane
Preston
PR1 2RE

Quarter Sessions	1835 to 1875	ref. QJC/3 to 55
	1889 to 1931	
Liberties	1821 to 1834	ref. QJC/2
Crown Prisoners	1801 to 1822	ref. QJC/1 & 1a
(Palatinate Court of Lancaster)	and 1832 to 1837	
ditto	1838 to 1847	ref. QJC/12

Calendars of prisoners prior to 1835 for Quarter Sessions are filed with Recognizances, ref. QSB.

Cumbria Record Office
140 Duke Street
Barrow-in-Furness
Cumbria
LA14 1XW

The following Lancashire calendars of prisoners are held by the Cumbria Record Office, Barrow-in-Furness:

Quarter Sessions	1873, 1880, 1887	ref. Z1635 to Z1672
and related papers	1842 to 1869	

For other Lancashire calendars see also Somerset Record Office.

Leicestershire

Leicestershire Record Office
57 New Walk
Leicester
LE1 7JB

Quarter Sessions	1753	ref. DG9/2231
Quarter Sessions	1815	ref. DG5/882
Quarter Sessions	1835	ref. DG9/2240
Assizes	1835	ref. DG9/2240

Calendars are also filed with Quarter Sessions Rolls for Leicestershire, 1714 to 1791, ref. QS3/1 to 1113. They are also filed with Sessions for the Borough of Leicester, 1606 to 1837, ref. BR 1V/1/1 to 203 & 205; and 1836 to 1971, ref. 31D71.

Lincolnshire

Lincolnshire Archives Office
The Castle
Lincoln
LN1 3AB

Assize Calendars	*c.* 1770 to 1850	ref. Mon.7/50 and ref. Hill 41/5

Calendars are also filed with Quarter Sessions Bundles.

Middlesex (including London)

Greater London Record Office
40 Northampton Road
London EC1R 0AB

Newgate Gaol	1550 to 1774	ref. MJ/CC
Middlesex House of Correction	1619 to 1825	ref. MJ/CC
Middlesex New Prison, Clerkenwell	1620 to 1821	ref. MJ/CC
Westminster Gatehouse	1620 to 1768	ref. MJ/CC
Westminster House of Correction	1660 to 1799	ref. MJ/CC

Post Trial Calendars New Prison	1690 to 1774	ref. MJ/CP
Middlesex House of Correction	1710 to 1774	ref. MJ/CP
Newgate Gaol	1711 to 1774	ref. MJ/CP
Westminster Gatehouse	1693 to 1765	ref. MJ/CP
Westminster House of Correction	1732 to 1758	ref. MJ/CP
Calendars of Prisoners Tried for each Middlesex Session	1802 to 1889	ref. MJ/CP
Newgate Calendars of those prisoners for trial at Old Bailey	1820 to 1853	ref. OB/CP

Monmouthshire

County Record Office
County Hall
Cwmbran
Gwent
NP44 2XH

Quarter Sessions	1808 to 1936	ref. Q/Cal of P 1 to 15
Quarter Sessions, Records of Convictions	1831 to 1872	ref. Q/R of C 1 to 3

Norfolk

Norfolk Record Office
Central Library
Norwich
NR2 1NJ

Quarter Sessions	1862 to 1971	ref. C/S10/1 to 16
Assizes, 1863 to 1971	1863 to 1971	ref. C/S10/17 & 18

Kings Lynn Sessions Books, 1726 to 1952, ref. KL/C 20/1 to 12 and Thetford Sessions Books, 1632 to 1639 and 1751 to 1951 ref. T/QS/1 to 8, contain calendars of prisoners.

Northamptonshire

Northamptonshire Record Office
Wootton Hall Park
Northampton
NN4 9BQ

Quarter Sessions	1832	ref. C(A) 8359
Quarter Sessions	18th century	ref. ASL 1223
Assizes	1612 and 17th century	ref. IL 2557 & IL 1962
Assizes	1735	ref. LT 225
Assizes	1814	ref. YZ 4763 & D 1710
Assizes	1815	ref. D 2889
Assizes	1818 to 1836	ref. ZB 68/1
Assizes	1831	ref. ZA 852 & Box 72 (QS)

Assizes	1837 to 1846	ref. ZB 68/2
Assizes	1854 to 1881	ref. Box X 328
Assizes	1882 to 1892	ref. ML 2033
Assizes	1892 to 1958	with QS

Calendars are also filed with Quarter Sessions Rolls for 1630 and 1657 to 1972. For other Northamptonshire calendars see also Somerset Record Office.

Northumberland

County Record Office
Melton Park
North Gosforth
Newcastle upon Tyne
NE3 5QX

Calendars of prisoners are filed with Quarter Sessions records from 1842 to c. 1878. Calendars for both Assizes and Quarter Sessions from 1878 to 1971 are filed with Quarter Sessions records.

Nottinghamshire

Nottinghamshire Record Office
County House
Nottingham
NG1 1HR

Assizes	1772	ref. DDN 231/11
Assizes	1790	ref. DDE 3/14
Assizes	1799	ref. DDBB 129/4
Assizes	1832	ref. DDFS 1/134 to 6
Assizes	1864	ref. DDM 105/22

Quarter Sessions calendars are also filed with Sessions records, ref. QJV/2, QSP and QAG2.

Oxfordshire

Oxfordshire Record Office
County Hall
Oxford
OX1 1ND

Quarter Sessions and Assizes	1822 to 1913	ref. QSP I/2 to 11
Quarter Sessions and Assizes	1778 to 1844	ref. QSP I/1
Post Trial Calendars	1882 to 1958	ref. Acc 2357

Calendars of prisoners for other counties held by Oxfordshire Record Office:

Buckinghamshire Post Trial Calendars	1882 to 1958	ref. Acc 2357
Berkshire Post Trial Calendars	1882 to 1958	ref. Acc 2357

For other Oxfordshire calendars see also Berkshire Record Office and Somerset Record Office.

Rutland

None identified.

Shropshire

County Record Office
The Shire Hall
Abbey Foregate
Shrewsbury
SY2 6ND

Quarter Sessions	1786 to 1930	ref. QS 38 to 51
Quarter Sessions	1830 to 1835	ref. QS Box 53
Quarter Sessions	1779, 1784, 1794, 1795, 1796, 1798, 1799	ref. 3719
Assizes	1830 to 1835	ref. QS Box 53
Assizes	1809 to 1866	ref. QS 43 to 47
Assizes	1768, 1772, 1778, 1787, 1788, 1790, 1793, 1796, 1798, 1832	ref. 3719

For other Shropshire calendars see also Somerset Record Office.

Somerset

Somerset Record Office
Obridge Road
Taunton
Somerset
TA2 7PU

Quarter Sessions	1812 to 1822	ref. Q/SCs 1 to 27
	1823 to 1830	ref. Q/SCs 28 to 59
	1831 to 1836	ref. Q/SCs 60 to 86
	1837 to 1841	ref. Q/SCs 87 to 119
	1842 to 1845	ref. Q/SCs 120 to 147
	1846 to 1848	ref. Q/SCs 148 to 170
	1849 to 1855	ref. Q/SCs 171 to 220
	1856 to 1862	ref. Q/Scs 221 to 252
	1863 to 1872	ref. Q/SCs 253 to 291
	1873 to 1882	ref. Q/SCs 292 to 330
	1852	ref. Q/SCz 2

Calendars of prisoners are also filed with Quarter Sessions Rolls, ref. Q/SR.

Assizes	1665	ref. DD/SF 1067
	1796, 1798, 1801 to 1805, 1813 & 1814, 1820 & 1821	ref. DD/MT Box 53

1799, 1806 to 1812, 1816 & 1817, 1819, 1822 & 1823	ref. DD/MT Box 59
1836 to 1847	ref. DD/MK Box 21
1803, 1809, 1819, 1827	ref. DD/SAS C/2402/37
1774, 1816	ref. DD/GF C/462
1816	ref. DD/FF C/281
1798	ref. DD/UK C/1068
1831	ref. DD/SAS C/909, 142
1866 & 1867	ref. DD/SF 3347, 3340
1777, 1787	ref. DD/MY 46
1815, 1821, 1823 to 1830, 1832, 1833, 1836, 1838, 1840	ref. Q/SCz 3
1810, 1815 to 1832	ref. Q/SCa 1 to 30
1833 to 1853	ref. Q/SCa 31 to 63
1854 to 1863	ref. Q/SCa 64 to 90
1864 to 1874	ref. Q/SCa 91 to 119
1875 to 1881	ref. Q/SCa 120 to 143
1882 to 1892	ref. Q/SCa 144 to 182
1893 to 1905	ref. Q/SCa 183 to 220

Calendars of prisoners for other counties held by the Somerset Record Office:

Assizes

Berkshire	1852	ref. Q/SCz 2
Cumberland	1852	ref. Q/SCz 2
Devonshire	1834, 1838, 1844, 1845	ref. Q/SCz 1
Devonshire	1838	ref. Q/SCz 3
Essex	1845	ref. Q/SCz 2
Hampshire	1830	ref. Q/SCz 1
Hampshire	1850	ref. Q/SCz 2
Kent	1851	ref. Q/SCz 2
Lancashire	1852	ref. Q/SCz 2
Northamptonshire	1852	ref. Q/SCz 2
Oxfordshire	1852	ref. Q/SCz 2
Shropshire	1851	ref. Q/SCz 2

Quarter Sessions

Buckinghamshire	1852	ref. Q/SCz 2
Cornwall	1851	ref. Q/SCz 2
Cumberland	1852	ref. Q/SCz 2
Derbyshire	1852	ref. Q/SCz 2
Devonshire	1852	ref. Q/SCz 2
Durham	1852	ref. Q/SCz 2
Essex	1844 & 1845	ref. Q/SCz 2
Glamorgan	1852	ref. Q/SCz 2

Hampshire	1852	ref. Q/SCz 2
Hertfordshire	1852	ref. Q/SCz 2
Kent	1851	ref. Q/SCz 2
Oxfordshire	1852	ref. Q/SCz 2
Shropshire	1851	ref. Q/SCz 2
Staffordshire	1852	ref. Q/SCz 2
Suffolk	1843, 1844 & 1852	ref. Q/SCz 2
Warwickshire	1852	ref. Q/SCz 2

Somerset Local History Library
The Castle
Castle Green
Taunton
TA1 4AD

| Somerset Quarter Sessions | 1846 to 1852 | ref. Shelf T 347 |
| Somerset Assizes | 1852 to 1853 | ref. Shelf T 347 |

Staffordshire

Staffordshire Record Office
County Buildings
Eastgate Street
Stafford
ST16 2LZ

None separately identified but calendars for Quarter Sessions and Assizes from 1780 are to be found in Quarter Sessions Bundles, ref. Q/SB. For other Staffordshire calendars see also Somerset Record Office.

Suffolk

Suffolk Record Office
Gatacre Road
Ipswich
IP1 2LQ

| Quarter Sessions and Assizes | 1882 to 1896 | ref. Acc 608/1 to 7 |

For other Suffolk calendars see also Somerset Record Office.

Surrey

Surrey Record Office
County Hall
Kingston upon Thames
Surrey
KT1 2DN

| Central Criminal Court | 1857 to 1889 | ref. QS 3/3/1 to 15 |
| Quarter Sessions and Assizes | 1848 to 1892 | ref. QS 3/4/1 to 18 |

Earlier calendars are to be found with Quarter Sessions Rolls.

Sussex, East

County Record Office
The Maltings
Castle Precincts
Lewes
East Sussex
BN7 1YT

Quarter Sessions	1815 to 1888	ref. QCR/1/4/E1 to E11
Miscellaneous		ref. QSR/1/4/E12

Sussex, West

West Sussex Record Office
Sherburne House
3 Orchard Street,
Chichester
PO19 1RN

None separately identified but some calendars are filed with Quarter Sessions Rolls.
See also East Sussex Record Office.

Warwickshire

County Record Office
Priory Park
Cape Road
Warwick
CV34 4JS

Quarter Sessions	1801 to 1971	ref. QS 26/2/1 to 16
Assizes	1801 to 1848	ref. QS 26/1/1 to 9

For other Warwickshire calendars see also Somerset Record Office.

Westmorland

Cumbria Record Office
Kendal
Cumbria
LA9 4RQ

Assizes	1656	ref. WDX/666

Some calendars are to be found with the Quarter Sessions Files, ref. WQ/SR.
Returns of prisoners are filed with Quarter Sessions records from 1821 to 1838,
ref. WQ/JC/1 & 2.

Wiltshire

Wiltshire Record Office
County Hall
Trowbridge
Wiltshire
BA14 8JG

| Quarter Sessions (includes Assizes from 1885) | 1728 to 1971 | ref. A1/125/1 to 101 |
| Assizes | 1862 to 1877 | ref. A1 125/102 |

Name index to calendars of prisoners, 1728 to 1820, ref. A1/125/1 to 52C on open shelves:

   The Goody Index, 2 volumes
   The Baddy Index, 2 volumes

Worcestershire

Record Office
County Hall
Spetchley Road
Worcester
WR5 2NP

| Quarter Sessions | 1839 to 1898 | ref. BA 772 |

Yorkshire, North

County Record Office
Malpas Road
Northallerton
North Yorkshire
DL7 8TB

| Quarter Sessions | 1765 to 1766, 1794, 1827 to 1834, 1843 } | ref. QSG (microfilm) |

North Yorkshire Record Office
The York Archives
Exhibition Square
York
YO1 2EW

| Quarter Sessions | 1828 to 1853 (two volumes) |

North Yorkshire County Library
Museum Street
York
YO1 2DS

| Assizes | 1785 to 1851 | ref. Y343.1 |

Yorkshire, West

Registry of Deeds
Newstead Road
Wakefield
WF1 2DE

| Quarter Sessions | 1816 to 1971 | ref. QS7 |
| Calendars (unspecified) | 1863 to 1915 | ref. C118/251 to 279 |

Yorkshire, South

South Yorkshire Record Office
Central Library
Barnsley
S70 2JF

Prisoners list for Sheffield Town Hall awaiting Trial, 1845 to 1846.

2.1.2 Wales

Anglesey

Area Record Office
Shirehall
Llangefni
Gwynedd
LL77 7TW

Quarter Sessions	1847	W/QA/G/1028a
	1856	W/QA/G/1029b & c
	1865	W/QA/G/1029d
	1866	W/QA/G/1029a
	1870	W/QA/G/1030
	1893	W/QA/G/1081
Assizes	1840 to 41	W/QA/G/1026 & 1027
	1845	W/QA/G/1028
	1850	W/QA/G/1029
	1878 to 79	W/QA/G/1031 to 41
Quarter Sessions and Assizes	1880 to 88	W/QA/G/1042 to 1081

Calendars are also filed with Quarter Sessions Papers from 1772 to 1974.

Brecon

County Archives Office
County Hall
Llandrindod
Powys
LD1 5LD

| Quarter Sessions | 1836 to 1912 | ref. Brecon Q/CRp |

Carnarvonshire

Area Record Office
County Offices
Caernarfon
Gwynedd
LL55 1SH

None separately identified but calendars for Quarter Sessions are filed with Quarter Sessions Rolls.

Cardiganshire

The National Library of Wales
Aberystwyth
Dyfed
SY23 3BU

Calendars of prisoners at the House of Correction at Cardigan	1830 to 1865	ref. Cardigan Printer's File

Dyfed Record Office
County Offices
Aberystwyth
Dyfed
SY23 2DE

Quarter Sessions	Midsummer 1881	ref. D/HL/27
Quarter Sessions	Michaelmas 1881	ref. D/HL/25
Quarter Sessions	Epiphany 1882	ref. D/HL/26

For other Cardiganshire calendars see also Pembrokeshire Record Office.

Carmarthenshire

Carmarthenshire Record Office
Dyfed Archives Service
County Hall
Carmarthen
SA31 1JP

Quarter Sessions and Assizes	1851 to 1880	ref. Museum 733

For other Carmarthenshire calendars see also Pembrokeshire Record Office.

Denbighshire

Clwyd Record Office
Ruthin Branch
46 Clwyd Street
Ruthin
LL15 1HP

None separately identified but some calendars for Quarter Sessions and Assizes are filed with Quarter Sessions Rolls, ref. QSD/SR.

Flintshire
Clwyd Record Office
Hawarden Branch
The Old Rectory
Hawarden
Deeside
CH5 3NR

None separately identified but some calendars for Quarter Sessions and Assizes are filed with Quarter Sessions Rolls, ref. AS/SR.

Glamorgan
Glamorgan Archive Service
County Hall
Cathays Park
Cardiff
CF1 3NE

Quarter Sessions and Assizes	1850 to 1912	ref. QSC 1 to 9
Quarter Sessions	1903 to 1920	ref. QSC 1B
Assizes	1882, 1903 to 1917	ref. QSB 1A
Quarter Sessions	1794	ref. D/DX 162/1

Merioneth
Area Record Office
Cae Penarlag
Dolgellau
Gwynedd
LL40 2YB

Calendars of Prisoners in County Gaol showing employment, crime, behaviour and attendance in Chapel	1828 to 1832	ref. Z/QA/G/14

Montgomeryshire
County Archives Office
County Hall
Llandrindod
Powys
LD1 5LD

None separately identified but calendars for Quarter Sessions are filed with Quarter Sessions Rolls.

Pembrokeshire

Pembrokeshire Record Office
Dyfed Archives
The Castle
Haverfordwest
Dyfed
SA61 2EF

Great Sessions (and Assizes)	1814 to 1900	ref. PQ 21
Quarter Sessions	1831 to 1850	ref. PQ 21
Quarter Sessions	1817 to 1901	ref. PQ 14
Quarter Sessions	1835 to 1854	ref. HQ 14
Great Sessions (and Assizes)	1882 to 1886	ref. HQ 21

Calendars are also filed with Quarter Sessions Rolls, 1779 to 1971, ref. PQ 7.

Calendars of prisoners for other counties held by the Pembrokeshire Record Office:

Cardiganshire Assizes	1816 to 1862	ref. PQ/C/1/20
Carmarthenshire Assizes	1816 to 1862	ref. PQ/C/1/20
Gloucestershire Assizes	1816 to 1862	ref. PQ/C/1/20

Radnorshire

County Archives Office
County Hall
Llandrindod
Powys
LD1 5LD

Returns of Prisoners committed for trial	1815 to 1824	ref. Radnor S 1646 to 52
Returns of Prisoners committed for trial	1829	ref. Radnor S 1653 to 6

2.2   PRISON REGISTERS AND JOURNALS

2.2.1   England

Bedfordshire

Bedfordshire Record Office
County Hall
Bedford
MK42 9AP

Register of Prisoners in County Gaol	1799 to 1836	ref. QGV 10/1
Register of Prisoners in County Gaol	1837 to 1849	ref. QGV 10/2

Register of Prisoners in County Gaol and House of Correction	1847 to 1856	ref. QGV 10/3
Register of Prisoners in County Gaol (with photographs)	1859 to 1876	ref. QGV 10/4
Registers of Prisoners for the New House of Correction	1820 to 1849	ref. QGV 11/1 & 2
Registers of Prisoners	1847 to 1878	ref. QGV 12/1 & 2
Register of Prisoners received from outside the County	1850 to 1865	ref. QGV 13/1
Register of Middlesex Prisoners and Government Convicts held in Bedford Gaol	1863 to 1879	ref. QGV 13/2
Commitment and Description Book for Bedford Borough Prisoners in the County Gaol and House of Correction	1847 to 1850	ref. QGV 16/2
Lists of Debtors in Gaol	1770 to 1854	ref. QGV 15/1
Sheriffs' Debtors Debtors	1846 to 1849 1846 to 1878	ref. QGV 15/2

Berkshire

None

Buckinghamshire

Buckinghamshire Record Office
County Hall
Aylesbury
HP20 1UA

County Gaol Gaol Receiving Books	Dec. 1870 to Sept 1878	ref. Q/AG 23 to 26
Chaplains' Character Books	Oct. 1853 to Dec. 1876	ref. Q/AG 27 to 29

Cambridgeshire

None

Cheshire

County Record Office

None

Chester City Record Office
Town Hall
Chester
CH1 2HJ

Chester City Gaol
Lists of Prisoners   Sheriff's Gaol   ref. SIG
                                     Indentures 1667 to
                                         1795

Cumbria Record Office
140 Duke Street
Barrow-in-Furness
Cumbria
LA14 1XW

Chester Gaol
List of Executions   1809 to 1877   ref. Z2729 & Z2730

Cornwall

None

Cumberland

None

Derbyshire

None

Devonshire

Devon Record Office
Castle Street
Exeter
EX4 3PU

Exeter Gaol

Reception Books	1857 to 1863	ref. ECA book nos. 293 & 294
Lists of Prisoners	1818 to 1863	ref. ECA book nos. 279, 279a, & 280
Chaplains' Diaries	1816 to 1863	ref. ECA book nos. 252 to 259
Surgeons' Journals	1823 to 1863	ref. ECA book nos. 283 & 284
Schoolmaster's Report Book	1857 to 1863	ref. ECA book no. 266

| Prisoners' Misconduct Book | 1851 to 1863 | ref. ECA book no. 261 |
| Occurrence Books | 1819 to 1863 | ref. ECA book nos. 285 to 292 |

Bradninch House of Correction

| Register of Prisoners | 1852 to 1865 | ref. 1978A/6/1 |

Tiverton House of Correction

| Prisoners | 1829 to 1879 | ref. R4/1/c309 |

Dorset

Dorset Record Office
Bridport Road
Dorchester
DT1 1RP

Dorchester Gaol

Criminal Process Registers	1782 to 1828	ref. NG/PRI/A1 to A4
Prison Registers	1812 to 1879	ref. NG/PRI B1 to B10
Descriptions of Prisoners	1858 to 1878	ref. NG/PRI/C1 to C4
Register of Debtors	1793 to 1842	ref. NG/PRI/D1

Durham

None

Essex

None

Gloucestershire

County Record Office
Clarence Row
Gloucester
GL1 3DW

County Gaol

Register of Prisoners	1815 to 1844	ref. Q/Gc 5/1 to 7
Register of Prisoners	1844 to 1879	ref. Q/Gc 6/1 to 7
Register of Prisoners	1841 to 1844	ref. Q/Gc 7a
Register of Prisoners	1817 to 1831	ref. Q/Gc 7b
Debtors' Registers	1838 to 1879	ref. Q/Gc 8/1 & 2
Register of Summary Convictions	1853 to 1879	ref. Q/Gc 9/1 to 9
Governors' Journals	1795 to 1873	ref. Q/Gc 3/1 to 3
Deputy Governor's Minute Book	1844 to 1845	ref. Q/Gc 14
Chaplains' Journals	1806 to 1872	ref. Q/Gc 15/1 to 6
Surgeons' Journals	1791 to 1820	ref. Q/Gc 16/1 to 3

Horsley House of Correction

| Register of Prisoners | 1825 to 1860 | ref. Q/Gh 10/1 to 5 |

Governors' Journals	1809 to 1843	ref. Q/Gh 1/1 & 2
Chaplain's Journal	1852 to 1858	ref. Q/Gh 11
Surgeon's Journal	1843 to 1844	ref. Q/Gh 12

Lawfords Gate

| Keeper's Journal | 1820 to 1826 | ref. Q/Gla |

Littledean House of Correction

Index to Prisoners	1844 to 1891	ref. Q/Gli 15
Prison Registers	1791 to 1923	ref. Q/Gli 16/1 to 8
Chaplain's Journal	1801 to 1815	ref. Q/Gli 3/1
Chaplain's Books	1816 to 1839	ref. Q/Gli 17/1 to 3
Governor's Journal	1837 to 1844	ref. Q/Gli 3/3
Keeper's Journals	1844 to 1854	ref. Q/Gli 3/4 & 5
Chaplain's Journal	1839 to 1844	ref. Q/Gli 17/4
Journal and Prisoner Character Books	1844 to 1850	ref. Q/Gli 17/5 & 6
Chaplain's Journal	1850 to 1854	ref. Q/Gli 17/7
Surgeon's Books	1806 to 1838	ref. Q/Gli 18/1 & 2
Surgeon's Journal	1842 to 1848	ref. Q/Gli 18/3
Medical Officer's Journal	1844 to 1854	ref. Q/Gli 19
Matron's Journals	1844 to 1854	ref. Q/Gli 21/1 & 2
Schoolmaster's Journals	1844 to 1877	ref. Q/Gli 22/1 to 3
Schoolmistress's Journals	1844 to 1851	ref. Q/Gli 23

Northleach House of Correction

Register of Prisoners	1791 to 1816	ref. Q/Gn4
Apothecary's Journal	1800 to 1818	ref. Q/Gn 5/1
Surgeon's Journals	1818 to 1841	ref. Q/Gn 5/2 & 3

Hampshire

Hampshire Record Office
20 Southgate Street
Winchester
SO23 9EF

County Gaol

Governors' Journals	1820 to 1877	
Deputy Governor's Journal	1849 to 1853	
Chaplains' Journals	1820 to 1872	no reference
Surgeon's Journals	1849 to 1856	
Committal Register	1836 to 1848	

County Bridewell

| Governors' Journals | 1820 to 1852 | no reference |

Herefordshire

None

Hertfordshire

County Record Office
County Hall
Hertford
SG13 8DE

County Gaol
Governor's Journals   1834 to 1878   (no ref.)

Huntingdonshire

County Record Office
Grammar School Walk
Huntingdon
PE18 6LF

County Gaol
Prison Record Book   1829 to 1833   ref. 806/HCP/2
General Register   1856 to 1873   ref. 318/HCP/2
Keeper's Journals   1833 to 1851   ref. 320/HCP/2
Habitual Criminals   1870 to 1878   ref. F37 & F38
  (with photographs)
Discharged Prisoners' Passes   1837   ref. 1895/5

Kent

Kent County Archives Office
County Hall
Maidstone
ME14 1XQ

Maidstone Gaol
Convict Book   1805 to 1833   ref. PC/M
Gaoler's Journals   1814 to 1824   ref. PC/M

Lancashire

None

Leicestershire

Leicestershire Record Office
57 New Walk
Leicester
LE1 7JB

Leicester Prison
Letter from William Newell   1894   ref. Misc 828
  (a prisoner)
Commitment of two persons for
  assisting in an escape from
  Leicester Gaol   ref. OS 1

County Gaol
Sentences of Prisoners	1797	ref. DE 1243/300
Prisoners sent to Hulks	1818	ref. 1577/1885

Lincolnshire

Lincolnshire Archives Office
The Castle
Lincoln
LN1 3AB

County Gaol
Governors' Journals	1848 to 1878	ref. Co. C5/1/4 to 8
Chaplains' Journals	1823 to 1878	ref. Co. C5/1/20 to 29
Surgeons' Journals	1823 to 1878	ref. Co. C5/1/11 to 19
Matrons' Journals	1848 to 1878	ref. Co. C5/1/9 & 10

Middlesex (including London)

Greater London Record Office
40 Northampton Road
London EC1 0AB

New Prison House of Correction
Register of Births, Baptisms and Deaths	1795 to 1835	ref. MA/G
Beer Book giving names of Prisoners	1852	ref. MA/G

See also Bedfordshire Record Office.

Monmouthshire

County Record Office
County Hall
Cwmbran
Gwent
NP44 2XH

Monmouth Gaol
Governor's Journals	1842 to 1869	ref. Q/MG 5 to 10
Chaplain's and Surgeon's Journals	1824 to 1843	ref. Q/MG 14 to 16
Chaplain's Journals	1822 to 1869	ref. Q/MG 13, 17 to 23
Surgeon's Book	1790 to 1823	ref. Q/MG 24
Surgeon's Journal	1840 to 1869	ref. Q/MG 25 to 39
Matron's Journal	1869	ref. Q/MG 40
Labour Yard Officers' Journal	1869	ref. Q/MG 41
Schoolmaster's Journal	1869	ref. Q/MG 42
Female Officers' Journal	1869	ref. Q/MG 43
Untried Yard Officers' Journal	1869	ref. Q/MG 44
Warders' Journal	1869	ref. Q/MG 45

Prisoners' Relief Fund	1851 to 1870	ref. Q/MG 52
Number Books of Prisoners	1843 to 1869	ref. Q/MG 59 & 60
Register of Prisoners received from and transferred to other Prisons	1844 to 1869	ref. Q/MG 61
Description of Prisoners Received	1867 to 1869	ref. Q/MG 62
Male Clothing Book	1856 to 1870	ref. Q/MG 63
Female Clothing Book	1856 to 1870	ref. Q/MG 64

Monmouthshire Reformatory, Little Mill

Register of Boys	1859 to 1914	ref. Q/MR 9 & 10
Register of Admissions and Discharges	1872 to 1922	ref. Q/MR 11 to 14

Norfolk

Norfolk Record Office
Central Library
Norwich
NR2 1NJ

Norwich City Gaol

Returns of Prisoners	1681 to 1682	ref. case 12 shelf c, bdl. 1
Returns of Prisoners	1702 to 1827 1793, 1815 to 1833 }	ref. case 12 shelf d, bdl. 1

At the Castle Museum, Norwich

Wylsham Bridewell

Register of Prisoners	1801 to 1825	ref. Castle Museum 30.1.73

Norwich Gaol

Keeper's Journal	1822 to 1835	
Surgeon's Journals	1843 to 1850	
Chapel Books listing debtors, felons, and convicts' misdemeanours }	1816 to 1839	

At Yarmouth Museum

Yarmouth Gaol

Gaol Books	1798 to 1865	ref. L2/1 to 3
Bridewell Book	1822 to 1838	ref. L2/4
Committal and Discharge Books	1819 to 1838	ref. L2/5 & 6
Index to Receiving Book	1838 to 1839	ref. L2/7
Receiving Book	1842 to 1845	ref. D 41/28
Gaol Registers	1808 to 1875 }	ref. L2/8 to 14
Bridewell	1837 to 1838 }	
Supplementary Register	1846 to 1851	ref. L2/15
Indexes to Registers	1838 to 1875	ref. L2/16 to 18
Registers of Prisoners' Belongings	1867 to 1875	ref. L2/26

Register of Employments	1868 to 1875	ref. L2/27
Register of Admissions	1868 to 1873	ref. L2/28
Journal of Admissions and Discharges	1869 to 1876	ref. L2/29
Particulars of Habitual Prisoners	1870 to 1873	ref. L2/30
Discharge Books	1850 to 1856 ⎫ 1862 to 1874 ⎭	ref. L2/31 to 33
Gaol Keeper's Journals	1825 to 1876	ref. L2/46 to 51
Surgeon's Journals	1838 to 1875	ref. L2/52 to 55
Chaplain's Journals	1847 to 1865	ref. L2/56 to 59
Schoolmaster's Journal	1853 to 1862	ref. L2/60
Misconduct Book	1849 to 1875	ref. L2/66
Register of Prisoners Remanded	1875 to 1877	ref. L2/67

Northamptonshire

Northamptonshire Record Office
Wootton Hall Park
Northampton
NN4 9BQ

Northampton Gaol

List of Prisoners	17th century	ref. IL 1962

Northamptonshire Police Museum
Wootton Hall
Northampton
NN4 OJQ

Stony Stratford Lock-up

Register of Prisoners	1887 to 1918

Thrapston

Return of Offences, Register	1860 to 1888

Northampton Borough Police Photograph Book of wanted Criminals	1867 to 1913
Divisional Sergeant's Statement re discharge of a convict from Northampton Gaol, with photograph of the prisoner	1884
Northampton Borough Police Book of Prisoners Photographs	1870 to 1871

Northumberland

None

Nottinghamshire

Nottinghamshire Record Office
County House
High Pavement
Nottingham
NG1 1HR

Nottingham Gaol
Prisoners' Character Book   1869 to 1893   ref. QAG 2/50

Oxfordshire

None

Rutland

Leicestershire Record Office
57 New Walk
Leicester
LE1 7JB

County Gaol
Conveyance of Morris Best and ⎫
   Mathew Beever from Oakham ⎬   ref. RQS/11/1
   to a hulk on the River Thames, ⎭
   1792

Shropshire

None

Somerset

Somerset Record Office
Obridge Road
Taunton
TA2 7PU

Ilchester Gaol

Occurrence Book (daily log of events in the Gaol)	1816 to 1821	ref. Q/AGi 7/1
Surgeon's Visiting Book (details of prisoners treated and medicines given)	1821	ref. Q/AGi 7/2
Gaol Returns	1809 to 1820	ref. Q/AG(i) 13/1 & 2
Registers of Prisoners	1808 to 1844	ref. Q/AG(i) 14/1 to 6
Description Books	1821 to 1844	ref. Q/AG(i) 15/1 to 4
Register of Sick Prisoners	1811 to 1821	ref. Q/AG(i) 16/1
Account Book of Receipt and Expenditure of bread and allowance to Prisoners	1811 to 1823	ref. Q/AGi 16/2
Felons and Debtors	1833 to 1839	ref. Q/AGi 16/3

Papers concerning escape of
   Prisoners being conveyed to a } 1835   ref. Q/AGi 16/4
   transport ship
Debtors Charged   1769 to 1772   ref. Q/AGi 17/1
Debtors' Books   1808 to 1844   ref. Q/AGi 17/2 & 3

Shepton Mallet Gaol
Gaol Returns   1809 to 1820   ref. Q/AG(s) 13/1 & 2
Registers of Prisoners   1856 to 1879   ref. Q/AG(s) 14/1 to 8
Index to Description Books   1855 to 1878   ref. Q/AG(s) 16/1 & 2
Register of Debtors   1842 to 1878   ref. Q/AG(s) 17/1
Governor's Journal   1876 to 1878   ref. Q/AGs 7/2

Wilton Gaol (Taunton)
Gaol Returns   1809 to 1820   ref. Q/AG(w) 13/1 & 2
Registers of Prisoners   1810 to 1879   ref. Q/AG(w) 14/1 to 5
Description Books   1807 to 1859   ref. Q/AG(w) 15/1 to 6
Receiving Books   1838 to 1866   ref. Q/AG(w) 16/1 to 8
Male Prisoners' Effects   1839 to 1870   ref. Q/AG(w) 16/9 & 10
Female Prisoners' Effects   1869
Prisoners Executed   1857 to 1861   } ref. Q/AGw 16/10
Clothing to Prisoners on
   Discharge   *c*. 1869

Register of Debtors   (see Ilchester ref. QA/Gi 17/3)
Registers of Prisoners' Letters,
   posted and received   1841 to 1879   ref. Q/AGw 11/11 to 21

General
Claims for expenses in
   conveyance of prisoners   1881 to 1917   ref. Q/AGz 12/6
Returns relating to employment
   of prisoners in County Gaols } undated   ref. Q/AGz 16/2
   throughout England & Wales

Staffordshire

Staffordshire Record Office
County Buildings
Eastgate Street
Stafford
ST16 2LZ

Stafford Prison
Registers of Prisoners   1712 to 1815   ref. D 1723/1 to 4

Suffolk

Suffolk Record Office
Gatacre Road
Ipswich
IP1 2LQ

Beccles Gaol
Prison Registers   1791 to 1848   ref. Acc. 1122/1 to 12

Woodbridge Gaol
Prison Registers   1802 to 1842   ref. B 106/3/8.1 to 8.4

Ipswich Gaol
Prison Registers   1840 to 1870   ref. Acc. 609/1 to 30

Ipswich Borough Gaol
List of Prisoners   1800 to 1824   ref. C1/6/20

Suffolk Record Office
Raingate Street
Bury St Edmunds
IP33 1RX

Bury St Edmunds Gaol
Gaol Books   1844 to 1878   ref. Q/HER/1

Surrey

Surrey Record Office
County Hall
Kingston upon Thames
KT1 2DN

Horsemonger Lane Gaol
Surgeon's Order Book   1867   ref. QS 5/4 (part)

County Gaol, Newington
Register of Deaths (includes six   1798 to 1818 ⎱
  baptisms)   1832 to 1838 ⎬   ref. QS 5/4 (part)
                                    1840 to 1878 ⎰
Prison Books
Insolvent Debtors   1737 to 1771   ref. QS3/2/1 to 14
Kings Bench and Marshalsea   1761 to 1781   ref. QS3/2/15 to 29

Sussex, East

County Record Office
The Maltings
Castle Precincts
Lewes
East Sussex
BN7 1YT

Battle House of Correction
Orders of Committal   1822 to 1853   ref. QDB/E1/1 to 22
Register of Committals   1822 to 1853   ref. QDB/2/E1 & E2
Keeper's Daily Journals   1823 to 1853   ref. QDB/3/E1 to E3

Chaplain's Journal and		
Attendance Books	1833 to 1853	ref. QDB/E4 & E5
Surgeon's Journal	1846 to 1853	ref. QDB/E7

Sussex, West

None

Warwickshire

None

Westmorland

None

Wiltshire

County Record Office
County Hall
Trowbridge
BA14 8JG

Fisherton Anger Gaol

Matron's Journal (women		
prisoners only)	1849 to 1853	ref. A1 507/5

Devizes Prison

Prisoners' Property Book	1865 to 1878	ref. A1 517/1
Chaplain's Journal	1867 to 1878	ref. A1 517/2
Surgeon's Journal	1873 to 1878	ref. A1 517/4
Minister's Register (prisoners'		
denominations)	1873 to 1879	ref. A1 517/5
Prisoners' Punishment Book	1875 to 1880	ref. A1 517/6
Minutes of Prison Visitors'		
Committee	1878 to 1914	ref. A1/517/8
Register of Prisoners	1879 to 1881	ref. A1/517/9

Devizes Prison and Fisherton Anger Gaol

Returns to the Secretary of State		
on the numbers of prisoners at		
Devizes and Fisherton Anger	1869 to 1877	ref. A1/507/3
(includes lists of prisoners)		

Worcestershire

Record Office
County Hall
Spetchley Road
Worcester
WR5 2NP

County Gaol

Chaplain's Journals	1858 to 1878	ref. Box Q/122

Roman Catholic Chaplain's Journal	1868 to 1893	ref. Box Q/122
Chaplain's Character Books	1861 to 1877	ref. Box Q/122 8A & 8B
Governor's Journals	1831 to 1875	ref. Box Q/122 12A & 12B

Yorkshire, South

None

Yorkshire, North

North Yorkshire County Library
Museum Street
York
YO1 2DS

York Castle

Chaplain's Books	1835 to 1867	ref. Y 365.66
Gaoler's Journals	1824 to 1863	ref. Y 365

Yorkshire, West

West Yorkshire Archives Service
Registry of Deeds
Newstead Road
Wakefield
WF1 2DE

Armley Prison

Register of Male Prisoners	1908 to 1909	ref. C187/1/3
Register of Female Prisoners	1913 to 1914	ref. C187/1/4

Wakefield Prison

Register of Prisoners	1801 to 1875	ref. C118/98 to 103
Indexes of Prisoners	*c.* 1878 to 1899	ref. C118/104 to 108
Register of Prisoners	1879 to 1951	ref. C118/109 to 243

2.2.2 Wales

Anglesey

None

Brecon

None

Carnarvonshire

None

Cardiganshire

None

Carmarthenshire

Carmarthenshire Record Office
County Hall
Carmarthen
SA31 1JP

Carmarthen Prison
Register of Felons   1844 to 1871   ref. ACC.4916
Gaoler's Journal   1845 to 1850   ref. ACC.4916

Denbighshire

County Record Office
46 Clwyd Street
Ruthin
Clwyd
LL15 1HP

Prisoners' Books   1847 to 1859   ref. QSD/SE/1
Prosecution Books   1844 to 1892   ref. QSD/SS/1 to 4

Both these series of books are records of the Denbighshire Court of Quarter Sessions; the references are mostly to Ruthin Gaol.

Photograph Books of Convicted
    Criminals   1862 to 1896   ref. DPD/5/1 to 2

Flintshire

None

Glamorgan

Glamorgan Record Office
County Hall
Cathays Park
Cardiff
CF1 3NE

Swansea Gaol
Governors' Journals   1829 to 1878   ref. Q/GJ G1 to G15
Surgeons' Journals   1829 to 1878   ref. Q/JG S1 to S9
Chaplains' Journals   1831 to 1877   ref. Q/JG C1 to C7
Punishment Books   1852 to 1878   ref. Q/GJ P1 & P2

Cardiff Gaol
Governor's Reports   1867 to 1878 ⎫
Surgeon's Reports   1867 to 1878 ⎬   ref. Q.G.
Chaplain's Reports   1869 to 1877 ⎭

Merioneth

Area Record Office
Cae Penarlag
Dolgellau
Gwynedd
LL40 2YB

County Gaol, Dolgellau

Surgeon's Journals and Attendance Books	1860 to 1871 1871 to 1875	ref. Z/QA/G/12 ref. Z/QA/G/13
Register of Prisoners' Employment	1870 to 1875	ref. Z/QA/G/15
Receipt Book of Gaol Keeper	1867 to 1878	ref. Z/QA/G/16
Account Book of Gaol Keeper	1860 to 1865	ref. Z/QA/G/17
Draft County Petition to Privy Council on account of the Gaol giving account of the County Rates	1817 to 1826	ref. Z/QA/G/18
Discharge Book	1867 to 1878	ref. Z/QA/G/19
Dietary Sheet recommended by the Secretary of State for Prisoners confined to County Gaol	1865	ref. Z/QA/G/20

Montgomeryshire

County Archives Office
County Hall
Llandrindod
Powys
LD1 5LD

Montgomery Gaol

Returns of Prisoners, Quarter Sessions	1818 to 1819	ref. Montgomery Q/AG/3 to 5
Returns of Prisoners Committed for Trial, Quarter Sessions	1834 to 1849	ref. Montgomery Q/CR/6

Pembrokeshire

The Record Office
The Castle
Haverfordwest
Dyfed
SA61 2EF

Haverfordwest Gaol and House of Correction
The general reference for the following is PQ/AG

Governor's Register	1813 to 1820

Governor's Register with list of Lunatics	1788 to 1824
Governor's Register	1822 to 1828
Registers of Felons	1828 to 1863
Registers of Debtors	1813 to 1836
Registers of Prisoners committed under summary convictions, etc.	1846 to 1854
Register of Prisoners removed from the County	1838 to 1853
Prisoners' Committal and Discharge Papers	1812 to 1864
Order for removal of Convicts for Transportation	1825 to 1864
General Daily Account of Prisoners	1833 to 1865
General Weekly Return of Prisoners	1842 to 1843
Surgeon's Journal	1820 to 1835
Chaplain's Character Book	1840 to 1856
Prisoners subsisted after Conviction	1847 to 1862

Radnorshire

None

APPENDIX 3

CRIMINAL RECORDS OF THE COURTS OF GREAT SESSIONS OF WALES AT THE NATIONAL LIBRARY OF WALES

3.1   Chester Circuit

Gaol Files

Flint	1543 to 1830	ref. WALES 4/966 to 1022
Denbigh	1546 to 1830	ref. WALES 4/1 to 74
Montgomery	1690 to 1830	ref. WALES 4/124 to 203

Rule Books[1], Minute Books, Order Books

Flint, Denbigh and Montgomery	1783 to 1830	ref. WALES 14/1 to 7
Flint	1574 to 1806	ref. WALES 14/71 to 86

Crown Books

Flint and Denbigh	1564 to 1667, 1707 to 1756	ref. WALES 14/68 to 70 and NLW MS 6298D

3.2   North Wales Circuit

Gaol Files

Anglesey	1708 to 1830	ref. WALES 4/250 to 261
Merioneth	1514 to 1830	ref. WALES 4/296 to 308
Carnarvon	1622 to 1830	ref. WALES 4/270 to 284

---

[1] These are mainly concerned with civil actions but contain details of verdicts and sentences of criminal actions.

Rule Books, Minute Books, Order Books

Anglesey, Merioneth and
   Carnarvon   1783 to 1830   ref. WALES 14/14 to 18

3.3   Brecon Circuit

Gaol Files

Brecon   1558 to 1830   ref. WALES 4/320 to 398
Radnor   1541 to 1830   ref. WALES 4/461 to 538
Glamorgan   1541 to 1830   ref. WALES 4/591 to 640

Black Books

Brecon, Radnor and Glamorgan   1726 to 1830   ref. WALES 28/31 to 36

Rule Books, Minute Books, Order Books

Brecon, Radnor and Glamorgan   1725 to 1830   ref. WALES 14/22 to 30

Calendar Rolls of Indictments

Radnor   1553 to 1659   ref. WALES 7/1 to 3
Glamorgan   1553 to 1601   ref. WALES 7/4 to 5

3.4   Carmarthen Circuit

Gaol Files

Carmarthen   1542 to 1630   ref. WALES 4/715 to 766
Pembroke   1547 to 1830   ref. WALES 4/775 to 837
Cardigan   1542 to 1830   ref. WALES 4/883 to 916

Rule Books, Minute Books, Order Books

Carmarthen, Pembroke and
   Cardigan   1661 to 1807   ref. WALES 14/52 to 56

Calendar Rolls of Indictments

Cardigan   1541 to 1602   ref. WALES 7/6 to 7
Pembroke   1541 to 1674   ref. WALES 7/8 to 11

APPENDIX 4

RECORDS IN THE PUBLIC RECORD OFFICE

Note on Classification

The document collections at the Public Record Office are arranged in *Groups*, each *Group* being designated a number of identifying letters. For example:

ADM = Admiralty
PCOM = Prison Commissioners
HO = Home Office

A *Group* is arranged in various *Classes* and each *Class* is given a coding by adding a number to the *Group* letters. For example:

ADM 1
PCOM 2
HO 12

Each individual document, bundle, file or volume within a *Class* is identified by a *Piece Number*. The full reference to a particular document, bundle, file or volume is made up by adding the *Piece Number* to the *Class* reference. For example:

ADM 1/1561
PCOM 2/312

In some instances individual documents may be identified by further sub-division. For example:

HO 12/1/5

The Division of Departmental Documents within the Public Record Office

The Public Record Office has two offices, one at Chancery Lane, London, and the other at Ruskin Avenue, Kew, Surrey. The following lists the location of the departmental documents referred to in this book:

DEPARTMENT	GROUP REFERENCE	LOCATION
Admiralty	ADM	Kew
Exchequer and Audit Department	AO	Kew

Clerks of Assize	ASSI	Chancery Lane
Court of Bankruptcy	B	Chancery Lane
Palatinate of Chester	CHES	Chancery Lane
Central Criminal Court	CRIM	Chancery Lane
Director of Public Prosecutions	DPP	Chancery Lane
Palatinate of Durham	DURH	Chancery Lane
Exchequer	E	Chancery Lane
Home Office	HO	Kew
Justices Itinerent	JUST	Chancery Lane
Court of King's/Queen's Bench	KB	Chancery Lane
Metropolitan Police Offices	MEPO	Kew
Ministry of Health	MH	Kew
Privy Council Office	PC	Chancery Lane
Prison Commission	PCOM	Kew
Palatinate of Lancaster	PL	Chancery Lane
King's/Queen's Bench Prison, Fleet Prison and The Marshalsea	PRIS	Chancery Lane
Public Record Office (Gifts and deposits, PRO 30)	PRO	Chancery Lane
Court of Star Chamber	STAC	Chancery Lane
Treasury	T	Kew
Treasury Solicitor's Department	TS	Chancery Lane
War Office	WO	Kew

4.1   ASSIZE RECORDS

Records of the Justices of Assize are arranged in circuits and are deposited at the Public Record Office. The various circuits' records are:

4.1.1   Home Circuit (1558 to 1876)

Essex, Hertfordshire, Kent, Surrey and Sussex.

ASSI 31	Agenda Books	1735 to 1875
ASSI 34	Cost and Account Books	1791 to 1890
	Instruction Books	1783 to 1827
	Postea Books	1791 to 1856
	Presentment Books	1786 to 1804
	Process Books	1773 to 1822
	Rough Entry Books	1834 to 1884
	Cause Books	1763 to 1768
	Record Book	1733 to 1786
	Rule Book	1737 to 1741

4.1.2   Midland Circuit (1558 to 1971)

Derbyshire, Leicestershire, Lincolnshire, Northamptonshire, Nottinghamshire, Rutland and Warwickshire. From 1864 to 1876 the Midland Circuit covered Derbyshire, Lincolnshire, Nottinghamshire, Warwickshire and Yorkshire. From 1876 to 1971 the Midland Circuit covered Bedfordshire, Buckinghamshire, Derbyshire, Leicestershire, Lincolnshire, Northamptonshire, Nottinghamshire, Rutland and Warwickshire.

ASSI 11	Minute Books	1818 to 1945
ASSI 12	Indictments	1860 to 1957
ASSI 13	Depositions	1862 to 1945
ASSI 15	Miscellaneous	1870 to 1890

4.1.3 Norfolk Circuit (1558 to 1876)

Bedfordshire, Buckinghamshire, Cambridgeshire, Huntingdonshire, Norfolk, and Suffolk. From 1864 to 1876 Leicestershire, Northamptonshire and Rutland were added to the Norfolk Circuit.

ASSI 33	Gaol Books	1734 to 1863
ASSI 34	Precedent Books	1831 to 1863
	Process Books	1831 to 1863
	Cause Books	1742 to 1746
	Indictment Books	1774 to 1775
	Postea Books	1829 to 1862

4.1.4 Northern Circuit (1558 to 1971)

Cumberland, Northumberland, Westmorland and Yorkshire. (In 1864 Yorkshire was transferred to the Midland Circuit.)

ASSI 41	Minute Books	1741 to 1889
ASSI 42	Gaol Books	1658 to 1811
ASSI 43	Postea Books	1830 to 1866
	Account Books	1730 to 1840
	Note Books	1730 to 1840
ASSI 44	Indictments	1607 to 1890
ASSI 45	Depositions	1613 to 1890
ASSI 46	Estreats	1843 to 1890
ASSI 47	Criminal Returns	1805 to 1890
	Nisi Prius Records	1830 to 1865
	Special Cases	1629 to 1890
	Miscellaneous Pleadings	1650 to 1890
	Correspondence of the Keeper of York Prison	1790
	Correspondence of the Clerk of Assize	1826 to 1874
	Miscellaneous Papers	1640 to 1890
ASSI 51	Indictments	1868, 1877 to 1890
ASSI 52	Depositions	1877 to 1890
ASSI 53	Orders	1879 to 1890
ASSI 54	Minute Books	1877 to 1892

4.1.5 North Eastern Circuit (1876 to 1971)

Durham, Northumberland and Yorkshire.

ASSI 41	Minute Books	1876 to 1889
ASSI 44	Indictments	1876 to 1890
ASSI 46	Estreats	1876 to 1890

ASSI 47	Criminal Returns	1876 to 1890
	Special Cases	1876 to 1890
	Pleadings	1876 to 1890
	Miscellaneous	1876 to 1890

4.1.6 Oxford Circuit (1558 to 1971)

Berkshire, Gloucestershire, Herefordshire, Monmouthshire, Oxfordshire, Shropshire, Staffordshire and Worcestershire.

ASSI 1	Minute Books	1803 to 1888
ASSI 2	Crown Books	1656 to 1948
ASSI 3	Crown Books (second court)	1847 to 1951
ASSI 4	Postea Books	
	Process Books	
	Note Books	1660 to 1888
	Fee Books	
	Certificates of Trial	
	Cost Books	
ASSI 5	Indictments	1650 to 1957
ASSI 6	Depositions	1719 to 1951
ASSI 8	Pleadings	1854 to 1890
ASSI 9	Estreats	1746 to 1890
ASSI 10	Returns as to Cases tried, Fees, etc.	1732 to 1890

Some records relating to Monmouthshire Summer Assizes, 1808, are to be found in PRO, ref. PRO 30/44/1.

4.1.7 South Eastern Circuit (1876 to 1971)

Cambridgeshire, Essex, Hertfordshire, Huntingdonshire, Kent, Norfolk, Suffolk, Surrey and Sussex.

ASSI 31	Agenda Books	1876 to 1940
ASSI 32	Minute Books	1876 to 1943
ASSI 35	Indictments	1876 to 1957
ASSI 36	Depositions	1876 to 1889
ASSI 37	Pleadings	1876 to 1890
ASSI 39	Accounts, Appeals, etc.	1876 to 1891
ASSI 40	Agenda Books	1876 to 1911

4.1.8 Western Circuit (1558 to 1971)

Cornwall, Devonshire, Dorset, Hampshire, Somerset and Wiltshire.

ASSI 21	Crown Minute Books	1730 to 1953
ASSI 22	Civil Minute Books	1656 to 1945
ASSI 23	Gaol Books	1670 to 1824
ASSI 24	Certificate Books	1876 to 1887
	Estreat Books	1740 to 1800
	Note Books	1629 to 1932

ASSI 24 (contd)	Transportation Order Books	1629 to 1819
	Process Books	1717 to 1820
	Bail Books	1654 to 1677
	Cost Books	1869 to 1890
ASSI 25	Indictments	1801 to 1953
ASSI 26	Depositions	1861 to 1947
ASSI 28	Pleadings	1812 to 1957
ASSI 30	Miscellaneous	1740 to 1902

4.1.9   North and South Wales Circuit (1830 to 1876)

Anglesey, Brecon, Carnarvonshire, Cardiganshire, Carmarthenshire, Denbighshire, Flintshire, Glamorgan, Merioneth, Montgomeryshire, Pembrokeshire, Radnorshire and Cheshire.

For records of this circuit see the records of the North Wales Division and the South Wales Division, Sections 4.1.10 and 4.1.11 of this Appendix.

In 1876 the North and South Wales Circuit was formally divided into two divisions, namely the North Wales Division and the South Wales Division. It is clear from the dates of the documents listed under these two divisions that the North and South Wales Circuit was previously unofficially organized in two divisions as the dates of these records predate 1876.

4.1.10   North Wales Division (1876 to 1945)

Anglesey, Carnarvonshire, Cheshire, Denbighshire, Flintshire, Merioneth, and Montgomeryshire.

ASSI 57	Civil Minute Books	1843 to 1878, 1911 to 1924
ASSI 58	Certificates	1914 to 1926
ASSI 59	Pleadings	1840 to 1927
ASSI 60	Returns	1867 to 1912
ASSI 61	Crown Minute Books	1831 to 1938
ASSI 62	Crown Books	1835 to 1883
ASSI 63	Miscellaneous Books	1694 to 1942
ASSI 64	Indictments	1831 to 1891, 1908 to 1945
ASSI 65	Depositions	1831 to 1891, 1909 to 1944
ASSI 66	Coroners' Inquisitions	1798 to 1891
ASSI 67	Miscellanea	1778 to 1800

4.1.11   South Wales Division (1876 to 1945)

Brecon, Cardiganshire, Carmarthenshire, Glamorgan, Pembrokeshire and Radnorshire.

ASSI 71	Indictments	1834 to 1892, 1920 to 1945
ASSI 72	Depositions	1837 to 1942
ASSI 73	Miscellanea	1839 to 1937
ASSI 74	Judgement Rolls	1841 to 1842

ASSI 75	Civil Minute Books	1846 to 1943
ASSI 76	Crown Minute Books	1844 to 1942
ASSI 77	Miscellaneous Books	1837 to 1884

4.2   CALENDARS OF PRISONERS

4.2.1   HO 77   Newgate Calendar

| HO 77/1 to 61 | Printed lists of prisoners held at New gate for trial | 1782 to 1853 |

4.2.2   PCOM 2   Calendars of Prisoners Held for Trial at Quarter Sessions and Assizes

PCOM 2/301 & 367	Assizes & Q.S. Glamorgan	1863 to 1869
304 & 305	Assizes, Wiltshire	1774 to 1799
306 & 307	Assizes & Q.S., Bor. of Leicester	1854 to 1868
311	Q.S., Louth and Spilsby	1854 to 1876
312	Q.S., Kirton and Lindsey	1858 to 1878
313 & 314	Assizes, Lincolnshire	1854 to 1878
319 to 329	Assizes, Liverpool, & Q.S. Lancashire	1840 to 1874
330 to 341	Liverpool Boro. Sessions	1812 to 1843
344 & 345	Sessions & Assizes, Town of Newcastle	1860 to 1876
346	Sessions & Assizes, Northumberland	1864 to 1866
347	Q.S., North Riding of York	1859 to 1881
348	Q.S., Norfolk	1825 to 1857
397 & 398	Q.S. & Assizes, Shropshire	1870 to 1877
405 to 410	Q.S. & Assizes, Somerset	1854 to 1877
412 to 416	Q.S. & Assizes, West Riding of York	1853 to 1869
417	Assizes, West Riding of York	1864 to 1869
418 to 420	Assizes, Hampshire	1816 to 1882
421 & 422	Q.S. Hampshire	1829 to 1867
439	Q.S., Louth and Spilsby for Parts of Lindsey	1831 to 1863
440	Lancaster, debtors and plaintiffs, Nominal Register	1792 to 1797
441	Lancaster, Crown Cases, Nominal Register	1820 to 1826
449	Q.S. & Assizes, Lancaster	1882 to 1888
450	Assizes, Lancaster	1894 to 1898
451	Q.S. & Assizes, Kendal & Lancaster	1899 to 1901
452	Q.S. Lancaster	1905 to 1913
453	Assizes Lancaster	1905 to 1913
454	Q.S. & Assizes	1914 to 1916
455	{ Q.S. Kendal	1905 to 1913
	{ Assizes Appleby	1905 to 1911
456 to 460	Defendants, Nominal Register, Lancaster	1884 to 1909

4.2.3 HO 16   Old Bailey Sessions 1815 to 1849

Returns of Prisoners committed for trial, charges and results of trial
(see also PCOM 1/1 to 156).

HO 16/1	1815 to 1818
2	1819 to 1822
3	1823 to 1826
4	1827 to 1830
5	1831 to 1834
6	1835 to 1838
7	1839 to 1842
8	1843 to 1846
9	1847 to 1849

4.2.4 CRIM 5   Old Bailey, Calendars of Indictments

CRIM 5/1 to 24   Manuscript Calendars, 1833 to 1971

4.2.5 CRIM 9   Old Bailey, Post-Trial Calendars of Prisoners

CRIM 9/1 to 95   1855 to 1949

4.2.6 HO 130

HO 130/1   Calendar of Prisoners at Winchester
                        Special Assize 18 December 1830

4.2.7 HO 140   County Calendars of Prisoners. Sessions and Assizes 1868 to 1909 (including Guernsey, Jersey and the Isle of Man)

HO 140/1	Anglesey to Gloucester	1868
2	Hampshire to Lincoln	
3	Merioneth to Rutland	
4	Shropshire to York, Guernsey, Jersey, Isle of Man	
5	Anglesey to Gloucester	1869
6	Hampshire to Lincoln	
7	Merioneth to Rutland	
8	Shropshire to York, Guernsey, Jersey, Isle of Man	
9	Anglesey to Gloucester	1870
10	Hampshire to Lincoln	
11	Merioneth to Rutland	
12	Shropshire to York, Guernsey, Jersey, Isle of Man	
13	Anglesey to Gloucester	1871
14	Hampshire to Lincoln	
15	Merioneth to Rutland	
16	Shropshire to York, Guernsey, Jersey, Isle of Man	

17	Anglesey to Gloucester	1872
18	Hampshire to Lincoln	
19	Merioneth to Rutland	
20	Shropshire to York, Guernsey, Jersey, Isle of Man	
21	Anglesey to Gloucester	1873
22	Hampshire to Lincoln	
23	Merioneth to Rutland	
24	Shropshire to York, Guernsey, Jersey, Isle of Man	
25	Anglesey to Gloucester	1874
26	Hampshire to Lincoln	
27	Merioneth to Rutland	
28	Shropshire to York, Guernsey, Jersey, Isle of Man	
29	Anglesey to Gloucester	1875
30	Hampshire to Lincoln	
31	Merioneth to Rutland	
32	Shropshire to York, Guernsey, Jersey, Isle of Man	
33	Anglesey to Gloucester	1876
34	Hampshire to Lincoln	
35	Merioneth to Rutland	
36	Shropshire to York, Guernsey, Jersey, Isle of Man	
37	Anglesey to Gloucester	1877
38	Hampshire to Lincoln	
39	Merioneth to Rutland	
40	Shropshire to York, Guernsey, Jersey, Isle of Man	
41	Anglesey to Gloucester	1878
42	Hampshire to Lincoln	
43	Merioneth to Rutland	
44	Shropshire to York, Guernsey, Jersey, Isle of Man	
45	Anglesey to Gloucester	1879
46	Hampshire to Lincoln	
47	Merioneth to Rutland	
48	Shropshire to York, Guernsey, Jersey, Isle of Man	
49	Anglesey to Gloucester	1880
50	Hampshire to Lincoln	
51	Merioneth to Rutland	
52	Shropshire to York, Guernsey, Jersey, Isle of Man	
53	Anglesey to Gloucester	1881
54	Hampshire to Lincoln	
55	Merioneth to Rutland	

56	Shropshire to York, Guernsey, Jersey, Isle of Man	
57	England and Wales (sic), Guernsey, Jersey and Isle of Man	1882
58	Anglesey to Gloucester	1882
59	Hampshire to Lincoln	
60	Merioneth to Rutland	
61	Shropshire to York, Guernsey, Jersey, Isle of Man	
62	Anglesey to Cumberland	1883
63	Denbigh to Gloucester	
64	Hampshire to Kent	
65	Lancashire	
66	Leicestershire	
67	Monmouthshire to Rutland	
68	Shropshire to Sussex	
69	Warwickshire to Yorkshire, Guernsey, Jersey, Isle of Man	

This series continues to 1909.

4.3   CONVICTS' LICENCES, CAPTIONS AND TRANSFER PAPERS

4.3.1   PCOM 3 and PCOM 4   Licences

These are licences for convicts to *live at large*, with references to revocation of such licences. They are endorsed on *Old Captions* and in some cases on *Transfer Papers*.

PCOM 3 Male. These are arranged numerically
PCOM 3/1 to 446, 1853 to 1877, Numbers 1 to 31,124.
This series is indexed by: PCOM 6/1 to 13 (1853 to 1864 only).

PCOM 4 Female. These are arranged numerically
PCOM 4/1 to 72, 1853 to 1887, Numbers 1 to 7,625.
This series is indexed by: PCOM 6/14 to 17.

4.3.2   PCOM 5   Captions

A Caption is a copy of an Order of Court for the imprisonment or transportation of a convict.

PCOM 5/1	⎧ 1847 to 1857	Hulk Captions
	⎩ 1843 to 1852	Old Captions
2 to 20	1857 to 1865	Old Captions
21	1851 to 1866	Deaths, A to H
22	1851 to 1866	Deaths, I to Z
23	1843 to 1852	Old Captions
24	⎧ 1854 to 1857	Old Captions
	⎩ 1856 to 1865	Transfer Papers

Captions are indexed by: PCOM 6/18 to 20.

4.3.3   PCOM 5   Transfer Papers

These record the order for the transfer of a convict from one government prison to another and contain the penal records and other particulars of the convict.

PCOM 5/24	1856 to 1865				
25	1863 to 1867		Nos:	1 to 47	A & B
26	1863 to 1867			52 to 98	C & D
27	1863 to 1867			100 to 153	D to G
28	1863 to 1867			155 to 217	G to K
29	1863 to 1867			218 to 265	K to M
30	{ 1863 to 1867			266 to 294	M to N
	{ 1864 to 1871			298 to 315	A to B
31	1864 to 1871			316 to 353	B to E
32	1864 to 1871			354 to 412	E to M
33	1864 to 1871			413 to 460	M to P
34	1864 to 1871			461 to 505	P to R
35	1864 to 1871			506 to 574	R to S
36	1864 to 1871			575 to 658	S to W
37	1864 to 1871			660 to 713	Female A to L
38	{ 1864 to 1871			714 to 767	Female L to W
	{ 1871			772	Male T
39	{ 1864 to 1871	Deaths		1 to 3	L to S
	{ 1864 to 1871	Deaths		4 to 34	A to R
40	1864 to 1871	Deaths		35 to 47	S to W
		Deaths		48 to 66	B to M
41	{ 1864 to 1871	Transfer Papers, Deaths		67 to 84	M to W
	{ 1864 to 1871	Transfer Papers, Deaths		85 to 125	A to W
42	1856 to 1865				
43	1856 to 1865				
44	1856 to 1865				
45	1856 to 1865				
46	1856 to 1865				
47	1856 to 1865	No numbers or letters given in these			
48	1856 to 1865				
49	1856 to 1865				
50	1856 to 1865	(contains photograph of Thomas Smith alias Hughes)			
51	1856 to 1865	(contains photograph of James O'Neil)			
52	1856 to 1865	Miscellaneous (contains photograph of William Wright)			

Since going to press further material in this series has been opened for public search including Registers of Licences (PCOM 6).

4.4   COURT OF BANKRUPTCY RECORDS

4.4.1   B1   Order Books

B1/1 to 214   1710 to 1877

4.4.2   B2   Gaolers' Returns

B2/15	Queen's Prison and Whitecross Street Prison	1862
16	Whitecross Street Prison	1864
18, 19	Whitecross Street Prison	1865
20, 22	Whitecross Street Prison	1866
23, 25	Whitecross Street Prison	1867
28, 29	Whitecross Street Prison	1868
31, 32	Whitecross Street Prison	1869
17	Horsemonger Lane Prison	1865
21	Horsemonger Lane Prison	1866
24	Horsemonger Lane Prison	1867
26, 27	Horsemonger Lane Prison	1868
30	Horsemonger Lane Prison	1869

4.4.3   B4   Docket Books

B4/1 to 56   1710 to 1833

4.4.4   B5   Enrolment Books

B5/1 to 15   1758 to 1825

4.4.5   B6   Certificates of Conformity Registers

B6/1 to 41	Certificates of Conformity	1733 to 1856
42	Commissioners of Bankruptcy	1777 to 1832
43	Town and County Sub-assignments	1813 to 1819
44	Town and County Sub-assignments	1819 to 1827

4.4.6   B6 and B8   Petitions of Prisoners

B6/45 to 47	Town and County	1813 to 1820
48 to 62	Town and County	1820 to 1861
63 to 71	Town and County	1820 to 1861
B8/1 to 69	Town	1825 to 1861

4.5   CRIMINAL REGISTERS

4.5.1   HO 26   Criminal Registers – Series I Middlesex only

HO 26/1 to 56   1791 to 1849

After 1849 Middlesex Criminals will be found in the county series HO 27.

4.5.2   HO 27   Criminal Registers – Series II

All England and Wales (including some of Middlesex before 1850), found in HO 26.

PIECE NUMBER	YEAR	COUNTIES		PIECE NUMBER	YEAR	COUNTIES
1	1805	All Counties		50	1835	M to Y
2	1806	All Counties		51	1836	A to L
3	1807	All Counties		52	1836	M to Y
4	1808	All Counties		53	1837	A to L
5	1809	All Counties		54	1837	M to Y
6	1810	All Counties		55	1838	A to L
7	1811	All Counties		56	1838	M to Y
8	1812	All Counties		57	1839	A to H
9	1813	All Counties		58	1839	K to R
10	1814	All Counties		59	1839	S to Y
11	1815	All Counties		60	1840	A to H
12	1816	All Counties		61	1840	K to R
13	1817	A to L		62	1840	S to Y
14	1817	M to Y		63	1841	A to H
15	1818	A to L		64	1841	K to R
16	1818	M to Y		65	1841	S to Y
17	1819	A to L		66	1842	A to H
18	1819	M to Y		67	1842	K to R
19	1820	A to L		68	1842	S to Y
20	1820	M to Y		69	1843	A to H
21	1821	A to L		70	1843	K to R
22	1821	M to Y		71	1843	S to Y
23	1822	A to L		72	1844	A to H
24	1822	M to Y		73	1844	K to R
25	1823	A to L		74	1844	S to Y
26	1823	M to Y		75	1845	A to H
27	1824	A to L		76	1845	K to R
28	1824	M to Y		77	1845	S to Y
29	1825	A to L		78	1846	A to H
30	1825	M to Y		79	1846	K to R
31	1826	A to L		80	1846	S to Y
32	1826	M to Y		81	1847	A to H
33	1827	A to L		82	1847	K to R
34	1827	M to Y		83	1847	S to Y
35	1828	A to L		84	1848	A to H
36	1828	M to Y		85	1848	K to R
37	1829	A to L		86	1848	S to Y
38	1829	M to Y		87	1849	A to H
39	1830	A to L		88	1849	K to R
40	1830	M to Y		89	1849	S to Y
41	1831	A to L		90	Number not used	
42	1831	M to Y		91	1850	A to F
43	1832	A to L		92	1850	G to L
44	1832	M to Y		93	1850	M to R
45	1833	A to L		94	1850	S to Y
46	1833	M to Y		95	1851	A to F
47	1834	A to L		96	1851	G to L
48	1834	M to Y		97	1851	M to R
49	1835	A to L		98	1851	S to Y

[contd]

PIECE NUMBER	YEAR	COUNTIES	PIECE NUMBER	YEAR	COUNTIES
99	1852	A to F	148	1867	Sur to Y, & Welsh Co's
100	1852	G to L	149	1868	B to K
101	1852	M to R	150	1868	L to Som
102	1852	S to Y	151	1868	South'ton to Y,
103	1853	A to F			& Welsh Co's
104	1853	G to L	152	1869	B to K
105	1853	M to R	153	1869	L to Som
106	1853	S to Y	154	1869	South'ton to Y,
107	1854	A to K			& Welsh Co's
108	1854	L to Mid	155	1870	B to K
109	1854	Mon to Y	156	1870	L to Som
110	1855	B to K	157	1870	South'ton to Y,
111	1855	L to Mid			& Welsh Co's
112	1855	Mon to Y, & Welsh Co's	158	1871	B to K
113	1856	B to K	159	1871	L to Som
114	1856	L to Mid	160	1871	South'ton to Y,
115	1856	Mon to Y, & Welsh Co's			& Welsh Co's
116	1857	B to K	161	1872	B to K
117	1857	L to Mid	162	1872	L to Som
118	1857	Mon to Y, & Welsh Co's	163	1872	South'ton to Y,
119	1858	B to K			& Welsh Co's
120	1858	L to R	164	1873	B to K
121	1858	S to Y, & Welsh Co's	165	1873	L to R
122	1859	B to K	166	1873	S to Y, & Welsh Co's
123	1859	L to R	167	1874	B to K
124	1859	S to Y, & Welsh Co's	168	1874	L to R
125	1860	B to K	169	1874	S to Y, & Welsh Co's
126	1860	L to R	170	1875	B to K
127	1860	S to Y, & Welsh Co's	171	1875	L to R
128	1861	B to K	172	1875	S to Y, & Welsh Co's
129	1861	L to R	173	1876	B to K
130	1861	S to Y, & Welsh Co's	174	1876	L to R
131	1862	B to K	175	1876	S to Y, & Welsh Co's
132	1862	L to R	176	1877	B to K
133	1862	S to Y, & Welsh Co's	177	1877	L to R
134	1863	B to K	178	1877	S to Y, & Welsh Co's
135	1863	L to R	179	1878	B to K
136	1863	S to Y, & Welsh Co's	180	1878	L to R
137	1864	B to K	181	1878	S to Y, & Welsh Co's
138	1864	L to R	182	1879	B to K
139	1864	S to Y, & Welsh Co's	183	1879	L to R
140	1865	B to K	184	1879	S to Y, & Welsh Co's
141	1865	L to R	185	1880	B to K
142	1865	S to Y, & Welsh Co's	186	1880	L to R
143	1866	B to H	187	1880	S to Y, & Welsh Co's
144	1866	L to R	188	1881	B to K
145	1866	S to Y, & Welsh Co's	189	1881	L to R
146	1867	B to L	190	1881	S to Y, & Welsh Co's
147	1867	M to Suf	191	1882	B to K

PIECE NUMBER	YEAR	COUNTIES	PIECE NUMBER	YEAR	COUNTIES
192	1882	L to R	208	1887	S to Y, & Welsh Co's
193	1882	S to Y, & Welsh Co's	209	1888	B to K
194	1883	B to K	210	1888	L to R
195	1883	L to R	211	1888	S to Y, & Welsh Co's
196	1883	S to Y, & Welsh Co's	212	1889	B to K
197	1884	B to K	213	1889	L to R
198	1884	L to R	214	1889	S to Y, & Welsh Co's
199	1884	S to Y, & Welsh Co's	215	1890	B to K
200	1885	B to K	216	1890	L to R
201	1885	L to R	217	1890	S to Y, & Welsh Co's
202	1885	S to Y, & Welsh Co's	218	1891	B to K
203	1886	B to K	219	1891	L to R
204	1886	L to R	220	1891	S to Y, & Welsh Co's
205	1886	S to Y, & Welsh Co's	221	1892	B to K
206	1887	B to K	222	1892	L to R
207	1887	L to R	223	1892	S to Y, & Welsh Co's

Hampshire is listed as Hampshire 1805 to 1837 and as Southampton from 1838 onwards. Shropshire is listed as Shropshire 1805 to 1808 and as Salop from 1809 onwards. The Welsh Counties of Anglesey, Brecon, Carnarvonshire, Cardiganshire, Carmarthenshire, Denbighshire, Flintshire, Glamorgan, Merioneth, Montgomeryshire, Pembrokeshire, Radnorshire, are listed after all English counties 1805 to 1814, alphabetically with English counties 1815 to 1854, and again after all English counties from 1855 onwards. Monmouthshire is always with the English counties. Bristol is listed after Gloucestershire.

4.5.3   PCOM 2   Alphabetical Register of Habitual Criminals in England and Wales

PCOM 2/404   1869 to 1876

4.5.4   MEPO 6   Habitual Criminal Registers

MEPO 6/1 to 24   1881 to 1912

4.6   DEBTORS' PRISON RECORDS

4.6.1   PRIS 1   Fleet Prison

PRIS 1/1a to 50   Commitment Books   1685 to 1842

4.6.2   PRIS 2   Fleet Prison

PRIS 2/1 to 160   Commitments   By number; the numbers are those given in the Commitment Books in PRIS 1, Nos 1 to 32,083

4.6.3 PRIS 3 Fleet Prison

PRIS 3/1 to 43	Discharges and Copy of Causes	1775 to 1842

4.6.4 PRIS 4 King's/Queen's[1] Bench Prison

PRIS 4/1 to 54	Commitment Books	1719 to 1862

4.6.5 PRIS 5 King's Bench Prison

PRIS 5/1 to 20	Abstract Books of Commitments	1780 to 1815

4.6.6 PRIS 6 Queen's Bench Prison

PRIS 6/1 to 3	Commitments to Strong Room	1847 to 1862

4.6.7 PRIS 7 King's/Queen's Bench Prison

PRIS 7/1 to 79	Discharges	1776 to 1862

4.6.8 PRIS 8 King's/Queen's Bench Prison

PRIS 8/1 to 10	Executions	1758 to 1851

4.6.9 PRIS 9 Queen's Prison

PRIS 9/1 to 2	Donation Book – Prison Charities	1843 to 1862
3 to 5	Receipt Book of Charities	1846 to 1862
6 to 14	Keepers' Journals	1843 to 1862
15	Chaplain's Journal	1848 to 1854
16 to 19	Governors' Letter Books	1843 to 1862
20	Gaolers' Letter Books	1851 to 1862
32	Maintenance of Poor Prisoners Book	1861 to 1862

4.6.10 PRIS 10 Miscellanea . . . King's Bench, Fleet and Marshalsea Prisons

PRIS 10/49 to 57	Entry Book of Discharges, Fleet Prison	1734 to 1842
114 to 115	Prison Complaints; Queen's Prison	1845 to 1862
140 to 148	Alphabetical lists of prisoners for debt who are in the custody of the Marshalsea	1794 to 1813
149 to 150	Register; Fleet Prison	1822 to 1842
151 to 155	Index to Marshalsea volumes 1 to 18	(undated)
156	Lists of Prisoners; Fleet	1754 to 1813
157	Prisoners committed and discharged; Fleet	1697 to 1702
158	Fugitive Book	1748 to 1750
	Prisoners committed and discharged (Prison not given)	1771 to 1781

[1] From 1842 the King's Bench Prison was known as the Queen's Bench Prison.

159 to 164	Prisoners committed and discharged (Prison not given)	1781 to 1829
165 to 166	Prisoners and securities (Prison not given)	1822 to 1825
167	Prisoners for contempt; committed by the Court of Equity (Prison not given)	1822 to 1842
168	Register of insolvent debtors (gives prisoners' addresses) (Prison not given)	1835 to 1842
171	List of Prisoners addresses; alphabetical (Prison not given)	(undated)

171 continued: *A rough note written inside the back cover reads: 'If lost to be brought to the lobby of the King's Bench Prison and no Questions asked.' Prichard*

177	Keepers' Returns of Chancery Prisoners (Prison not given)	1843 to 1862
228	Register of Evening Visitors and List of Servants (Prison not given)	1845 to 1855
235	Medical Certificates for Nightly Nurses (Prison not given)	1853 to 1862
238	Includes papers relating to individual prisoners (Prison not given)	1845 to 1849

4.6.11   PRIS 11   Marshalsea Prison

PRIS 11/1 to 14	Day Book of Commitments	1812 to 1842
15 to 17	Entry Book of Admiralty Prisoners	1773 to 1842
18	Original Orders for Commitment and Discharge of Admiralty Prisoners	1812 to 1842

4.7   PALATINATE COURTS' CRIMINAL RECORDS

4.7.1   Palatinate of Chester

CHES 24/1 to 225	Gaol Fines and Indictments	1341 to 1832

4.7.2   Palatinate of Durham

DURH 15/1 to 10	Minute Books	1770 to 1876
DURH 16/1 to 7	Crown Books	1753 to 1876
DURH 17/1 to 197	Indictments	1582 to 1877
DURH 18/1 & 2	Depositions	1843 to 1876

4.7.3   Palatinate of Lancaster

PL 25/1 to 317	Assize Rolls	1422 to 1843
PL 26/1 to 284	Indictments	1424 to 1868
PL 27/1 to 18	Depositions	1663 to 1867

4.8   PRISON BOOKS AND JOURNALS

PCOM 2/84 to 89	Pentonville	Minute Books	1842 to 1850
90	Pentonville	Commissioner's Visiting Book	1843 to 1854
91 & 92	Pentonville	Directors' Order Books	1854 to 1885
93	Pentonville	Visitors' Book	1862 to 1863
94	Pentonville	Visitors' Minute Book	1842 to 1849
95	Pentonville	Visitors' Observation Book	1880 to 1885
96 & 97	Pentonville	Visitors' Order Books	1842 to 1850
353	Pentonville	Chaplain's Journal	1846 to 1851
159	Wormwood Scrubs	Governor's Order Book	1860 to 1878
160 & 161	Newgate	Chaplain's, Surgeon's and Sheriff's Journals	1825 to 1839
466	Newgate	Pardon, Thomas Ragner	1828
467	Newgate	Misc. Correspondence	1832 to 1883
162 & 163	Gibraltar	Officers' Sickness and Absence Book	1859 to 1875
164	Millbank	Question & Suggestion Book	1855 to 1863
293 to 295	Bedford	Governors' Journals	1852 to 1877
315	Lindsey	Visiting Committee Minute Book	1872 to 1904
316	Lindsey	Chaplain's Journal	1872 to 1876
317 & 318	Lindsey	Governor's Journals	1872 to 1878
349	Oxford	Gaoler's Journal	1823 to 1827
351	Oxford	Commissioners' and Inspectors' Minute Book	1859 to 1890
354 to 366	Portland	Governors' Journals	1848 to 1878
368	Portland	Register of Staff	1853 to 1880
392 & 393	Reading	Entry Book of Pardons	1818 to 1896
394	Reading	Visiting Justices' Order Book	1841 to 1863
395	Reading	Judges' Orders	1847 to 1883
399	Spalding	Chaplain's Journal	1873 to 1881
426 to 429	Chatham	Governor's Journals	1857 to 1869
367	Chatham	Register of Staff	1847 to 1869
442 to 446	Lancaster	Governor's Journals	1815 to 1856
448	Lancaster	Letter Book	1849 to 1856
463	Clerkenwell	Visiting Committee, Minutes	1878 to 1886
468	Montgomery County Gaol	Order for removal of two convicts to the Hulk *Justitia*	1837
469	Montgomery County Gaol	Discharge of Richard Evans	1839
471	Various Prisons	Audit Queries and Replies Book	1855 to 1856

4.9   PRISON HULK RECORDS

4.9.1   HO 7/2   Irish Hulks and Convict Establishments

Essex, Dublin (1835); *Surprise*, Cove of Cork, 1835; Convict Department, Cork, 1835. Officers and individuals belonging to these; no convicts' names except invalid convicts on *Essex*.

4.9.2 HO 7/3 Hulks in Bermuda

Antelope, Bermuda, 1823 to 1826; *Coromandel*, Bermuda, undated (*c.* 1827 to *c.* 1829); *Dromedary*, Bermuda, 1825; *Weymouth*, Bermuda, 1828 to 1829.

4.9.3 HO 9 Registers of Convict Hulks

HO 9/1	*Cumberland*, *Dolphin* and *Ganymede* at Chatham, 1820 to 1833
2	*Euryalus* and *Fortitude* at Chatham, 1825 to 1836
3	*Captivity*, *Ganymede* and *Discovery* at Devonport and Woolwich, 1821 to 1833
4	*Prudentia* at Woolwich, 1803 to 1809; *Retribution* at Woolwich, 1803 to 1814; *Justitia* at Woolwich, 1814 to 1836
5	Index to *Justitia*
6	Index to *Retribution*
7	*Retribution* at Woolwich, *c.* 1802 to 1834; *Bellerophon* at Sheerness, 1816 to 1825
8	*Fortunée* at Portsmouth, 1801 to 1816; *Captivity* &/or *Laurel* at Portsmouth, 1801 to 1822; *Leviathan* at Portsmouth, 1810 to 1836
9	*York* at Portsmouth, 1814 to 1836; *Hardy* at Portsmouth, 1824 to 1832; *Laurel* at Portsmouth, *c.* 1805 to 1836
10	*Euryalus* at Chatham, 1837 to 1843
11	*Fortitude* at Chatham, 1837 to 1843
12	*Ganymede* and *Warrior* at Woolwich, 1837 to 1845
13	*Justitia* at Woolwich, 1837 to 1844
14	*Leviathan* at Portsmouth, 1837 to 1844
15	*York* at Gosport, 1837 to 1845
16	Convict Hulk Establishment Letter Book, 1847 to 1849

4.9.4 T 38 Prison Hulks – Quarterly Lists

T 38/310	*Bellerophon* at Sheerness	1816 to 1818
311	*Captivity* at Portsmouth	1802 to 1804
312	*Captivity* at Portsmouth	1805 to 1806
313	*Captivity* at Portsmouth	1807 to 1808
314	*Captivity* at Portsmouth	1809 to 1811
315	*Captivity* at Portsmouth	1812 to 1814
316	*Captivity* at Portsmouth	1815 to 1817
317	*Justitia* at Woolwich	1814 to 1818
318	*Laurel* at Portsmouth	1804 to 1806
319	*Laurel* at Portsmouth	1807 to 1809
320	*Laurel* at Portsmouth	1810 to 1812
321	*Laurel* at Portsmouth	1813 to 1815
322	*Laurel* at Portsmouth	1816 to 1818
323	*Leviathan* at Portsmouth	1817 to 1818
324	*Portland* at Portsmouth	1802 to 1804
325	*Portland* at Portsmouth	1805 to 1807
326	*Portland* at Portsmouth	1808 to 1810
327	*Portland* at Portsmouth	1811 to 1813
328	*Portland* at Portsmouth	1814 to 1816
329	*Retribution* at Woolwich	1810 to 1811
330	*Retribution* at Woolwich	1812 to 1814
331	*Retribution* at Sheerness	1814 to 1815

332	*Retribution* at Sheerness	1816 to 1818
333	*Retribution, Prudentia* and *Stanislaus* at Woolwich	¦1804
334	*Retribution, Prudentia* and *Savage* at Woolwich	1804 to 1806
335	*Retribution, Prudentia* and *Savage* at Woolwich	1807 to 1809
336	*Zealand* at Sheerness	1810 to 1811
337	*Zealand* at Sheerness	1812 to 1813
338	Inspector's Accounts	1802 to 1815
	Report by John Henry Capper,	
	Messrs. Bradley, Erskine, and Wm. Kinnard.	

4.9.5 ADM 6

ADM 6/418	*Cumberland*	1830 to 1833
419	*Cumberland* Index[2]	1830 to 1833
420	*Dolphin*	1823 to 1833
421	*Dolphin*	1829 to 1835
422	*Dolphin* Description Book	1814 to 1831
423	*Dolphin* Index to 420 to 422	1825 to 1830

4.9.6 PCOM 2

PCOM 2/105	*Stirling Castle*	1847 to 1853
131	*Defence*	1857 to 1860
132	*Defence*, 1849 to 1851; *Stirling Castle*	1852 to 1856
133	*Defence*, 1856 to 1857; *Stirling Castle*	1850 to 1852
134	*Stirling Castle*	1837 to 1850
135	*Retribution*	1837 to 1841
136	*York*	1841 to 1852
137	*Europa* at Gibraltar	1840 to 1856

4.9.7 HO 8   Quarterly Prison Hulk Returns

Piece Numbers	Hulk	Place	Year/Quarter to Year/Quarter	
1	*Alexander Lamb*	Portsmouth	1824 Sept. only	
1 to 32	*Antelope*	Bermuda	1824 Sept.	1844 Sept.
1 to 6	*Bellerophon*	Sheerness	1824 Sept.	1825 Dec.
8 to 39	*Captivity*	Devonport/ Plymouth	1826 June	1834 March
8	*Coromandel*	Bermuda	1826 June and	
16 to 114			1828 June	1852 Dec.
23 to 37	*Cumberland*	Chatham	1830 March	1833 Sept.
9 to 32	*Dasher*	Woolwich	1826 Sept.	1832 June
100 to 108	*Defence*	Gosport	1849 June	1851 June
112 to 132	*Defence*	Woolwich	1852 June	1857 June
2 to 30	*Discovery*	Deptford	1824 Dec.	1831 Dec.

[2] This item is a box containing the Index Book (marked 1a) to the *Cumberland*. The box also contains two other Index Books to the *Cumberland* but a note in each states 'Entries in red refer to convicts on *Fortitude*'.

Piece Numbers	Hulk	Place	Year/Quarter to Year/Quarter	
31 to 38	*Discovery*	Woolwich	1832 March	1833 Dec.
1 to 22	*Dolphin*	Chatham	1824 Sept.	1829 Dec.
1	*Dromedary*	Woolwich	1824 Sept. only	
8 to 55	*Dromedary*	Bermuda	1826 March	1857 June
7 to 78	*Euryalus*	Chatham	1826 March	1843 Dec.
92 to 110	*Euryalus*	Gibraltar	1847 June	1851 Dec.
38 to 79	*Fortitude*	Chatham	1833 Dec.	1844 March
1 to 61	*Ganymede*	Woolwich	1824 Sept.	1839 Sept.
1 to 39	*Hardy*	Tipner Lake	1824 Sept.	1834 March
1 to 111	*Justitia*	Woolwich	1824 Sept.	1852 March
64 to 66	*Leven*	Deptford	1840 June	1840 Dec.
1 to 88	*Leviathan*	Portsmouth	1824 Sept.	1844 Dec.
95 to 150	*Medway*	Bermuda	1848 March	1861 Dec.
74 to 127	*Owen Glendower*	Gibraltar	1842 Dec.	1856 March
6 to 10	*Racoon*	Portsmouth	1825 Dec.	1826 Dec.
1 to 39	*Retribution*	Sheerness	1824 Sept.	1834 March
63 to 81	*Stirling Castle*	Devonport	1840 March	1844 Sept.
82 to 111	*Stirling Castle*	Portsmouth	1844 Dec.	1852 March
112 to 129	*Stirling Castle*	Gosport	1852 June	1856 Sept.
77 to 119	*Tenedos*	Bermuda	1843 Sept.	1854 March
67 to 77	*Thames*	Deptford	1841 March	1843 Sept.
78	*Thames*	Chatham	1843 Dec. only	
82 to 120	*Thames*	Bermuda	1844 Dec.	1854 June
62 to 128	*Warrior*	Woolwich	1839 Dec.	1856 June
19 to 47	*Weymouth*	Bermuda	1829 March	1836 March
1 to 58	*York*	Portsmouth	1824 Sept.	1838 Dec.
59 to 111	*York*	Gosport	1839 March	1852 March

4.9.8   T 1   Treasury Board Papers for the transportation period to Australia

T 1/653 to T 1/6848 (1788 to 1868)

These papers are arranged in bundles and boxes, among which are to be found lists of convicts on board prison hulks. There is an index (T 2) to this series which dates from 1777 and is arranged in annual volumes. The index gives the names of persons paid by the Treasury for all manner of contracts and also includes the names of those persons petitioning the Treasury for agreement to perform certain tasks and duties. In order to locate lists of convicts on hulks it is, therefore, necessary to know the name of the Overseer of Convicts for the particular port at which a hulk was moored. Against his name in the T 2 index for the year required will be found a document number.

In many instances documents were moved by the Treasury clerks from one bundle to another, thus collecting together several papers all relating to the same matter. Movement and relocation of such documents is recorded in T 3 Annual Registers of the document numbers. If there is a tick against a document number this indicates that it has not been moved from its original bundle and has been preserved. If it has been moved the number of the document to which it has been attached is shown. It is then necessary to check this second number to ascertain whether the papers have been kept or have been linked with later papers. Many documents were weeded out and destroyed by the Treasury in 1852; such documents have T.O. (Taken Out) against the number in T 3.

The T 1 class list is arranged annually with several piece numbers for each year, each piece containing a range of document numbers. By referring to the year required in the T 1 class list and cross-referring the document number found in the T 2 index (or the repositioned number in T 3), the present piece number can be found.

An incomplete survey of the T 2 index has revealed the following Overseers of Convicts:

Messrs. Campbell (Duncan and J. Campbell): Woolwich 1785 to 1801; Portsmouth 1786 to 1791.
Messrs. Bradley (James and Henry Bradley): Plymouth 1786 to 1791; Portsmouth 1790 to 1796, 1800 to 1802; Woolwich 1790 to 1800.
Mr. Dyne (Andrew Hawes Dyne): Portsmouth 1797 to 1800.

It should be noted that some documents referred to as Taken Out in T 3 have in fact survived, having been located in their rightful place in T 1. Other documents which should be in place have not been found. Additionally lists of convicts on hulks, which are not listed in T 2 have been found in T 1. It is, therefore, advisable to search T 1 direct if the required hulks have not been identified in T 2.

Other occasional references to convicts on prison hulks are found in:

4.9.9   HO 6/1 to 25   Judges' Circuit Letters

Returns by Judges and Recorders of convicted persons recommended for mercy, lists of convicts, letters from governors of convict prisons etc., 1816 to 1840.

4.9.10   HO 47/1 to 75   Judges' Reports on Criminals, 1784 to 1829

4.9.11   PC 1/67 to 92   Correspondence relating to transported convicts, 1818 to 1844

4.9.12   PC 2/132 to 269   Privy Council Office Registers, 1787 to 1868

The piece numbers given here cover the period of transportation to Australia. This series of registers actually begins in 1540 and finishes in 1901.

4.9.13   AO 3/292 to 296   Accounts of Convict Hulks, 1830 to 1837

4.10   PRISON REGISTERS

4.10.1   HO 23   Registers of County Prisons

HO 23/1	Aylesbury	1864 to 1865
2	Bath	1848 to 1855
3	Leeds	1848 to 1864
4 to 7	Leicester	1848 to 1865
8	Northampton	1848 to 1855
9	Northampton	1863 to 1865
10	Nottingham	1864 to 1865

11	Preston	1848 to 1855
12	Reading	1847 to 1855
13	Somerset	1864 to 1865
14 to 20	Wakefield	1847 to 1866

4.10.2 HO 24   Prison Registers and Returns

HO 24/1 to 14	Millbank	1843 to 1874
15	Parkhurst	1838 to 1863
16 to 19	Pentonville	1842 to 1875
20 to 29	{ Statistical information for various prisons in England and Wales. Names of prisoners are rarely given.	1860 to 1869

4.10.3 PCOM 2   Prison Registers

PCOM 2/1 to 9	Chatham	1865 to 1891
10	Dorchester	1853 to 1854
11 to 13	Gibraltar	1851 to 1875
60	Millbank	1816 to 1826
20 to 58	Millbank	1837 to 1877
161 & 166 to 229	Newgate	1770 to 1881
59	Parkhurst	1853 to 1863
61 to 83	Pentonville	1842 to 1885
	(Includes prisoners' photographs	1875 to 1885)
368 to 391	Portland	1853 to 1865
105 to 114	Portsmouth	1847 to 1877
	(Portsmouth Convict Prison was opened 1 April 1852. Entries in PCOM 2/105 before this date are for the *Stirling Castle* Prison Hulk.)	
115 to 125	Portsmouth working parties	1847 to 1877
126 to 130	Portsmouth	1867 to 1894
138	Shorncliffe	1849 to 1851
139	Westminster Penitentiary [Millbank]	1816 to 1871
140	Westminster Penitentiary [Millbank] Burials	1817 to 1853
141 to 151	Woking	1846 to 1889
152 to 153	Wormwood Scrubs, working parties	1874 to 1890
154 to 158	Wormwood Scrubs, separate confinement register	1882 to 1890
165	Millbank, Deaths and Inquests Register (Most of burials were in Victoria Park Cemetery)	1848 to 1863
230 to 289	Wandsworth	1858 to 1879
290 & 291	Wandsworth (prisoners photographs)	1872 to 1873
292	Bedford	1844 to 1857
430 to 434	Birmingham, Habitual Criminal Register	1871 to 1875
435 to 437	Birmingham, Register of Convicts	1799 to 1893
296 to 299	Birmingham, Habitual Criminal Register	1872 to 1875
300	Cambridge, Habitual Criminal Register	1875 to 1877

302	Derby	1836 to 1844
303	Durham	1848 to 1850
308 to 310	Lincoln	1808 to 1846
342	Louth	1852 to 1859
343	Newcastle	1859 to 1860
350	Oxford	1845 to 1851
352	Oxford (Prisoners' photographs)	1870 to 1881
392 & 393	Reading, Entry Books of Pardons	1818 to 1896
396	Shrewsbury, Debtors' Register	1855 to 1861
400	Spilsby, Discharge Register	1826 to 1848
401 to 404	Stafford	1841 to 1876
411	Wakefield	1856
425	Worcester	1874
438	Lindsey	1872 to 1873
456 to 460	Lancaster	1884 to 1909
440	Lancaster, Debtors and Plaintiffs	1792 to 1797
441	Lancaster, Crown Cases	1820 to 1826

4.10.4   HO 8   Quarterly Prison Returns

Piece Number	Prison	Place	Year/Quarter to Year/Quarter	
115 to 155	Boaz Island	Bermuda	1853 March	1863 March
201 to 207	Borstal	Kent	1874 Sept.	1876 March
126 to 182	Brixton, female	Surrey	1855 Dec.	1869 Dec.
183 to 206	Brixton, male	Surrey	1870 March	1875 Dec.
153 to 171	Broadmoor, convict	Berkshire	1862 Sept.	1867 March
159 to 206	Broadmoor, male and female lunatics	Berkshire	1864 March	1875 Dec.
130 to 207	Chatham	Kent	1856 Dec.	1876 March
106 to 207	Dartmoor	Devonshire	1850 Dec.	1876 March
131 to 207	Fulham, female	Middlesex	1857 March	1876 March
121 to 202	Gibraltar		1854 Sept.	1874 Dec.
133 to 143	Lewes	Sussex	1857 Sept.	1860 March
162 to 182	Parkhurst	Isle of Wight	1864 Dec.	1869 Dec.
162 to 202	Perth, criminal lunatic	Scotland	1864 Dec.	1874 Dec.
98 to 206	Portland	Dorset	1848 Dec.	1875 Dec.
112 to 207	Portsmouth	Hampshire	1852 June	1876 March
102 to 109	Shorncliffe	Kent	1849 Dec.	1851 Sept.
140 to 174	Woking	Surrey	1859 June	1867 Dec.
175 to 207	Woking, invalid	Surrey	1868 March	1876 June
180 to 207	Woking, female	Surrey	1869 June	1876 June

4.10.5   HO 20/13   Bethlem Asylum Register (Criminal Lunatics), 1819 to 1841

4.10.6 WO 25 Savoy Prison and Hulk Registers (Army Criminals and Deserters)

WO 25/2956	1799 to 1806
2957	1803 to 1819
2958	1807 to 1812
2959	1809 to 1815
2960	1815 to 1821
2961	1821 to 1823

4.10.7 KB 32/23 Millbank Prison Returns, 1826

4.11 SHERIFFS' ASSIZE VOUCHERS, SHERIFFS' CRAVINGS AND PAYMENTS AND TREASURY WARRANTS

4.11.1 Sheriffs' Assize Vouchers

Lists of persons convicted at Assizes (see 4.11.2).

4.11.2 Sheriffs' Cravings

Requests for payments relating to hanging, whipping, the pillory, and other punishments for prisoners. Prisoners' names are given.

Sheriffs' Assize Vouchers and Sheriffs' Cravings appear together in the following:

E 370/35	1714 to 1741
36	1741 to 1760
37	1760 to 1765
38	1765 to 1770
39	1770 to 1775
40	1775 to 1780
41	1780 to 1785
42	1785 to 1790
43	1790 to 1795
44	1795 to 1800
45	1800 to 1805
46	1805 to 1810
47	1810 to 1815
48	1815 to 1821
49	1821 to 1825
50	1825 to 1829
51	1829 to 1832

T 64/262	Sheriffs' Bills of Cravings 1745 to 1785.
	The following years are missing from this series: 1748, 1750, 1752 to 1756, 1758 and 1773.

4.11.3   T 90   Sheriffs' Payments

Payments made by the Treasury to County Sheriffs. These are arranged by county and include Justices' expenses for keeping prisoners in gaol, conveying to prison hulks, executing etc. Criminals' names are given.

T 90/146	1733 to 1735
147	1735 to 1739
148	1752 to 1753
149	1754 to 1755
150	1756 to 1757
151	1757 to 1761
152	1758 to 1759
153	1760 to 1761
154	1762 to 1763
155	1764 to 1765
156	1766 to 1769
157	1768 to 1769
158	1770 to 1771
159	1772 to 1773
160	1774 to 1775
161	1776 to 1777
162	1778 to 1779
163	1780 to 1781
164	1782 to 1783
165	1784 to 1787
166	1788 to 1789
167	1791 to 1794
168	1794 to 1799
169	1807 to 1813
170	1814 to 1822

4.11.4   T 207   Sheriffs' Payments

T 207/1	1823 to 1836
2	1837 to 1853
3	1854 to 1869
4	1870 to 1885
5	1886 to 1897
6	1897 to 1908
7	1909 to 1920
8	1921
9	1920 to 1941
10	1941 to 1959

4.11.5   T 53   Treasury Warrants

Entry Books of warrants for payment. These include Conviction Money which is payment made to County Sheriffs or Undersheriffs for expenses incurred in apprehending and convicting criminals. They also give criminals' names. See the index at the back of each volume under *Sheriffs' Conviction Money*.

T 53/29	1721 to 1722
30	1722 to 1723
31	1723 to 1725
32	1725 to 1726
33	1726 to 1728
34	1728 to 1729
35	1729 to 1731
36	1731 to 1733
37	1733 to 1735
38	1735 to 1737
39	1737 to 1739
40	1739 to 1742
41	1742 to 1745
42	1745 to 1748
43	1748 to 1751
44	1751 to 1753
45	1753 to 1756
46	1756 to 1759
47	1759 to 1761
48	1761 to 1763
49	1763 to 1765
50	1765 to 1768
51	1768 to 1771
52	1771 to 1773
53	1774 to 1777
54	1777 to 1780
55	1780 to 1782
56	1782 to 1784
57	1784 to 1785
58	1785 to 1787
59	1787 to 1790
60	1790 to 1793
61	1793 to 1797
62	1797 to 1801
63	1801 to 1805
64	1805 to 1810

No Conviction Money after 1805

4.11.6   T 54   Treasury Warrants

Warrants not relating to money. These include Conviction Money from 1806 to 1827.

T 54/50	1806 to 1808
51	1808 to 1811
52	1811 to 1814
53	1814 to 1818
54	1818 to 1824
55	1824 to 1827

4.12   TRANSPORTATION TO AUSTRALIA: LISTS OF CONVICTS

4.12.1   HO 11   Convict Transportation Records arranged by ships, giving names of convicts

HO 11/1	1787 to 1809
2	1810 to 1817
3	1818 to 1820
4	1821 to 1822
5	1823 to 1825
6	1826 to 1828
7	1829 to 1830
8	1831 to 1832
9	1833 to 1834
10	1835 to 1836
11	1837 to 1838
12	1839 to 1841
13	1842 to 1843
14	1844 to 1845
15	1846 to 1848
16	1849 to 1850
17	1851 to 1852
18	1853 to 1863
19	1864 to 1867

4.12.2   TS 18   Contracts for the transportation of convicts, naming convicts, with date and place of trial, and sentence

Piece no.	Ship	From	Year of Departure	Destination
460	*Canada*	Spithead	1842	VDL
461	*Waterloo*	Sheerness	1842	VDL
462	*Emily*	Sheerness	1842	VDL
463	*Moffatt*	Plymouth	1842	VDL
464	*Garland Grove*	Woolwich	1842	VDL
465	*Duchess of Northumberland*	Sheerness	1842	VDL
466	*John Renwick*	Portsmouth	1842	VDL
467	*Gilmore*	Sheerness	1843	VDL
468	*Emerald Isle*	Sheerness	1843	VDL
469	*Lord Petre*	Woolwich	1843	VDL
470	*Tasmania*	Woolwich	1844	VDL
471	*Hydrabad*	Woolwich	1844	VDL
472	*Sir Geo. Seymour*	Woolwich	1844	VDL
473	*Mountstuart Elphinstone*	Woolwich	1845	VDL
474	*Tory*	Woolwich	1845	VDL
475	*Theresa*	Woolwich	1845	VDL
476	*David Malcolm*	Woolwich	1845	VDL
477	*Marion*	Woolwich	1845	VDL
478	*Equestrian*	Woolwich	1845	VDL
479	*Lloyds*	Woolwich	1845	VDL

Piece no.	Ship	From	Year of Departure	Destination
480	*Stratheden*	Woolwich	1845	VDL
481	*Mayda*	Woolwich	1845	VDL
482	*Pestonjee Bomanjee*	Woolwich	1845	VDL
483	*Joseph Somes*	Woolwich	1845	VDL
484	*Emma Eugenia*	Woolwich	1846	VDL
485	*Lady Palmira*	Woolwich	1846	VDL
486	*Sea Queen*	Woolwich	1846	VDL
487	*John Calvin*	Woolwich	1846	VDL
488	*Elizabeth & Henry*	London	1846	VDL
489	*Pestonjee Bomanjee*	Woolwich	1846	VDL
490	*Thomas Arbuthnot*	Spithead	1847	VDL
491	*Asia*	Spithead	1847	VDL
492	*Eden*	Plymouth	1848	NSW
493	*Hashemy*	Portsmouth	1848	NSW
494	*Fairlie*	Plymouth	1852	VDL
495	*Sir Robert Seppings*	Woolwich	1852	VDL
496	*Pestonjee Bomanjee*	Plymouth	1852	VDL
497	*William Jardine*	Plymouth	1852	W. Aust.
498	*Lady Montague*	Plymouth	1852	VDL
499	*Oriental Queen*	Plymouth	1852	VDL
500	*Pyrenees*	England	1852	W. Aust.
501	*Ramilies*	London	1854	W. Aust.
502	*Sultana*	Plymouth	1859	W. Aust.
503	*Palmerston*	Portland	1860	W. Aust.
504	*Lincelles*	Portland	1861	W. Aust.
505	*Norwood*	Portland	1862	W. Aust.
506	*Merchantman*	Convict Establishment Bermuda	1862	W. Aust.
507	*Lord Dalhousie*	Portland	1863	W. Aust.
508	*Clara*	London	1864	W. Aust.
509	*Merchantman*	Portland	1864	W. Aust.
510	*Racehorse*	Portland	1865	W. Aust.
511	*Vimiera*	Portland	1865	W. Aust.
512	*Belgravia*	Portland	1866	W. Aust.
513	*Corona*	Portland	1866	W. Aust.
514	*Norwood*	Portland	1867	W. Aust.
515	*Hougoumont*	London	1867	W. Aust.

[VDL = Van Diemen's Land (Tasmania)]

4.12.3 PC 1 Privy Council Correspondence

PC 1/2715: Lists of Convicts embarked on the *Eden* for New South Wales, with correspondence, 1840.

PC 1/2716: Lists of Convicts embarked on the *Tortoise* for Van Diemen's Land, with correspondence, 1841.

PC 1/2717: Lists of Convicts embarked on the *Elphinstone* for Van Diemen's Land, with correspondence, 1842.

PC 1/2718:   Lists of Convicts embarked on the *Anson* for Van Diemen's Land, with
             correspondence, 1843.

4.12.4   PC 2   Privy Council Office Registers

These contain 'Orders in Council' which list convicts sentenced to transportation. (They
do not usually include those sentenced to transportation for life.) The following registers
cover the transportation period to Australia:

PC 1/132 to 266   1787 to 1867

4.12.5   HO 31/1   'Orders in Council'

These give lists of transported convicts for the following:

27 April 1785
13 May 1785   (two lists)
 2 December 1786   (two lists)
22 December 1786   (three lists of female convicts)
12 February 1787
20 April 1787   (two lists)
15 May 1789
14 October 1789
18 November 1789
25 January 1792
 2 May 1792
 2 May 1792   (Scottish convicts)
 1 August 1792   (female convicts)
31 December 1795   (Joseph Gerald, convicted Edinburgh – no others)
 8 January 1794

APPENDIX 5

CRIMINAL RECORDS HELD IN POLICE ARCHIVES FOR THE PERIOD UP TO *c.* 1900[1]

5.1 Cambridgeshire

Cambridgeshire Constabulary
Huntingdon
PE18 8NP

Cambridge Borough Gaol Book, 'John Payne's Accounts', 1822 to 1839
Register of Habitual Criminals (8 vols), 1887 to 1895

5.2 Derbyshire

Derbyshire Constabulary Headquarters
Ripley
DE5 3RS

Convict Registers, Blakewell District (3 vols.), 1866 to 1946
Index of Prisons, 1873 to 1904
Register of Convicts and Convictions, 1876 to 1920
Criminal Portraits and Record Albums, 1888 to 1910
Register of Returned Convicts on Licence, 1880
Calendar of Prisoners, Derby Quarter Sessions, 1893 to 1897
Criminal Register, Ilkeston, 1890 to 1920

5.3 Devonshire

Devon and Cornwall Constabulary
Exeter
EX5 1DD

Unexecuted Warrants and Convicts on Licence:

  G Division, 1864
  X Division, 1865
  H Division, 1865, 1879

---

[1] See also Appendix 2.2.

5.4 Dorsetshire

Dorset Police
Winfrith
DT2 8DZ

Criminals Photographic Register, *c.* 1870

5.5 Glamorgan

South Wales Constabulary
Bridgend
Mid Glamorgan

Cardiff, Habitual Criminals Register, 1882 to 1885

5.6 Hertfordshire

Hertfordshire Constabulary
Welwyn Garden City
AL8 6XF

Register of Prisoners in the Cells, Baldock, 1886 to 1922

5.7 Huntingdonshire

Address as 5.1 above

Petty Sessions Book, Huntingdon, 1873 to 1878

Habitual Criminals (2 vols), 1877, 1883 and index
Assizes and Sessions (3 vols), 1882 to 1916
Convicts on Licence, 1879 to 1954
Quarter Sessions Orders and Minutes, Huntingdon, 1856 to 1888
Huntingdon County Gaol, Rules and Regulations, 1863
Huntingdon County Gaol, Habitual Criminal Returns (2 vols), 1870 to 1878

5.8 Kent

Kent Constabulary
Maidstone
ME15 9BZ

Petty Sessions Register, Elham, 1895 to 1903

5.9 Leicestershire

Leicestershire Constabulary
Force Headquarters
Narborough
LE9 5BX

Registers of Convicts Liberated on Licence:

    Hinckley, 1866 and 1884
    Melton Mowbray, 1866
    Market Bosworth, 1871
    Leicester Division, 1874

Gaol Photographs, Leicester Borough Gaol, Female, 1880 to 1922

Calendar of Prisoners, Leicestershire Quarter Sessions, 1891 to 1903

5.10 Lincolnshire

Lincolnshire Constabulary
Lincoln
LN5 7PH

Convicts on Licence, Boston, 1875 to 1896

5.11 London

City of London Police
37 Wood Street
London
EC2P 2NQ

4th Division Bow Lane
Photographic Register of Convicted Criminals, 1870

5.12 Monmouthshire

Gwent Constabulary
Cwmbran
NP44 2XJ

Register of Criminals (3 vols), 1869 to 1939 and indexes
Convicts on Licence, 1882 to 1916

5.13 Norfolk

Norfolk Constabulary
Police Headquarters
Norwich
NR1 2DJ

Thetford Gaol
Surgeon's Visiting Book, 1840
Chaplain's Visiting Book, 1841
Register of Convicted Persons, 1859
Habitual Criminals Register, Loddon Division, 1870
Norfolk Assize and Quarter Sessions Calendars, 1891 to 1944

5.14 Northamptonshire

Address as 5.1 above

Borough of Peterborough Conviction Register, 1889 onwards

5.15 Northumberland

Northumbria Police
Newcastle upon Tyne
NE20 0BL

Tynemouth Police, Criminal Register Book, 1872 to 1949

5.16 Oxfordshire

Thames Valley Police
Reading
RG7 4DX

Criminal Register, Bampton East, 1865
Prison Register, Watlington Prison, 1888 to 1947
Prison Register, Burford Prison, 1888 to 1947
Register of Prisoners, Bampton East Division, 1888 to 1921

5.17 Somersetshire

Police Headquarters
Taunton

Pensford Petty Sessions, Meeting Books (5 vols), 1850 to 1884

5.18 Yorkshire

West Yorkshire Police
Police Headquarters
Wakefield

Recognizances from the Session Rolls
Liberty of Ripon, 1753   ref. A136 159 HQ919

Returns of Persons Committed to Gaol
Liberty of Ripon, 1828   ref. A54 47–48 HQ71

House of Correction Bread Book
Liberty of Ripon, 1847 to 1849 (2 vols)   ref. A90 352 HQ44441

West Riding Quarter Sessions Minute Book, 1856 to 1889
ref. A60 1HQ 120

Ticket-of-Leave Men, Huddersfield, 1864 to 1949   ref. A90 19

Registers of Prisoners (Photographs), Leeds, 1896 to 1899

APPENDIX 6

CRIMINAL RECORDS CURRENTLY HELD BY THE PRISON SERVICE

For completeness of the survey of criminal records given in the appendices of this book the following list gives eighteenth- and nineteenth-century documents currently held by the Prison Service which will be of particular interest to historians. At the time of going to press these are not available for public search but will in due course be deposited at the Public Record Office or the appropriate County Record Offices.

6.1   Bedford Prison

Magistrates' Visiting Book, 1878 to 1907

6.2   Bristol

Registers of Prisoners, 1884 to 1900

6.3   Brixton, Millbank, Woking and Fulham Prisons

Reception Register, females, with photographs, [?] to 1873

6.4   Cardiff

Calendars of Prisoners; Assizes and Quarter Sessions, 1896

6.5   Cornwall County Gaol, Bodmin

Register of Prisoners, 1815

6.6   Devon County Gaol, Exeter

Female Receiving Book, 1852 to 1855
Officer's Pay Book, 1830
Chaplain's Journal, 1797 to 1842
Rules and Regulations, 1841
Minute Book, 1867 to 1868
Further records, details not available

6.7   Everthorp, Wormwood Scrubs, and Coldbath Fields

Papers and Photographs

6.8   Gloucester

Reception Photographs; male and female, 1890
Calendar of Prisoners, 1885 and 1899

6.9   Hull

Execution Register, nineteenth century

6.10   Lancaster

Chaplain's Journal, 1862 to 1871

6.11   Leicester

Borough of Leicester Court Calendars, giving previous convictions and current convic-
    tions, 1866 to 1877
County of Rutland and Leicester Court Calendars giving previous convictions and current
    convictions, 1872 to 1894
Leicester Prison, Reception Registers, 1868 to 1880
Leicester Prison, Register of Officers, eighteenth to early nineteenth century

6.12   Lincoln

Reception Register, 1878 to 1879
Register of Executions, nineteenth century

6.13   Maidstone

Nominal Register of Prisoners, 1882 to 1900
Chaplain's Journal, 1847 to 1858

6.14   Manchester Borough Gaol

Register of Felons, 1794 to 1801
Register of Prisoners, 1853 to 1856

6.15   Manchester, Strangeways

Nominal Register of Prisoners, 1853 to 1871

6.16   Millbank

Prison Accounts, 1884

6.17   Newgate

Newgate and Tyburn Calendar, 1751
Rules and Regulations, 1873
Newgate and Pentonville; various papers

6.18   Norwich

Nominal Register of Prisoners, 1888 to 1900
Board of Visitors' Journals, 1878 to 1900
Execution Register, 1880 to 1900

6.19   Salford

New Baily Prison, Register of Misdemeanants, 1847 to 1872

6.20   Northampton

Register of Officers, 1800 to 1900

6.21   Nottingham

Nominal Register of Prisoners, 1759 to 1880
Register of Officers, 1800 to 1900

6.22   Parkhurst

Register of Prisoners, 1845
Register of Inmates, 1845 to 1847
Surgeons' Reports, 1838 to 1883
Medical Reports, 1888 to 1900
Register of Officers, 1880 to 1900
Registers of Inmates, 1882 to 1900

6.23   Portland

Governor's Journal, 1844

6.24   Preston

Calendar of Prisoners, 1842 to 1846

6.25   Shepton Mallet

Registers of Prisoners, 1883 to 1890

6.26   Shrewsbury

Magistrates' Visiting Book, 1823 to 1830
Registers of Prisoners, nineteenth century

6.27   Southwell Prison, Nottinghamshire

Visiting Committee Minute Book, 1878 to 1880

6.28   Stafford

Nominal Registers of Prisoners, 1878 to 1900
Reports and Correspondence on the Deaths of Prisoners, 1883 to 1895
Assizes Committal Books

6.29   Swansea

Nominal Registers of Prisoners, 1845 to 1900

6.30 Usk

Inspectors' Minute Books, 1888 to 1900
Register of Officers, 1894 to 1900
Visiting Committee Minute Book, 1878 to 1900

6.31 Wakefield

House of Correction; Calendar of Prisoners, 1803 to 1835
Prison; Calendar of Prisoners, 1866 to 1868
Prison; Rules and Regulations

6.32 Wetherby Sessions

Register of Felons, 9 January 1821

6.33 Wolverhampton

Register of Prisoners, *c.* 1800 to 1820

6.34 Wormwood Scrubs

Register of Inmates, *c.* 1890 to 1900
Staff Register, *c.* 1874 to 1900

6.35 Westminster House of Correction

Nominal Register of Prisoners, 1866 to 1877
Photograph Albums of Prisoners
Nominal Registers of Prisoners Convicted at Assizes and Sessions, 1872 to 1879

6.36 General

Free Pardon, 1851
Reports of Inspector of Prisons
Report on Diarrhoea and Typhoid Epidemic, 1875
Digest of Gaol Returns, 1845
Reports of Inspectors of Prisons, 1836

Records are also held for Rochester and Wandsworth Prisons but details are not available.

APPENDIX 7

COUNTIES, WITH COURTS OF JURISDICTION

Counties in England and Wales giving their related Assize Circuits and other Criminal Courts with jurisdiction (not including Quarter Sessions).

ENGLAND

Historic County	Assize Circuit		Other Courts with Jurisdiction
	Name	Dates Covered	
Bedfordshire	Norfolk Circuit Midland Circuit	1558 to 1876 1876 to 1971	
Berkshire	Oxford Circuit	1558 to 1971	
Buckinghamshire	Norfolk Circuit Midland Circuit	1558 to 1876 1876 to 1971	
Cambridgeshire	Norfolk Circuit South Eastern Circuit	1558 to 1876 1876 to 1971	
Cheshire	North & South Wales Circuit North Wales Division Wales & Chester Circuit	1830 to 1876 1876 to 1945 1945 to 1971	Palatinate Court of Chester up to 1830
Cornwall	Western Circuit	1558 to 1971	
Cumberland	Northern Circuit	1558 to 1971	

[contd]

Historic County	Assize Circuit		Other Courts with Jurisdiction
	Name	Dates Covered	
Derbyshire	Midland Circuit	1558 to 1971	
Devonshire	Western Circuit	1558 to 1971	
Dorsetshire	Western Circuit	1558 to 1971	
Durham	North Eastern Circuit	1876 to 1971	Palatinate Court of Durham up to 1876
Essex	Home Circuit South Eastern Circuit	1558 to 1876 1876 to 1971	Central Criminal Court 1834 to 1971
Gloucestershire	Oxford Circuit	1558 to 1971	
Hampshire	Western Circuit	1558 to 1971	
Herefordshire	Oxford Circuit	1558 to 1971	
Hertfordshire	Home Circuit South Eastern Circuit	1558 to 1876 1876 to 1971	
Huntingdonshire	Norfolk Circuit South Eastern Circuit	1558 to 1876 1876 to 1971	
Kent	Home Circuit South Eastern Circuit	1558 to 1876 1876 to 1971	Central Criminal Court 1834 to 1971
Lancashire	Northern Circuit	1876 to 1971	Palatinate Court of Lancaster up to 1876
Leicestershire	Midland Circuit Norfolk Circuit Midland Circuit	1558 to 1863 1864 to 1876 1876 to 1971	
Lincolnshire	Midland Circuit	1558 to 1971	
Middlesex	None		Old Bailey up to 1833 then named Central Criminal Court in 1834

Historic County	Assize Circuit		Other Courts with Jurisdiction
	Name	Dates Covered	
Monmouthshire	Oxford Circuit	1558 to 1971	
Norfolk	Norfolk Circuit South Eastern Circuit	1559 to 1876 1876 to 1971	
Northamptonshire	Midland Circuit Norfolk Circuit Midland Circuit	1558 to 1863 1864 to 1876 1876 to 1971	
Northumberland	Northern Circuit North Eastern Circuit	1558 to 1876 1876 to 1971	
Nottinghamshire	Midland Circuit	1558 to 1971	
Oxfordshire	Oxford Circuit	1558 to 1971	
Rutland	Midland Circuit Norfolk Circuit Midland Circuit	1558 to 1863 1864 to 1876 1876 to 1971	
Shropshire	Oxford Circuit	1558 to 1971	
Somersetshire	Western Circuit	1558 to 1971	
Staffordshire	Oxford Circuit	1558 to 1971	
Suffolk	Norfolk Circuit South Eastern Circuit	1558 to 1876 1876 to 1971	
Surrey	Home Circuit South Eastern Circuit	1558 to 1876 1876 to 1971	Central Criminal Court 1834 to 1971
Sussex	Home Circuit South Eastern Circuit	1558 to 1876 1876 to 1971	
Warwickshire	Midland Circuit	1558 to 1971	
Westmorland	Northern Circuit	1558 to 1971	

[contd]

Historic County	Assize Circuit		Other Courts with Jurisdiction
	Name	Dates Covered	
Wiltshire	Western Circuit	1558 to 1971	
Worcestershire	Oxford Circuit	1558 to 1971	
Yorkshire (all Ridings)	Northern Circuit Midland Circuit North Eastern Circuit	1558 to 1863 1864 to 1876 1876 to 1971	

WALES

County	Courts of Great Sessions	Assize Circuit		
Denbighshire Flintshire Montgomeryshire	Chester Circuit 1543 to 1830		North Wales Division 1876 to 1945	
Anglesey Carnarvonshire Merioneth	North Wales Circuit 1543 to 1830	North & South Wales Circuit 1830 to 1876		Wales & Chester Circuit 1945 to 1971
Brecon Glamorgan Radnorshire	Brecon Circuit 1543 to 1830		South Wales Division 1876 to 1945	
Cardiganshire Carmarthenshire Pembrokeshire	Carmarthen Circuit 1543 to 1830			

APPENDIX 8

EXISTING PRISONS IN ENGLAND AND WALES WHICH WERE IN USE PRIOR TO 1900

Gaol	Historic County	Date first used for Custody of Offenders	Purpose for which Built	Remarks
Aylesbury	Bucks	1845	County Gaol	Now a Youth Custody Centre
Bedford	Beds	1848	County Gaol	
Birmingham	Warwick	1845	City Gaol	
Bristol	Gloucester	1883	City Gaol	Built by the Prison Commissioners
Brixton	Surrey	1853	Female Penitentiary	
Broadmoor	Berks	1863	State Criminal Lunatic Asylum for men & women	Built by Convicts from Woking Prison
Canterbury	Kent	1808	County Gaol	Rebuilt 1852
Cardiff	Glamorgan	1830	County Gaol	

[contd]

Gaol	Historic County	Date first used for Custody of Offenders	Purpose for which Built	Remarks
Chelmsford	Essex	1819	County Gaol	Now a Prison for Young Offenders
Dartmoor	Devon	1850	French Prisoners of War	Built in 1808 by Prisoners from the Napoleonic Wars
Dorchester	Dorset	1855	County Gaol	Rebuilt by Prison Commissioners 1879
Durham	Co. Durham	pre 1877	County Gaol	Rebuilt 1881
Exeter	Devon	1853	County Gaol	
Gloucester	Gloucester	c. 1800	County Gaol	Rebuilt 1840
Holloway	Middx	1853	City of London Gaol	Now a Prison for Women
Hull	Yorks	1869	City Gaol	
Lancaster	Lancs	17th century		Castle with Norman Keep
Leeds	Yorks	1840	City Gaol	
Leicester	Leics	1828	County Gaol	Rebuilt 1850
Lewes	Sussex	1855	County Gaol	
Lincoln	Lincs	1869	County Gaol	
Liverpool	Lancs	1854	City Gaol	
Maidstone	Kent	1817	County Gaol	
Manchester	Lancs	1869	County Gaol	

Gaol	Historic County	Date first used for Custody of Offenders	Purpose for which Built	Remarks
North Allerton	Yorks	1850	County Gaol	Now a Youth Custody Centre
Norwich	Norfolk	1892		Built by the Prison Commissioners
Nottingham	Notts	1890	City Gaol	Rebuilt 1912
Oxford	Oxford	1858	County Gaol	
Parkhurst	Isle of Wight, Hants	1838	Male Juvenile Offenders	
Pentonville	Middx	1842	Convict Prison	Built as a 'Model Prison'
Portland	Dorset	1848	Convict Prison	
Portsmouth	Hants	1878	City Gaol	
Preston	Lancs	1799	County Gaol	
Reading	Berks	1845	County Gaol	
Rochester	Kent	1873	Built as a Convict Prison	Now a Prison for Women
Shepton Mallet	Somerset	1610	House of Correction	Was Military Prison, 1939 to 1966
Shrewsbury	Shropshire	1795	County Gaol	Rebuilt 1885
Stafford	Staffs	1845	County Gaol	
Swansea	Glamorgan	1859	County Gaol	
Usk	Monmouth	1838	County Goal	Now a Detention Centre for Boys

[contd]

Gaol	Historic County	Date first used for Custody of Offenders	Purpose for which Built	Remarks
Wakefield	Yorks	1820	House of Corr'n	
Wandsworth	Surrey	1849	County Gaol	
Winchester	Hants	1855	County Gaol	
Wormwood Scrubs	Middx	1874		Completed in 1891 by Convict Labour

INDEX OF PLACE NAMES, PRISON HULKS AND SHIPS

Entries in italics refer to names of prison hulks or transportation ships; page references in italics refer to illustrations including illustrations of documents.

INDEX OF PERSONAL NAMES

When the same name occurs for more than one person, entries are distinguished by places and dates connected, in the text, to the individual.

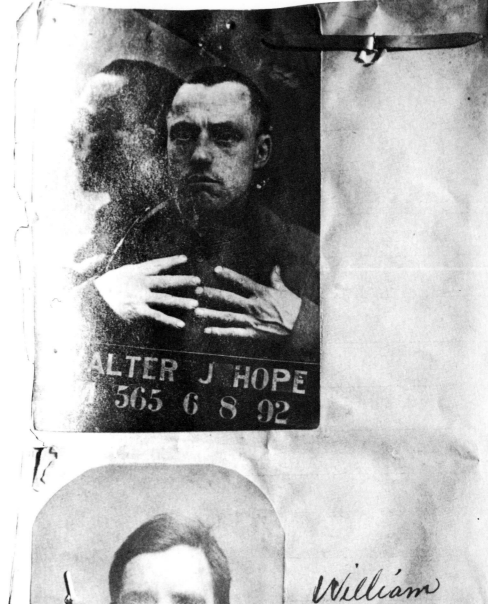

ALTER J HOPE
565 6 8 92

William Bailey

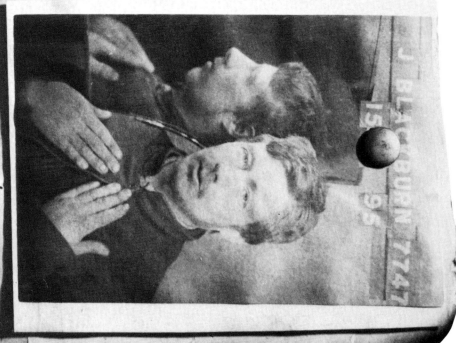